THE BEAUTIFUL GAME IS OVER:

The Globalisation of Football

THE BEAUTIFUL GAME IS OVER:

The Globalisation of Football

John Samuels

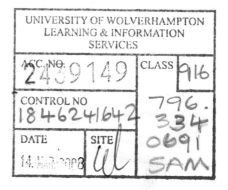
Book Guild Publishing

Sussex, England

First published in Great Britain in 2008 by
The Book Guild Ltd
Pavilion View
19 New Road
Brighton, BN1 1UF

Second printing 2008

Typesetting in Times Roman by
SetSystems Ltd, Saffron Walden, Essex

Printed in Great Britain by
Athenaeum Press Ltd, Gateshead

A catalogue record for this book is
available from the British Library

ISBN 978 1 84624 164 2

Dedicated to the memory of my parents
John Owen and Mary Price Samuels

CONTENTS

ACKNOWLEDGEMENTS

My first thanks must be to the many excellent players and to the many not so good but hardworking players that I have watched over the last five decades. Unfortunately, living in the West Midlands has meant much excitement, but little success. This has not been as a result of lack of effort on the players' part, but rather to a lack of vision on the part of the directors of the local clubs.

After many years of being starved of success and of little prospect of improvement in the future, I am not surprisingly 'grumpy'. If I had been a fan of Manchester United, Liverpool or Chelsea my 'interpretation' of the take-over of the game by commercial interests might have been different.

Many thanks are also due to the many excellent writers on football. These include many of the journalists who fill the sports pages of newspapers with stories, analysis, rumours and facts about the game.

These reports are very often much more interesting to read than what appears on the front page of the papers, and often in fact more enjoyable than watching a match on television or being in attendance at a game.

Unfortunately, however, now quite often, the game is over-hyped. The investigatory journalists deserve special praise as do the co-authors of some of the 'autobiographies'.

Association Football was once referred to as an activity which gave the working man something to talk about. Now it is an activity that gives men (and some women) all over the world, something to talk about. Football has also become a respectable subject for academics to research and write about. I am indebted to the work of many of these economists, sociologists and political and sports scientists. I am also indebted to Deloitte's for their excellent Annual Review of Football finances.

I would like to thank Carol Biss, Joanna Bentley, Janet Wrench and the staff at Book Guild for taking on the publication of this book. The work began as a study that was to be entitled 'Whatever Happened to Football in the Midlands?' This topic did not, however, excite publishers, and so the study was expanded to one that could be called 'Whatever is happening to Football?' I am particularly grateful to the editing work of Kim Hjelmgaard. I also wish to thank Cynthia Pickering, Jennie King, Karen Hansen and Jean Wakefield for their work over many years on the manuscript of the book. I also thank Dr Irshad Zaki for his recent help.

Finally, extra special thanks to my wife, Valerie, not only for her love and suppport, but also for her word processing skills.

Introduction

'When money becomes the all important consideration, football a secondary one, the game in general and the football supporters are likely to be the main sufferers.' *Sir Stanley Rous, 1978 former President of FIFA.*[1]

What is happening in football today is almost entirely predictable. The dominance of a few clubs, the take-over of Manchester United, the foreign ownership of English clubs, the influence of the media, the significance of foreign managers and players and the headhunting of talent are all the result of the globalisation of the football business and the impact of free market forces. Unfortunately as a result of these economic forces the results of domestic football competitions have also become quite predictable. The rich clubs are becoming richer and the less rich becoming of little importance. The winning of major competitions is now largely over for clubs from the Midlands, North East and most other parts of the country. Success for them is now judged as avoiding relegation, or at best, finishing higher than seventh place in the Premiership.

The lack of competitive balance is not good for the majority of football supporters, for the majority of clubs and the majority of players. However, it is good for the media, for the commercial interests of a few elite clubs and for the top players. It is the stakeholders who have the power who are benefiting. The situation is made worse by a lack of effective leadership in the game and by the fact that the numerous bodies who attempt to regulate and control the sport and the business of football are in competition with each other. Each makes decisions based on their own preferences rather than those of the customers (the fans).

The game has been taken over. What was once a game based on local communities, local support and local pride has become a

1

product to be sold around the world. Those running the top clubs still make a token effort to be seen as part of the community, but their main interests are in expanding their fan base around the world. They now boast that they have many more fans outside the UK than in it. Furthermore, the clubs are now owned by people whose main business interests are outside the UK.[2]

The game was once administered and governed by national bodies. Even though those running the Football Association, the Football League and later the Premier League, did not like each other, they at least ran the game in what they each saw were the best interests of those interested in football in England. Now these national-based organisations are of minor importance.

The game is now run by those interested in maximising the income of the game globally. We are told to reduce the number of clubs in the top domestic league so that more games can be played in competitions with a foreign interest. We are told to stop playing football in January and February and to play in the summer months. Why? Because it would be more convenient to clubs and national teams from other countries. The reason these changes have been proposed has to do of course with money.

Changes in traditions in the game

The typical football fan in England is being brainwashed. Most games in the Premier League are not of a high standard. The English national team continues to be mediocre. Most football grounds are of poor quality, particularly the catering facilities. The crowds still use foul language. Yet the media regularly lead us to believe the Premier League is the best in the world, that the English team has a good chance of winning each competition in which it is involved, and that football grounds are now pleasant places full of well-behaved middle class people.

The more football can be packaged by marketing people to be sold in the global market, the more it will attract the really big money. Coca-Cola will sponsor the World Cup, television companies will pay huge sums for the right to broadcast matches.

This is progress, it is globalisation, it makes the players richer, the owners of clubs richer, the administrators and regulators of the game richer, the agents richer and the sponsors richer. But globalisation does not make everyone richer, the trickle down process does not work very well. Does the globalisation of football benefit the clubs outside of the elite few? Does it benefit the fans of such clubs? Does it benefit the majority of football fans in England?

Football has already become a television sport. With the Euro 2008 qualifying games beginning only a few weeks after the 2006 World Cup finals, the saturation coverage of football did not stop. The disappointment of England's performance in the World Cup was soon forgotten with matches such as England against Macedonia and Wales against Cyprus to watch. These matches, shown live on TV, had to be squeezed between those of the Premier League, the UEFA Champions League and UEFA Cup. No wonder football fans are not rushing to watch Wigan play Sheffield United or Aston Villa play Charlton.

This book is about the 'not so beautiful' aspects of professional football.[3] It is about how the game, driven by business interests, has been taken away from the majority of football fans. It is now a game where, when those who are responsible for its regulation talk about protecting the sport's integrity, they mean that whilst a penalty is being taken advertising hoardings should be frozen for a few seconds. (The Premier League guidelines on electronic advertising hoardings also feel it necessary to say that the home club cannot attempt to distract the visiting team during free kicks and corners by altering the speed or brightness of the moving images. So we are now at a stage in the evolution of the sport where there is a danger that advertisers could affect the result of a game.)

Professional football, especially the Premier League, is a multinational business. As with all multi-national businesses there is a good side (the occasional beautiful game) and a dark side (scandal). Those running football businesses behave no differently to those running other global businesses. Those at the top make large sums of money. Those lower down can struggle financially. As a result of the, in vogue, free market economic approach, and the corresponding minimum level of regulation, inequality in the sport has been increasing. To an extent the inequality in terms of income and wealth distribution of the players and managers may not matter, but the increasing inequality between one club and another does matter.

The Premier League is now a competition in which there are 16 clubs who face the danger of relegation and four clubs who have a chance of being champions. At the national level those who govern the league are being told, by those who 'control' global competitions, to reduce the number of clubs that can participate at the top level, so relegating yet more clubs to lower leagues and depriving their supporters of seeing the best players live. FIFA and UEFA, the FA and the Premier League have a difficult task—how to maximise their wealth—when there are only 52 weeks in a year and so many commercial sponsors wanting to be associated with the major competitions. In whose interests are they acting?

This book is also about those football clubs who have under-performed for the last decade or so and for whom it is now too late to join the elite. It is written for those lovers of football who are fed up with reading about the successes, the transfer dealings, the wage negotiations and the scandals of the few 'elite' clubs. It is written for those who do not care whether or not Chelsea pay £20 million or £25 million for a squad player, whether or not Rio Ferdinand is paid £5 or £6 million a year, and whether or not Jose Mourinho stayed at Chelsea. It is written for those football sup-porters who do not care whether Manchester United are owned by an English family who made their money, partly, through selling poor quality meat to schools, or by Irish racehorse owners, or by an unusual family from the US who know little about soccer. This book is about football clubs and the effects of globalisation.

What is happening with the ownership of Premier League clubs is wholly predictable. In all industries globalisation has resulted in the market leaders selling their product around the world. At the same time globalisation has resulted in an 'extraordinary boom' in global merger and acquisition activity in what is known as the market for corporate control. In football, from a time when only one top club, Fulham, were owned by a foreigner we have moved quickly to a situation where over one half of the Premier League clubs are already (or soon will be) in foreign hands.

British companies have been a leading target in the take-over 'boom' of the twenty-first century. Steel companies, banks, airports and car manufacturers have all been purchased by foreign com-panies, as have football clubs. The level of merger and acquisition activity is increasing. Where will it stop? One cannot say. Global-isation cannot continue at its present pace indefinitely. The admin-istrators of the football industry in the UK talk about putting a stop to more foreign ownership, but they do not have the power to do so. They talk about tests for 'fit and proper' owners, but most of the new owners are fit and proper, and those that are not cannot be shown to be unsuitable.

A major factor behind the latest 'wave' of activity in the market for corporate control is the growth of private equity finance and hedge funds. In the 1990s the stock markets boomed, with institutional investors buying and selling shares of companies listed on stock exchanges. This has changed; now it is money privately, often secretly, owned, that is being used to buy the shares of companies.

The demand for the game of football and its by-products has, over the last 20 years, shown a phenomenal increase; there is now an obsession with the game. This growth in demand is the result of a number of factors: the decisions made by those outside the game, the decisions made by those with power inside the game and because of the development of new technology. Unfortunately this increase in demand for the game has not benefited all those involved with the supply of the game; the increase has become concentrated around the activities of a few clubs and a few individuals.

The comparatively rapid decline in competitive balance in the game, in the increase in the structural rigidity in the game, does not at present appear to have put off most customers. The interest in the matches played by the top clubs, and in international competitions such as the World Cup and the UEFA Nations Cup, is greater than ever. FIFA earned over one billion from the sale of the 2006 World Cup's broadcasting rights. This was 40% higher than they obtained from the rights to the 2002 World Cup.[4]

The FIFA 2006 World Cup was watched by a cumulative worldwide audience of more than 26 billion—in other words, 7 times more than those who watched the 2004 Olympics. The average worldwide viewing figure per match exceeded 500 million. In England, over 20 million watched the matches involving the national team live at home, with over 3 million watching in pubs.

Whatever one thinks of the political skulduggery and questionable financial dealings at FIFA, there is no denying that they know how to sell a sporting event. The World Cup gives pleasure to many billions of people around the world, many of whom would not normally watch a football match. The 2006 tournament, in which it was generally agreed the standard of football was not high (few matches were exciting and too many coaches, including England's, adopted defensive tactics), provided a festival for the 'people'.

The highly paid players often misbehaved (perhaps more often than the fans) and adopted cynical tactics such as deliberately attempting to have their opponents sent off. Many 'stars' under-performed. The organisation of the World Cup and of the festival by the German hosts was, however, a great success, so much so that FIFA immediately began to worry about whether the 2010 World Cup, to be held in South Africa, would be able to maintain the same standards (and attract the same amount of money). The President of FIFA was, however, in a difficult position, because he needed the votes of the African members of FIFA if he was to be re-elected to the Presidency in 2007.[5]

It is easy to criticise the commercialisation of the sport, the ridiculous level of coverage and promotion in the media, and the selfishness of some of those involved, even at the highest level, but it cannot be denied that the game now provides excitement to more people than ever before. The fact that only a very few clubs now have a chance of doing well in the Premier League, that the power in the game is now in the hands of large multi-national companies and a few wealthy individuals, that the cost of watching football is increasing dramatically and considering that one cannot escape the hyperbole about the game, does not seem to worry most football fans.

Perhaps the fact that now at the domestic level football does not provide the balanced sporting competition it used to does not really matter. The logic of the free global market, which is at present generally accepted as being good for us, means that we should expect that the ultimate competition in the market for any product will necessarily be between that produced by one or two companies from one country and that produced by one or two companies from another country. This is what we should expect to be the outcome from a free global market in football.

It is, however, interesting, and perhaps significant, that in the 2004–5, 2005–6 and 2006–7 seasons the most excitement and the greatest drama in the Premiership occurred on the last days of the season, when the bottom clubs played in matches which decided which three would be relegated.[6] It is at the bottom end of the league, amongst the relatively poorer clubs, where there is arguably true competitive balance. Within England, the vast majority of supporters had far more fun on the final Sunday of the 2004–5 season (when within a few minutes West Bromwich Albion moved from twentieth position to sixteenth) than that enjoyed over the previous four or five weeks, during which time Chelsea established a twelve point lead over the second place team Arsenal, who finished with a five point advantage over Manchester United, who in turn had an incredible sixteen point advantage over the fourth place team Everton. In 2005–6 a similar situation developed with Chelsea finishing eight points above the second placed team. Perhaps competitive balance is not important to fans.

In our consumerist society, dependent for its success on a high rate of consumption and spending, Premier League football is a product to be sold. It is the media that are responsible for the increase in the wealth in the game. It is the media that sell the glamour and the excitement of the game and feed the public's obsession with celebrities, with gossip and scandal. Many of the people inside the game, involved in the supply of football, have benefited financially from the changes over the last decade, and in return for selling the game have allowed media interest to dominate. Not only do the elite teams dominate the headlines during the nine-month season, but stories about them fill the back pages of newspapers during the summer months. Will player x stay at Liverpool, will player y sign a new contract at Manchester United? How much will Chelsea be prepared to pay for a promising player from one of the lesser clubs? Meanwhile, the only news from the lesser clubs is whether they can afford to pay two or three million for a player few supporters have ever heard of, or for one who is past his best.

An enquiry by the London Assembly into the implications of Wimbledon Football Club moving their home to Milton Keynes found that clubs brought economic, community and regenerative benefits to a city. Football matches provided local businesses with extra revenue, and football clubs could be significant employers in a local area. From a community point of view the position of players as role models for young people was useful in addressing social, health and educational problems. In addition football matches helped create a 'stimulating environment' for young people. In other words football clubs were more than just a business enterprise. In particular, Charlton Athletic was praised by the London Assembly for its community approach and for the work it does to create a good relationship with fans. The report 'Away from Home' called for action to stop clubs devastating communities when, for business reasons, they make decisions to move away.

7

This is of course just one set of opinions. In the US, where American football has a similar role in society, it is not uncommon for a football club to transfer its base from one city to another. It is, however, accepted that if they do move they can harm the community they leave. New Orleans following the hurricane disaster were desperate to keep the 'Saints' NFL team in the city. Owners know this and squeeze local politicians for funding.

A successful local football team can also improve local productivity. People, whether in a factory or in an office, are more likely to feel good, and bond more easily, if they have a good local team to support. One study found that 62% of men believed their team's results had an impact on their approach to work, thus increasing their motivation when the club was successful.

Football is a game that undoubtedly gives pleasure to many millions, and which arouses passion, sometimes strong, sometimes base, in many of its followers. It is even now possible for the really fanatical supporter to not only follow his (or her) club whilst alive, but also to continue to be associated with his (or her) club after death. Certain undertakers offer coffins decorated with football club crests, with interior lining in club colours, with a memorial brick at the team's stadium and with the possibility of the deceased's ashes being scattered on or near the pitch.[7]

Those who see the game as in a crisis situation, as being in an unhealthy condition, can point to the inequality in the game, to the success being limited to a few clubs, to the gap increasing between the elite and the 'also-rans' and to the scandals involving match-fixing, drugs, gambling and racism. They can point to the weak state of governance in the game, and to the conflicts of interest of many of those who govern the game.

Football followers in Germany have recently been shaken by the revelation that certain referees in their domestic competitions had been accepting bribes to favour one team against another. A few weeks before the 2006 World Cup began, information about match-fixing in Italy's Serie A was made public. In 2006 there were, as so often in the past, a number of scandals surrounding Italian football. One of the goalkeepers in their World Cup squad, Gianluigi Buffon, was being investigated for gambling irregularities. The player admitted betting on matches in the past, but claimed he had stopped once the Italian Football Federation banned such action. The investigators examined the movement of large sums of money

8

between a number of bank accounts and analysed the contents of certain phone calls.

Investigators were also looking into a possible corruption scandal in which Marcello Lippi, the coach of the Italian World Cup team, was involved. It was claimed that Luciano Moggi, a former director of Juventus, had tried to influence Lippi in his selection of players for the squad. Why this alleged pressure might be corrupt has to do with the fact that the players Moggi wanted selected were all clients of the GEA World football agency. GEA was run by Moggi's son. (Lippi's own son also worked for the agency.) As it happens, GEA's activities were at the time also being investigated for 'unfair competition'; they had allegedly used violence and threats to further their business interests. The third Italian scandal of note involved certain Juventus directors seeking to influence the results of matches by ensuring that the referees appointed to take charge of matches in which they were involved would be 'favourable' to the club. This turned out to be the biggest scandal of the lot.

In the twenty-first century sport has become of major importance in society. Its significance has grown over time. Some would argue it is now of disproportionate importance, others would suggest it is the only escape from the real troubles that daily surround us.

Nevertheless, when the President of FIFA—a representative body for football with a dubious governance record involved in secret dealings with little accountability, and with Coca-Cola as their main partners—has meetings with the Pope, the Secretary General of the UN, the Presidents and Prime Ministers of most of the powerful countries, and talks to them about football helping to bring about world peace, not to mention assisting with world economic development, one wonders if the lunatics are beginning to run the asylum. For at the same time as FIFA talk about football being a force for good in the world, they themselves are being investigated by the Swiss legal authorities and there is evidence of corruption and match-fixing in football in many countries.

Similarly, when a major newspaper such as the *Sunday Times*, in a review of the year 2005 (which it names 'a year of catastrophe'), mentions in its 62 word introduction, the bomb blasts in London, an earthquake in Pakistan, a US City laid waste, slaughter in Iraq and 'a thrilling Ashes victory', one does wonder whether sport has

9

not become too important. One also wonders what (or who) has 'driven' sport into this central role.

In December 2004, Indonesia played Malaysia in a football match that attracted a crowd of 110,000. What was remarkable about the match was that it was played only a few days after the earthquake and the resulting tsunami that killed thousands of people and devastated large swathes of both of these countries. People still went to the stadium to watch football and the police and organisers still wanted the event held—such is the power of sport.

This 2005 victory in the Ashes was judged to be so important that the Queen of England announced that she was to honour all the cricketers that took part with the award of an MBE. This for a victory in a competition that only involves two teams and which takes place every two years.[8] Times have changed: in 1966 the England football team won the World Cup but the players were not similarly rewarded. It is true that over the next few decades some of the squad did receive honours, including knighthoods, but the fact that these awards were not given until many years had passed is significant.

The Royal family and their advisors are very good at judging public opinion, and as with all businesses they need to keep up with changing values and tastes. In 2005 they appreciated the importance of sportsmen and sportswomen in popular culture. They were even prepared to confer very high honours on the administrative team that successfully fought off the opposition to bring the 2012 Olympic Games to London. Sport, like it or not, is now extremely important.

Yet, just 20 years ago football was on the decline, crowds were falling, the Prime Minister proposed that those who wanted to see live matches should carry ID cards, and the chairman of at least one club wanted to fence in spectators. What has changed? Money. There is now so much money in sport that the major companies of the world take an interest in it. Competitions are no more exciting than they were in the past (despite what the media tell us) but businessmen have realised that as a result of changes in technology they have a product that can be sold in the global market place. People have more money than ever to spend on entertainment.

In the 1880s and 1890s many football clubs were formed because football was seen by those 'in charge' as a pursuit that was a healthy activity for young working class men. (It would take their minds off sex.)[9] One hundred plus years later football is seen by those 'in charge' as a means of making profits, not necessarily for the football clubs themselves, but for the companies 'supporting' the game. To be fair, it is also about allowing a few 'young men' to become very rich and giving great pleasure to a large number of people from all sectors of society.

Those controlling the game on a day-to-day basis, whether they be at FIFA, UEFA, the FA, the Premiership or at one of the top clubs, continue to make decisions that are in their own interests. In the past the top clubs were happy, for instance, that BSkyB had exclusive rights to broadcast live matches because they feared (incorrectly) that the total money coming into the game would fall if BSkyB had to share these rights. The fact that consumers might have benefited if the exclusivity deal had ended did not concern them. Similarly, they now argue against the UEFA initiative that would encourage a proscribed number of home-grown players being in each club's squad. This is ignoring the wider interests of football in the country. This is the problem. This does not, however, have to be the situation, changes could be made to protect the weaker clubs and give all clubs a chance of achieving some success.

But those who benefit from the way the game is at present organised do not want to rock the boat. They pay lip service to change, but only propose cosmetic change. Typical of such an approach were the views expressed by the then UEFA chief executive, Lars-Christer Olsson, in December 2005.[10] He was proposing that players' salaries be controlled, but the version of salary capping he was proposing would do more harm than good. Olsson suggested that if clubs wanted to obtain a UEFA licence, then 'clubs can only spend a percentage of their turnover (revenue) on players' salaries. If they want to pay big stars, they can pay other players less, or try to boost their revenue.' This scheme would, if implemented, increase inequality in the game, not reduce it. It is the sort of scheme—a control on the percentage of revenue spent on salaries—favoured by clubs such as Manchester United.

In 2003–4, Manchester United spent only 45% of their revenue on wages and salaries. Portsmouth, by way of contrast, spent 64%, and Leicester City (who were relegated) 61%. If UEFA-licensed clubs could only spend 50% of their turnover on players' wages it would not harm Manchester United, but would weaken other clubs.

Perhaps Mr Olsson could tell weaker clubs how to increase their revenue — one way of course is revenue sharing, but he would not agree to that.

At the end of 2005 Dave Whelan, owner of Wigan, called for a £25 million annual salary cap at Premier League clubs in order to prevent the competition becoming monotonous every season. With Chelsea paying twice that amount on wages there would clearly be problems in introducing a cap at such a low level. However, before arguments can begin on an appropriate level, there is the problem of getting Premiership clubs to agree on the need for any limit, plus the problem of balance in European wide competitions.

In 2002 Paul Tagliabue, the Commissioner of the National Football League in the US, in articulating the fear of regulators in his country, said: 'if you allow the revenue side of the structure to change in fundamental ways, then the whole structure will change in fundamental ways, including what the players are prepared to accept. If you end up having have-nots and haves when it comes to revenue, you end up having have-nots and haves when it comes to talent. And then you have a league with a product that is less attractive, and you've started a downward spiral.'[11]

Mr Tagliabue might have been describing what has happened to football in Europe over the last decade or so. The revenue structure has changed in fundamental ways and we have ended up with haves and have-nots in terms of revenue and in terms of talented players. We now have domestic leagues, which despite the hype, are arguably less interesting than they used to be. Consumers have shown that they find this to be so; attendance figures at many grounds are falling. The winning game has been over for some time for most clubs.

We know what steps need to be taken to achieve balanced competition, but the European Commission regard the football industry as primarily a business activity and so prevent clubs and official football associations from introducing restrictive practices that would, as they see it, limit economic competition. In any case it is not clear that the top bodies such as FIFA, UEFA, and the Premier League really want to change anything — they are, after all, still winning.

In December 2005, the European Commission agreed to look at areas in which football might be given exemption from European laws. This was agreed at a meeting between sports ministers of a number of European countries (including the UK), the European Commissioner for Sport and representatives of FIFA and UEFA. The meeting itself was an achievement, although how significant it will be will not be known until we know the outcome. In return UEFA agreed to set up a task force that would look at ways in which football could tackle its problems. FIFA had already at its annual congress set up a task force to see how it could tackle corruption in the game. There is talk of change, but do those benefiting from the game as it now is really want to alter anything fundamentally?

In 2006 the 'Arnaut Report', which was the result of the deliberations of a number of ministers of sport from European countries, did show how the EU could, within its 'Articles', treat football (and other sports) as a special case.[12] Football could, it indicates, introduce certain rules, certain practices, with the parties involved reaching collective agreements, on a range of issues, that would not offend the principles of the EU. Football could therefore, if it wanted to, take steps to improve the competitive balance in the game, and improve its own governance. It is one thing, however, to be able to bring about change, it is another thing to agree on what changes to make. In fact the authors of the report believe that 'only the direct involvement of political leaders' can save football. They may be right, but there are many in football that do not want governments and politicians to interfere in the governance process. There are those who are suspicious of the motives of politicians when they become involved with sport.

There are so many different pressure groups and non-governmental bodies involved in football, each with their own goals (and strategies), that it would take an absolute disaster before they could agree on meaningful reforms. Governmental bodies have shown they do not want to intervene, so if any change is to take place, it will be up to FIFA, its big multi-national business partners, the national associations, the confederations (including UEFA), the executives who run the domestic leagues, the elite clubs, players, agents, TV companies and football fans to agree on what is 'for the good of the game'.[13]

The current boss of FIFA, Sepp Blatter, has expressed regret that a few elite clubs now dominate football competitions, and is concerned that as a result 'consumers' will lose interest in the game, but it is the values of officials at FIFA and other governing bodies and the decisions they have made that have contributed to the crisis. It is now possibly too late for the majority of clubs to ever compete again on equal terms with the elite clubs.

In 2004 Freddie Shepherd, at the time chairman of Newcastle United, pointed out, 'ten years ago there were twelve rich guys in control of football clubs. Now there are seven.'[14] He was right, this is the direction in which the game is moving, away from successful owners of local small businesses, and away from individual fans owning shares. Freddie Shepherd used the word *control*, that is correct, the game at domestic and international level, at club and establishment level, is now controlled by just a few people. The rest of us are just pawns.

The traditional supporters of football have become of minor importance, they have been taken for granted. It is the sponsors, advertisers and the media that have 'bought' the game off the authorities. The important consumers are those who watch football on TV, watch it in pubs or bars and those who buy replica club football shirts. This is why the sale of broadcasting rights is so important to those who run the game. (The credit card companies estimated that because England qualified for the 2006 World Cup finals in Germany, an extra £1 billion was spent in pubs and stores as fans ate and drank whilst watching televised matches. If they had reached the final, the total projected spend would have risen to £1.8 billion.) Some of this broadcasting revenue and advertising and sponsorship income will 'trickle down,' but the amount being redistributed will not be enough to alter the outcome of future competitions.

There are three themes to this book. The first is that the winning game is over for all but a few clubs. The chance of any of these 'other' clubs winning a major competition is minute. The globalisation of the game combined with the values of those who govern the game has resulted in inequalities that now appear to be too big to overcome. This does not, however, have to be the outcome.

The second theme is that those clubs who are benefiting from globalisation are those that have had superior leadership over the last decade or two. The long-term success of any business depends on decisions made by boards of directors—football is no different. There are now clearly four elite English clubs: Chelsea, Manchester United, Liverpool and Arsenal. If we go back to the beginning of the Premier League in 1992–3, the clubs generating the highest levels of revenue per season were Manchester United, Liverpool, Tottenham, Arsenal, Leeds, Sheffield Wednesday and Aston Villa. Where did four of these go wrong? This book is concerned with why such clubs missed out. It is also about whether or not they will ever be able to compete again on equal terms with the present elite.

Which brings us to the third theme of this book. Unless something is done to change the direction in which the industry is moving football will become just another form of TV entertainment. It will have its scandals, its match-fixing, its drugs, its disputed decisions, but it will be of little consequence beyond entertainment value. It will have its moments of excitement, but it will not be a beautiful game.

→ and no social or community value will remain - only point will be profit & economics.

1

The Present Football Environment

Over one hundred yeards ago, James Hamilton Muir wrote 'the best you can say for football is that it has given the working man a subject for conversation.'[1] Seventy or so years later it was still a subject mainly for the working man, but now it is a subject for all social classes all over the world. Top footballers are now global celebrities.

Even Tony Blair claims to have been a football fan in his youth (he is said to have watched the legendary Newcastle United player Jackie Milburn and to have sat behind the goals at St James's Park to watch his hero play). There are only two things wrong with this story: Tony Blair was only four years old when Jackie Milburn retired from football; and at that time there was no seating behind the goals at St James Park.[2]

Three days of mourning in the newspapers and on the television followed the death of George Best in 2005. People who had never seen him play, including the Prime Minister, lined up to say that he was one of the best players the world had ever seen. They had of course seen his goals on video. He was a great footballer, who lived the life he wanted to. He was also somewhat of a folk hero amongst the lads, having enjoyed not only the best of football, but also the best of women and the best of drink. But did this justify the coverage? On the day he died the BBC evening news programme devoted the first ten minutes to a eulogy of George Best. It was a pity they, too, jumped on the bandwagon at the end.

James Walvin, who has for many years argued that football is the 'people's game', recently wrote that 'football remains the people's game, however lavish and absurb the antics of the wealthy minority.'[3] It is true that the game of football was not the creation of businessmen, but the formation of the Football League, the

17

Premier League, the European Champions League and the World Cup have been the creation of businessmen.

Deloitte and Touche (one of the so-called Big Four accounting firms) in their 2003 'Review of Football Finance' re-examine the old question of what is the purpose of a football club.[4] The answer they give is that its purpose is 'to provide a unique focus for local pride, to provide entertainment for this generation and future generations.' This is exactly what William McGregor and the other football enthusiasts that started the Football League over 100 years ago would have said. So does this mean little has changed over time? Unfortunately it does not. Deloitte and Touche in the above quote were referring only to the objective of clubs 'below the Premier League.' Their advice to the leading football clubs is to convert their exceptional top line (i.e. Revenue) growth into 'sustainable bottom line profit.' If this were to happen, explain Deloitte and Touche, the biggest financial winners would be the Premier League clubs themselves and in particular those clubs that are financially well managed and have a 'consistent track record of Premier League status since its inception.'

The Premier League in 2001–02 celebrated its tenth birthday anniversary, and in the opinion of Deloitte and Touche it was 'a stellar decade of growth and commercial success in English football.' It was not, however, a decade of football success for the England national team, nor in fact on the pitch for the few English clubs that compete in Europe, not to mention for most of the English clubs that did not compete in Europe. It was a decade of growth, but one of increasing financial inequality and domination by a few. This is of course the expected outcome of the globalisation of an industry.

The State of Play

The end of the 2005–06 season merged with the beginning of the 2006–07 season. There must be no break from the opportunity to sell. The very commercially successful FIFA 2006 World Cup ended as Newcastle United and a number of other clubs started to compete for the Intertoto Cup. The UEFA Champions League matches started on 5 August. England's miserable performance in the World Cup would soon be forgotton, with the competition

18

beginning in September for the UEFA Euro 2008 Cup. The success for England in the two early matches against Andorra and Macedonia would result in the followers of the game being led to believe that this was a competion England could be expected to win.

Wayne Rooney published the first volume of his (expected to be five or six part) autobiography.[5] He had been shown a red card in the last game of the 2005–06 season and was shown another in the first game of the new season. A number of clubs were hoping to attract new owners (including Liverpool and Aston Villa), while others were seeking new managers. Ashley Cole was still talking about a move.

Those with power at the Football Association were still squabbling. They had not provided leadership in the year or so leading up to the World Cup and gave little indication that they would be able to do so afterwards. They had not agreed on how to implement the key proposals in the 'Burns Report' on restructuring.[6] The representatives of the amateur game were reluctant to see their importance reduced and independent non-executive directors had still not been appointed. The sports minister was becoming increasingly frustrated with the lack of progress on reforming the FA. Although the FA, as a private body, was free to do as it liked, which could mean making no changes, the government made it clear that if the proposals in the 'Burns Report' were not implemented this would seriously harm the relationship between the FA and the government.

Chelsea had reported a record £140 million pre-tax losses for the 2004–05 season, the largest loss in football history. It beat the club's loss in the previous year of £87.8 million.[7] Roman Abramovich had invested £166.6 million in the club in 2004–05, bringing his total investment in the club to £381.5 million. (This was in addition to the £60 million he paid to the previous owners of the club.) The club were Premier League champions in 2005–06, as they had been the previous season. Despite talk of planning to financially break even in the future and of developing English talent, they continued to spend. In preparation for the 2006–07 season they paid a record sum for the UK of £30 million for Andriy Shevchenko.

In fact perhaps the most significant events of the summer of 2006 were the scandals surrounding refereeing and match-fixing in Italy. It reminded 'the people' that there is a side to football that the regulators and the bossess who run the game would prefer to ignore. People only want to watch sporting contests because they believe the outcome is uncertain—it is the uncertainty that makes the contest exciting. If it has been decided in advance what the outcome will be the contest is meaningless. A match is 'fixed' to enable those involved to make money. It is those who follow football, the consumers, who lose. There have been match-fixing scandals in football since the game started.

The football environment in 2006 was one full of contradictions. The FIFA World Cup finals had more national teams taking part than ever before and the games generated record levels of revenue. The event was the most watched event ever in the history of sport and it gave pleasure to billions of people. There was talk of holding a World Cup competition every two years. FIFA had signed up Coca-Cola as their main partners (sponsors) until 2022. In England the Premier League had sold the TV broadcasting rights for the three seasons beginning 2007–08 for record amounts, with the result that the revenue from TV for the average Premier League club would increase by over 30%. Yet despite these 'successes' the 'Arnaut Report', closely associated with UEFA, and submitted to the European Commission, referred to football as being 'not in good health.' This was not the only report that referred to a crisis in the game, a FIFA working party was looking at ways of dealing with a number of problem issues. How could this contradiction arise?

The Game is Healthier Than Ever?

The last eight in the UEFA Champions League in the 2005–06 season included the biggest club in France (Lyon), the two top teams from Milan (AC and Inter), Juventus from Turin, Arsenal and Chelsea from London, and Barcelona and Villarreal from Spain. Only Villarreal's presence was a surprise. For they were (with Chelsea) the only club not a member of the G14 Group.[8]

In the 2004–05 season in the Champions League the last 16 teams contained the usual names with two clubs from London (including Chelsea), Manchester United, Real Madrid, Liverpool, Barcelona, two clubs from Milan, Bayern Münich, Juventus and the previous years' two finalists. Thirteen of the clubs were members of G14. Only three of the teams could be seen as a surprise. In fact one of the least fancied of these clubs, Liverpool, beat one of the most fancied, AC Milan, in the final, proving the game is not entirely predictable.

In Europe 2003–04 was an unusual season, with two of the four major national leagues being won by a club that was not one of the elite clubs of the country. In Spain the champions were Valencia, whose captain claimed that the triumph of his club's 'very human squad' showed that 'money in this life is not everything.' In Germany the champions were the unfashionable Werder Bremen, with Bayern Münich coming second. In the UEFA Champions League the two teams in the final were Porto and Monaco. One of these clubs plays in the Portuguese league, the other in the French league; 2004 was the first season since 1991 in which the two finalists were from outside the big four leagues.

These surprising outcomes in 2004 led some of those interested in football to point out that money cannot guarantee success. The Minister of Culture in the Bremen regional parliament in Germany claimed that his local club's success was a victory over 'capital arrogance.' It was, however, a mistake to start claiming that the game had changed yet again—money does help. In England, Arsenal were champions with Chelsea runners up, and in Italy, AC Milan were champions with Roma second; none of these are small or even medium-sized clubs. After 2004 things returned to normal.

In 2007 in the US, by way of comparison, the winner of the Super Bowl was the unfashionable Indianapolis Colts. In 2006 the last eight teams competing in the National Football League (NFL) Super Bowl were from Pittsburg, Seattle, Denver, North Carolina, Washington DC, Boston, Indianapolis and Chicago. Only three of these clubs had been in the final eight the previous season. Half of these clubs were from smaller cities. There were no teams from New York, California or Texas, the largest states.[9] In 2005 the teams in the last eight were from Pittsburgh, New York (the Jets), Minnesota, Atlanta, St Louis, Indianapolis, Boston and Philadelphia. One team was this time from New York, and unusually for the years since the introduction of a salary cap, four of the teams had appeared in the quarter finals the previous season. In fact in 2005 the New England Patriots won the Super Bowl for the third year out of four, which was a big surprise to many. The introduction of a salary cap in the 1994 season had been intended to keep all the teams in the NFL at an approximately equal strength. One of the judges who had been involved in the decision to allow the

NFL to engage in certain restrictive practices said that this action was necessary 'in order to try to protect the weaker teams from the stronger teams.'

In 2004 the final eight teams competing for the Super Bowl were from the cities of Indianapolis, Green Bay (Wisconsin), Boston (New England), St Louis, Kansas City, Philadelphia, Nashville (Tennessee) and Charlotte (North Carolina). With the exception of Boston none of the clubs were from major cities. There were no teams from New York, Chicago, Los Angeles, Houston, Dallas or Miami. By way of contrast the last eight teams competing in 2004 for the UEFA Champions League included clubs from Milan, Madrid and London; in other words, the larger cities in Europe.

One other very significant difference between success in football in Europe compared with success in American football in the US is in the ability of some European clubs to dominate over long periods of time. In the UEFA Champions League final and its predecessor, the European Cup's, 51-year history, Real Madrid have appeared in 12 finals, AC Milan in 10, and Bayern Münich, Benfica (Lisbon) and Juventus (Turin) in 7 finals each. In the Super Bowl over the last 11 years, 15 teams have appeared in a final. Of these, 1 team has appeared in 3 finals, and 5 teams appeared in 2 finals. Why this difference? Basically it is because in the US professional sport has been allowed to protect itself from the adverse effects of a free, competitive market place. In Europe professional sport has not been allowed to do so.

Which approach is best? To the suppliers of football, the European system results in the greater risks, but also the greater potential financial reward. In the US, the restricitive practices in place in the NFL allow for such benefits as revenue sharing, equal distribution of young talent and salary capping. For consumers, the European system offers the greater level of satisfaction for a minority of the followers of the game; those who support the elite teams can see them continually performing well.[10] However, it will be argued that for the majority of the followers of the game, the US structure and regulatory framework offers the greater satisfaction because the outcome of competitions is less predictable. In the US the clubs are closer together in terms of ability and so supporters of all the clubs involved have a chance of seeing their respective team win. In England, satisfaction for most supporters of even

Premier League clubs is just to see their team survive relegation and occasionally to watch the elite teams play.

According to UEFA, and to the 'Arnaut Report', the European model for football is based on a pyramid structure. This can be differentiated from the US model, which they portray as having the top part of the pyramid (the pointed part) separated from the base. In the European model there is possible progression from the base to the top, in the US model there is not. There is a separation. UEFA and FIFA talk a lot about the need for solidarity and the need for a united football family in order to create a stronger than ever football pyramid. They are saying this is what should happen in an ideal world. But we do not have an ideal world—we have a world driven by economic market forces and by globalisation. A world in which over 30% of tickets for World Cup matches, in the final stages, are reserved for FIFA and their business partners. The supporters of the clubs involved are struggling for tickets for the remaining seats. A world in which the rich clubs become richer, and the poor relatively poorer, does not result in a pyramid structure. In terms of wealth the top seven clubs in the Premier League obtain over one half of the revenue earned by the Premier and Championship league clubs and the remaining thirty-seven clubs share the remainder. This is not a pyramid structure.

There are two main reasons why we now have a situation in football in Europe in which a few clubs dominate, a situation that will become worse unless changes are made. Firstly, we now live in a world in which the people with power believe that an unregulated free market global economic system is the best. Second, politicians and administrators in Europe have for some time regarded football as an economic activity so that therefore any restrictive practices within the industry have been frowned upon. The inevitable outcome is an industry with a lack of competitive balance. Even Deloitte's, in their 2006 'Review of Football Finance', agree that a key concern about the game is that success is becoming 'A closed shop for a privileged few clubs, with it becoming more and more difficult for clubs to break into this elite handful.'[11]

The Game is Not in Good Health

In 2005 UEFA produced a document entitled 'Vision Europe' in which they revealed how they would like to see football develop.[12] In an ideal world they would like to see clubs owned by their members and supporters (as at Barcelona) not by plcs or wealthy individuals. They would like to see clubs run on democratic grounds, and they would like to prevent unsuitable owners and directors from being involved in the game. This would be 'ideal' but is unlikely in an industry in which money decides who are the winners.

Not to be outdone, FIFA established a task force 'For the good of the game.'[13] The five main financial matters FIFA considered were: player transfers, multiple club ownership, betting, players' agents and club management. All these are major issues affecting the reputation and future of the industry. There are of course many other dark sides to the game, including drugs, violence and racism. In 2006 Jose Arnaut, who chaired the so-called 'Independent Report on Sport', said that he was 'deeply concerned' about the state of football in Europe. He thought it was not in good health.

UEFA say they would like to see an appropriate level of competitive balance in the game. The trouble is what is appropriate? Is the balance to be between the elite teams in Europe, or between the teams in a domestic league? UEFA, not surprisingly, are in favour of self-regulation for the sport—which as an ideal is fine. The problem is that in practice self-regulation has only bene-fitted the few, and the different regulatory and governing bodies historically fight each other. There is a need for more independent, non-executive directors to be involved in the governing process.

FIFA, the top self-regulatory body for the sport, is not itself an example of good corporate governance. Its recent history contains many stories of corruption, the people involved in running it are too close to big business, and the organisation is simply too commercial. UEFA's 'Vision Europe' document calls for greater solidarity in the sport, but at present the game is littered with different interest groups fighting one another. Some want a more balanced redistribution of the money coming into the game. Others want stricter 'fit and proper' tests on the owners and directors of clubs. Yet others want no change.

24

'Vision Europe' is referred to as a strategy document. It is (as are many strategy documents) based more on a dream world than on reality. It has more to do with how UEFA would like their own future to be than on the future for football in Europe. According to UEFA, an ideal world would be one where UEFA deals with all questions relating to European football. But unfortunately they are just one stakeholder, they do not represent everyone, they do not represent consumers. In their ideal world 'football represents integrity, sportsmanship and loyalty.'

In fact the UEFA document is political. It seeks to differentiate itself from FIFA. UEFA are also involved in a power struggle with G14, and so their strategy document criticises the 'elite clubs' who are asking for more money for the release of players to national teams. They believe such action is an 'erosion of the solidarity principle.' The solidarity principle is their own. They believe that for clubs to release players to a national team is a form of solidarity that has existed since the creation of football (to be more exact since the 1880s) and must be protected. They support the 'European Club Forum' which involves more than the elite few, and fits in better with their preferred pyramid structure.

UEFA representatives have had discussions with representatives of the European Union in the hope of 'establishing a platform for co-operation.' Written into the European constitution (which was not adopted) was an article dealing with sport. This article refers to the specific nature of sport, and states that 'The Union shall contribute to the promotion of European sporting issues, while taking account of its specific nature.' Furthermore, it states that when framing laws the European Commission must take account of the social and educational functions inherent in sport. There have been discussions with the EU on such matters as the transfer system and the central marketing of media rights. Getting football treated differently to any of the other businesses competing in the European free market economy is an uphill struggle.

There are those who criticise the current values in the game. In fact they are the same values as in the rest of society, no better, no worse. There are those who want to reduce the amount of commercialism in sport, but there are also those who want to increase this amount. Those with power in football have used the people's affection for the game to make themselves wealthy. The astronomical salaries of the game's biggest stars reflects what is happening in all of business. Jules Tygiel, writing about what has happened in sports in the US, said it reflects 'a transformation in the economy whereby the gaps between the people at the very top, and the people not even at the very bottom but in the middle, have advanced dramatically.' A contention borne out by recent economic data.[14]

UEFA write about integrity and loyalty in the game. But some would say 'Now cash is the one true goal.' This was the heading to Hugh McIlvanney's column in the *Sunday Times* on 24 April 2005. This observation resulted from the controversy surrounding Rio Ferdinand's treatment of Manchester United. McIlvanney raises the question as to whether 'it is legitimate to ask if our best footballers have arrived at the point where no other consideration can compete seriously with the desire for more and more money as a motivator of career moves.'

Sir Alex Ferguson had stated that he was running out of patience with Ferdinand over his reluctance to sign a new contract. The club had been extremely supportive of the player when he forgot (for two days) to take a drugs test. The club tried to protect him, and continued to pay his wages through his eight-month ban from the game. There were similar comments made about the lack of loyalty amongst players when Ashley Cole moved from Arsenal to Chelsea. He dismissed the offer of nearly £3 million a year Arsenal offered him, saying the directors were 'taking the piss'.

Growth in Demand for Football

The professional football business is part of the entertainment industry, and with the growth in wealth of much of the world's population, there is now money available to be spent on leisure and recreational activities. Historically, the game of football was rooted locally, but television, mass marketing and international organisations have taken the game and its top teams to a global audience, and like it or not the globalisation process rolls on.

For the first 70 to 80 years of the professional game matches were played on a Saturday and because of the absence of floodlights, the kick-off in the winter months had to be quite early in the afternoon. Many people worked Saturday mornings, so they just had enough time for a beer and perhaps a pie before paying to watch their local team. Of course for big matches, some supporters would travel by rail to watch their clubs in away games. For the first two thirds of the life of the professional game TV did not exist and even when it first appeared it was regarded with suspicion by the football authorities. However, certain club directors saw the opportunities that could result from the advances in broadcasting technology, particularly from TV. From the 1970s, teams such as the 'Busby Babes' attracted wide support nationally and inter-nationally, and together with clubs such as Liverpool and Real Madrid became global names.

When in the 1990s BSkyB purchased the rights to broadcast Premier League games, and broadcast these around the world, the top English clubs attracted even further support. Clubs travelled to other countries to play exhibition matches in order to increase their exposure. Of course only a few clubs had sufficient glamour, and a history of success to mean that young (and not so young) men wished to be identified with them.

For a handful of clubs the global market offered great potential, and the directors of some of these clubs were wise enough to be able to exploit this potential. Manchester United, at their annual general meeting in November 2003, were able to report that they had sold 2.6 million replica shirts in the last year, over half of them being sold outside the UK. It was claimed that Real Madrid had only sold 200,000 over the same period. It was also claimed that 75 million people around the world were supporters of Manchester United and that the club planned to expand their global appeal, aiming in particular at the North American and Asian markets. In the summer of 2003 they had toured the US (with David Beckham still a member of the team) and the following summer they toured China. They had even signed up a promising young Chinese player, which would help their marketing and promotional work in that country.

The point is that many clubs now see their market place as global. Sheffield United's chairman announced at their 2005 annual general meeting that they were taking the club global. He told the shareholders that they were purchasing a Chinese second division club. The club is in Chengdu, a city with a population of 11 million, which is itself located in a province with a population twice as large as that of the UK. As the chairman said 'this does represent a potential fan base which we can use to develop both the Five Bull (the name of the local club) and Sheffield United's brands.' The

27

plan was to develop a Sheffield United shop at the stadium in Chengdu to sell merchandise, and to be involved with a bar in the city centre to show football on TV and sell drinks. The two clubs hoped that an exchange of players and staff would benefit both sides. This was an imaginative plan, which is necessary if a non-fashionable English club is to be successful in distracting the global consumer from the hype surrounding the new elite clubs.

Of course the elite clubs are not standing still, at the same time that Sheffield United are trying to develop a base in the North East of China, certain elite clubs continue to try to crack the lucrative US market. Peter Kenyon, chief executive of Chelsea, signed a 'special club to club relationship' deal with one of the US major league soccer clubs, and established link-ups with three other US soccer clubs. This was part of an attempt to establish Chelsea, by 2014, as the most dominant football club in the world. In fact in 2001 the same Peter Kenyon, whilst at Manchester United, had established similar links between United and the New York Yankees baseball team. At the time there was talk of synergy, potential joint marketing opportunities and shared commercial goals. It did not seem to excite the American sports fans, but it might have been the spark that led to the owners of another US sports club taking over Manchester United.

Such is the demand for the modern game. This demand results from a mixture of a genuine love for the sport, from a wish to be entertained, and from clever advertising and marketing of the game and players. What will happen once the 'genie of market forces has escaped the bottle' is uncertain. In Europe in 2004–05, in the UEFA Champions League, 74 teams took part in the competition. In the UEFA Cup, 140 teams took part (although 16 of these qualified for a place because they had been eliminated from the Champions league). This means that 198 teams in Europe took part in one of the two 'Super' competitions. One result of this is that the top players are under pressure to play in an increasing number of games for their clubs and country, and this has led to the elite clubs and FIFA wishing to change once again the structure of domestic competition.

The Consumers

The demand to watch and be involved with football comes from four different categories of consumer. Two of these include people who actually attend matches and two include people who watch broadcast matches. Of the former, those who actually attend matches, there are the traditional supporters of a club (people who in the past stood on terraces, but now sit) and those who sit in the executive seats, or boxes, eat prawn sandwiches or better, and enjoy all the hospitality the club can offer. The traditional supporters are the 'fans', they buy the season tickets, the shirts and all the other merchandise that the clubs sell. The 'business' guests come to the match to enjoy the atmosphere but they do nothing themselves to create an atmosphere. This group have, nevertheless, become increasingly important financially to the clubs and will be vital to the financial success of the new stadium at Wembley and the new home for Arsenal. This group of consumers will be more likely to watch games if the local team is winning. Another factor affecting their attendance is whether or not the local team has a 'highly recognised marquee player', one who such people want to be able to say they have watched.

The other two categories of consumer, those who watch broadcast football matches, are those who watch in their homes and those who watch in pubs, clubs or hotels. These groups can watch matches played in any country. Many Asian countries and parts of Africa, for example, have become obsessed with the Premier League. The TV companies (particularly those in which Rupert Murdoch is involved) have been remarkably successful in marketing the Premier League around the world.

Far away islands such as Mauritius are divided between Manchester United and Liverpool supporters (with one village named Arsenal supporting that team). The bars in Singapore and Hong Kong show three or four Premier League games each weekend. Unfortunately, this overseas marketing of the English game only extends to the Premier League, and these far away fans are only interested in supporting a club if it has a chance of winning something. The bars are not full unless an elite team is playing.

Of the four categories, the traditional 'fan' was the most important for the first 100 years of the professional sport, but within the last 15 years it can be argued that for the top clubs these fans have become the least important part of their game. The steps taken by many clubs over the last 20 years to build new stadiums or refurbish old ones were motivated by a wish to improve their revenue producing assets. They were concerned with increasing the number of executive seats and boxes. Roy Keane has commented on the lack of passion shown by spectators who sit in such accommodation. The Wembley Stadium company sold Corporate Boxes, Premier Seats, Executive Gold Seats, Executive Silver Seats and more modest Club Seats, with licence terms ranging from three to ten years. The price of a box at the new Wembley was in 2005 being sold for £210,000 per annum, while the price of a Premier Seat was going for an initial fee of £16,100 plus an annual season ticket price of £5,450. One can see why the more traditional supporters, buying a modest season ticket or even a more modest ticket to watch one match at a time, are seen by clubs as of minor importance.

Football clubs have tended to regard the traditional type of supporter as an unquestioning consumer of their product; as people who will continue to purchase the product through bad times as well as good, as a captive audience. A football club is often referred to as a 'passion brand'. But times have changed. Research has shown that 'modern supporters are more discerning and their patterns of consumption more variable and unpredictable than they were.' Nevertheless, the clubs, in order to satisfy a new audience via television, have broken away from the traditional pattern of match days and times, and local spectators' interests have consequently been sacrificed.

One of the primary factors on which the wealth of the game now depends is 'the depth of the corporate consumer market.' This is the view of Gerry Boon of Deloitte.[15] The corporate customer will stay with the market as long as it is the leading spectator sport in the world, and as long as people are prepared to spend money on products associated with the sport and with the celebrity players. One danger to football is that an alternative sport or an alternative form of entertainment will increase in popularity and capture some of football's share of the market. The NFL has tried to increase American football's share of the world market for sport, but so far has not been successful. In the 1970s and 1980s the cinema business lost a share of the entertainment market but has since fought back. It is a mistake to think that nothing changes.

There are uncertainties surrounding the future demand for football. One is that it will be overexposed, with the market becoming saturated. Already the game is being played for almost twelve months of the year, and in England matches are shown on TV five or even six days a week. Yet another danger is that the scandals and dark side of the game will turn spectators and sponsors away. A further danger is that all but the most loyal supporters of a club will lose interest because of the real loss in competitive balance in the game.

It is the elite teams that attract the crowds and the TV audiences, it is not the romance of European competition. In 2005–06 when Bolton and Middlesbrough provided their fans with the opportunity to watch European opponents, there was not a big rush. When Bolton played a team from St Petersburg, there was only a very small crowd present.

It is easy to become blasé about football, to become complacent. The game has survived despite past crisis. In the mid-1930s two writers on football, one of them an insider in the game, expressed concern about the future.[16] The question they raised was 'could football remain a national sport in face of growing opposition and attraction of greyhound racing, the dirt tracks, tennis and other games?' They did see a promising future because football is a clean pastime, unaffected by betting, like greyhound and dirt track racing, and there is very little unsporting instinct shown anywhere either on the part of players or spectators. W. Capel-Kirby and Frederick W. Carter were correct about the future but for the wrong reasons.

There is a sociological concept of 'sport space' that seeks to explain why once a nation's sport space is filled it is difficult for a new sport to push in. This is the reason why soccer has found it hard to be accepted in the US and American football has problems in attracting support in Europe. In the US in the nineteenth century football as a recreational and spectator sport was crowded out by baseball. The key period when baseball took up this space was between 1870 and 1930 when modern mass societies became established. Baseball became the working class sport in the US, one with which immigrants wished to identify. (American football was the university sport.)

But it should be remembered that things do change. Baseball was for nearly 100 years the sport of the people in the US. From the 1960s, thanks partly to the interest in the sport by the TV companies and partly due to clever leadership in the NFL, American football began to increase its share of the space, until now it is clearly the most popular US sport.

Sport faces competition from other parts of the entertainment industry. For a new generation of consumers pop concerts, clubs and the cinema provide a known and guaranteed level of excitement, and so arguably have more appeal than watching two mediocre Premier League teams, either live or on TV. On TV, commentators often have to struggle for viewer attention; their fear is that viewers will change channels. They frequently resort to promising that the game will improve in the second half, or as time goes by, that it will improve in the last 30 minutes or even in the last 10 minutes. They are forever predicting that goals will come.

A headline in the *Daily Express* described the Premier League as 'overrated, over hyped and over paid.'[17] But those businessmen who run TV or other media companies, or who are on the periphery of the game and rely on football to sell their products, cannot afford to let such views become widely accepted. They need to keep emphasising the excitement of the game, the glamour of the players, and the pride that goes with supporting a winning club or national team.

Many Premier League games are not exciting. The *Guardian* correspondent who was unfortunate enough to watch the Boxing Day 2003, game between, at the time, potentially two of the top teams in the country, Leeds and Aston Villa, commented: 'The days immediately after Christmas are traditionally a time for taking things back, items that do not fit or are just plain unacceptable. Sadly for the 38,000-odd here, they will never be able to get these 90 minutes back, not even with a valid receipt. An afternoon that was meant to be about spice, bile and personality clashes—turned out just bland. No goals, no real football.' In January 2005, Fulham visited Birmingham City, and the report in the local paper referred to the match as a terrible advert for the Premiership. It was the reporters view that words 'had not yet been invented to adequately convey just how bad the first 45 minutes were.'

Reference is sometimes made to a crisis in football but it has to be remembered that the FIFA World Cup finals are now the biggest sporting event in the world. They provide interest and excitement to many millions of people. It is good that so many countries want to take part. The main influence on the structure of the tournament is, however, money. In the qualifying stages all countries are treated equally, very democratic. This meant that in the 2004–05 season France had to play the Faroe Islands twice, that Holland played Andorra twice, that Spain played San Marino twice and Russia played Liechtenstein twice. Do such matches really add anything to football? They increase the number of international matches that can be shown on television, but unfortunately it leads to calls to reduce the number of matches in domestic competitions, and to disputes between clubs and FIFA. Whose interests are most important?

Television

The most significant factor in transforming the game over the last 20 or so years has been the income from TV broadcasting. People will pay to watch films and sport. This fact was appreciated by the new pay-to-view channels. In May 1992 Rupert Murdoch outbid the UK's other independent TV companies for the rights to broadcast Premier League matches. This coup enabled him to broadcast top football matches all around the world, thus ensuring that millions subscribed to his cable and satellite channels.[18]

At the end of the 1990s the Office of Fair Trading brought a case against the Premier League because they believed the collective selling of TV rights was anti-competitive. They also did not like the fact that one TV company, BSkyB, was given the exclusive rights to broadcast live Premier League games. Such exclusive selling rights and exclusive broadcasting rights, it was argued, were against consumer interest.

Surprisingly, the Restrictive Practices Court, to whom the Office of Fair Trading took the case, found in favour of the Premier League; they did not find that the collective selling of rights was inherently against consumer interest. The court accepted the Premier League argument that without the collective agreement, less money would be available at the lower level of the game, and that on balance the collective agreement brought positive benefits to the game. These benefits included the opportunity to share TV income fairly between the Premier League clubs and to use some of this income to subsidise grass roots football.

Richard Scudamore, chief executive of the Premier League, argued that without the collective selling agreement other football leagues in England would suffer. He claimed that when a match is shown on TV the impact of an attendance at other grounds at the time of the televised match is 'a reduction of about 10%.' Without the collective agreement, he argued, there would be an increase in the number of televised matches, which would reduce still further attendance at grounds and 'undermine the long-term viability of the Football League.' The Football Task Force set up by the UK government welcomed the court's decision. The Task Force believed that there would be little or no income to redistribute to clubs outside the Premiership if the collective selling arrangement was brought to an end, and that this could lead to bankruptcy for many clubs.

A few years after the decision certain of the arguments used to justify the collective selling agreement could be seen to be somewhat dubious. First, not as much of the TV money was redistributed to the grass roots as had been expected, only 5% of the total, not 10%. Secondly, the actual allocation of the TV income to the Premier League clubs was not one designed to maintain a competitive balance. The successful teams received much more than the less successful.[19]

The Restrictive Practices Court decision was not the end of the issue. The European Union were concerned about the sale of rights exclusively to one company. A number of TV cable companies were becoming interested in purchasing the right to show Premier League games, and the elite Premier clubs were developing their own TV channels. The European Commission challenged the Premier League practice of selling all their matches to one TV company. There was also the question of whether or not selling the exclusive rights to one broadcasting company did produce more money for the league than selling individual packages of matches to more than one TV company.

In 2003 the Premier League, in order to try to satisfy the European Commission's policy, divided their matches into four packages. The intention was that one media company would purchase the rights to show one package of matches, another company another package and so on. It was thought at the time that BSkyB would as a result of a competitive bidding process buy the 'golden' package, which would enable them to select the most attractive 38 matches. It was also thought that BSkyB would purchase the 'silver' package, which meant the next best 38 matches. It was thought that ITV and the BBC would then compete for the two 'bronze' packages, which consisted of 31 games each.

The hoped for competitive bidding process and spreading of live matches over different channels did not materialise. In August 2003 the Premier League announced that BSkyB had won the right to screen all live matches for the next three seasons, commencing with the 2004–05 season. In other words, BSkyB had purchased all four packages. The European Commission were unhappy that another exclusive broadcasting rights deal was in place. Richard Scudamore expressed the view that 'we are confident that we have met all the EC concerns.' Not everyone interested in football was so confident—to many the deal looked as if it had been fixed. Once again business interests won and the consumer lost.

The Premier League received £1.19 billion for this three year deal, which was less than that received for the previous three years. Nevertheless, the deal was heralded by Richard Scudamore as good for football, by which he meant good for the Premier League.[20] BSkyB were reported to have admitted they had an interest in maintaining the quality of top flight British football. They were not talking about an interest in maintaining the sport. BSkyB acquired the right to show more matches (138) than pre-viously (106), at a lower price, and for the first time they had the right to show live matches at 1.00 p.m. and 5.00 p.m. on Saturdays. These times fit in well with TV programming and are times when it is convenient to show live matches in pubs.

Rupert Lowe, the then chairman of Southampton, and a member of the FA's executive board, was one notable figure critical of the European Commission's intervention into the selling of TV rights.[21] He blamed them for lowering the value of the Premier League's highly lucrative TV deal. At the time Southampton were in the Premier League. 'The insistence on splitting the broadcast deal into packages and the continual moving of the goal posts has quite simply cut the value of the deal to the clubs. The EC does not understand the structure of the game. I do not like the presence of unelected bureaucrats in Europe showing unwanted interest in our game. We are supposed to live in a capitalist society in which we can sell what we want to whom we wish. It's interesting, isn't it, that money is pouring in from former Communist Russia to the Premiership while Brussels is taking it out. England has the most successful league in the world but it is crucial that the people who run the game are allowed to do so as they please.'

Rupert Lowe was chairman and in control of Southampton for ten years. He also became an influential person at the FA. He was an unusual type of club chairman having little background in football. Gordon Strachan, who was manager of Southampton for a time, believes that Lowe's favourite sports are probably hockey and rugby.[22] He made some unconventional managerial appointments at Southampton, including England's former Rugby Union coach, Sir Clive Woodward. Unfortunately for Lowe, he disappointed the supporters of his club; the club did move to an exciting new stadium at St Mary's during his time in charge, and took part in the 2003 FA Cup final, but were relegated from the Premier League in 2005. Lowe was not an easy person to work with. There were eleven managers at the club during his time in office. In 2006 the major shareholders at the club wanted him to leave. There were wealthy investors who were prepared to put money into the club if Rupert Lowe was removed.[23]

There was a big surprise in 2006 when the auction by the Premier League of TV broadcasting rights resulted in more money coming into the game from this source than ever before. The clubs and BSkyB had fought to retain an exclusive deal, as it was thought that if one broadcaster did not have the exclusive rights to show all Premier League games that the total revenues from selling the rights would fall. They did not, they increased. BSkyB paid £1.3 billion for the right to broadcast four out of six packages of games for the three years from 2007–08, and Setanta, an Irish media company, paid £392 million for the rights to the other two packages. (This was in total a 66% increase on the amount received from the previous three-year deal.) In fact, the £1.7 billion is not the total income from broadcasting Premier League games; once mobile phone, internet highlight programmes and overseas rights are added in, the total became £2.7 billion.[24]

As Deloitte point out, for 'top quality' football, the collapse in the value of broadcasting rights, which had been forecast by some, has not happened. In France and Germany, as well as in the UK, there have been large increases in the value of the broadcasting deals. They go on to say that 'we must admit that like other industry commentators, we were surprised that the value of the new broadcasting deal was as high as it was.'[25] The top clubs become richer and TV becomes more and more obtrusive. It is projected that the TV reach of the Premiership will increase by 63% over the next ten years. That is, from 249 million to 407 million.

Spectators, both those attending the match and those watching on TV, were first exposed to moving advertising messages in 2001. Channel Five, who were at the time broadcasting an England World Cup game, were after the match heavily criticised on account of the rolling images being a distraction. But advertisers were prepared to pay large amounts to be able to make use of this very effective form of promotion. Because the pictures move around the boards surrounding the pitch, people do read them. Whose interests were most important? The advertisers. A few years later such electronic advertising hoardings had become the norm, particularly in the Premier League.

Advertisers find moving messages a particularly effective way of catching the eye of potential customers. At one time the Europeans mocked American football on account of the fact that sixty minutes of actual playing time could take three (or more) hours to complete, partly due to advertising breaks during the game. Soccer, in contrast, flowed more or less non-stop for the two, forty-five minute periods. Now soccer has gone one better than American football, it can show adverts continually whilst the game is in progress. The business interests override the sporting interests. Jim Smith, a respected football manager, said whenever changes take place now in football 'they will be dictated by the revenue football is getting from television and not by the paying public.'[26] The tail now wags the dog. However, to be fair most of the changes in league football from the time when it began have been dictated by those who provide the money.[27]

Football, as with all businesses, provides an opportunity for many people involved with the supply side of the industry to make money, some to earn a good living, for the chosen few a remarkably good living. The problem is of course that although professional football is a business, it is not like any other business. Clubs attract many fans, or as they are now called customers, who care passionately about their team. Football brings people together, who share a common 'faith', and who form bonds with like-minded people.

37

The fans care passionately about their team. They share a common history. They have an identity. This is being eroded as television and mass marketing take-over the game. Perhaps this does not matter to the top teams to whom the fans have become of less importance than the corporate customer. It is only when clubs are in financial difficulties that the support of the fans becomes of crucial importance.

What is happening in football is what sociologists call the mediaisation of popular culture. Those in control of the modern game have been successful in that they have increased the size of the total market for the game, and they are certainly bringing into the industry more money than ever. BSkyB were able to build up their empire by selling football all around the world. Sports goods manufacturers were also able to build up big empires because they sell products that are associated in consumers minds with sports stars and sporting clubs. Nike, for instance, are associated in football-related products with Arsenal and Manchester United. An international company with roots in the US, Nike are the market leaders with annual sales of over £7 billion, followed by Adidas (based in Germany) with sales of £4.5 billion, and Reebok (based in the UK) with sales of £2 billion. These companies compete for sponsorship of the top football clubs, the top players and the leading sporting events.

The Producers

It is an obvious point that two of the principal parties involved in the supply of football matches are the club owners and the players. Two other parties involved with the supply of football matches are the administrators of the leagues and cup competitions, and the regulators, inside and outside the game.

As it now stands, power is not shared equally between these four parties and over time the balance of power has swung from one to another. For the first 80 years of the sport, the players had little power—they have been referred to as being for many years little better than 'serfs'. It has been suggested by some that the balance of power has now swung too much the other way. Sepp Blatter has said that 'the most important people in football are the players,' but this is what one would expect a 'modern' head of FIFA to say. The most important people in the modern game are in fact just a small elite. This includes a few top players, but also includes a small group of administrators, club owners, managers, agents and business executives. It is they who are shaping the modern game. This elite group includes executives of the media companies who are now the main buyers of the game, but it does not include representatives of other consumer groups, such as fans or armchair supporters.[28]

One party influencing the supply of football at a domestic level is the government. Football has to follow the laws of a country (and in the UK those of the EU) and the rules and regulations of regulatory bodies. In the UK, the government has intervened in football over such matters as ground safety, the sale of alcohol and work permits, but on many issues it allows football to regulate itself. There has been pressure on the government to appoint an independent regulator for football, but after some initial interest they appear to have decided not to become too closely involved with football. The most important regulatory influence now on what happens in football is arguably the European Union, whose laws on employment and competition have led to major changes. Political parties and bureaucrats pay lip service to football being the people's game, and to it having a wide role in society, but they do little to protect the sport from free market forces. In his 1994 book, *The People's Game*, James Walvin referred to football as just that: a game of the people. In his later book of 2004 he observed that the game had been taken away from the people. It was no longer those who played the game who paid to attend matches or local businessmen who were directors of clubs, nor was it the case that the national administrators who served the game were the most important figures in the professional game. In one sense the game still belongs to the people, but to different people.

2

The Globalisation of Football

On St George's day, 2005, Chelsea were on their way to the English Premier League Championship. They had two English players in their team, a team with a Portuguese manager and a Russian owner. Their rivals Arsenal had only a few weeks earlier fielded a team with no players from either the UK or Ireland. The largest block of shares of the then third best team in England, Manchester United, were already owned by foreigners, and were soon to be taken over by an American who had only ever seen one soccer match. In fact, the majority of the players in the Premier League then (as now) came from outside the UK and Ireland. Each month there is a new rumour of a wealthy foreign investor wishing to take-over an English club. Is this what followers of football in England want?[1]

We are told it is. We are told that the Premier League is the best in the world. The evidence is right there in the level of demand to watch games on TV, and can be seen also in the insatiable demand to purchase products associated with football, for this is what the consumer wants.[2] We are told that the game is now an important part of popular culture. In fact the game has been taken over by big business. For it is big business that has sold the game to those who can afford to purchase the product, and they in turn have sold it globally.[3]

The political and economic philosophy currently in vogue, combined with changes in technology, have led to the globalisation of football. The game, which was once locally based, is now driven by a multitude of competitions, involving either elite club sides or the many national sides. Each year it seems a new 'global' competition is introduced, each new one helping to reduce the importance of domestic competitions. Of the four fundamental economic freedoms strongly promoted by the European Union—the free movement of goods, persons, services and capital—two have fundamentally changed football. The English clubs (some more than others) have embraced the free movement of people and capital: foreign players, foreign managers and foreign capital. Some clubs have, nevertheless, failed to take advantage of these new opportunities. This book is, at least in part, about the clubs who were left behind, those who failed to join the elite. Why did they fail? What will happen to them in the future? Can they catch up?

Globalisation is not some God given solution to help the world become a better place. 'It is not some inevitable kind of end-state, but rather, a complex, intermediate set of processes.'[4] It is not necessarily better than what has gone before, and it is not necessarily worse, it is just different. Although at present globalisation is an economic steamroller, it will not go on forever, there will be change, there always is. 'These (globalisation) processes are worked out through the actions and interactions of two major groups of actors—trans-national corporations and states—set within a volatile technological environment.' It was one set of politicians (in the 1980s) who decided to let the globalisation process loose; another set of politicians could one day stop the steamroller.

What Peter Dicken describes above is happening in every industry. Technological changes have allowed football to become part of the global entertainment industry. Because of the appeal of the sport to very large numbers of people, it has attracted the multi-national company and the state. The game is now run by trans-national businesses, both on the supply side, in FIFA, UEFA and G14, and on the demand side, in TV companies and multi-nationals such as BSkyB and Nike. This has meant a decline in the importance, on the supply side, of all but the top few clubs, and of the national football associations; on the demand side, it has meant a decline in the football spectator.

As with all globalisation, there is a good side and a bad side. The good side is that so many people in the world now have an opportunity to enjoy a broad range of products and watch top class football. The danger is that a few suppliers will continue to become very rich at the expense of football in general and football fans in particular. The current political view is that free markets are best and that if business in any industry is left to itself with as few restrictions as possible, then this will lead to the best possible outcome for all concerned. The free market economic system, combined with the elimination of tariffs and the removal of restrictions on the movement of labour and capital, leads to globalisation. It is argued by those who support the free market philosophy that globalisation leads to the greatest possible total returns. There is reason to believe, though, that not everyone benefits from the system. Joseph Stiglitz, who was Chief Economist at the World Bank from 1997–2000, suggests that the failures of globalisation can be traced to the fact that 'in setting the rules of the game, commercial and financial interests and mind-sets have seemingly prevailed over all other interests.'[5] The game Stiglitz is referring to is the free market for products and services. The failings he refers to apply equally to the market for the game of football. Stiglitz believes that 'the most fundamental change that is required to make globalisation work (and the free market system) in the way it should is a change in governance.' By this change in governance he means that interests other than financial should be taken into account in the decision-making process. There are in fact a number of respected economists who go as far as to argue that the globalisation process is already collapsing, but that Western governments are at present reluctant to admit that they have got it wrong.

The winners in the global economy are the 'elite trans-national capitalist class.' These are the owners and controllers of the major businesses, 'the globalising bureaucrats and politicians, the globalising professionals (with particular technical expertise), merchants and media people.'[6] The winners in football are those involved with the elite clubs, the owners, and the directors of these clubs and the regulators and organisers of the game that operate at the global level. The winners also include the top professional players and the merchants and media involved with the game and its products.

Suffice to say, the way the globalisation process has been allowed to develop is controversial. Free markets with some interference and regulation have the potential to benefit all, but the way it is being allowed to operate is leading to increasing inequality in income and wealth distribution. This applies at the international level to inequality between countries, at the personal level to inequalities between rich and poor, and at the corporate level to increasing inequality between large and small companies. All of

43

these failings apply to the globalisation of football. The market-based economic system, to be efficient, requires competition, but in fact effective competition in football at the top level is limited (in an economic and sporting sense).

In England, we have one Premier League (a private organisation) and then a number of weaker leagues (also private). We do not have two major leagues competing against each other. We do not now realistically have the possibility of a new league being formed to compete with the Premier League. Even the FA does not now stand up to the Premier League. At the European level, we have one (private) organisation controlling all the European-wide competitions. In terms of the domestic competitions within Europe, the same picture is emerging.[7] The gap between leagues is increasing. The Premier League is now by far the richest league in Europe. In 2005–06 the total revenue of the Premier League clubs was €600 million greater than that of the second biggest league, Serie A in Italy. In 1999–2000 the gap was under €100 million.

The magnitude of the difference between the revenues of different leagues is the same problem as that faced by individual clubs within a league. The rich clubs are becoming richer, the other clubs are fighting for the crumbs, either to obtain the last place available in a European competition or to avoid relegation. Clubs that once had the potential to be amongst the elite are finding that they have been left far behind. They have missed the opportunity; the financial gap is now too big. This is the situation at big city clubs such as Tottenham, Aston Villa, Everton, Leeds and Manchester City. These clubs once enjoyed success, but at a crucial time they were let down by their directors, by those who were responsible for strategic decisions.

There are of course good aspects of the global market in football. The standard of play of the top teams is outstanding. Consumers all around the world benefit from having the opportunity to see, in the UEFA Champions League, matches between Chelsea and Barcelona and AC Milan versus Real Madrid. The top players enjoy very good rewards.

Not surprisingly, BSkyB boss Rupert Murdoch once described himself as being a total 'internationalist'. Murdoch has admitted that the globalisation process, to which his TV companies contribute, is not without its dangers. One such danger being that globalisation will 'homogenise the whole world with satellite and with no room for local culture.' But Murdoch also believes that most people will benefit and the world will be a better place for having free markets.[8]

The Globalisation of Capital

The ownership of clubs is becoming increasingly controversial. For a number of years the actual funds to purchase many of the clubs has come from mysterious sources, chiefly funds in offshore financial centres (tax havens). This money is kept offshore not only to avoid tax, but also for secrecy. Many of those who own the money do not want the authorities to know how it was obtained. Much of this secret money is dirty money, obtained from drug dealing, arms trading, people smuggling and corruption. Some of it is even 'earned' by taking advantage of the weaknesses or faults in governmental control. A third of the world's wealth is now secret money. It is not surprising that some of it finds its way back into football.

Funds can flow easily from one country to another; barriers to capital mobility have been removed. Individuals and companies with funds in one country, whether that country is one of the major industrial nations or a tax haven offering anonymity, can purchase control of companies in almost any country. Companies engaged in football are no different to companies in any other business. Japanese, Chinese, German and American companies have taken over control of much of England's manufacturing industry.[9] Americans, Russians, Icelanders, Lebanese, Egyptian and others have taken over control of certain English football clubs.

Nick Leeson, the rogue trader who brought down Barings Bank in 1995, and who spent time in prison in Singapore, has expressed an interesting opinion on the financing of football clubs. Writing in the *Guardian* in 2005 he asked 'Does mismanagement in football make it vulnerable to something more sinister than incompetence?'[10] Leeson was referring to the lack of controls on the ownership of football clubs. His answer was 'Yes, the idea of money-laundering is to put dirty money into something and take a reduced, clean amount out. These people are quite happy to lose some along the way. So why not at a football club? Whenever

45

someone is prepared to invest a lot of money you have to ask where it comes from.'

A particularly worrying aspect about the global capital market is that it actually increases uncertainty. People associated with Manchester United were relatively happy with life until 2005. They believed their club was something special, that it was safe and successful, but they discovered that if you become involved in the global markets you could lose. Shareholders of Manchester United had demonstrated on a number of occasions that they were willing to sell their shares when offered big enough gains.

Most Manchester United supporters were devastated when 'their' club was taken over by Malcolm Glazer, yet such an event was predictable. It was the fifth attempt to take-over the club, and sooner or later one such attempt would succeed. Between 1985 and 2005 Manchester United were extremely successful both financially and on the pitch. The directors of the club, however, made one, possibly two, crucial mistakes. The first was to have their shares listed on a stock exchange; the second was that they forgot or chose to forget, that as a public company they needed to keep their shareholders satisfied.

In the late 1980s and early 1990s a number of clubs made the decision to go public and Manchester United were just one of them. At the time football clubs desperately needed an additional source of funds. The big crowds seen in the 1950s and 1960s were a thing of the past, while TV money was minimal. In 1983 Manchester United received just £25,000 a year from TV, the same as Rochdale. Tottenham had already raised money on the stock market. In 1984, prior to Manchester United's float, Martin Edwards, chairman and majority shareholder in Manchester United, was informed that Robert Maxwell, who at the time owned Oxford United, was interested in purchasing his stake in the club. Maxwell was an unpopular figure, once labelled 'the unacceptable face of capitalism.' In the end, Edwards decided against selling his controlling interest to Maxwell.

In 1989 a new bidder appeared on the scene, Michael Knighton. Knighton had made money out of property development. Football was at a low point at the time following the Heysel and Hillsborough disasters and Knighton told Edwards that not only would he buy his shares for £10 million, but that he would invest in ground improvements at Old Trafford. Edwards was tempted, he could not afford to invest in the ground, he owed a bank over £1 million, and his house was mortgaged. He gave Knighton an option to buy his shares. When news of the possible deal between Edwards and Knighton became known there was an outcry. It soon became clear that Knighton was not what he said he was. He personally did not have the amount of money behind him that he had led Edwards to believe he did. It became known that two well-known businessmen were backing Knighton's bid but following the public criticism of Knighton they withdrew their support.[11]

In June 1991 the club finally floated their shares on the stock market. A number of football clubs were persuaded by their financial advisers to have their shares listed on a stock exchange and were told about the advantages of a listing (access to more finance and existing shareholders having an opportunity to real-ise financial gains) but not about the dangers. One of the dangers of a listing, is that a listed company can become a take-over target.

According to Sir James Goldsmith, the stock market is a jungle in which only the strong survive. In the jungle you have predators who prowl around eating the weak, and so it is in the stock market.[12] But there is one difference; all the studies on mergers and acquisitions show that in the stock market it is not only the weak, the unsuccessful that are taken over, sometimes the strong become the victims of predators, too. This is particularly the situation if the predator is knowledgeable about the latest financial engineering techniques.

Football clubs never considered they would become a part of what is called 'the market for corporate control'; the target of take-over battles. In September 1998 Rupert Murdoch's BSkyB tried to take-over Manchester United. Articles quickly appeared in the Murdoch-controlled press arguing that this would be good for the club, but supporters did not think so and they conducted an impressive and effective campaign to prevent the take-over. The supporters had the backing of MPs, the FA and, it is said, club manager Alex Ferguson. There was a widespread fear that a leading broadcasting company owning a leading club would not be good for the game.

BSkyB bid £623 million for the club, a big increase on the £20 million that Michael Knighton had valued the club at 9 years earlier. Martin Edwards himself had been in discussion with BSkyB prior to the announcement of the bid, and if the bid was successful, it was rumoured that Edwards was to join the board of BSkyB.

After two months of lobbying against the bid the proposed take-over was referred to the Monopolies and Mergers Commission. It is surprising that there was ever any doubt that the proposed take-over would be investigated. With the political mood so much in favour of free and fair competition, how could the largest purchaser (BSkyB) of football be allowed to take-over the most prestigious supplier (Manchester United) of football? Not surprisingly the Commission found that if BSkyB took over Manchester United it would damage competition amongst broadcasters for Premier League rights and also harm the quality of British football.

The reasons the Commission gave for arriving at this conclusion are illustrating. First, the Commission said that such a deal 'would reinforce the existing trend towards greater inequality of wealth between clubs, thus weakening the smaller ones.' Second, they argued that 'it would give BSkyB additional influence over Premier League decisions relating to the organisation of football 'which did not reflect the long-term interests of football.'

It has been said that if the Commission had allowed the bid to go ahead, then BSkyB had the support of 'close' to enough shareholders to have been able to take-over the club. Martin Edwards was prepared to sell his shares, as was the chairman, Sir Roland Smith, and Peter Kenyon, the then deputy chief executive. Such matters as balanced competition and the long-term interests of football are of course not relevant to shareholders of individual clubs. The Trade Secretary, however, blocked the take-over bid.

It is necessary at this juncture to differentiate the take-over of a club such as Leeds in 2004 with the take-over of Manchester United. In Leeds' case, the club needed new owners in order to survive. It had suffered from bad management, the club was unsuccessful on and off the pitch, and it had huge debts that had to be paid off. Manchester United were the complete opposite. They appeared to be well-managed, successful, with no debts. But in the stock market, in the fight for corporate control, the strong are sometimes victims just as much as the weak.

The characteristics of Manchester United shareholders changed over the 1990s. In 1990, Martin Edwards was the largest share-holder, with a major percentage of the balance held by financial institutions. In 1991, Phillips and Drew Fund Management were the second largest shareholder (10.9%). In 1995 Marathon Asset Management were the second largest investors, owning approximately 6%. But by the end of the decade institutional investors were becoming increasingly disillusioned with football club shares, while private investors were becoming more interested, some attracted by the possibility of financial returns and some because of the chance it provided to control and be involved with a high profile activity.[13]

Martin Edwards, who at one time owned over 50% of the clubs equity, began to disinvest. In October 1999 he sold 19.5 million of the shares of the club for just under £41 million. (This amounted to 7.5% of the total shares in the club.) He had been approached by stockbrokers, who were looking for Manchester United shares and Edwards clearly thought this was a profitable time to sell (at a price of £2.10 per share), following, as it did, on the treble success of the club in the previous season.

Edwards had a few months earlier been approached by two Irish racehorse owners, J.P. McManus and John Magnier, but he turned down their offer to buy his holdings, 'aware that there were voices in Old Trafford who were not happy at the prospect of a racing syndicate owning a large slice of shares.' He sold his final block of shares in the club, 17.0 million (6.5% of the total) to Harry Dobson (who made his money in the mining industry) in May 2002. Dobson said that he bought the shares as a 'punt'. As it happened, Dobson did very well with his £20 million purchase. His holding (in the name of Mountbarrow Investments) doubled in value in two years.

Towards the end of 2002, Manchester United shares were trading close to their five-year low. There was talk at the time of turning the club into a mutual organisation, owned for the benefit of the fans and partly run by the fans. The idea was for a supporters organisation to borrow on the security of the guaranteed part of the club's revenues (ticket sales, sponsorship deals) and to use the funds raised to purchase shares and to take the club off the stock market. The bank behind the plan was Goldman Sachs. In the end the plan was not pursued. Two years later, the same financing technique was used to support the take-over of the club by Malcolm Glazer, with Goldman Sachs as advisors.

By 2004 the shares of the club had become concentrated in a few hands. BSkyB had sold the 10% holding they acquired at the time of the unsuccessful take-over attempt. The holdings of J.P. McManus and John Magnier, through their investment company Cubic Expression, had been steadily increasing, from 6.8% in October 2001 to 28.9% in September 2004. Another private investor who had appeared on the scene at this time was Malcolm Glazer. He held 3.2% of the shares in September 2003, and 19.2% a year later. When in October 2004 Glazer was seeking to add to the size of his holding of shares with a view to a possible take-over, a key purchase that he made was the holding of the Swiss bank, UBS, who offered him 8 million shares (about 3% of the total) at a price of £2.85 per share. Glazer purchased these shares, and on the same day acquired another 7.8 million shares at the same price. This raised his holdings from 19.2% to 25.5%. UBS had previously gone on record as having a long-term interest in Manchester United, but here they demonstrated that if the gain from a sale is big enough, an institutional investor's first obligation is to realise the profits in the interests of those whose money they manage.

At first the interest of Glazer in the club was not taken too seriously. In the US he had built up a reputation as a person who regularly tries to buy sports clubs. At one time or another he had attempted to acquire three American football clubs, and three baseball teams. Before buying the Tampa Bay Buccaneers he had tried to purchase the New England Patriots. He had been described at the time as a 'tyre kicker', someone who likes to try out a new car, to look at it, to kick its tyres, but someone who in the end does not go ahead with the purchase. Clearly in the Manchester United case, having kicked the tyres he did not walk away. McManus, Magnier and others sold to him, he acquired Manchester United plc, took the company private, and put his children on the club's board.

Although it was predictable that Manchester United would be taken over, it was a surprise that the person who became the new owner was an American who knew nothing about football. The price that he paid was high, based more on the recent valuation levels of American football teams than of European football clubs. He valued the club at over four times its annual turnover (revenue), whereas the market value of other Premier League clubs was closer to the size of their annual turnover. The market value of Aston Villa in mid-2005, for example, was in the region of £43 million, and its 2004 revenue was £56 million. Tottenham's market value in mid-2005 was £30 million, its revenue was £66 million. Are

English football clubs worth four times their annual revenue? This will be discussed further in the chapter on Finance. Time will tell who is right. There is more than one way of valuing a business, and perhaps profitability is more important than revenue. In fact every NFL club (franchise) is profitable (including Tampa Bay). Much of the credit for this is usually given to the policies and abilities of those running the NFL, and in particular to their strict salary cap policy and a very lucrative TV deal.

Malcolm Glazer handled the public relations side of the bid badly. He tried to bully the Manchester United board. He asked to be allowed to examine the financial records of the club (to conduct due diligence on the club's books), and warned the directors that if they did not allow him to do so, he would at the annual general meeting vote against the directors who were standing for re-election. He was advised against taking such action by his public relations firm and by his bank. He ignored the advice, voted against the three directors standing for re-election, and as a result the club's legal adviser, the club's commercial director and an important member of the financial community were voted off the board. McManus and Magnier (still significant shareholders) did not vote on the re-election proposals. Glazer was able to show what a nuisance he could be. Glazer lost the support of some of the financial community, and J.P. Morgan, his main financial backer, withdrew their support. Later his public relations firm also stopped working with him. In the end, however, all that mattered was money. He proved that if he offered a high enough price he would win.

The directors of Manchester United could not truthfully recommend to shareholders that they reject the take-over on the grounds that the price offered for their shares was too low. All they could say was that they believed that the amount of debt being raised by the Glazer family in order to raise cash to pay for the Manchester United shares would be harmful to the football club. Of the £831 million needed to purchase the club (including £41 million paid out as fees) £284 million was being financed by debt secured against the club's assets, at an interest rate which could vary between 7.35% and 11.10%. There was little to worry about with this part of the borrowing. The problem arose over the £275 million 'pay in kind loans' (PIK). Such loans are expensive for the borrower because the investors who advance the money, usually hedge funds,

51

take on a considerable level of risk. (The interest charge varies between 14% and 20%.) The securities are close to equity in terms of risk but are loans because the money obtained has to be repaid. The annual interest on a PIK does not have to be paid to the investors each year, but can be rolled up and paid when the PIK is redeemed. The annual interest that is not paid is of course added to the debt and itself earns interest. This can result in the end in very high interest charges.

The PIK's issued to obtain funds to acquire Manchester United are secured against the Glazer family's business assets (their own resources), which of course now include the assets of Manchester United. If the PIK's cannot be redeemed at the agreed date, the family's stake in Manchester United could be transferred to the three hedge funds that purchased the notes (that advanced the money).[14] No wonder the Manchester United supporters were worried, but like it or not this is the world of global business.

Against such powerful financial players, what hope do traditional fans have of being of significance in the people's game? The local fans are only important to the club if the club has failed to attract the interest of those who control the global market place (or if there are high interest charges to be covered.)[15] Although the motives of many 'predators' are financial, this does not mean that all predators are asset strippers. The majority of the hostile take-overs in the last five years have been more strategically focused than financial. Such take-overs are motivated by factors as diverse as market power, economies of scale and business growth. In such take-overs the buyer is seeking the long-term development of the business, although even in such cases this usually means much restructuring of the acquired firm.

Peter Kenyon (who had been chief executive of Manchester United from August 2000) had warned that the club would always be faced by the insecurity of being 'in play' for a take-over bid. This was because it was a public limited company. He contrasted this position with that of Chelsea, the club he moved to as chief executive, who as a private company had security. He said that he was glad he was no longer on United's board, and that he was much happier operating under private ownership. 'Within the industry the preference would always be for private ownership over public. There was a time when it was seen as a golden goose for clubs to go to the stock market. Manchester United gained liquidity in shares, which allowed key shareholders to benefit, but apart from about £16 million the bulk of the £150m to £160m we invested in players and stadia came from within the football club. As a public company you are always in play, and in terms of long-term planning that makes life difficult. As a private business it means that literally three of us (at Chelsea) can decide what to do.'

Kenyon was of course speaking as chief executive of a club that was about to win the Premier League and had got to the semi-finals of the UEFA Champions League, but also as chief executive of a club that had just made huge monetary losses. Very few private owners of a business are prepared to put up with large losses. As the directors, managers and players of Manchester United might discover, private ownership can also have its problems.

The relationship between the amount of debt finance used by a company and the amount of its equity finance is referred to as the level of financial gearing (or leverage). For many years it was accepted by those in the financial community in the UK and the US that the optimal level of such gearing is about 50:50. This means that for a profitable company somewhere in the region of 50% of the assets of the company should be financed by borrowed money and the remainder by equity finance. One reason why gearing is advantageous is because interest paid on debt is, for a profitable company, tax deductible. At an optimal level of gearing the cost of money used to run the business is at its lowest and the value of the equity shares is the highest. What is an acceptable level of debt changed dramatically with the growth of private equity.

Manchester United were proud of the fact that they had no borrowing. Too much borrowing (as at Leeds United) is obviously dangerous but, less obviously, too little borrowing is dangerous. Manchester United had for many years been a profitable company, paying taxes. The financial predators in the stock market prey on companies that do not follow wise financial policies. If the Manchester United directors were not prepared, on the strength of their assets, to borrow money then there were financial operators who were. The much-hated Malcolm Glazer was just following the basic rules of finance. Debt finance is cheaper than equity finance, and so by borrowing up to the optimal levels of gearing and investing wisely, directors are able to raise the total value of the

y and to provide shareholders with large gains. The shareholders of large public companies are usually investors interested
in making money. Glazer, by following the rules of finance, was
able to raise the value of Manchester United. The high profile and
experienced directors of Manchester United must have thought
they could ignore the way investors in the stock market behave.
They might also have thought that the basic rules of finance did
not apply to them. They were wrong.

There is no better example than Manchester United of the fact
that football clubs are now principally global businesses. With the
free movement of labour and capital not only can they easily
become foreign-owned, the managers and workers (players) can
come from anywhere.

It is ironic that one of the two clubs that Malcolm Glazer owns
plays in a league in which there is a good level of competitive
balance, and the other one, the one in England, plays in a league
where four teams dominate. Glazer of course will be happy to be
owning one of these dominant clubs in a league where there is not
much threat to his club's elite position, and where the authorities
and media do not seem to be worried about the position—as long
as the money continues to flow in.

The take-over of Manchester United was controversial. The
subseqent take-over of English clubs by foreign investors, including
that of Liverpool, have been less so.[16]

Globalisation and Players

Concern over the number of foreign players in English football is
not new. One hundred years ago the worry was about the number
of Scottish players in the English League. Now there are occasions
when clubs such as Chelsea and Arsenal field teams with no
English players at all. The recent success of some clubs, for
example Arsenal, has been based almost entirely on foreign
players.

To put it in perspective, from 1978 to 1990, only 11 non-British
players were recruited by Manchester United; in the next 10 years
they recruited 33 non-British players. In the 1992–93 season (the
first of the Premier League) the proportion of foreign players in

the league was 13%; by 2004–05 it was 50.6%. A similar situation now exists in the other major leagues in Europe, with very few local players being given the opportunity to develop. In the Euro 2004 tournament, when the national sides from England, France, Italy, Spain, Germany and Holland all performed badly, this failure was put down to the failure of each of these countries to develop their own domestic talent. In the past, national football associations were allowed to impose quotas on the number of foreign players that could be included in any one team. Such practices are now illegal.[17]

As the European Union becomes larger, the pool of footballers that can move freely from one country to another increases. In 2003 the President of the German Football Association urged officials in the EU to protect home-grown talent. He said that he would like to limit the number of foreigners playing in the German league, but regretted that this was not possible because of the laws to do with the free movement of people within the EU. He noted that 'European law rules over football, which suffers from EU decisions that are hostile to sport.'

A similar concern had been expressed in England by the Professional Footballers Association, who have found that more youth players in England are dropping out of the game than ever before. The PFA are concerned that the enlargement of the EU will result in more foreign players than ever before being attracted to leagues such as the Premiership with its high salaries.

When Arsenal beat Real Madrid in the UEFA Champions League in February 2006, Gordon Taylor of the PFA noted that Arsenal's victory was 'not an English success. It's probably a greater reflection of youngsters from France and elsewhere in Europe. It's hard to say that it speaks volumes for English football when none of the players are home-grown.' There were in fact two English players that took part in the match, David Beckham and Jonathan Woodgate, but they played for Real Madrid.

When the Premier League was first formed one argument the FA used to support its introduction was that it would result in a stronger national team. It clearly has not worked. England continue to do badly in international competitions, good enough to beat the weaker sides, but not so good so as to get through to the finals of competitions. Despite paying the national manager in the region of £4 million a year, double what any other country at the time paid their manager, and eight times what the winners of Euro 2004 (Greece) paid theirs, we did not get results. The Premier League might be the richest league in the world, but this wealth does evidently very little to help build a world-class national team.[18]

The European Commission, with its role of promoting a community-wide approach to such issues, might not like the idea of a home-grown quota, yet it needs to be recognised that there is a problem. Most football followers like to identify with their own national side. If their national side performs badly all the time they will lose interest in international competitions.

In the years up to 2006 (when they won the World Cup) Italy had also been very disturbed by the lack of success of their national team. There had been a call for each Italian sports club to be made to field teams in which at least half of the players were Italian. The Italian Football Federation had been suggesting such changes for some time 'as the only way to safeguard their national identity.' The situation has been made even worse by the decision made in the so-called Kolpak case. In 2003 a Slovakian handball player named Maros Kolpak won a legal ruling that suggested that he could play in the European Union as a non-foreigner because his home country had an 'associate agreement' with countries of the EU. Prior to this ruling it was of course known that citizens of any member state could play in any other member state as a non-foreigner, but it had not been thought that this free movement of labour rule applied to citizens of 'associate' countries. The ruling worried many people as it allowed players from many parts of the world theoretical entry into the major European leagues.[19]

UEFA recently tried to take steps to slow down the trend that results in the majority of players in the major European leagues being from outside the home country of the league in question. The UEFA plan announced in April 2005 was to introduce quotas for clubs for home-grown players. The plan was that from the start of the 2006–07 season, clubs entering the Champions League and UEFA Cup must name at least four home-grown players (with at least two of these from their own academy and the other one or two trained by clubs in the same country) as part of their 25-strong squad.

The plan was that the quota would rise to six players the next season and then to eight—almost a third of their squad – by the start of the 2008–09 season. Home-grown players were defined not by nationality but rather by nurture. Those eligible would need to spend at least three years between the ages of fifteen and twenty-one being developed by their club or by another club or academy from the 'home' country. This policy was approved by UEFA's national federations.

Clubs competing in European competitions will be bound by this ruling, but it will not apply to domestic competitions, despite the efforts of UEFA to have the rule more widely applied. The Premier League clubs were, with two exceptions (Norwich and Charlton) against the introduction of this rule, and the FA decided to follow the line of the 'big' clubs and to argue against the quota system. (The FA is technically responsible for 43,000 registered clubs.) Of significance, however, is the fact that the representatives of the major leagues in Spain, Germany and France supported the quota system, seeing it as a way to increase opportunities for good young home-grown players.

David Dein, at the time a member of the FA Council, and a director and owner of 16% of the shares of Arsenal, argued against the introduction of quotas, claiming that 'the product is good' already, by which he meant Premier League football, and that 'we don't want to debase it.' Dein could certainly argue that his club's product had sold very well over the last decade. There is, however, more to football than the Premier League, and the UEFA proposals were designed to look after wider interests in the game.

The quota arrangements are a step forward, if only a minor one. It should, however, be appreciated that there is the possibility that none of the home-produced players in a squad might be selected to play in a match. Nevertheless it is a step in the right direction. It suggests a long-term approach to the dangers of market forces.[20]

Globalisation and the Fans

In England, the traditional supporters of clubs have continued to be loyal to their local team, even though it may be owned, managed, and on occasion, staffed exclusively by foreign players. Why? Is this the power of globalisation, or is it the power of traditional loyalty, of clinging to one's 'roots'? Joel Glazer, son of

Manchester United owner Malcolm Glazer, maintained that the 'true ownership' of the club still resided with the fans. Whatever that means!

A large percentage of the fans in England, as in most European countries, are very nationalistic—some are racist and some are xenophobic—but they do not seem to care who owns their club, who manages it or who plays for it. They do not care as long as the foreigners produce results. The 'people' who are traditional supporters of, say, Arsenal, Chelsea, Liverpool or Manchester United, are happy to see their clubs owned by rich people from Russia and the US. They are happy to see their clubs managed by educated French, Spanish, Portuguese and Italians, and they are happy to see their teams made up of skilled players from anywhere in the world. Yet these same people are often fanatical when it comes to supporting the English national team. They are willing to hurl abuse, to show hatred against the French, German, Irish, Turkish and even the Welsh and Scottish national teams. Yet they welcome players from these countries into their own club sides. Football supporters are illogical, perhaps that is why it is easy for business to exploit them. The owners of the clubs are not so illogical.[21]

3

Competitive Balance

'Competition is nice, but if you want to be profitable it helps to write
your own rules.' *Economist 27 April 2006*

The underlying market for professional sport is somewhat different
to that for other products. The economics of the industry has been
referred to as 'peculiar'.[1] One reason for this difference is arguably
because it is not in the financial interests of any one club (one
producer) to dominate the sport. The demand for sporting contests
depends partly on the uncertainty of the outcome. Once the result
of a match becomes easily predictable football loses its appeal to
many potential spectators. This means that it is necessary to
regulate competition in order to ensure that no one team achieves
too much market power. But it is not sufficient to have uncertainty
over the outcome of an individual match, it is also necessary to
have uncertainty over who will be champions in an individual
season. Balanced competition clearly results in more exciting and
greater spectator interest. So how does this fit in with the fact that
in the 15 years we have had the Premier League, Manchester
United have won the league 9 times, Chelsea twice and Arsenal
3 times?

Stefan Szymanski and Andrew Zimbalist raise the question of
whether the lack of competitive balance really matters? They point
out that football is currently the world's most popular sport even
though competitive balance has been on the decline for a decade
or two.[2] They refer to the case of Tottenham Hotspur where it
might appear 'balance' does not matter. The club still fill the
ground regularly, even though they have not been serious chal-
lengers for a European place for some time, or fighting against
relegation. 'Despite the fact that Tottenham's season was undistin-
guished, to say the least, its fans had plenty of excitement.' It is

possible, however, to look at other clubs, such as Aston Villa, Blackburn, Middlesbrough, and Bolton where the lack of excitement, and the lack of uncertainty, does appear to keep the fans away. Even Arsenal, in 2006, could not fill their new stadium for a local derby match against Tottenham.

Szymanski and Zimbalist believe that competitive balance does matter, but the reasons why they believe that the problems associated with imbalance are important are 'mostly financial rather than emotional.' They have to do with the management of clubs rather than the preferences of fans. They are worried that a club, in order to stay 'competitive', will spend more than it can afford.

Jonathan Michie and Christine Oughton have shown that over the period 1947–2004 there has been a decline in competitive balance in English football.[3] The rate of decline has been more marked since the introduction of the Premier League, and is getting worse. The decline is associated with the widening gap in wage expenditure, the unequal distribution of broadcasting revenue and the widening revenue gap between the Premier League and the Championship. Yet something can be done about all these issues if the will to do so existed.

There is evidence that competitive balance is good for sport. The evidence is based on what has happened in sports leagues around the world. Jeffrey Borland and Robert MacDonald have shown that in England uncertainty about overall success in a season has more effect on attendance levels than uncertainty about the outcome of a particular match.[4] This can be clearly seen at Villa Park, where modest final league positions have been shown to reduce average attendance figures. Borland and MacDonald review the literature on the subject and find that all the research on 'seasonal competitive balance' confirm that uncertainty of outcome (of final league position) is good for attendance figures.

In the US, Martin Schmidt and David Berri have shown that in basketball a good competitive balance encourages attendance and that the longer in time a lack of competitive balance continues the stronger a spectator deterrent it becomes.[5] When the Cleveland Browns won the American football Conference (AFC) four years in a row, between 1946 and 1949, this dominance resulted in declining spectator interest and led to the AFC merging with the NFL in 1949. There are similar stories from other sports and other leagues around the world. There is evidence that 'fan interest at the weaker franchises dries up and ultimately fan interest at the stronger franchise dries up as well.'

There is more competitive balance within the lower divisions in England than in the Premier League. A survey of supporters of Football League clubs found that in 2006 89% supported the proposition that Football League games (as opposed to Premier League games) were 'unpredictable and competitive.' The financial inequality is not so great between the teams in the Championship as it is in the Premiership.

In Italian football 'there has been a marked deterioration in competitive balance since 1992.' In Germany, the deterioration had been less marked than in other major countries but it is still possible to identify a decline in competitive balance over the last ten or so years. In Spain, the evidence of a decline in competitive balance is also identifiable.

Nobody should be surprised by this trend, it results from an increasing inequality between rich and poor clubs and from an industry that is run almost entirely on free market economic principles. If, instead of football clubs, one thinks of nation states as engaged in economic competition with one another, then the same trends are evident. The gap in wealth between the rich countries and the poor countries is increasing. Despite the efforts by the economic regulators to ensure level playing fields there is a decline in competitive balance between nations.

Maximising Wealth

Football (soccer) is the most popular sport in the world. It is not, however, the most profitable team sport, and the Premier League clubs are not the most valuable. It is the clubs in the NFL that are the most valuable. In 2004, the average NFL team was worth $733 million (approximately £431 million). To put this in perspective, West Ham United were, in 2006, worth about £100 million, and Liverpool about £250 million. What accounts for this difference?

In Europe the owners of clubs squabble with each other over the league structure that will maximise their individual wealth. By the standards of the US, football teams in England are ridiculously undervalued. The typical club in the NFL is valued at four and a half times its annual revenue. In 2004 the Washington Redskins, the most valuable club in the NFL at the time, was valued at $1.1 billion (approximately £660 million), and its annual revenue in 2004 had been $245 million. The club had been purchased by Daniel Snyder in 1999 for $750 million. (The Redskins have a reputation for being 'brilliant at maximising stadium and sponsorship revenues,' but they have not been particularly successful at football.)

A more recently successful NFL team have been the New England Patriots, who were valued in 2004 at $861 million, based on annual revenue of $191 million (again a valuation ratio of just over four times turnover). The Patriots are unusual for the NFL in that they financed a new stadium without having to use public sector money. The private sector borrowing to fund the stadium was backed by revenue to be generated from use of the new stadium. The Patriots owner is Robert Kraft, the same person whom Liverpool at one time had discussions with when they were looking for new owners.

These valuations are for the club in total, so include both the debt and equity contribution. If one looks at a club like Aston Villa, whose annual revenue in 2005 was £51 million and whose debts were zero, it might be thought that based on US valuation methods the value of its equity would be around £200 million. In 2006 they were sold for just under £63 million. Newcastle United's 2006 revenue figure was close to £87 million, which might suggest a total value of £300 million plus. (The club had debts of about £60 million.) In June 2007 their equity was purchased for close to £135 million, which taking into account the debt, valued the club at near £200 million; 2.3 times the revenue.

When Malcolm Glazer took over Manchester United he paid in the region of £800 million, which was five times the club's annual revenue—very high by English standards but not out of line with the valuation of US sports clubs.

In the US sports clubs have realised that competitive balance can be in their collective interests. The risks for NFL teams are less than those of European football clubs insofar as there is no danger of relegation and revenue and costs are more certain, more in control. A high proportion of total NFL revenue is shared between the clubs and this revenue sharing arrangement means that any one club is unlikely to suffer very much of a financial downturn.[6] Add this to the strict salary capping arrangements in place and this results in costs that are reasonably predictable. Similarly, the NFL collective bargaining arrangements have been successful. There has not been a strike since 1987. The players may have had lower annual salary increases than players in other US sports, but they have also over recent years avoided costly labour disputes.

The NFL can be said to control the supply of American football insofar as it takes pains to make sure the game is not over sold by the media, particularly by TV. The American football season lasts for less than five months and the days when live football appears on TV is limited, as is the size of the league. This is not to suggest that club owners in the US are less greedy than those controlling soccer in Europe. The Americans are simply more concerned with long-term returns, whereas FIFA, UEFA and those running the domestic leagues in the UK are more concerned with short-term benefits.

In the past each NFL club has been allowed to keep the revenue it generates from certain sources, such as its local TV and media revenue and the revenue it earns from its executive boxes and hospitality. From 2006, though, there was a reduction in the amount of self-generated revenue a club could retain. The NFL operate a strict salary cap, with clubs taxed heavily if they break the agreed levels.[7] The NFL club owners have been referred to as '32 fat cat Republicans who vote socialist' on football matters.

In 2005 the NFL national TV contract was worth $17.6 billion over eight years, which is shared between the clubs in the league. 'But the pecking order of team values and profits is determined by stadium economics. The eight most valuable teams control or own their stadiums and are therefore able to rake in millions of dollars in corporate sponsorships and advertising. The nine teams with the lowest valuations play in antiquated stadiums that are controlled by municipalities.'[8]

In other US sports leagues (as in football in Europe) corporate ownership has replaced the traditional local family-oriented business; but not in American football. The NFL does not allow corporate ownership of its clubs. The NFL is also the only US sports league with a hard salary cap (all the others have a soft cap).

The 1990s was 'a decade that produced astonishing player salaries, widespread corporate involvement and skyrocketing ticket prices and broadcasting rights fees.' The above quote could easily apply to football in Europe, but it actually refers to US sports teams.[9] However, despite tremendous growth, 70 out of the 116 US sports teams lost money during this period.

James Gladden, Richard Irwin and William Sutton believe that in an attempt to become more profitable (successful) in the future the strategy of owners of US sports clubs will be to seek to strengthen their relationship with fans at the same time as trying to sell a more attractive package to corporations.[10] The first is necessary because of the disillusionment of the 'average fan'. The disillusionment (erosion of loyalty and apathy towards the teams) results from very large increases in the cost of admission to games, and the rapid movement, and decrease in loyalty, of players to a club. This does not apply so much to NFL clubs as to clubs in other US sports. If we are considering disillusionment with football in England two other reasons could be added: one, the over exposure of the sport on TV; and two, the complete indifference by TV towards the personal interests of fans when TV wish to alter the date and starting time of matches. A season ticket holder buys his or her ticket and has little idea, until a few weeks before a match, when exactly a particular game will take place. Neither of these two 'problems' exist for fans of the NFL.

Not a Commercial Enterprise?

Professional sport in the US is sometimes referred to as being 'above the law'. There are historical reasons for this. In 1879 baseball club owners were worried about the high wages they needed to pay their star players and hit upon the idea of a 'reserve clause'. This was an agreement amongst club owners that each team could select five of its best players (the stars) and exclude them from the end of the season market when players were transferred. The five best players from each club were effectively 'reserved', which meant that the players concerned could not increase their salaries by moving to another club. (Each club agreed only to play against other clubs that honoured the reserve clause.) The situation was made worse by the fact that clubs in one league agreed to honour the reserve clause of clubs in another league. The reserve clause was challenged a number of times in US courts, but survived for many decades.

At the time, baseball, regarded as 'The American Sport', was in a bad way, despite the reserve clause. Twenty baseball leagues went out of business between 1910–20. In 1922 the Supreme Court ruled that organised baseball was exempt from the Sherman Antitrust Act, an act that was designed to prevent organisations and companies from acting as monopolies. Exemption was granted basically because the Supreme Court believed baseball was of paramount importance to the people of the US. The judgement itself was based on the rationale that baseball was not interstate commerce in the sense of the Act. In other words, the judge ruled that the business of baseball clubs was 'giving exhibitions of baseball' and that such exhibitions took place within an individual state and so therefore could not really be deemed 'commerce'. The clubs themselves argued that the provision of baseball matches was not in any way related to producing anything and so should not be subject to the rules of commerce.

The decision was highly controversial and has since been challenged many times. Individual points in the judgement have been overturned, but 'notwithstanding, organised baseball has continued to receive exemption from the antitrust laws up to the present day.' Other sports tried to adopt similar rules to baseball and attempted to avoid the monopoly laws on the grounds that they also were putting on 'exhibitions' and not producing an item for commerce. In 1936 the NFL were successful in introducing rules that amounted to a restriction on the freedom of players. They introduced the college draft system, which is still a key feature of the American football system. The draft, it is argued, helps bring about competitive balance. It has also, however, lowered salaries and bonuses for players entering the league. The new players to the league are not free to join any club they might choose.

In the years up to the 1960s, despite the 'restrictive practices' that were allowed, American football, baseball and basketball, had problems with uncompetitive leagues. This was good for the teams that dominated their sport, but resulted in falling attendances at matches of clubs not in the dominant group. It was decided that it would be in the interests of both owners and players to seek to obtain a reasonable balance of competition.

In the 1960s Congress passed legislation that exempted sports leagues from the antitrust laws as they applied to nationwide television contracts. This allowed a league such as the NFL to negotiate a collective agreement for nationwide coverage of all its league games. This exemption from the collective selling laws still applies and has been a key factor in the growth of the wealth and the popularity of American football. It is this issue the European Commission is still wrestling with 40 years later, with respect to European football.

The rules of the NFL only allow a limited number of teams to compete in their league, with limited competition within a geographical area. This provides each team with something of a regional monopoly. The revenue sharing system introduced was a means of subsidising the members of the league who had less income earning potential. All of these measures helped to create competitive balance in the sporting sense and to reduce the risk of those investing in the sport. They were not based on the principles of a free market system.

Collective Bargaining

In the 1970s the players in the various US sports succeeded in organising themselves into very powerful trade unions. This meant that the players' unions could challenge the club owners in the courts. Prior to this it was both costly and professionally dangerous for an individual player to take on club owners. In baseball the players sought free agency, with an end to the reserve clause system. This confrontation with the owners led to lockouts and strikes, to collective bargaining agreements, and then to further strikes and collusion between owners (and in the end to a free agency system). In American football, there were strikes before the signing of the first collective bargaining agreement in 1970. The courts decided that 'collective bargaining may potentially be given pre-eminence over the antitrust laws where the restraint on trade primarily affects the parties to the collective bargaining agreement.' A key word in this judgement is 'primarily,' which suggests consumers interests are not primary.

At various times this collective bargaining decision has been challenged by individual players. The draft system has also been challenged, as have the rules regarding contracts, free agency and annual salary caps, but the courts have decided in every case that where there is a genuine negotiated settlement between the players union and the NFL, that individual players should be bound by the agreement.

The law in the US sees the main economic competition in football as being between one league and another—not between the teams in a league. Rival football leagues to the NFL can be formed and have been formed, and these other leagues are free to compete with the NFL for players and customers. Sport in the US has managed, through the clever use of lawyers, to avoid the Federal laws designed to encourage economic competition in the market place.

James Quirk and Rodney Fort refer to the 'murky and equally controversial court decisions that have been handed down regarding the antitrust status of pro team sports leagues.'[11] They raise the question of why the sports industry in the US has been able to get away with practices that minimise consumer interest and maximise the interest of suppliers. In professional sport in the US over the last 30 or so years what economists refer to as 'monopoly rents' have been shared between club owners and players. Monopoly rents arise when suppliers in an industry are able to limit the supply of the product to a level lower than that which would be achieved with free market forces at play. The result of this is that the consumer pays more than they would in a free market and the producer receives more. There has, in fact, been much criticism of the restrictive practices in US sports.

For their part the NFL and other professional sports leagues have been able to justify these restrictive practices on the grounds that they are necessary to achieve competitive balance. Competitive balance is said to be what spectators want, but this is not the complete picture. The number of people that watch a match live and on television is a function not only of 'the closeness of the match' but also of the likelihood that the ultimate victor will be the team that most fans support. Not all teams are equally supported. In general those from big cities or conurbations are better supported than teams from smaller towns. Therefore, if the owner of a club wants to maximise revenue it is not sufficient for all matches to be meaningfully close and the results uncertain. It is also necessary for the clubs from the larger cities to (more often than not) be the winning teams. This is worrying, for it suggests that if the owners collectively wish to maximise league revenue, they need 'to ensure that, over the long run, it is the teams with the largest

67

number of fans that are successful.' In one match between, say, the New York Giants and Seattle Seahawks, the owners want there to be a good chance of either team winning, but with respect to their collective interests over the long-term they want New York to be more successful than Seattle. This is of course because New York's greater population is capable of generating greater revenue on TV and in stadiums.

In the 2005 American football season it was encouraging to see the success of unfashionable teams such as the Indianapolis Colts (who won the first 11 games of a 16 game season) and Seattle Seahawks (who qualified for the playoffs as early as November). These two clubs consistently beat big city clubs, such as the New York Giants and Los Angeles Rams. This simply could not happen in European football competitions, yet we are led to believe what is happening in Europe is normal under the auspices of free market competition.

There are many aspects of the US system that are instructional and can provide useful lessons to other countries. There are also many aspects that are best avoided. The notion that a small number of clubs should not consistently dominate a competition is certainly an attractive one. It is not by accident that in American football, historically, one club is at the top for, say, a three to four year period, and then reverts to being an average team. Over the last 30 years the Chicago Bears, Dallas Cowboys, Washington Redskins and San Francisco 49ers have all enjoyed a few years of domination to only then to move back to an average position. The rules of the NFL are designed to ensure this happens. This is very different to the situation with football in Europe. In the US the owners of individual clubs would obviously like their own teams to dominate, in the way of Manchester United or Arsenal, but they have also accepted that it is in the collective interests of club owners to maintain a competitive balance within their leagues.

In baseball, by contrast, the competition has for many years been dominated by one team: the New York Yankees. This is because that club's wealth is so much more than that of other teams, but also because of its location and because of the rules in baseball relating to the distribution of revenue. Major League Baseball in the US has in fact been losing its appeal. The fact that in 2002 the New York Yankees spent $126 million on wages, and the thirtieth ranked team, Tampa Bay Devil Rays, only spent $35 million on wages, would indicate a lack of competitive balance. Baseball did introduce a new salary cap scheme in 2003; the cap was set at $127 million and clubs that spent above that were to pay a 'luxury tax'. This was designed to start improving the competitive balance. But it was only a start. Only the Yankees were paying above the level of the cap and they had to pay only $10 million in tax.

Michael MacCambridge, in his story of the NFL, expresses the opinion that American football in the early years of the twenty-first century has been better than ever, 'the games [are] more consistently exciting, fluid, intense contests ... [They are] not merely closer, but more free flowing.' In 2002, with two weeks to go, 'thirteen of the sixteen teams in the NFL were still in contention for the playoffs.' This is in sharp contrast to the situation in the new century in the Premier League. It does have to be admitted, however, that in the NFL, in the early years of the twenty-first century, the New England Patriots did appear to create a 'little' dynasty.

Paul Tagliabue, who in 1989 took over the post of commissioner, referred to the system in place in the NFL as 'a very even playing field and an unforgiving system. It is a merit-based system and there are no advantages that one team can secure that another team can't secure.'[12] This is again in sharp contrast to the system in Europe. The Premier League system is not a level playing field, a handful of teams have been able to build up clear advantages.

Early History

Football has been played in the US in one form or another since Colonial times. By the mid-nineteenth century versions of the game were being played in universities. In 1873 a football team (of eleven players) from Eton played a match against Yale University. In 1877 a number of US universities adopted the rules of the game as played at Rugby school in England and so played the game with 15 men on each side. Three years later modifications were introduced which included playing with 22 men per team. This became American football.

American football began to develop as a professional sport at the same time as did soccer in England. In the 1890s in Pennsylvania, in small towns and cities near the Ohio River Valley, and in Wisconsin, Michigan and Minnesota, teams began to emerge who were willing to pay players for playing the game. As in England there was a clash between these new working class 'professionals' and those running the game at colleges who believed the game would be better if it was motivated by ideas of 'Muscular Christianity' rather than money. In order to be successful, however, some of the college teams resorted to deception. Universities such as Purdue (in Indiana), in order to physically strengthen their squad (the college boys were not muscular enough), hired some local manual workers to play for them. The college team subsequently became known as the 'boilermakers', because of the occupation of the hired help. By 1915, it had become quite common for stars of a college team to move into the professional game upon leaving university.

Both countries set out to achieve what we now call 'competitive balance' based on the belief that the game would have more appeal to the paying public if the teams competing in a game were of more or less equal ability. However, the business history of American and English football ultimately developed along very different lines. In the first half century or so of both games the governing bodies controlled the game, so as to protect the interest of the owners of the clubs, and arguably to provide the best football for fans to watch. In the US, league regulators limited the supply of football matches, restricted the movement of players between clubs and adopted a policy of revenue sharing. In England, the authorities also introduced restrictions on the transfer of players, enforced maximum player wages, and sought to share revenue, but they did not limit the supply of matches.

At the end of the Second World War the owners of the NFL clubs were 'a hidebound and tightly knit fraternity, loath to accept outsiders, reluctant to change.' Many businessmen in cities without a top professional football club wanted to acquire a franchise, but the officials running the NFL were reluctant to expand. Not surprisingly, a new rival league, the AFL (American Football League) was formed in 1959. The entrepreneur behind the new league was Lamar Hunt, the son of (at the time) one of the richest people in the world. Then, as now, money helps in sport.

In 1960 Pete Rozelle became the NFL Commissioner. He proved able to provide leadership for the sport, and was able to unite all the owners. In the mid-1980s, when the business of professional sport in the US as well as in Europe was going nowhere, those with power and authority in American football adopted a very different strategy to that which was being followed in Europe. The NFL, led by Pete Rozelle, pursued a policy referred to as 'League think', based on the belief that the greater the equality of the playing strength of teams, the greater would be the uncertainty of outcome and therefore the greater the interest of consumers in the competition.

The way this was achieved was to control who owned and operated the clubs and to not allow corporate ownership, as this was thought to potentially lead to a conflict of interest between those seeking profits for the club and those who wanted what was good for the league. Relatedly, the public was not allowed to own the clubs. Instead, ownership of a club by a few individuals was encouraged, with at least one individual to own 51% of the club's shares. No owner was allowed to have an interest in more than one club. The reason why the NFL wanted a major shareholder for each club, rather than widely dispersed ownership, was that it would make decision-making easier, as there would be less dispute at boardroom level. Publicly listed companies would also require the need for greater disclosure of financial matters.

The NFL have been partly successful in their ownership policy. There has been stability in the ownership of clubs, with no acrimonious take-over battles. There have, however, been a few problems with certain owners at times acting in the best interest of their own clubs. One such problem, from a supporter's point of view, is that periodically the owner of a club will wish to move the club franchise from one city to another. The NFL challenged in court owners' right to do this but lost. It is now not uncommon for a franchise to be relocated if the owner thinks it is in the club's interest.

The NFL has had its share of problems, however. In 1974 and 1982 there were player strikes, and in 1987 and again in 1992 there were strike threats. The threat of the 1992 strike was ended when a solution, which had first been proposed 40 years earlier, was adopted. Namely, to limit the level of salaries that a club can pay. In 1953, 'in order to keep teams at an approximately equal strength,' a salary cap was one of a number of measures that had been proposed. In 1992 this was a key element of a new agreement.

The players were offered the right to free agency after they had played for four years in the league and were offered a guaranteed aggregate salary level per club, which would improve over time. The offer was accepted.

The salary cap per club is based on the revenue generated collectively by the NFL clubs. This base is called the 'Gross Defined Revenue' (GDR), which is the total received from most (but not all) sources. It obviously includes all television income (which is negotiated through collective selling), most match day receipts, and income from NFL merchandising. For a number of years it did exclude certain revenue generated locally by clubs (this is now known as the 'Old Model') but the definition was changed in 2006 and so now includes even the revenue from local naming rights and local advertising. (This is the 'New Model'.)

The owners and players agree as a result of collective bargaining on the maximum percentage of this GDR that will be paid to the players. This has been increasing over time; the percentage to be paid as salaries under the Old Model was 63% in 2000, and 65.5% in 2005. Under the New Model the players share in 2006, of the enlarged GDR, was set at 59.9%. This aggregate salary figure is then divided by the number of teams in the NFL (in 2006 this was 32) to give the unadjusted salary cap per team. In 2006 this resulted in a figure per team of $102 million. This is the cap on the amount to be paid to current and former players; it does not include the amount paid to the manager and coaches. A minimum salary level is also agreed upon.

The NFL owners have generally worked together, acting in the best interests of the league. Between 2001 and 2005 the NFL as a body raised approximately $500 million by selling bonds in the capital markets, and the money raised was lent to clubs to assist them in building new stadiums. One cannot imagine the FA or the Premier League adopting such forward thinking leadership. The NFL also have a rule which limits the amount of borrowing of each individual franchise club. This prevents each club from moving into dangerous levels of financial gearing.

As explained, the NFL does not permit corporate ownership of its clubs. In the other major US professional sports there has, however, been a move in this direction—the trend being away from local, family private ownership to ownership by companies. Fox Broadcasting Company owns the Los Angeles Dodgers, Time

Warner at one point owned the Atlanta Braves, and Cablevision has ownership interests in the New York Knicks and New York Rangers. This ownership structure, with media companies controlling sports clubs, has not been allowed in England, with the possible acquisition of Manchester United by BSkyB thought to be not good for the game. Those running the NFL would agree with the Monopolies and Mergers Commission decision on this matter.

American football is now the most popular sport in the US but it has only become so since it reorganised itself around the NFL. Before that baseball was the 'people's game'. Now the popularity and the TV ratings for American football increase each year, whilst baseball, basketball and ice hockey are losing support. One amazing thing about American football is not the way, as in football in England, it has been able to benefit financially from TV coverage of matches, but the way it has, unlike football in England, been able to exploit uncompetitive practices such as limiting supply, for financial gain. The result is that for most Americans watching top level American football means watching TV, which is good for advertisers, but not the real thing. Not surprisingly, therefore, to football clubs in the US revenue from the sale of TV rights is much more significant than it is to football clubs in Europe. In the US such income is approximately 65% of the total revenue of clubs, whereas in England for the typical Premier League club it is in the region of 33%. There is a danger that if a European Super League is formed that television revenue will, as in the US, become the most important source of all revenue.

Restrictive Practices in Europe?

In 1999 Thomas Hoehn and Stefan Szymanski published a thought-provoking paper entitled 'The Americanisation of European Football.' Their message was one that would have excited capitalists but one that would alarm football supporters. Hoehn and Szymanski argue that because of the growth of a single market in Europe the importance of national football associations and national football leagues is on the decline. We have already seen a number of attempts to form a European-wide Super League, driven by the wish of a few clubs to make the most that they can out of the sport. Because of the value of TV rights a new Super League would bring more money into the game, but national competitions would become of less importance. The elite teams, it follows, would eventually wish to discontinue with the system whereby on an annual basis they need to qualify for the Super League and so would jettison their other commitments to concentrate on the more profitable Super League.

European football would then be more like American football, with a few large teams, each team having a monopoly of supply in a certain catchment area and with the owners and players making very large sums of money. With owners of the elite clubs now attempting to maximise their revenue there is a move towards the Americanisation of European football, as there is a move towards the Americanisation of most industries.[13]

In European football, traditional followers of the game are not just interested in who wins a league, they are also interested in relegation issues. With meaningful competition for places at both ends of the league, fans and TV spectators have more to hold their interest throughout the season. The creation of a Super League would bring to an end the relegation drama. A second difference to the system in the US is that at present national leagues feed into international competitions and therefore although one or two teams might dominate a national competition they will encounter balanced competition at the international level. Both of these differences are attractive to consumers.

European football opinion is divided upon the advisability of salary capping and improved revenue sharing. More and more official reports including, the 'Arnaut Report', refer to such measures as a possible way forward, and some clubs have said they support the idea. But salary capping means different things to different people.

By way of comparison, Rugby League's attempts at financial reform have shown that it is possible. They introduced a salary capping system based on two important 'Rules'. No club would spend more than 50% of its revenue on salaries, and no club would spend more in total than an agreed amount on the salaries of its players. In 2005–06 this upper cap was £1.8 million, a paltry sum by English football's standards.

In August 2006 an 'Independent Judiciary Panel' found that Wigan Warriors had breached this salary cap. In the 2005–06 season the club had spent somewhere in the region of 55% of their revenue on player salaries. As a consequence they suffered a penalty of a two point deduction for the following season and a fine of £50,000. Wigan admitted they were guilty of breaching the salary cap, but said it was the result of an administrative error. Some of their rivals were not as charitable, the chief executive of Leeds Rhinos referred to it as 'brilliant cheating'. The audit of the 2005–06 salary cap returns found that four other clubs had committed minor breaches of the Rules (two had to pay small fines and two were just warned). Rugby League have in fact been successfully operating the two-pronged salary cap for a number of seasons. In 2003, three clubs had been found to have broken the cap, and each suffered a two point deduction. The maximum points deduction allowed is six points. The points deduction approach would certainly deter even the rich soccer clubs, were the system to be introduced in the Premier League. It could mean, under the present arrangements, the difference between qualifying for European competition or not.

The ex-footballer, successful businessman and now respected owner of Wigan Athletic, David Whelan, added his voice to those who would like to see a salary cap. He believes that with Chelsea (and Manchester United) continuing to win 'it will end up killing the game.' 'A salary cap is the only way to restore competitiveness before fans, sponsors and television companies desert the national sport.' When he made similar proposals during the 2005–06 season, Blackburn, West Bromwich Albion, Sunderland and Charlton were the only Premiership clubs to back him.

In May 2006, during a European Parliament debate, Bayern Münich's President, Karl-Heinz Rummenigge called for a Europe-wide salary cap. He was frustrated because whereas his club, which is roughly the same size as Chelsea, was achieving little success on the pitch and in 2005 made a profit of €35 million, Chelsea, who were extremely successful on the pitch, made a €204 million loss. Rummenigge was right to point out the lack of competitive balance in the game, but his suggested solution was the wrong one. It would have helped Bayern to compete with Chelsea but would not have helped the clubs outside the elite group. He proposed that 'we should have an overall salary budget capped at, say, 50% of turnover. Across Europe there should be harmonisation.'

But a percentage system would not help the clubs outside the elite, only a cap on total salaries paid by a club would do that.

Rummenigge was speaking out of self-interest. He wanted clubs such as Bayern Münich to be guaranteed places in the lucrative UEFA Champions League. He argued that since Bayern Münich had 'taken part in the Champions League on 12 occasions it was fair that they should be guaranteed participation.' Fair of course is a meaningless word in this context. Rummenigge wants to end the present pyramid structure, and so allow a group of clubs who happen to be the richest at one point in time to remain so for ever.

To refer back to the 'Arnaut Report', one of the conclusions the authors reached was that the top players and their agents were taking too much money out of the game. They were also worried that a few owners were putting too much money into the game. The report recommends 'the establishment of an effective salary cap.' The problem is that the various interest groups will never agree on what is an 'effective' cap. The report discusses placing 'an overall limit on the amount a club can spend on player wages' in order to 'preserve a degree of competitive balance between teams' and to 'prevent extremely wealthy individuals purchasing teams' and then signing all the best players and paying them more than anyone else. The 'Arnaut Report' comments that 'in this respect' the decision-makers in Europe could usefully look to the system in the US.

Opinions are, not surprisingly, divided. Some clubs have said they would support the idea of a salary cap as long as it was based on a percentage of the revenue of a club. This method is unfortunately meaningless, it would perpetuate the present inequalities. Salary capping can work, as the US has shown, if it is based on an absolute limit that each club can spend on salaries each year.

A hard cap, with a rigid upper limit, would be difficult to enforce in European football, particularly in the early years of its introduction. However, with a soft cap where an individual club can pay out to its players more than the agreed upper limit if it is prepared to pay a 'luxury tax', there is an increased chance of success. The proceeds from this soft cap tax are shared out amongst the clubs in the league who have not exceeded the cap. This tax helps to hold back the high spending clubs.

Of course the threshold at which the tax started would initially have to be set at a high enough level to accommodate the superior wealth of clubs like Chelsea and Manchester United, but if the rate of increase each year were set at a lower rate than the rate of increase in football revenue, over time it would allow other clubs to catch up.

One suggestion for improving the game made in '*FourFourTwo*' the football monthly was 'a fat cat tax.'[14] High spending teams could be taxed and the money raised used to support the less well-off clubs. In a way this is already happening, with the Premier League paying a percentage of the TV revenue the clubs generate into a fund. One problem with the idea of cross subsidisation is that a mechanism needs to be in place to ensure that it is not the inefficient and badly managed clubs that are subsidised.

A belief in the superiority of the free market system over any other system is based on a concept called the 'invisible hand'. This is supposed to work to ensure that even though everybody pursues their own interest, in the end this collective striving works in everyone's interest. This theory, which was brought to prominence by Adam Smith, is based on the system being free from distortions.[15] In theory it means that the size of the 'cake' produced as a result of the free play of market forces will be greater than that which can be achieved by any other economic system. One problem with this approach is that the amount of the cake the different interest groups receive depends upon the distribution system. This is the problem with football. Directors are only interested in their own club; owners are interested in their own rewards; administrators are interested in their own power; players are interested in their own income; agents are interested in the players they represent; and football fans are there to be exploited. The current EU laws on competition seek to encourage decisions to be made on the basis of free market forces with intervention only applicable when absolutely necessary. In Europe nobody checks to see if in fact the consumer is benefiting; it is assumed that, based on the 'invisible hand' concept, consumers will automatically benefit.[16] By contrast in the US the sports business is not left to 'faith' in a political ideology. Intervention is encouraged in order to produce a meaningful sporting competition.

Of course such intervention will not happen in the immediate future in Europe because of the current belief in the advantages of free competition, and because of the greed of some of the present decision-makers in the game. As Tom Bower points out, the behaviour of many club chairmen has 'mirrored pertinent truths about modern Britain.' Unfortunately it is not just Britain.[17]

Stephen Morrow points out the main conflict faced by football is the prioritisation of sporting outcomes versus the prioritisation of economic or market solutions.[18] It is Morrow's belief that all recent trends suggest that 'there is little or no likelihood of the policies that would improve competitive balance being implemented in practice.' In the short run, unfortunately, Morrow is almost certainly right. The best hope for the long run is that there will be a sea change in economic thinking about sport. There is the danger that if those running the game do not make changes they could ruin the professional game and harm themselves financially.

There are of course a number of problems with restrictive practices such as salary capping. One is the enforcement problem. With subsidiary companies now comprising a substantial element of a football club's financial structuring, coupled with the secrecy of offshore financial centres, money can quite easily be channelled to players. How successful a salary cap is, as a means of distributing talent across clubs, also depends on how easy it is for teams to get around the spirit of the agreement by offering non-financial rewards. Creative accounting presents a significant barrier in this regard.

To enforce this restrictive practice requires a strong regulating unit. If, as is the case in some US sports, there is an agreed minimum that clubs have to pay with respect to salaries, this also has to be carefully monitored to ensure smaller clubs pay at least the required amount.

Baseball is one sport where wage capping has not succeeded in improving competitive balance. In 2002 the total payroll of the New York Yankees was $126 million, with the average salary for a player at the club being $4.3 million. The total payroll of the Tampa Bay Devil Rays was $35 million, with the average salary being $1.2 million. Since 1923 the Yankees have won one third of World Series Championships, which has made them an extremely popular team. Even though Major League Baseball has a system of revenue sharing, the revenue sharing is based on national revenue only and the Yankees benefit from the local media interest. The baseball experience suggests that a revenue sharing agreement, where the revenue level used as a base excludes too may sources, does not work.

The potential dangers of a salary capping system can also be seen in the National (Ice) Hockey League in North America. In

78

2004–05 the NHL was in a bad way financially; it was not attracting the audiences or the sponsors. The owners of the clubs wanted to introduce cost saving measures, and they hoped a new collective bargaining agreement could be introduced that would be favourable to them.

The season was due to commence in October 2004, but it did not start. The owners of the clubs and the players union could not agree on the level at which to cap salaries. The proposal on the table from the NHL at the beginning of 2005 was that for any club a maximum team payroll for a season should be $42 million, with a payroll floor of $32 million. Some owners were worried about whether or not they would be able to afford to pay even the floor level of wages. The League proposed a 'linkage' so that salary costs at any club would not in any season exceed 53% of club revenue. Many players did not like the idea of a salary cap, and even more disliked the idea of a 'linkage'. The Players Association said they would accept a '24% rollback of all players' salaries' through the term of existing contracts. This meant over time each player taking a 24% cut in salary. These were quite dramatic proposals. They would save the employers over $1 billion over 3 years. It effectively took one season for the disagreement to be resolved and a settlement was not reached until May 2006.

Two Possible Schemes for Football

A redistribution scheme that would restore competitive balance in domestic leagues is needed. The objective in England would be to reduce the financial gap between the rich and the relatively poor in the Premier League. As explained, in the US sports competitions have been granted exemption from that country's generally very strict antitrust legislation. Some of those who have looked at this issue in Europe, including Stefan Szymanski in his review of the 'Economic Design of Sporting Contests', conclude that the European Union would not allow similar exemptions. There are, however, now signs that EU officials would listen to such proposals, and already there are salary caps operating in rugby.

One important difference between the US and the European position is that in the US the players and club owners operate under collective bargaining agreements. Even if some form of restraint on free market forces were to be allowed by the EU there would still be the need for players and employers to reach agreement. If there was to be a salary cap, the owners would presumably be happy but the players would need to agree to the restrictions. Whether the higher paid stars would agree to have their salaries constrained in the interests of better-balanced competitions is far from certain. It is likely that initially they would resist. It is possible that the owners of the top five or six teams would also react in a negative way; they are benefiting from the present winner take all approach. The history of collective bargaining in professional sport in the US demonstrates that initially, and then every few years, when the agreements have to be renegotiated, there occurs a difficult time with the sides involved posture, but eventually agree on, what is for the 'collective' good.

One possible scheme for European Football would be based on a soft salary cap accompanied by financial penalties and subsidies. Another scheme would be a form of luxury tax. Both of these would, however, require those who run a league, and all the clubs involved, to agree to tax the richer clubs and redistribute the tax revenue received to the poorer teams. The principle of redistribution has already to some extent been accepted in England. The Premier League passes on to the grassroots in the game, via the Football Foundation, a percentage of the TV revenue it attracts. In 2006, 5% of TV income was redistributed, and this percentage is to rise, following the auction of the rights to broadcast games, for the 2007–08 season and beyond. The UK government, through the Department for Culture, Media and Sport, helped the Premier League settle its dispute with the European Commission over the collective selling of TV rights. In return for this help the Premier League agreed to increase the percentage being passed to the grassroots.

This redistribution is good for the game and none of the schemes being proposed, if introduced, need interfere with this arrangement in any way. The objective of the Football Foundation is to help the game at all levels. The objective of the redistribution schemes discussed below would be to improve competitive balance at the higher levels of the game.

Model One—A Wages and Salaries Cap

Numerous studies have shown that the amount a club spends on wages and salaries in a season is the key determinant of the final league position of that club. In 2003–04 Chelsea spent £115 million on salaries whilst Wolves spent £19 million—a staggering difference. The salary bill of Chelsea was exceptional, the second highest was Manchester United with £77 million. The average payment on salaries for Premier League clubs was £40 million, but only 7 of the clubs in the league paid more than that (one of which was Leeds United, who were relegated). Clubs at the lower end of the ranking included Birmingham City who paid £23 million and Leicester City who paid £24 million.

The total revenue (turnover) of Premiership clubs in 2003–04 and 2004–05 was just over £1.3 billion. Of this approximately 31% was what is called match day revenue (being mainly gate receipts in all their forms), 43% was media (broadcasting) revenue, and the remaining 26%, commercial revenue (covering sponsorship and merchandising). The breakdown of course varies club by club. It is not proposed that all this revenue be used as a base to determine which clubs pay a tax. First the revenue from European games needs to be excluded. It is very lucrative for the clubs who qualify for the Champions League and the UEFA Cup competitions, and in order to encourage clubs to qualify and to do well when they are in these competitions all revenue from these competitions would be excluded from the revenue base.

In 2003–04 Manchester United's match day revenue from European Champions League games was £4.9 million, and the media revenue they received from these games was £20 million. Other clubs that take part in European competitions do not necessarily benefit to the same extent as Manchester United. The amount of media revenue depends on the stage of the competition that is reached. Assuming 6 English clubs qualify for Europe and generate average extra revenue of £25 million each, this gives a total European generated revenue figure of £150 million, which if deducted from the total brings the base down to approximately £1.15 billion.

The next source of revenue that it is argued should be excluded from the base is commercial. Clubs earn this income themselves. It is the club, afterall, that attracts sponsorship, the club that sells replica shirts, the club that provides good (or bad) catering. If all commercial income is excluded (say £250 million) this brings the base down to £900 million. The final source of revenue that is proposed be excluded from the base is the 'merit award' part of the media income. The amount an individual club receives depends on final league position. In 2003–04 each place in the league was rewarded with about £600,000 more than the place below. In total, this source of revenue amounts to about £100 million. This means the 'adjusted' revenue is £800 million and it is this figure that will be used as the base for the luxury tax.

The related revenue figure (defined net revenue) divided by the twenty clubs gives £40 million per club. In fact in 2003–04 the unadjusted (including European, commercial and merit money) average revenue per Premiership club was £67.7 million, but the distribution was very skewed, with the figure for Manchester United being £171.5 million and that for Wolverhampton Wanderers (who were relegated) £38 million. This difference indicates the need for something to be done if balanced competition is to be achieved.

Having calculated the 'defined' base as £800 million, the next step is to agree on the percentage of this figure that can be paid out to players as salary. Let us say it is agreed that the upper band is set at 60%, and the lower band at 50%. This means that for each of the 20 Premier League clubs the salary cap based on the league's defined revenue would be £24 million (£800 million x 60% ÷ 20) and the salary floor £20 million. Each club would, of course, be allowed to spend more than this amount because the revenue from European matches, from commercial income as well as the merit award, has been excluded from the base.

Manchester United received revenue of approximately £25 million from Europe, £72 million from commercial sources (including £20 million from Nike) and £10 million from a merit award. This is in total £107 million, on top of the league 'defined' revenue.

The next key issue that would need to be decided, hopefully as a result of collective bargaining, is the percentage of the 'self-generated revenue' that can be paid out as salary. If it was agreed that the appropriate figure would be 40%, then for Manchester United this would add £43 million to the salary pool, giving a total of £67 million. In fact the actual wage bill for 2003–04 was £77 million. This would mean, based on the above assumptions, and taking the tax rate as £1 for every £1 of overspend, that the club would be taxed £10 million.

By way of contrast, Tottenham had no European revenue, commercial revenue of £34 million and £4 million merit revenue. With 40% of this £38 million to spend on salaries, the total pool would be £39 million. The club in fact only spent £34 million; near the salary floor. At Aston Villa there was no European revenue, £24 million commercial revenue and an £8 million merit award. This £32 million of self-generated revenue would add £13 million to the salary pool, giving an overall 'cap' of £37 million. The club actually spent only £33 million, again no tax with salary payments near the agreed floor.

The club with serious problems under this scheme would be Chelsea. In 2003–04 the club participated in the UEFA Champions League which generated over £30 million extra revenue, the commercial revenue was £50 million and the merit award £10 million. This £90 million of self-generated revenue would enable the club to push up its salary cap to £60 million. Its actual wage bill was £115 million resulting in a fine of £55 million.

The figures above are, of course, only indicative. Much discussion would need to take place to arrive at an agreement on what is an acceptable percentage of revenue to be paid as salaries on the league-based 'defined revenue' and on the self-generated club revenue. It would also be necessary to agree on which salaries are covered by the cap. Is it just player salaries or does it include managers and coaches?

There are various ways in which a figure could be arrived at for a salary cap. A simple version would be to just base it on the actual salary costs of all clubs at a given point in time. In 2003–04 the average salary bill in the Premier League was £40 million. If the maximum team payroll was set at, say, £50 million (the average plus 25%), and the floor for the payroll at £40 million, this would mean that Birmingham City would need to increase their wage bill by £7 million. How could a redistribution of revenue take place that would allow such a salary band to exist?

The answer is a tax. A club would be able to spend more than the level of the cap (if it could afford it) but it would have to pay a tax for everything spent above the upper figure. In fact in 2003–04 only 4 clubs had a wage bill above the £50 million being used as a suggested maximum. The 4 clubs paying above the £50 million would pay a tax and the income raised from the tax would be used to subsidise the poorer clubs and so assist them in being able to afford to pay the £40 million minimum wage bill. The result would be that some players would receive more than under a completely free system but some would receive less. That is why a collective agreement would be needed. It may also be thought necessary to adjust the maximum for clubs taking part in European competitions.

Model Two—A Luxury Tax

Another approach at redistributing income would be to tax some clubs, and give a subsidy to others, based on the revenue figure of a club. Again, a base figure would need to be established, the so-called football-related revenue (FRR) of the club.

The steps to be followed to arrive at the tax or subsidy figure for an individual club would be:

- Calculate the aggregate revenue figure for Premier league clubs
- After adjusting for revenue to be excluded, calculate the average FRR per club
- Agree on a 'corridor'—a range around this average. If an individual club's FRR is within this corridor, the club will not be taxed or subsidised
- Calculate each club's actual FRR. If it is below the lower band of the corridor the club will receive a subsidy equal in amount to the deficit. If the club's FRR is above the upper band of the corridor, it will be taxed on the amount it is in excess.

The purpose of the corridor is to allow flexibility. The size of the corridor would be a matter of negotiation. In the early years of the scheme the corridor could be generous—that is it would be wide, so as to be not too severe on the wealthy clubs. For illustrative purposes we will say the upper band of the corridor is the average FRR plus 25%. Using the 2003–04 example this would amount to £50 million. We will leave the lower band at £40 million, but this could of course be lowered which would benefit the poorer clubs. In the NFL, in 2006 (12 years after the cap system was first introduced), the upper level of the corridor used to establish the salary cap was $102 million per club, and the lower limit $75 million per club.

The FRR of Manchester United in 2003–04 was £65 million (this excludes the media merit money, the European media income, the European match day revenue and commercial revenue). The upper level of the corridor of the tax base is £50 million. This would mean Manchester United would be taxed £15 million (based on a £1 tax on £1 excess). This money would be put into a 'pool' to be distributed to the poorer Premiership clubs.

Fifteen million pounds might seem to be a lot, but it must be remembered that self-generated revenue, the non-relevant revenue of the club that was excluded from the tax base, was £79 million. To pay this 'league' tax would mean diverting revenue at present used for other purposes. This would of course mean a sacrifice for the club; its pre-tax profits in 2003–04 were £28 million (down from £39 million the previous year). Its 'staff costs' (salaries and wages) were £76.8 million, which would probably have to be cut; the object of the exercise. This example is based on a tax of £1 for every £1 surplus, but this rate would be a matter for negotiation.

Amongst the relatively poorer clubs are Birmingham City, Aston Villa, Manchester City and Tottenham. In 2003–04 the FRR of Birmingham City was only £32.2 million, so they would therefore receive a subsidy (from the pool) of £7.8 million. Not a lot but a start, enough to buy one good player, or to improve the wages they can offer and so attract the better players to the club. The FRR of Aston Villa was £31.5, which means that they would receive a £8.5 subsidy from the pool. For Manchester City the FRR was £40 million, and so they would not need to pay a tax and would not receive a subsidy. Tottenham would be another club that had no tax to pay and no subsidy to receive. Their FRR was approximately £48 million, within the safety range.

With this luxury tax system there is no salary cap. Revenue is redistributed between rich and poor and then it is up to each club to decide how much it wishes to spend on salaries and wages.

A simpler version of the luxury tax scheme would be just to redistribute gate receipts for Premier League games. In England up to the 1980s the match day receipts from a game were divided between the two teams taking part. The criticism of this approach was that it worked against the interests of those clubs that had invested in a large stadium. The bigger clubs were able to change the rules, so that for league games the home team kept all the receipts.

In 2003–04 the average league match attendance at Manchester United was 67,640, whereas at Fulham it was only 16,240; at Portsmouth it was 20,000 whilst at Birmingham City it was 29,100. It does not require a genius to realise the impact on club revenue resulting from such differences in attendance figures. How was it ever thought that with such differences in income generating capacity that competitive balance could be maintained?

In 2003–04 the total match day revenue of Premier League clubs was £395 million. This averages out to nearly £20 million per club. The match day revenue for Manchester United (excluding European games, cup games and tour games) was £48 million, over double the average. The figure for Birmingham City was around £21 million. A division of match day receipts, not necessarily an equal division, would help reduce inequality. It might be possible to share the gate receipts from Premier League games, but the revenue from games in European competitions would need to be excluded.

Revenue sharing might be thought to reduce the incentive for a club to spend money on improving its stadium: the club would receive only part of extra revenue generated. For the revenue sharing approach to benefit all, it would be necessary for all clubs in the league to have more or less equal-sized stadiums. In the US, clubs in the NFL act as a cartel. The NFL make loans available to enable clubs to improve their stadiums, thus overcoming the problems caused by big differences in stadium size.

4

Finance and Ownership

In the current football climate a necessary condition for club success is access to finance, and access to finance depends on ownership. But having access to finance is one thing—spending it wisely is another. A number of clubs who have had access to funds have wasted their money by purchasing players (and paying them high wages) who have failed to live up to expectations. Newcastle, Leeds and Birmingham City are all guilty of this. By making the best use of what is available a good manager (or director of football) can show his value. In the 'old days', clubs were usually owned by reasonably wealthy, local businessmen who were not expecting much back in terms of financial returns. Football was organised in such a way that the more successful clubs shared revenue with the less successful clubs, and thus were costs controlled. Things changed once it appeared that football might be able to attract new sources of revenue (such as TV) and become profitable.

When a new wave of directors entered the game in the late 1980s, a new type of investor became interested in the game and financial institutions began to persuade clubs that it was in their best interests to have their shares listed on a stock exchange. Any restrictive practices within the game were changed or by-passed. A number of media companies concurrently became interested in obtaining 'strategic holdings' in football clubs. A few years later when it became clear that the large amounts of money coming into football would not necessarily result in large returns for shareholders, the financial institutions lost interest in football club shares. Another new breed of investor then appeared on the scene, the wealthy private individual, who had earned his money, one way or another, in the global marketplace. His motives were often complex and his interests did not usually extend to investing in the less fashionable clubs.

The particulars of ownership of course varies from country to country within Europe, but it seems fair to say that football clubs in England did not in the past attract the 'top' businessmen in the way that football in Italy attracted that country's top industrialists. Piero Pirelli, who founded the giant rubber business, ran AC Milan from 1908 (and was responsible for the construction of the famous San Siro Stadium in 1926). By the end of the First World War, Fiat was one of the biggest companies in Italy, controlled by the Agnelli family. In 1923 Eduardo Agnelli, son of the founder of Fiat, acquired control of Juventus and the family have been linked to the club ever since. 'In a way that is unique, Italy's biggest company has run Italy's biggest football club.'

The link between Italian football and 'big' business has continued to the present day. A recent example is Silvio Berlusconi's ownership of AC Milan. By 1980, Berlusconi was the richest person in Italy—amongst other things he controlled three national television channels and the country's biggest publishing business. He purchased and became president of the Milan football club in 1986. In 1994 he became Prime Minister of Italy, promising to manage the country like he managed his football club. He also reportedly used his position as Prime Minister to intervene in the world of football.[1]

Such a situation has never existed in English football, where for a long time clubs were owned and run by 'local' plumbers, builders, brewers, butchers, etc. Italy have won the World Cup four times, England once. Not until Roman Abramovich appeared on the scene was a major industrialist involved with an English club.[2]

If we assume that to be successful a club needs money the question that arises is: where is that money to come from? To supporters of a club the answer is very simple: the money should come from the owners of the clubs. In the minds of supporters, ownership of a club implies a commitment to invest money. Although the shareholders are the legal owners of the club, the supporters of the club see themselves as the moral owners. Shareholders and directors come and go, as do managers and players, but the 'true' supporter usually remains loyal to the club through thick and thin.

Unfortunately, from the point of view of supporters, to purchase control of a club does not necessarily imply investing any money in a club. The shares acquired are usually bought off another investor and it is the shareholder who is selling that receives the cash. Supporters of course hope the person who purchases control of a club has plenty of 'spare' finance available which they also hope he will invest directly in the club in one way or another. But often the supporters are disappointed. It is easy for the supporters to 'live the dream' but not so easy for the individuals who have to provide the money for the club to fulfil that dream. This situation has changed a little at some smaller and medium-sized clubs where 'supporters trusts' have shown that financial support from fans can make a difference.

One source of equity finance is retained profits. This is the money that is each year left over after all costs have been met, including interest on loans and possibly dividends paid out to shareholders. But very few clubs are profitable. Despite the large amount of revenue flowing into the game from broadcasting, commercial activities and match day receipts, very little of this becomes available to finance long-term success. Nearly all the annual revenue is paid out each year in wages, salaries, operating costs, and on the purchase of players. Very few clubs make very much profit. As Deloitte point out the number of Premiership clubs that reported pre-tax profits fell from 14 in 2004–05 to 9 in 2005–06.

The relative significance of each of the different sources of finance has changed over the last few years. In the early years of the Premier League, which coincided with a period of stock market boom, it was new investment in the clubs by shareholders that was the main source of finance. In the 1996–97 season there were 12 clubs that floated their shares in the market, and this raised £262 million of new money for clubs. Newcastle alone raised over £50 million. The 'Review of Football Finance' commented at the time that 'Flotations provide a good opportunity [for clubs] to spread the sources of finance.' They did, however, warn that the game would not benefit if the money were to 'speed out again on bank repayments or overseas transfers.'

In the mid-1990s it was thought that new finance would come into the clubs through the sale of equity shares on the stock market. It was thought that the market in football club shares would continue to be popular with both individual and institutional investors. However the collapse of stock market prices generally towards the end of the 1990s, combined with the lack of profitability of most football clubs, meant that the possibility of raising new finance by selling new equity shares to the public or to financial institutions more or less disappeared.

Members of the financial community are inventive, and seemingly tireless at devising new techniques for supplying finance to those in need. A particularly novel way of financing the acquisition of players was offered to football clubs in the late 1990s through sale and leaseback deals. Another way of obtaining money quickly was through securitising ticket sales. The problem is that money obtained through means other than equity has to be paid back and the higher the amount of borrowed money or money received in advance (in whatever form), in relationship to shareholder money, the greater the risk to the company involved.[3]

It became possible for only a few clubs to attract new equity finance, the rest had to rely on bank or other loans. In 2003–04 the financing cash flows the Premier League clubs raised from shareholders amounted to £123 million, from new loans £443 million, from working capital £9 million, and from the sale of investments £5 million. Of the £123 million of new equity, £100 million was provided by Roman Abramovich for Chelsea. The major user of the debt funds was Arsenal, who were financing their new stadium. The Premier League clubs had moved collectively from a position in 1998–99 in which the total amount of borrowings equalled 42% of equity to a position in 2002–03 when the borrowing figure was 204% of the equity figure. In 2005–06 the financial gearing ratio was 220%.[4]

It goes without saying that equity is in a way the most important source of capital for any company. It is the risk capital, those who provide it are the last each year to receive a financial return and in the event of liquidation they are the last to receive their money back. The amount of risk capital invested in a business is a key factor influencing how much other finance the business can attract. In theory, companies engaged in a risky business need a higher proportion of equity finance to debt finance than those engaged in a safer business. Football is now a very risky business. Premier League clubs need to invest large sums just to survive in that division. Money helps to buy survival, but with some clubs spending large sums just to survive it means that the directors of the less successful clubs have little option but to try to match that level of expenditure.

Even John Madejski, one of the wealthiest men in the UK (in 2006, ranked 174th on *The Times* Rich List) and said to be worth £350 million, cannot afford to keep a club in the Premiership. After he helped Reading to the top tier he announced in July 2006 that he was willing to sell all or some of his shares in the club. He simply could not afford to spend the amount of money needed if the club was to survive at that level. 'If there is some person out there who has the financial resources and would like to be the chairman of a football club, then they should come and see me. I am prepared to let go and clear the way for someone who would like to take up the challenge. I have been doing this for 16 years now and when I came here my goal was to get us into the Premiership. I have achieved that but now it is time for someone else to take up the reins.'

The Good Old Days?

In the past and still in the vast majority of cases, the people who owned the football club, the shareholders, also controlled the club. The major shareholders would usually be the directors, and even when they began to appoint directors who were not significant shareholders they would usually appoint friends and business associates (grey directors). There was a brief time at some clubs, following the listing of some clubs' shares on the stock market, when there was a divorce of ownership and control. At this time, for some clubs, including Tottenham, Leeds and Manchester United, the majority of shares were owned by financial institutions. This created its own problems to do with goal congruence. The shareholders were worried that the directors were more interested in building up, over time, a winning team, than in earning profits in the short run. The supporters of the club for their part were worried that the directors were more concerned with earning profits than in winning competitions. We now seem to have moved through that time, with private equity coming back into football and with the owners, either as directors or as shadow directors, controlling the club.

Of course in the past, and at some clubs now, directors were willing to sell some shares (a minority) to supporters. Sometimes these shares had restricted voting rights, sometimes the shares could not be easily traded. For example, the purchasers might only be allowed to sell their shares to another person with the approval of the club's directors. This meant the directors could control who would be the new shareholders.

From the early days both the FA and the Football League took steps to ensure that the owners of clubs could not exploit the financial opportunities open to them. Directors of clubs were not to be paid for their services, for instance. In 1896, Rule 34 was introduced which limited dividend payments each year to 5% of paid-up equity capital. This limit was raised to 7.5% in 1920, to 10% in 1974 and 15% in 1983. Also from the beginning rules were introduced to prevent directors selling off the club's assets.

The people running the football clubs found a way around the tight financial rules and regulations. They created holding companies that through subsidiaries owned and controlled some of the income-earning assets associated with a football club. These subsidiaries, which were not football clubs, could pay dividends to the holding company. The holding company in turn could pay dividends to shareholders. Only the football club need abide by FA rules.

In January 1981 the Executive Committee of the FA gave serious consideration to amending Rule 34, which covered the formation of holding companies. In fact, by February 1981 Chelsea football club (along with Brighton and Crystal Palace) were already owned by holding companies, with the directors of these holding companies being paid fees. The rules of the FA had been overtaken by commercial reality.

In the 1980s everything began to change, there was talk of breakaway leagues and the leading English clubs were now playing in competitions that had another set of rule makers. The laws of the European Union were also beginning to affect how these private football organisations could treat their members. The FA and the Football League continued to squabble.

Public and Private Companies

The main difference between public and private companies relates to share ownership. In a private company the sale and purchase of the shares has to be controlled. In a public company there are no limits on the number of shareholders and there are (normally) no restrictions on the transfer of the shares.

One advantage that private companies have is that they do not have to deliver short-term financial performance to outside shareholders. In the past a significant disadvantage of private companies was that it could be difficult for them to borrow large amounts without bringing in new equity finance. It was because of this financial constraint that some football clubs wished to 'go public' and offer their shares to a wider group of investors. This limitation has now largely disappeared and many companies owned by private equity funds have very high levels of borrowing.

Another advantage of a private company is that it can get away with lower levels of disclosure and so has no corporate governance standards to worry about. A danger to a club in having its shares traded on a stock market is what is known in corporate finance as 'the market for corporate control'. This arises when one investor or group of investors attempts to take control of a company away from its existing owners. This happens in normal businesses either because the target company is under-performing, or because it is undervalued or because of troubles within the existing company governance structure. Take-over battles such as those seen at Tottenham and Manchester United are normal in the corporate and financial world, but not in football. This is one reason why in football more and more clubs will in future be owned by private companies rather than public. In the private world it is much easier to retain control.

Why would wealthy people or financial institutions want to invest in football clubs? If their sole objective is to make money there are many safer, more profitable investment opportunities. Those institutional investors who invested in clubs in the late 1990s lost money and soon got out of the market. Private investors clearly do not want to lose money but in many cases they have motives for becoming involved that are not just financial.

In the Premier League there are now three distinct types of publicly-owned clubs. One is a listed company with dispersed ownership; another is the listed company with ownership and control in the hands of a small group of people (Newcastle, Birmingham City); and the third is unlisted plcs that are tightly controlled, but whose shares can be traded outside the main stock markets (such as Arsenal).[5]

It is interesting that in the US, in the NFL, it was decided that ownership of the clubs should remain in private hands, despite the temptation of the nearby, largest capital market in the world. The owners wished to retain control and to act in their collective interest, which is not possible in a public company because of directors' responsibility to outside shareholders. Private companies can take a long-term view; the owners of NFL clubs did just that and in doing so made a lot of money for themselves.

The shares of some of the larger English football clubs are now traded on the London Stock Exchange (LSE), either in the main market, or in the secondary market, the Alternative Investment Market (AIM). Some of the more tightly controlled public companies (such as Arsenal) have their shares traded on PLUS (formerly OFEX), which is classed as off-the-market. It is an independent market. It is not part of the LSE, but it is regulated by the Financial Services Authority (FSA). Some other tightly controlled clubs have their shares traded through JPJL. These clubs include Everton, Sunderland, West Bromwich Albion, Nottingham Forest and Derby County, and at one time included Liverpool. Technically this is not a market, trading is conducted on a matched bargain basis. The stockbroker behind JPJL is J.P. Jenkins. Dealing in shares is conducted on an online basis.

As at the end of 2006, 51.6% of Liverpool shares were owned by David Moores, the club chairman. There was talk in 2004 of the Prime Minister of Thailand wishing to buy control of Liverpool and in 2005 and 2006 other foreign consortiums were said to be interested in acquiring the club. In particular, at the end of 2006, Dubai International Capital was interested in taking over the club. They are a state-owned private equity fund. Nobody could acquire the club without David Moores agreeing to the take-over. This position contrasts markedly with that of Manchester United, who were taken over in 2005 partly because their shares were listed on the London Stock Exchange and ownership was quite widely dispersed. At the end of 2006 a rival bidder appeared on the scene at Liverpool in the form of Americans George Gillett and Tom Hicks. Their offer was attractive to the major Liverpool shareholders and they took over the club early in 2007.[6]

There are a number of lessons that football clubs and directors have learned as a result of their experiences in the stock market

94

and a number of lessons the market has learned about football clubs. During 2003–04 season the directors of Tottenham moved their company's listing from the main list to the smaller AIM. They did this partly because the shares were not being traded very much (the club have a concentrated shareholder base, with over 50% of the shareholding being held in three names) and partly because of cost. Another reason could have been because there are personal tax benefits of owning shares in an AIM-listed company. The three major shareholders of Tottenham at the time were ENIC Sports, Sir Alan Sugar (who although having lost a fight for control of the club still owned over 13% of the shares) and Polys Haji-Ioannou, brother of the well-known owner of Easyjet who owned 9.0%.[7]

When Aston Villa went public in 1997 Douglas Ellis, the club's Chairman, had a nasty surprise. After the flotation the market value of the shares went down rather than up. The stock market at that time turned out to be a sellers' market, in other words one with more people who had shares wishing to sell than people without shares wishing to buy. A significant portion of those selling were those who had held shares in Aston Villa before they were listed on the market. Ellis commented in his autobiography that 'None of us imagined that the original 8,000 shareholders dating back to the 1969 flotation would sell their shares as they did.' They were, however, not the only people cashing in. Even one of the directors who Ellis had brought on to the club's board in the early 1970s sold shares for a 'very handsome profit.' Similarly, a little old lady whose father had invested £30,000 in Villa shares sold them for £1 million.

None of this should be seen as surprising given that the above shareholders were simply profit-taking. They were acting rationally. Success in investing depends as much on the timing of when to buy and when to sell as on the choice of companies in which to invest. Take your profits while they are there, for no one knows what will happen to share prices in the future. Selling was a sensible decision for the Villa investors—it showed that football clubs should not regard supporters as a soft touch financially. Ellis himself sold some of his shares at the time of the public issue for a sum reputed to be £10 million.

Undoubtedly some of the investors who came into football in the 1980s have made a lot of money. David Dein's £1 million investment in Arsenal became worth £30 million or more.[8] Martin Edwards' investment of £600,000 in Manchester United became worth over £80 million, whilst Sir John Hall's family investment in Newcastle of a few million pounds became worth £55 million. Some investors did well out of football, but they were taking risks. Football was certainly not fashionable at the time they became involved and they could have invested in other business activities and made similar gains.[9]

The Edwards family made money out of their investment in Manchester United, but it must not be forgotten that when in June 1991 shares in the club were offered to the public less than 50% of those offered were purchased. Eighteen months later the shares were still trading at a price below their original offer price. This was at a time when the Premier League existed, TV money was coming into the game and the image of the game had improved. Supporters and the public have at various times been given a chance to invest in football. In 1983 Peter Hill-Wood, the Chairman of Arsenal, offered friends the chance to buy a 17% stake in the club, and they turned down the offer. Football was in the doldrums at the time. The mood of investors is hard to predict. The flotation of Tottenham shares on the stock market in October 1983 was oversubscribed four times. Yet to the disappointment of those who acquired the shares by 1990 the price was slightly below that of seven years earlier.

During the mid-1990s football club shares were popular, the market was booming and it was thought a place in the Premier League gave a club a licence to print money. The future looked rosy both for the financial institutions who bought shares in football clubs, and for the clubs themselves. Stephen Morrow has estimated that by December 1997, 40% of the equity shares of Manchester United, Leeds and Tottenham were in the hands of financial institutions.[10] Soon, however, the investors became disillusioned. Aston Villa shares were valued at £11 each at the time (May 1997) that they were listed on the market; two years later the price was down to £4.40; a further two years after that they were down to £2. Ken Bates' investment in Chelsea was once worth £50 million, but he sold out for £16 million.

What went wrong? Well the first point to make is that share prices in general fell when the stock market price bubble burst and football shares fell in value more than others. The analysts had correctly forecast the growth in the football market as a result of globalisation, increased sponsorship and with the additional income from broadcasting increasing. The problem was that they did not anticipate that the costs of just surviving in the Premier League would be so high. They underestimated the financial difficulties that would follow relegation.

The revenue of Premier League clubs did show phenomenal growth, in six years (1997–2003) it more than doubled from £582 million to £1.2 billion. Wages, however, grew at a faster rate, from £305 million to £761 million. The wage/revenue ratio increasing from 52% to 61%.[11] Over this time operating costs also doubled, but profits hardly grew at all. Where did the extra cash flowing into the clubs go?

The trading cash flows of the Premier League clubs show a tremendous outflow to non-English football clubs to buy players. If one English club sells a player to another English club, the money stays in the system, less the amount paid to agents, but if an English club buys a player from a Spanish club the money leaves the system. The net annual outflow from Premier League clubs (purchases less sales) to non-English clubs over the last few years has averaged well over £100 million per annum.

The large amount spent on the purchase of new, foreign players plus increased salary costs means that many clubs, despite increases in revenue, have been short of cash. With the lack of growth in profitability and low or no dividends being paid, it is not surprising football club shares declined in value. Eighty percent of the shares of companies listed on the UK stock markets are owned by institutional shareholders. The savings of individuals are mainly channelled into pension funds, insurance companies and unit trusts, and it is the managers of these savings vehicles who decide where to invest the funds. Most football clubs now have little appeal to such institutions.

In the past, Leeds United attracted institutional investors. In their 2002 Annual Report and Accounts the club stated that the strategy they had adopted was designed to deliver long-term shareholder value. They went on to explain that 'the combination of the actions taken since the year end and ongoing actions surrounding the playing squad will help ensure that we deliver against this strategy' The most obvious action they were taking in connection with the squad was to sell a number of big name players. This action seemed more designed to satisfy the club's bankers than to deliver long-term value to shareholders, but still one needs to survive to be of any value. Such language as that used in the Leeds report was designed to keep institutional investors happy, and such investors at the time owned approximately 56% of the shares in the club. The club in fact failed to deliver long-term shareholder value, and the institutions sold their shares to a consortium of private investors.

Some venture capital companies have made mistakes when valuing football clubs. In 1997 Electra purchased 25% of the shares of Derby County, which cost them £10 million. They clearly had expectations that the club would become firmly established in the Premier League, would become profitable and would be in a position to float their shares on the stock market. The club were in fact relegated from the Premiership in 2002, with large debts. They had spent more money than they could afford, and owed the Co-operative Bank millions. The club went into administration and Electra lost their money. The football club were then purchased by a consortium which itself was financed by a £15 million loan from a Panama-registered company. Panama is what is known as a base tax haven, one of the most secretive in the world. It attracts companies that have something to hide.[12]

There are similar stories at other clubs. In 1997, 37% of the shares in Sheffield Wednesday were purchased by a venture capital company, Charterhouse Development Capital, for £16 million. It had only intended purchasing 20% of the shares, but because existing shareholders and supporters did not want to take up a sufficient number of shares in a rights issue, the venture capital company as the underwriters were left to purchase the balance. Again there was talk of success in the Premier League, and floating the shares on the stock exchange. It all seemed so easy. A Charterhouse director even referred to Sheffield Wednesday as good value, as a team securely placed in the lucrative Premier League. The trouble was there were directors and investors at so many other clubs who thought they also were securely placed, and that with a little further investment the club would be among the elite. Charterhouse had been taken for a ride, they paid a high price for their shares. The directors of the club who sold their shares made money. Sheffield Wednesday were relegated, and Charterhouse sold out to two existing directors and to the man who would become chairman, a local casino and dog track owner.

Strategic Investment

A strategic investment is an investment undertaken by a company in one industry in the shares of a company in another industry due to mutual interests. Media companies such as BSkyB and cable TV companies have in the past purchased blocks of shares in the leading football clubs in order to have an influence in the clubs' decision-making process. Nevertheless this policy has, for the media companies involved, only been a limited success. BSkyB were prevented by the Monopolies and Mergers Commission from having too much influence at Manchester United and NTL made some bad investment decisions. NTL made a total of 32 acquisitions during the 1998–2000 period, including purchasing cable TV businesses and shares in Newcastle United, Aston Villa, Middlesbrough, Leicester City and Glasgow Rangers. All of these clubs benefited at the time from an injection of funds, but NTL were not particularly successful with any of these investments from either a strategic or financial point of view, and the shares purchased did not gain in value.

BSkyB bought shares in a number of clubs, usually buying just under a 10% stake. In 1998 they paid £8 million for a shareholding in Leeds United in what turned out to be a poor investment. The TV company had argued that 'there is a natural alliance between media companies and sports clubs and we can bring a certain expertise in promotion and marketing of the club and securing worldwide contracts.' They could not, however, save Leeds. Media companies will be more careful when making strategic investments in football clubs in future.

Another form of strategic investment is when those retail companies who sell football-related clothes and merchandise, or the owners of such companies, buy shares in football clubs. One such company is the John Davis Group, who invested heavily in Manchester City. Another example is that of Dave Whelan and his investment in Wigan Athletic. The Whelans are major shareholders in the sports goods manufacturer JJB Sports, which is based in

99

Wigan. Along with a controlling interest in the local football and rugby club the Whelans have helped finance the football stadium in the town. It might be more accurate to class the Whelan support of Wigan as less a strategic investment and more of a 'benefactor relationship', however. The relationship has been very successful. Wigan were promoted to the Premiership in 2005.

JJB Sports and its chairman have nevertheless experienced the odd difficulty. The Office of Fair Trading claimed that JJB Sports and a number of their rival companies had fixed the price of replica football kits, in particular those of England and Manchester United. It was known, as a result of information supplied by a whistle-blower, that a meeting of sports goods retailers had taken place, but not surprisingly, no minutes of the meeting were taken. The Competition Appeal Tribunal decided that the companies who took part in the meeting subsequently became involved in price fixing. Such price fixing was designed to enhance the profits of the companies involved at the expense of the consumer. Manchester United directors were aware of the agreement relating to the sale of their replica shirts; a director of Umbro who manufactured the shirts wrote to the club to point out how hard their representatives had worked in agreeing a consensus to the price of the new Manchester United jersey. The companies involved were found guilty and paid an £8.4 million fine. An example of the dark side of football, with the consumers, in this case the buyers of replica football shirts, being exploited.

Benefactors

A benefactor is a person who gives financial aid to a cause or institution. There clearly have been genuine benefactors in football. Jack Walker at Blackburn, Jack Hayward at Wolves and Elton John at Watford are obvious examples. Often these figures want to do something to help their local club, the club being in a region in which they have an emotional attachment. They do not generally invest for a financial return, although they do not want to throw their money away. Jack Hayward has shown, however, that even benefactors can, after time, become fed up with a lack of success.[13]

It is not always easy to decide whether the interest of an investor in a club is motivated by genuine beneficial concern or whether it is financial in nature. To have a business link does not mean one is not a supporter of the team, however. There are a number of major investors at football clubs who, although not benefactors, have an emotional link with the club in which they are, or have been, involved. David Moores and Steve Morgan at Liverpool are a notable example, as are Steve Gibson at Middlesbrough, Delia Smith at Norwich, the True Blue consortium at Everton and Eddie Davies at Bolton.

In 2000 Bolton were a struggling club going nowhere until Eddie Davies began to invest in the club. Three years later he took the company off the stock market (the AIM) and made it private. By 2006 he had built up his shareholding in the club to 94.5%. Davies had made his money through his involvement with an Isle of Man-based company that makes thermostats. He sold this company in 2005. He has helped finance a £35 million new stadium for Bolton.

Middlesbrough were locked out of their ground in 1986 by receivers. It was uncertain whether the club could continue and they played the first game of the 1986–87 season at Hartlepool's ground. Steve Gibson, Middlesbrough born and bred, saved them. At the time he was only 28, but he still took on the responsibility for a club which at the time had an annual revenue of £2 million and debts that turned out in total to be greater than this revenue figure. One of the problems Gibson had to deal with were the existing directors and shareholders. Some of these were from families that had been involved with the club for three generations, 'great grandchildren of the original shareholders delving back to 1876.' Over the years these 'old' directors had lent the club money and this had to be paid back. They had also mismanaged the club. Steve Gibson became the club's Chairman and the key person involved in turning the club around. Under his leadership a new ground was built, the club established themselves in the Premiership, played in a European Cup Final, and established a respected football academy for young players—all the result of local initiative and enthusiasm.

Tom Cannon and Sean Hamil argued in 2000 that the 'track record of the multi-millionaires going in and buying football clubs is appalling.'[14] They argue that the 'benefactors' or 'entrepreneurs' have benefited considerably from such action, but the clubs involved have only won a paltry number of trophies. The names of the multi-millionaires they mention include Alan Sugar and Irving

Scholar at Tottenham, Jack Walker at Blackburn, John Hall at Newcastle and Peter Johnson at Everton. Canon and Hamil argue that the case for ownership by stakeholder corporations, not carpetbaggers, is a stronger one. This view was expressed a number of years ago and since then we have learned a lot. It appears that no one would support carpetbaggers, yet stakeholder corporations have also been discredited.

In the September 2004 edition of the *FourFourTwo* football magazine one question raised was 'Can Sugar Daddies rot your club?' Two alternative views were offered, one was that sugar daddies are 'knights in shining armour'; the other was that they are 'short-term egotists.' Of course each sugar daddy is different, each has different motives and so not surprisingly the outcomes can be different. A number of cases were discussed in the article: the fans of Fulham that were consulted were grateful for Mohamed-Al-Fayed's contribution, as were the fans of Blackburn grateful for Jack Walkers involvement at their club. The fans of Oxford United and Darlington were not happy with their experiences of benefactors.

Oxford United supporters may have believed that they had attracted a true benefactor when in 1999 Firoz Kassam, through a Jersey-registered company, took over the club for £1. He took the club into a 'Compulsory Voluntary Arrangement' which resulted in all the larger unsecured creditors of the club receiving only £0.10 for every £1 they were owed. He then helped finance a new £15 million stadium, to which the club moved. By 2006, however, the supporters knew they didn't really have a benevolent benefactor. Kassam had sold the football club to Nick Merry (a US-based businessman) for £1, but retained ownership of the new ground and the commercial development surrounding the ground. In 2006 the club were relegated from the Football League. Kassam had made a great deal of money from the sale of the club's old ground. He owned the stadium, not the club. He had purchased the land on which the new ground was built and the area around it at a comparatively low price. Kassam's business interests are hotels and property development. He did very nicely out of his involvement with Oxford United. On leaving the club he admitted that he was not an expert on football and said that he was not prepared to invest millions of pounds in a football club. His interest was property, not football.

Not all property developers who come into football are as successful as Kassam. At Wrexham two businessmen took over the town's football club in 2002 with the intention, they claimed, of developing the club's old ground and rejuvenating the football club. They said they wanted to develop the site of the old ground and the land around it for commercial purposes and that the money raised would be used to pay off the club's debts, to develop the football club and to build a new stadium. There was, however, evidence that they wanted to develop the old ground for their own benefit; to asset strip the club.

Alex Hamilton and Mark Guterman arranged for ownership of the old ground to be transferred to a company they owned. They then cancelled the existing 125-year lease, the terms of which allowed the football club to use the ground, and introduced a new lease that enabled the new owners to remove the club with twelve months notice. Not surprisingly these moves were not popular. The result of legal action was that the High Court decided that the ownership of the old 'Racecourse Ground' should be transferred back to its former owner and the club should continue to use the ground. The court said that Guterman had breached his duty as a company director when he transferred the club's main asset to one of Hamilton's companies.

The views of fans at Darlington were mixed about the contribution of the former safecracker, George Reynolds. He had paid off the club's debts, financed a new stadium (bigger than was needed) and given the club one good season before succumbing to administration. Reynolds was an unusual benefactor, a 'former gangster and ex-Kray associate.' He had spent four years in prison, before becoming a successful businessman. In 1999 he sold one of his businesses and purchased the Darlington football club. He promised a 25,000-seat new stadium, and promotion to the Premier League within five years. But by 2006 Darlington were still in League Two (the fourth tier). They had a new stadium, but could not fill it. Unfortunately, despite George Reynolds' good intentions, he was not lucky with the Inland Revenue and had to go back to prison for three years for illegal tax avoidance.

Darlington are not the only club to have a 'benefactor' who finished up in prison. In 2000 Darran Brown purchased Chesterfield Football Club. Brown was a 29-year old entrepreneur who owned an ice hockey club and a basketball club, both Sheffield-based.

Brown brought some success to Chesterfield, they went to the top of the then Third Division (fourth tier) but there were financial shenanigans. Brown had bought the club from its previous owner, Norton Lea, for £1.2 million but Lea later revealed that not all of this amount had been paid to him. Lea also pointed out that when he had left the club it was not short of funds, but twelve months later not all the players' wages had been paid and Brown had transferred nearly £400,000 out of the club to one of his other companies.[15]

The club were investigated by the FA Compliance Officer, and found guilty of providing false information. The club were fined by the FA and had points deducted. The police were brought in, and it was discovered that the club's ground had been used to guarantee a loan, that the club had debts of £2 million, and that some of this money had been transferred to one of Brown's other sports companies, whilst other funds had been used by Brown to buy a house and luxury cars. A Serious Fraud Office investigation led to charges of false accounting and theft. It was found out that Brown was really a con-man, he had little money of his own, had used borrowed money to purchase Chesterfield, and had used the club's funds to pay his own creditors. Not all 'benefactors' are what they seem. Despite its problems the club were promoted to Division Two (third tier).

Supporters Trust

For many years supporters have purchased shares in the clubs they support. Sometimes when the opportunity arises they sell the shares and make a profit, but often they just hold onto the shares. Louis Edwards was able to take-over control of Manchester United by diligently tracking down supporters who owned a few shares and then purchasing the shares.

The power of supporters has increased since the supporters trust movement became active in 2000. There are now supporter trusts involved in over 100 clubs. In 2002–03 they raised over £2 million to benefit clubs. Although most of the teams they support financially are in the lower divisions they do have an involvement in over half the Premier League clubs.[16]

They not only buy shares in clubs but also assist in organising the financial rescue of clubs in distress. In three clubs—Exeter City, York City and Lincoln City—local supporters trusts are majority shareholders, and in a number of other clubs they own a sufficient percentage of the shares to give them a significant interest. At Chesterfield the football club is now wholly owned and controlled by a supporters trust.

Brentford are another example of a club now owned by its fans. In 2003 the company that had been the controlling shareholder agreed to transfer its interests in the club to the Brentford Community Society Ltd, the supporters' mutual society. The fans had raised £5.5 million to help refinance the clubs. The debts were rescheduled and are to be paid off over time. The club appointed Greg Dyke, the experienced businessman, as their Chairman.

Over 90% of the trusts are registered as Industrial and Provident Societies. The objectives of such trusts include the strengthening of the bonds between the club and the local community, the encouragement of the club to take proper account of the interests of its supporters and of the community, and the promotion of the principle of supporter representation on the board of any company owning or controlling a club.

From a financial point of view supporters trusts are a vehicle for acquiring an equity stake in a club. They are based on the principle of mutuality. The growth of supporters trusts is a promising development that could lead to changes in the power structure within some clubs. For a time it looked as if the ownership of shares by a club's supporters would only have a significant impact at the smaller clubs but developments at clubs such as Leeds and Leicester have shown that the growth of well organised and well advised supporters can at times produce results. In Deloitte's 2006 'Review of Football Finance' they acknowledge that the 'supporters trust movement has started to play a major role in the changing landscape of British football.'

Secret Money

At one time clubs like Manchester City and Birmingham City were alleged to have been controlled by small groups of businessmen who had links through local branches of the Freemasons. When Matt Busby was manager of Manchester United he is said to have 'worked the Manchester Catholic background to his advantage.'[17] Now that much of football has become global, there is even more secrecy surrounding the ownership of clubs and the relationship between different parties in a transaction.

A number of football clubs have blocks of their shares (often the controlling interest) registered in the names of offshore Investment Trusts. These trusts are registered in tax havens such as the Channel Islands, the Cayman Islands and the British Virgin Islands, and because of the secrecy laws in these countries it is not always known who are the beneficial owners of these trusts. The source of the owner's wealth is not known. In fact, the true owners of somewhere in the region of 35% of the wealth in the world is unknown, and each year the percentage held secretly increases; much of this money is 'dirty money'.

As this book goes to press one cannot say with any certainty whether or not dirty money has been used to buy the shares of English football clubs, although it is known that this has happened to football clubs in some other countries. It is known that in many countries in the world criminals are linked to football clubs. Criminal organisations have used football clubs to launder money. Drug traffickers in Columbia have invested money in that country's football clubs. In Western Europe, football clubs in Italy and France have been found to be connected to criminal gangs.

Considering that football is the biggest sport in the world and money-laundering is the third biggest business in the world, it is not surprising that the two activities on occasion come together. In his book *Dirty Dealing* Peter Lilley gives details of how legitimate businesses that have not traditionally been used for money-laundering are now being used for that purpose. The industries he cites as examples are real estate development, car dealerships and football clubs.

Drug traffickers are known to have invested their funds in several Scottish football clubs including Glasgow Celtic (it should be stated that this happened without the club's knowledge). In the 1996–99 period, Lilley reports that law enforcement investigators in Scotland tracked the finances of 43 prime criminals and of those 6 had funds invested in football clubs.[18] The law enforcement agencies are not winning the war against money-laundering. There is no reason to doubt that what has happened in Scotland has also happened in England.

106

UEFA are aware of this problem, but perhaps not surprisingly find it difficult to do anything about it. Criminal gangs, and those involved in dirty money, are very efficient and very well organised and there are dozens of countries (so-called tax havens) willing to allow them the 'secrecy' necessary to move their vast wealth around the world. As David Blunkett (at the time British Home Secretary) pointed out the criminal groups are better organised than the official bodies trying to fight and defeat them. This would certainly apply to UEFA (and the FA)—they do not have the expertise to find out how the private funds coming into football were first earned. Dirty money could have passed through ten different bank accounts on its way to being used to purchase football shares, with each account potentially in a different tax haven.

UEFA have argued it is the responsibility of the UK government to know who owns any sector of the UK economy, including football. FIFA and UEFA are private bodies running football competitions—they could ask to be given details about any club that takes part in one of their competitions. But even if they had the will to do so they do not have the ability to be able to detect the ultimate owners of clubs and to ascertain how the people concerned acquired their wealth. In 2005 UEFA asked the European Parliament to request the Financial Action Task Force on Money-laundering to investigate the large amounts of money being pumped into football by investors.

When Ken Bates purchased his equity interest in Chelsea in 1982 for £1, a large percentage of the shares in the club were already held by offshore companies. By 1996, when the shares in Chelsea were floated on the stock market, 66% of the shares were owned by Rysaffe Ltd, a Hong Kong-based company with a secret owner or owners. At the end of 1996 the shares held by Rysaffe were transferred to Swan Management Holdings. The trust was registered in Guernsey. In 2002 it owned 26% of the shares of the club. The identity of the person or persons behind Swan Management was unknown, but was the subject of much speculation. The presumed person behind the trust was Stanley Tolman. Tolman had been a friend and a business associate for over 25 years of Ken Bates; for nine years they jointly owned a flat in Monte Carlo. Tolman became a director of Chelsea in 1982, but resigned in 1992. In April 2002 he was indicted in the US on suspicion of fraud, tax evasion and making false statements. He was accused of tricking Wall Street banks into writing off both his own debts and those of his associates.

Tolman denies ever having owned Chelsea shares. Bates has said that the investors behind Swan Management Holding were the people who had backed his purchase of Chelsea in 1982. At the end of June 2002 the mystery beneficiary of Swan Management Holdings sold his Chelsea shares. Who was the buyer? Ken Bates purchased some of these shares. Presumably he did know who had been the beneficiary or beneficiaries. Bates paid for the shares he acquired through a company of his registered in the British Virgin Islands.

When Swan Management sold its holding in Chelsea, Ken Bates purchased the major amount, but some of the shares were sold to other people. It was necessary for Bates to keep his holding in Chelsea below 30% because if he owned over that amount, then stock exchange rules would require him to make an offer to purchase the remainder of the club's shares. The top regulatory body in the UK, the Financial Services Authority (FSA), carried out an investigation to ascertain who owned the balance, and in particular whether Ken Bates owned or controlled more of the shares in Chelsea Village than he had disclosed.

In 2006, the FSA, announced that following a two-year investigation into the status of certain shareholdings in Chelsea, they could not conclude anything. There were five mystery offshore companies that had held shares in Chelsea and it was unclear whether or not Ken Bates had owned shares in these companies and how much control he had over these investments. So in a sense it was not known who had owned Chelsea. The FSA report stated that they 'could not form a conclusive view as to whether Mr Bates had any degree of control over the five said companies, and if so the extent of any such control.'

One reason it was an issue was that when in July 2003 Roman Abramovich took over Chelsea, Ken Bates had said that he personally only controlled 29.5% of the shares of Chelsea. This statement by Bates was later challenged and it was claimed that he had misled the stock market insofar as through secret offshore companies he had a much greater level of control. Because the FSA could not form a 'conclusive' view they closed the case. If the FSA cannot

108

find out what is happening in the global financial markets, what hope do the FA, UEFA or FIFA have of deciding on the truth?[19]

Foreign Investors

When the stock market lost interest in the equity shares of football clubs, and after media companies had all the strategic holdings they required, it appeared an equity gap might develop. Most clubs were not earning enough profits to be able to finance their own needs. The big hope became private equity investors. Fortunately for the clubs, not only had English football become a global product, but the financial markets had become global. The clubs did not have to find an English investor who was in love with football, there were now foreign investors who one way or the other had accumulated great wealth, and who for one reason or another wished to be associated with an English football club.

With respect to the world of private equity, the potential wealth of a club depends upon the size of the wealth of the owner or owners of the club, and upon their willingness to spend their money. Liverpool were once thought to be lucky to have the wealth of the Moores family behind them. Wigan Athletic, with the wealth of Dave Whelan behind them, have performed very well to get into the Premiership. The £650 million of Jack Walker enabled Blackburn Rovers to win the Premiership and since his death family trusts have continued to financially support the Rovers. Such investments were motivated arguably by the love of a local club or of a city, town or region. But now the situation has changed.

When the international businessman Mohamed Al-Fayed took over Fulham and invested a part of his estimated wealth of over £600 million to assist the club in its drive for promotion to the Premiership, and even more of his money to keep them there, it was the beginning of a new era in the financing of clubs. If a man who operated in the global markets, who had only recently become involved with a local community through his ownership of Harrods, who was worth over four times more than the traditional type of wealthy local businessman interested in football (for example David Moores), if such a man became interested in a Premier

109

League club it indicated that a gap could open up between the rich and the poor clubs. But surely nobody wealthier than Al-Fayed would appear on the scene. Someone did: Roman Abramovich changed everything.

Roman Abramovich's life is a story of rags to riches. Born in 1966 in poor family circumstances, over 1,000 miles from Moscow, his mother died when he was one-year-old, and his father died a year later. By the time he was 36 years old he was the second richest man in Russia. In 2005 he was the eleventh richest man in the world. Abramovich is clearly a skilled businessman. He also had the ability and the good fortune to be able to take advantage of the badly handled Russian privatisation process in the 1990s. The state-owned industries were being sold off at well below their true value. The first stage of the privatisation process had been a success, the consumer sector was revolutionised. The problem came with the second stage, when thousands of large and medium-sized enterprises were sold off. This second stage, for which the Russians received advice from a subsidiary of the World Bank, the International Finance Corporation, involved all Russians (including children) receiving a voucher worth 10,000 roubles. These vouchers could be sold either for cash, swapped for shares in a company or invested in an investment fund. The opposition party referred to the scheme as 'smash and grab'.

The result was that the ownership of Russian companies, which had previously been state-owned, was not widely dispersed amongst the population. The vast number of Russians sold their vouchers for cash, which enabled those who knew what they were doing to build up big shareholdings in the newly privatised companies. There were also a number of other scandals at the time, for example the granting of foundation licences to companies to trade in gas and oil. Meanwhile the Russian mafia had infiltrated the banks and various state departments, leading to speculation that 'cabinets over which Yeltsin had presided had been riddled with corruption.' Even before the collapse of Communism there had been strong links between the Russian Mafia and many people in authority. 'Privileged' people were given export licences. A company called Sports Academy had licences for the export of many items including fuel oil, cement and aluminium. The head of this company, a known member of the Mafia, was eventually murdered but not before Yeltsin gave Sports Academy complete freedom from export and import taxes for the period from 1993 to 1995. There were other scandals involving Russian companies overpaying for work undertaken by foreign companies and the overpaid amounts finding their way into secret bank accounts in Switzerland and other tax havens. There was certainly a great deal of money 'leaving' Russia at the time

Roman Abramovich was a member of Boris Yeltsin's 'family' or 'cabinet'. These were a small group that surrounded Yeltsin in his final months as President of Russia. Yeltsin was unwell and it was the 'family' who became of increasing importance in decision-making matters. It was this group who were influential in promoting Vladimir Putin to be, first Prime Minister of Russia, and then President. Roman Abramovich has been close to two Russian Presidents, he has friends and business associates who are amongst the most powerful people in the world. What hope does a club have whose owner's wealth is based on a local, or even national business?

Abramovich purchased a state-owned mining company in Russia for just over $100 million at the time when Boris Yeltsin was privatising many public sector companies. It was a good buy, at the time of the purchase it was said to be worth $12 billion. He sold a part of the company, Sibneft, in 2003 for $3 billion. In 2005, when the Russian Government wished its huge oil assets to move back into state ownership, Abramovich wisely sold his remaining holding in Sibneft for £13 billion. As well as being a wise financial move, it took political pressure off him. His wealth in 2005 was estimated to be $10 billion.

Another wealthy financier who took over a top English football club at more or less the same time was Malcolm Glazer, but his wealth was estimated to be only £650 million, four times more than David Moores, but only one fifteenth that of Roman Abramovich. One big difference between these two investors is that at the time of the acquisitions Abramovich was passionate about football, but Malcolm Glazer knew little about the game. The Glazer family are, however, serious investors. They have used the financial markets to give them power beyond their own wealth. They borrowed two thirds of the money they needed to take-over Manchester United. (The pros and cons of such a strategy are discussed elsewhere in this book.) The extent to which private investors use borrowed funds is not always known. They do not have to publish accounts.

Ken Livingstone, the Mayor of London, apparently backed a campaign to attract Russia's super wealthy to England. It is a well-known fact that London does receive funds from all over the world and that it has a reputation for not asking too many questions about the original source of these funds. The UK tax laws are also favourable to such funds. A large number of very wealthy Russians have homes in England in order to protect their wealth from the Russian government. Roman Abramovich is in many respects the spiritual leader of these oligarchs. In 2006 he stated that he was cutting his political activities in Russia.

The director-general of Juventus, Luciano Moggi, in answering a question on how to compete with Roman Abramovich and Chelsea's wealth, expressed the view that 'those who haven't got that kind of money available will have to use their imagination to make up for it. And sometimes you get better results with imagination.' Imagination might make up for a small difference, but to make up a monetary difference of a magnitude of 10 or more times requires not imagination but pure fantasy.[20]

One thing that is remarkable about Abramovich's investment is that he is in no hurry to obtain a return. Chelsea talk about breaking even in five years time (by 2010), but between July 2003 and August 2005 they invested £218 million on new players. Chelsea have, so far, been lucky with their foreign 'benefactor'.

One other club that was acquired by a foreign businessman is Portsmouth. In 1998 the Serbian-born businessman, Milan Manderic, bought the club from the administrators for £5 million of his own money. When he bought the club they were in the Championship (the second tier) and their future uncertain. The club did well, and were promoted to the Premiership for the 2003–4 season. The net assets of the club more than doubled between the time Milan Manderic took over the club and 2004. Nevertheless, in 2005–06 the club were struggling to survive in the Premiership. Then, in January 2006, somewhat surprisingly, it was announced that Alexandre Gaydamak, the son of a Russian billionaire, was to pay Milan Mandaric £15 million for a 50% stake in the club. It was said that the new owner would invest up to £70 million in the club. They desperately needed to buy new players.[21] There was nothing surprising about more Russian money coming into English football but questions were asked about where Gaydamak's money came from. (Gaydamak was, in fact, a French citizen, of 30 years of age

112

with a number of business interests.) He claimed his wealth had been accumulated as a result of his own activities in the finance and real estate fields, with much of this being earned on property deals in Russia.

If this is the position Gaydamak is fortunate. His billionaire father (Arkady Gaydamak) has been the subject of a criminal investigation. In 2000 Paris magistrates issued an arrest warrant for him for questioning over an alleged arms-for-oil deal with Angola in the early 1990s. It was in connection with the same deal that the son of the former French President, Francois Mitterand, was found to have broken the law and sentenced to a 30-month suspended sentence.

Arkady Gaydamak has banking and industrial interests in Russia and is the owner of a football club in Israel, where he now lives. In 2005 and in 2006 he was questioned by Israeli police investigating money-laundering activities. In March 2006, the Israeli police recommended that charges be brought against him. He is alleged to have transferred hundreds of millions of dollars through an Israeli bank, in suspicious circumstances. Arkady Gaydamak denies money-laundering but admits that he did not report the monetary transfers as Israeli law requires. Alexandre Gaydamak has had his own problems with some of his business ventures in Britain. He has been a director of seven UK companies now defunct — not bad for a ten-year business career.

Alexandre Gaydamak was introduced to Portsmouth by the Israeli-based, so-called super agent Pini Zahavi, who also put Roman Abramovich in touch with Chelsea. There is now a European-wide inquiry into foreign investment coming into football clubs. There is concern that the source of the money should be transparent; easy to say but not easy to achieve.

Arkady Gaydamak's investment in an Israeli football club reveals something about the motives of certain international investors. He once said that Beitar (the Jerusalem football club) cost him $1 million, but that 'it was worth much more for him in terms of publicity.' He is now a permanent resident of Israel, but he was virtually unknown in that country until he bought a football club and began courting the sporting elite of that country. He is said to be the second richest person in Israel and to 'crave respectability.' This he seeks to obtain through football. There are different stories on how he built up his wealth. One intelligence agency concluded

113

that he 'succeeded in profiting remarkably from the opportunities offered by the collapse of the USSR.'

In November 2006 West Ham United became the sixth Premier League club to become foreign-owned. The take-over of West Ham was in a way a surprise. The club had a reputation as a good local club, with strong community links, and a family-type atmosphere. Its Chairman, Terry Brown, owned 36.6% of the club's shares, and with two other directors, they and their families controlled over 90% of the club's shares. The club could not be taken over unless Terry Brown and one of the other two major shareholders agreed.

The consortium that first showed interest in the acquisition was led by Kia Joorabchian, a London-based investor, who was born in Iran. Through a company called Media Sports Investment Joorabchian and group of investors had, in 2004, purchased control of Corinthians, the top Brazilian club. The source of the money behind the consortium was at first uncertain; there were rumours that the Russian oligarch Boris Berezovsky was backing the investment. Berezovsky was wanted in Russia on fraud charges, but has been granted political asylum in Britain. There were suggestions that the acquisition of Corinthians had been used to launder money. Joorabchian denied that Berezovsky was involved.

Another name linked to the consortium was Badri Patarkatshisum, who was the wealthiest man in Georgia, and who had links with Media Sports Investment and the Corinthians. He was also owner of the football champions of Georgia. UEFA are of course concerned about individuals owning more than one club. Joorabchian would not disclose the identities of the investors in Media Sports Investment, arguing that they do not want publicity, and that Media Sports Investment, like the vast majority of private equity funds, do not reveal the identity of their investors.

The Corinthians, once one of the most successful clubs in Brazil, have not performed well under the 'leadership' of Kia Joorabchian and Media Sports Investment.

At the end of 2006 they were near the bottom of the Brazilian championship. Two of the clubs better young players (both from Argentina) had been 'exported' to West Ham, much to the disgust of Corinthian fans. Media Sports Investment owned the two players and there was some complicated arrangement involving the football club and the investment company regarding the manner in which the players would be integrated into the West Ham team and what would happen to transfer fees if and when the players were sold. This arrangement might have worked out satisfactorily if the Joorabchian consortium had also taken over the club.

One investor said to be associated with the Joorabchian consortium was Eli Papouchado, who owned a multi-national property company based in Israel. Papouchado, who was born in Egypt, had little knowledge of football but was interested in the £70 million plus of tangible assets the club owned. The value of the club's land could, it was said, be worth very much more than this if planning permission for residential property could be obtained. Papouchado is reported to have said that he wanted the club because of its real estate. His interest in football made even more sense when it was revealed that West Ham were interested in moving to the Olympic Stadium when the 2012 Games were over. They hoped to conclude a similar deal to that of Manchester City, with the City of Manchester Stadium. If West Ham could move it would mean their existing ground, Upton Park, could be redeveloped—an attractive proposition for a property developer.

The leader of the consortium, Kia Joorabchian, resigned as head of Media Sports Investment. Strong financial links have developed between Russia, Israel, and Premier League football clubs.[22] Football supporters who are interested in this type of thing might wonder why this has happened. Israel is a country that does not have a good reputation in financial circles. In the past it has certainly been a money-laundering centre. Until recently, in fact, money-laundering was not a crime in that country. The reason given for this was that secrecy was necessary because of the country's long running conflict with its neighbours. Secrecy enabled wealthy supporters of Israel around the world to quietly help the country financially. The problem was that it also allowed criminal organisations around the world to use Israel to launder money. Israel has also been a very popular destination for Russian émigrés and their money. 'In 1996 between 3 and 4 million dollars were deposited in Israeli bank accounts by such émigrés. Many criminals posed as Jewish refugees and took advantage of liberal money transfer regulations.'[23]

The rival consortium that became involved in the battle for control of West Ham comprised a group of Icelandic businessmen, coincidentally a group in which the largest investor also had

115

Russian connections. This consortium was fronted by Eggert Magnusson, president of the Football Association of Iceland, and an executive committee member of UEFA. The members of this consortium were thought to be wealthy Icelanders and the bid was backed by an Icelandic financial institution. Magnusson was clearly a man of considerable importance in football circles. Whether or not a bid from either consortium would be successful depended on the decision made by Terry Brown and the other two major shareholders of West Ham, however. Terry Brown said he would be more interested in an Abramovich-type purchase than a Glazer one. The club already had debts in the region of £25 million. The football club's directors and its bankers were worried about the amount of debt any new owners of the club would need to take on in order to fund the purchase.

The Icelandic bid was successful. The company they established, W.H. Holdings, paid £85 million for the equity and took on responsibility for the club's debts. Terry Brown made a gain in excess of £30 million on his investment in the football club. The main investor in W.H. Holdings is Bjorgolfur Gudmundsson. (He is said to own 95% of the company.) He has had a colourful business career. He was a senior executive at Iceland's second largest shipping company until he and the company got into trouble. In December 1985 the company was declared insolvent and Gudmundsson was arrested and charged with false accounting and embezzlement. He was said to have used company money for his own purposes. He was found guilty and in 1991 sentenced to twelve months in prison, but the sentence was suspended and he was put on probation.

Gudmundsson went to Russia, where he and his son ran a very successful brewing company, which they were able to sell for $400 million. Upon returning to Iceland they then took over a major bank, one that before privatisation had been the National Bank of Iceland. He later acquired other financial institutions, a shipping company—and in 2006 a football club.

Other Premier League clubs who at the end of the 2006–07 season were having discussions with foreign investors were Manchester City and Arsenal. Foreign investors do not always win, Newcastle United were taken over by a wealthy Englishman.[24]

But it is not just Premier League clubs that interest foreign investors. Cardiff City, a Championship club, are an example of a club with unusual owners. In October 2006, Sam Hammam, the Lebanese businessman who had been Chairman and major shareholder at the club for six years, sold his 81.5% shareholding to a consortium of city investors. Members of the consortium were not known, but Peter Ridsdale (of Leeds United fame) announced that it did not consist of individual members but of two or three hedge funds. He intimated that the hedge funds were London-based financial institutions, and that in future he, as the club's new chairman, would be running the club as a public company with transparency. Nevertheless, this transparency does not go as far as disclosing where the money comes from that is being invested by the hedge funds.

Ridsdale said that he had been working on this take-over of Cardiff for over six months. He highlighted certain problems with the financial side of the club under Hammam's leadership. The club were £24 million in debt for a start, and this borrowed money had been obtained through the sale of 'loan notes' in Switzerland. There had always been a question of who had purchased the notes, and thus effectively loaned the club money. The new consortium planned to repay half of these loan notes when they had the money and when they knew who owned the notes. Many financial securities, bonds, notes and equity shares are in certain countries issued in 'bearer' form, which means the owner's name is not registered. A good example of football's mysterious and questionable financing if ever there was one.

Another club with interesting owners are Queens Park Rangers. The club had emerged from administration in May 2002. It had been purchased for £10 million in 1996 by Chris Wright, who made his money in the music and media business. The club were not successful on the pitch nor financially, and were put into administration in 2001. The club then experienced a number of boardroom changes before Gianni Paladini, an Italian businessman and former footballer and football agent, came on the scene to help the club. He invested £0.6 million of his own money to purchase 21% of the club's shares, put his wife on the board of the club, and helped attract new money from an ex-Brazilian footballer as well as from two Monaco-based companies with Italian owners. One of Paladini's business associates, who became involved with the running of QPR, is Antonio Caliendo, once a top football agent in Italy. Caliendo claims that he at one time represented 12 of the 22 players who played for Italy in the 1990 World Cup final. Unfortunately for him, whilst an agent, he got into difficulties with the Italian tax authorities. In 1991 he was arrested, and in a deal agreed with the tax authorities, he accepted a ten-month suspended prison sentence for attempted corruption. In 1992 he was investigated in connection with his involvement with an Italian football club that got into financial difficulties.

Another strange 'financier' said to be involved with QPR is Michael Hunt. When the club were in difficulty in 2002 they accepted a £10 million loan from the Panama-registered ABC Corporation: a loan with a 10% annual rate of interest. This was the same ABC Corporation that lent £15 million to Derby County when they were in trouble. It is thought Michael Hunt's money is behind the ABC Corporation. Hunt has also had tax problems, having in 1993 been sentenced to eight years in prison for fraud. ABC also purchased an equity stake in QPR. Caliendo arranged for the two Monaco-based companies to increase their equity stake, which meant that in 2005 Paladini, the Monaco consortium and ABC were the major investors in the club. There were, however, another group of investors who owned 30%. This lead to trouble.

In August 2005 police were called to the QPR's ground because Paladini had been involved in a fight with a group of men who he said forced him to sign a letter of resignation. Following this incident, one of the QPR directors and three other men were charged with conspiracy to commit blackmail and joint possession of a firearm with intent to cause grievous bodily harm. What a way to run a football club![25]

Another Russian, Vladimir Romanov, became the majority shareholder in Heart of Midlothian, in the Scottish League. Romanov was born in Russia, but made most of his money in Lithuania. He acquired several businesses in the Baltic states in the years following the break up of the USSR. He is the owner of a bank in Lithuania and is said to be worth £200 million. He has financed a football team in Lithuania and another in Minsk. When he took over Hearts he took on responsibility for the club's £20 million debts, provided finance to enable them to remain in their existing stadium and invested in new players.

Romanov brought into the club as Chairman George Foulkes, a respected local politician, to ensure that the club were 'on the right track in the political context.' But soon after he obtained control of the Scottish club Romanov began to exercise his power. He fell out with the very popular manager George Burley. (It was said that Romanov wanted to pick the team.) Burley left because of 'irreconcilable differences'. Shortly afterwards the chief executive was sacked, and George Foulkes resigned in protest.

As with all acquisitions of football clubs by foreign investors the question arises as to their motives. Romanov's answer was that he had 'been in football for 15 years as a sponsor of FC Kaunas in Lithuania. We won the league six seasons in a row but Lithuania is not a football country. I was intrigued by the paradox of those clubs elsewhere that spend lots of money and do not achieve success. That is because everyone in football is out to make money, and everyone does, except the club owner. So this is a challenge. I want to be responsible for a project, the like of which does not exist anywhere in the world. The [proposed] stadium has to be more than just a sporting facility, it has to be cultural, something that enhances the lives of children.'

All this sounds very impressive. Romanov does, however, have his critics. It has been pointed out that the ground the club have occupied for over 100 years is near the centre of Edinburgh, and should the club move to a new ground, the old site could be sold off, very profitably, for housing and commercial development. (The property is said to be worth £22 million.) Another worry about Vladimir Romanov was that his Lithuanian bank had not been all that successful. In fact, a City report referred to its 'very modest financial strength.' The uncertainty over Romanov's wealth was one reason why Foulkes resigned as Chairman of the club. Football in Scotland is in a bad way financially and it is in need of wealthy benefactors, philanthropists, or even entrepreneurs. It is not clear whether Romanov is such a person.

Many people are worried that the new breed of investor coming into football will in the long run harm the game. The Premier League, the Football League, and the FA say that they will conduct tests to ensure that all directors have a clean business record. All club directors and 'shadow' directors must now sign a declaration undertaking that they have not been convicted of any of 25 listed offences including theft, fraud, false accounting or have been the subject to a football banning order. If they have been guilty of any of these offences they cannot be a director of a football club.

The fit and proper persons test also prevents anyone who may in the past have been declared personally bankrupt from being on

119

the board of a Premier League club, and also bans anyone who has suffered insolvency on two separate occasions or has been involved with two different football clubs that have been declared insolvent.

A problem with this policy is that there are wealthy people who have accumulated vast wealth yet have not been found guilty of any criminal offence, but who are still not fit and proper persons to own a football club. There is much the authorities do not know about how certain people have accumulated their wealth. The football authorities in England do not have the resources, the skill or the real desire to find out where and how many of the new breed of football club owners acquired this wealth.

The danger of clubs falling into the wrong hands has been recognised by the authorities, but their approach to solving the problem has been halfhearted at best. Possibly they do not want to rock the boat, whilst the clubs need the money and supporters are happy with any money whatever the source. Hopefully the regulators will improve their monitoring procedures.

Ownership in Other Countries

The ownership situation varies from one country to another. In Italy, as noted previously, most clubs are owned by leading businessmen in a private capacity. Furthermore, with ex-Prime Minister Silvio Berlusconi owning AC Milan, the oil magnates Angelo and Massimo Moratti owning Internazionale Milan, the Agnelli family in charge at Juventus, oil 'baron' Roberto Mancini at the helm of Sampdoria, and Roma enjoying success under Francesco Sensi, the necessary conditions for success are quite clear. Lazio (from Rome) were floated on the Milan Bourse in May 1998, but this move has not been financially successful.

Even Parma enjoyed success under the ownership of the local multi-millionaire Calisto Tanzi, but unfortunately for the club Tanzi was found guilty of financial fraud. His company, Parmalet, collapsed and the football club lost its elevated status.[26] There are many scandals in Italy concerning multi-millionaire owners and the management of their football clubs.[27] Italy won the 2006 World Cup just as the match-fixing scandals in Serie A were revealed. One noticeable feature about the ownership of these clubs in Italy is that all the owners are Italian.

Until 1998, only sports clubs, that is to say sporting societies, could compete in the German Bundesliga. In 1991, Hamburg, and in 1992 Werder Bremen, tried to take steps which would lead to them acquiring company status and having their shares traded on the stock market. They were blocked by the Bundesliga. The statutes of the German FA provided that only licensed clubs can play in the Bundesliga, and licences would only be granted to sporting clubs. In fact, one club was funded by a company, but the company was not allowed to interfere in the running of the club. A number of German clubs argued that they would not be able to compete successfully in Europe unless they could obtain access to similar amounts of finance as other European clubs. The Bundesliga reluctantly agreed to change their rules, but subject to certain conditions. The restrictions they introduced were that if a football club did go public, at least 50% plus one of the shares must be retained by the sporting club members.

One can see why these restrictions in Germany are attractive to a club's supporters, or to be more precise to a club's members, but they do mean the shares in the football companies are not particularly attractive to investors. Control of the companies remains in the hands of members who are more interested in football than in business. The restrictions also protect weaker clubs and therefore help balance competition.

Bayern Münich did turn themselves into a limited company, but mainly so that Adidas could buy a 10% stake in the business, and so provide some extra finance without influencing control. (The other shares in the club are held by members.) Borussia Dortmund also took on company status and floated its shares, but it did not spend its new funds wisely; it built up debts and had to sell its stadium and lease it back. Not a dissimilar story to that of Leeds United. The result of this poor experience in Germany with the stock market is that all but a few German clubs have retained their sporting club legal status. Most clubs have, however, changed their constitutions so that they are now run in a more professional manner. They now have full-time executives who are paid to run the club, and as is normal in Germany, a supervisory board who approve or disapprove of the work being done by the management team.

One feature of German clubs is that most of the grounds are still council-owned. The Bundesliga has the highest league attendance

121

figures in Europe. Two possible reasons for this are the low price of admission to matches (£10) and the competitive balance between teams in the league. Surprisingly, however, despite the attendance figures, and with Germany being the wealthiest of the large European countries, the football clubs are not prosperous. One reason for this is TV income. In Germany, football followers are reluctant to subscribe to cable channels, there being good coverage of football on the free channels. In the global television markets matches in the German league do not attract viewers to the same extent as other big European leagues. There is also less of a commercial environment surrounding football in Germany compared to other countries; because it does not attract the revenue, it cannot pay the top wages and thus the players with global market appeal.

Discussion on possible changes in the ownership and organisational structure of football clubs in Germany continues. There have been proposals to establish a type of company that would be a combination of a partnership and a public company. The German FA have recommended that clubs and their members continue to control over 75% of the companies shares, as this level would allow members to push through any constitutional changes. If the clubs were allowed to sell off more than 25% of shares it would allow financial investors to block any changes. This is the reverse to what was the Manchester United position where supporters wanted to obtain control of over 25% of the companies shares to prevent investors (in particular Glazer) from making constitutional changes.

In Spain, Barcelona belongs to its 142,000 members. The club are very much identified with the politics of the Catalan region. Every four years members decide who the president and directors of the club will be. Such a situation is not necessarily so ideal, the club not so long ago had debts of £100 million and the club in of fact has now become very commercially minded. The present directors have, however, delivered playing success, being winners of the UEFA Champions League in 2006, and twice champions of the Spanish League in recent years. The fans are happy. This ownership structure is similar to that of many other Spanish clubs.[28]

5

The Confusing State of Governance

Internationally

The winning game is over for most clubs because the most powerful governing bodies in the game are happy with the way the game has developed. One governing organisation may squabble with another, but this is basically just a disagreement as to who gets most of the gains. Occasionally one of the governing bodies will make a case for a change of one sort or another, but nothing fundamental.

Of the many bodies and associations that claim to be involved in the governance of the game, some are non-governmental, some governmental. Some are international, others are national, while yet others are private-member organisations. The picture is confusing, which makes it difficult to introduce change, even if the individuals with the power really wanted change.

The numerous organisations involved in the governance process, and the people who they represent, each have their own agendas. Between them they have responsibility for organising competitions, regulation and for planning the future of the game. Very often the objectives of one organisation are in conflict with those of another. The FA, for instance, claim to look after the interest of all levels of football in England, but the Premier League are just interested in the top few clubs. Similarly, the group of 18 clubs known collectively as G14 look after the interests of the top European clubs, whereas UEFA are interested in a very much larger group of European clubs. FIFA's self-proclaimed remit is to 'Develop the game, touch the world, build a better future', whereas G14's objectives relate to member clubs only.

G14's objectives are to promote the co-operation, amicable relations and unity of the member clubs; to safeguard the general interests of the member clubs; to promote co-operation and good relations between itself and FIFA, UEFA and any other sporting institutions and/or professional football clubs, paying special attention to negotiating the format, administration and operation of the club competitions in which the member clubs are involved. G14's primary interests are club competitions, whilst FIFA's main activity is organising international competitions. Clearly the two organisations are bound to clash over the club versus county issue.

G14 was initially a lobbying group. In 2005 they stepped up a level when they became involved in the case brought against FIFA by the Belgian club, Royal Charleroi. They argued that FIFA were illegally abusing their position as the game's top regulator when they became involved in decisions on the release of players by clubs to take part in FIFA-organised international games. This case concerned a player registered with Charleroi who was injured whilst playing for his country, Morocco, in an unimportant friendly match against Burkina Faso. The club claimed compensation from FIFA for the financial loss they suffered as a result of the player's injury in an international match that was the responsibility of FIFA. The international association refused to pay, so the club, with G14 support, took the case to court, claiming abuse of a 'dominant position' by FIFA.

The Football Supporters' Federation have referred to the clubs in G14 as an arrogant elite who are trying to hijack the game. The problem is that most players who represent their countries play for the elite clubs. If more money were to be paid by national football associations or FIFA to these top clubs, for the release of these players, it would mean less money would be available elsewhere in the game.

John Sugden and Alan Tomlinson, in their book on FIFA, explore the question of who rules the people's game.[1] They make the point that it is easy to 'romanticise' earlier phases of the game but that 'In terms of ownership, in its modern form, football has never been the people's game.' The two writers investigate the history of the control exercised by FIFA on the game around the world and conclude that 'since its formation in 1904 FIFA has been the power base for a small elite.' The same could be said about the FA and football in England. Since the formation of the FA, and later the Football League and Premier League, a small elite have owned and controlled the people's game.[2] The people 'just play it, or stand on the periphery of the increasingly mediated and commodified football spectacle.'

FIFA has become 'more and more dependent upon partners outside of football.' In turn, powerful corporate entities have come to see that there are increasingly lucrative gains to be made through the use of FIFA. 'Prominent partners in the commercial, cultural and media industries [have] assumed more power.' The words Premier League could be substituted for FIFA in this quotation.

The key governance question is can industry 'insider' private member bodies such as the FA, UEFA and FIFA be trusted to run their sport in the interests of all stakeholders. In 2006 a number of the governing bodies and a group of sports ministers from various European countries produced reports in which they came up with proposals on what was needed to make the football environment healthier. They all agreed on what were the important issues, but not on the solutions. Not surprisingly they also did not agree on which of the bodies should be the most important agent of change, they could not agree upon which body was the most virtuous. One of the important issues highlighted in these reports is the level of salaries of the top players. FIFA believed these were too high, but not surprisingly the Premier League did not agree.

FIFA were worried about certain club owners 'throwing pornographic amounts of money' into their clubs, but not even their own working group who looked at this issue as part of the 'Good of the Game' study, could come up with recommendations on how this could be controlled. FIFA, the 'Arnaut Report', and UEFA argued for a more equal distribution of the income coming into the game, but not surprisingly they were opposed by the organisations representing the top clubs (G14 and the Premier League). UEFA established a 'European Club Forum', which they hoped would become the acceptable voice of football clubs; it was set up to counterbalance the voice of the G14 clubs.

UEFA and the sports ministers for many European countries want football, because of its social educational and cultural importance, to be protected from the Wild West-style capitalism. A very worthy intent. UEFA want to be recognised by the EU as the governing body for football in Europe, but if one looks at the recent behaviour of UEFA and particularly its parent body FIFA, it is as questionable as the behaviour of any of the top clubs and leagues.

The Premier League clubs are worried that the European Union and UEFA will try to tell everybody how to run the game. They do not want the top governing body to be seen as FIFA, and in Europe, UEFA. At the moment FIFA and UEFA run certain competitions, but that does not give them a right to say how all aspects of football should be run. At the moment a group of clubs could, if they wanted to, break away from the existing structure and form their own national and international competitions. The worry is that if governmental bodies, such as the EC become involved, the whole of the game, including new competitions that might be established, would have to follow a common set of rules on issues such as salary capping, ownership and agents.

Those who organise competitions have a right to set rules for their own competition. If a club does not want to follow this set of rules, it can drop out of the competition. This is effectively what the Premier League clubs did when they dropped out of the Football League. It is what the G14 clubs have threatened to do in respect of the UEFA Champions League. Whatever UEFA may prefer, it does not have the right to a monopoly on football competitions in Europe that involve teams from different countries. FIFA 'own' the World Cup but another body could set up a rival global competition.

FIFA — Federation of International Football Associations

FIFA is the most powerful non-governmental football organisation in the world. It has an impressive public relations machine to remind people of the good work it does. It was founded in Paris in 1904, but moved to neutral (and secretive) Switzerland after the First World War. When it started it had seven members, a member being a national football association. By 2006 there were 207 football association members of FIFA. Between 1975 and 2002, more than 60 associations were accepted as new members. FIFA is often referred to as the 'United Nations of Football'. FIFA uses some of the vast revenue it generates to support football associations around the world. Together with their commercial sponsors (partners) FIFA also has programmes for assisting development projects in poorer countries. One such programme is entitled GOAL. As at 2006, the number of countries to have benefited from this GOAL programme was 176.

In its early days FIFA was a relatively low-key organisation. It was in fact so low-key that England tried to ignore its existence, believing that as the father of the game they were above such upstart international bodies. The French were responsible for FIFA's early development. England believed that they were the best football nation in the world and so there was no need for them to prove it by playing in the World Cup competitions. (England didn't enter the competition until 1950 when they performed very badly.)

Sir Stanley Rous, who had been president of the FA, was president of FIFA between 1961 and 1974. He was respected for the way in which he sought to modernise the international association, but he could not control the political and commercial forces that were beginning to affect his beloved game. He was defeated in an election for president in 1974 by the charismatic Brazilian, Joao Havelance. The Brazilian had more appeal to the many representatives of Third World countries who had joined FIFA. There was also a problem in that Rous had to deal with the possible sporting boycott of South Africa. He was also seen by many as being too close to the old football establishment.

When Stanley Rous was defeated things began to change at FIFA. In the words of Andrew Jennings, by the mid 1980s 'the world of football, he [Rous] had led was under the control of the spivs he'd fought to keep at bay.'[3] To be fair, FIFA had become very successful at bringing money into the game. But many were unhappy about the increased commercialism in the game, particularly at the way in which some people, usually those close to the football establishment, had been able to benefit from this money. Complaints arose as far back as the 1970 World Cup held in Mexico. One of the sponsors of the World Cup, Televisa, bought the TV broadcasting rights. During televised matches they showed advertisements whenever they wished. They sold the broadcasting rights to companies all around the world and made big profits. Televisa, based in Mexico, was one of the biggest media companies in the world. Like BSkyB it has made huge amounts of money out of football. It not only owns hundreds of TV companies across

South America, it also owns football clubs. The company showed great foresight, it bought its first club (América) in 1961. The ownership of the club allowed the company to have a representative in the Mexican Football Association, and so to be able to influence the future direction of the game and the awarding of television contracts in the country.

The person who represented the football club owned by the TV company became Mexico's representative at FIFA and then became a vice president of FIFA. Somewhat of a conflict of interest. In other words, what was best for the Mexican television company, what was best for Mexican football and what was best for world football? In Mexico the regulators were not worried about multiple ownership of clubs and so Televisa bought a second club during the 1980s, and a third club during the 1990s. The three clubs frequently swapped players.

A similar, more recent example of a conflict of interest concerns Jack Warner. Even the FIFA ethics committee were concerned about Warner, an executive committee member of FIFA. His family owned a travel company in Trinidad, and it was this family company that in 2006 were the sole distributor of Trinidad's allocation of World Cup tickets. Warner had in the past purchased the exclusive rights to broadcast, in the Caribbean, the World Cup matches of 1990, 1994 and 1998 for the price of one US dollar. Not only was Warner on FIFA's executive committee, he was President of the Regional Football Conference for all the Americas (except South America). He was said to be able to deliver 35 votes for the candidate he supported in the election for FIFA president. He had no need to worry about the criticisms of his conflict of interest.[4] The FIFA ethics committee found there was a conflict. So Warner sold his shares so that he could remain as a vice president of FIFA. What had happened in the past was to be forgotten.[5]

This is not to suggest that the people running FIFA have not done a lot to bring money into the game. FIFA have been closely involved with Coca-Cola for over 25 years. Coca-Cola have paid for a programme to train football coaches which has been of particular help to developing countries. In turn, FIFA have helped Coca-Cola get their 'feet in the door' in China and many countries in Africa, Eastern Europe and the Middle East. When football is seen by spectators and young players in these countries, the name of Coca-Cola is linked to the sport. As the sponsorship manager of

Coca-Cola explained, 'What the World Cup does for the brand is it allows us to connect with fans globally.' He went on to expand on this by explaining that the World Cup 'encompasses not just fans, but brings in a bigger target range than any other event.' Many people watch World Cup matches, even though they are not particularly interested in football.

The 2006 World Cup was shown on TV in 214 countries, 'virtually every country in the world.' The cumulative audience was 26.3 billion viewers. Perhaps suprisingly 32% of this global total were viewers in Asia, with 20% of the viewers in Europe. The most watched match attracted 715 million viewers. As the marketing people at FIFA point out, football matches are the perfect vehicle for sponsors (advertisers) to deliver their message. FIFA claim that the annual revenue — worldwide — of the football business is greater than that of any company in the world. This total revenue figure of course includes not just receipts from spectators but also that paid into football by TV and media companies, corporate sponsors and in fact any companies wishing to advertise their products.

The World Cup is not just a sporting contest, it is a massive commercial enterprise. The event, FIFA point out, is privately funded (one would hope it is) and costs over €1 billion to put on. Most of the 2006 revenue came from the sponsors (over €482 million), and from the sale of television rights (€862 million). It is clearly important for FIFA to have a close relationship (a partnership) with those they refer to as their 'commercial affiliates'. The sale of the right to use the title '2006 FIFA World Cup' is very important. The 15 official sponsors (including Coca-Cola and McDonalds), along with 6 official suppliers, 'are the only commercial entities officially allowed to claim any direct association with the World Cup. FIFA are willing to take cases to court to 'ensure that their partners get the exclusivity they deserve.'

Criticisms of FIFA

Recent criticisms include: financial mismanagement, control by a small elite, money and favours being used to affect the result of the election of the FIFA president, committee members benefiting financially from related party dealings and sponsors money, failure to enforce rules to control football agents, and attempting to control the football calendar and the size of leagues in member countries.

One major criticism of the association is that it has for a long time been run by a small elite. For a start, it has only had two presidents in the last 30 years: Joao Havelange from 1974 to 1998, and then Sepp Blatter from 1998 to the present. (Blatter announced in 2006 that he was willing to run for a further term as president.)[6] 'FIFA today is run like a dictatorship.' This was the view in 2002 of Michael Zen-Ruffinen, at the time the second most important person in FIFA. He also claimed that FIFA was inefficient and that Sepp Blatter had cost FIFA $500 million (£340 million) during his first few years as president as a result of financial mismanagement, cronyism and widespread corruption. It was claimed that Blatter had rewarded those who had helped keep him in office by channelling them cash and lucrative contracts.[7] He is also reputed to have paid fees and expenses of representatives of various national associations that supported him.

In 2002 Lennart Johansson, then president of UEFA, complained to the Swiss authorities about corruption and financial mismanagement at FIFA. Not surprisingly he fell out with Sepp Blatter, and not surprisingly he was not re-elected in 2007. FIFA's accounts have in the past been heavily criticised. KPMG, FIFA's auditors, scolded them for booking future World Cup income too early in their accounts—what is known as front-end loading. At the end of 2001, after taking out the window dressing in the accounts, KPMG raised the 'negative' equity figure of FIFA from $37.1 million to $142 million. Negative equity is the excess of liabilities over assets. This is not as bad as it seems, FIFA is a cyclical business, and the revenue comes in, in large amounts, every few years. Before the 2002 World Cup, FIFA would have incurred a large amount of expenditure. The problem was that the finances of FIFA were not transparent. There is still not enough openness about who runs the beautiful game.[8] What hope is there for developing a well-balanced game when the organisation and control at the international level is in the hands of people whose primary concern is their own power and importance?

FIFA have set up a high profile committee to investigate corruption in the game, but they themselves are still the subject of an investigation by the Swiss authorities. In 2005 agents from the office of an investigating magistrate obtained access to the FIFA offices in Zurich, under warrants issued in connection with a possible embezzlement. There were questions to be answered about the collapse of FIFA's main marketing agency (partner), ISL, who were over $60 million in debt. ISL (International Sport and Leisure) had won the contract to sell the TV broadcasting rights to the 2002 World Cup to all countries outside Europe, but collapsed before the final matches took place. FIFA lost a large sum of money (said by the report to be $115 million) as a result of the failure of their partner. This collapse became the subject of a criminal investigation.

The trouble began before the 2002 World Cup, when not only ISL but a company called IMG wanted the marketing contract. The rights to the 2002 and 2006 World Cup were to be sold by FIFA as one package. IMG felt that FIFA were not considering their bid on a properly competitive basis. But ISL were having trouble getting banks to back their bid, so they turned for financial support to Leo Kirch, a German entrepreneur, who had the rights to show on television much of the football played in Germany. As a result of a vote at a controversial meeting of the executive committee of FIFA, in July 1996, ISL, together with their partner Leo Kirch, were awarded the contract.

Over the next few years there was talk of a special 'relationship between FIFA and ISL, with rumours of kickbacks and bribes'. Andrew Jennings writing in 2006 refers to 'evidence of wrongdoing' coming to light. The evidence included a standard UBS (United Bank of Switzerland) transaction form, which showed that ISL has transferred one million Swiss francs (£414,000) into FIFA's account. Jennings and others believe that the intention was that the money was to be paid to an individual who was 'a senior official in football. The money was in fact moved out of FIFA's account to the man named on the payment order.' Who that person was has not been disclosed. Jennings has tried many times to get Sepp Blatter to name that person, but he has refused to do so. FIFA tried unsuccessfully to get Jennings' book banned. FIFA's lawyer claimed that Jennings had been attacking FIFA and Blatter for years with dubious criticisms. Although Blatter would not disclose the name of the payee, records are in existence that disclose that name. UBS would have to keep such records until the winter of 2008.

In November 2005 Swiss investigators, as a result of the investigation into the failed ISL, moved into FIFA headquarters to obtain documents relating to the financial spin-offs that they had uncovered. One accused ISL manager admitted that money had been paid to people who were 'decision-makers in world sports'. It was alleged ISL made payments in excess of 10 million Swiss francs (£4 million) to certain FIFA officials, in order to obtain the marketing rights. FIFA would not discuss who had been receiving money, but the legal investigators might come forward with a name. This is, however, far from certain. FIFA paid some money back to ISL, and it has been suggested that they did this so that the names of the official or officials who received the kickbacks would remain a secret.[9]

The decision-making process within FIFA, which led to ISL being awarded marketing contracts, was not one designed to give confidence in an organisation which claimed to be the sport's leading governing body. Whilst Joao Havelange was president, ISL were given contracts to market five World Cups. In fact it was, on occasion, not the executive committee that decided to give the work to ISL, it was the president who informed the executive committee after the contracts had already been awarded. This is the organisation that wishes to ensure that those who are directors of football clubs should be 'fit and proper' persons. What about these who direct the governing bodies? More and more money has been coming into FIFA, particularly with the success of the World Cup competitions. This money has been distributed with little accountability.

FIFA are often referred to as football's governing body.[10] The truth is that it is a self-appointed governing body that only has power over certain competitions. It is true that if a club or a league does not do as FIFA say that players from that club or that league cannot play in the international matches (including the World Cup) organised either by FIFA or one of its confederations, however.

When Sepp Blatter announced that the top domestic competitions in the world, including the Premier League and Serie A, should reduce the number of clubs taking part to 18 by the 2007–08 season, he had no authority to enforce such a move. The FA, however, is a member of FIFA and is in a weak position. It did not challenge the proposed change when it was voted on at the 2006 congress of FIFA. Not surprisingly, Blatter's proposal to reduce league size received support from 194 delegates—only 5 voted against. The proposal only affected a few countries and so most delegates were willing to go along with Blatter, who in one way or another was providing them or their national associations with financial support.

The FA could try to persuade the Premier League to do as FIFA want, and part of the case they could make would be that if the Premier League do not do as FIFA want then players from that league cannot play for England. The chairman of the Premier League clubs run their competition, not FIFA or the FA. The case FIFA make for reducing the number of teams in the top domestic competitions is that less games being played means more time for players to relax and recover from injury. An alternative motive of FIFA could be that it gives more time for players to take part in FIFA-organised international competitions. In whose interests are FIFA really acting, the players, the clubs, the fans, or their own? There have even been suggestions that the World Cup should be held every two years.

Organisational Structure

One problem with FIFA is that each member country has one vote, and this works against the interests of the rich football nations, such as England, Italy, Germany and Spain. Each country is entitled to one vote, irrespective of the size of the population and irrespective of success in past competitions. This democratic voting pattern turns out to be very significant at the time of electing the president of this extremely powerful body. A president of FIFA has a lot he can offer a poor country from, say, Africa, but little he can offer to football in Italy, Spain or the UK.

FIFA has the legal status of an 'association' under Swiss Law. This is because it is recognised as pursuing a good cause (similar to religious, scientific and charitable organisations) and as being non-commercial in nature. As a registered 'association' it does not have to be as accountable as would a commercial business. One of FIFA's objectives is 'the promotion of football in every way it deems fit.' This is very nice for those running FIFA, particularly if they only have to be accountable to their own members. For the last 30 years the presidents of FIFA have run the organisation 'in an essentially oligarchic style' and have been 'fiercely protective of the power of FIFA.' John Sugden and Alan Tomlinson's 1998 book about FIFA carried the subtitle 'Who rules the people's game?' They then wrote a second book on the subject that was titled *Badfellas* and largely answered their earlier question.[11]

Joao Havelange became president of FIFA in 1974, and held the post for 15 years. He was a successful businessman, a 'smooth talking and ruthless international wheeler-dealer.' Sepp Blatter was FIFA's Secretary General during the Havelange Presidency; the two were close. Blatter was also a successful businessman, who had built up a big business empire in transport and in finance. He became President of FIFA in 1998. He has at times come forward with some pretty crazy proposals. One was that all games should have a winner; drawn games at full-time being settled with penalty shoot-outs. He has also suggested that goals should be made wider, and that in women's football shorts should be shorter.

Blatter has brought onto FIFA committees people with business experience who are key members of existing global business networks. Many of these committee members have mutual business and commercial links with other FIFA people. There are also strong business networks internal to FIFA, similar to that which one would find in a family business. 'A combination of powerful and strongly networked individuals and tame committees were to prove effective for the implementation of FIFA strategies and plans.'

FIFA officials have also revealed a certain degree of arrogance. They have, for instance, expressed displeasure with the European Union for making decisions that would have affected the freedom of movement of footballers. FIFA stated that it was their belief that 'a small group of countries (that is European Union countries) cannot be granted an exemption from sports regulations which are effective in all parts of the world.' FIFA are a non-governmental body based in an offshore financial centre, they do not decide law, they make rules that only apply to their members. They are a pressure group, representing the interests of their members; in other words, national football associations. They do not represent the players, the clubs or the supporters. The European Union is a democratic organisation making decisions on the basis of their effect on a wide variety of interested parties. But Blatter believes that football is above national politics. He has said that 'politicians are of course important, but the autonomy of football must be maintained above all else.' Not only do FIFA believe that their views are more important than politicians, they also believe that they can dictate to national football associations.[12]

UEFA have pursued a similar expansionist policy as FIFA. There are now over 180 clubs that qualify for either the UEFA's Champions League or the UEFA Cup. This policy has upset the elite clubs in the G14 group, because in order to allow more teams to be involved the Champions League competition has had to be restructured, cutting the final group stages from two to one. Under this format if one of the elite clubs wins the competition they do so having played fewer games than under the old format. The result is that the elite teams believe they are missing out financially, and have threatened to stop playing in UEFA-organised competitions. A battle of football politics based, as always, on who gets the money. Not much to do with the consumer interests or with sport.

In March 2006, UEFA denounced the G14 clubs as money grabbers, and passed a resolution that declared that 'football is about fairness, opportunity, excitement and variety'. What UEFA said is undoubtedly true, but is a little rich considering UEFA's past record on financial matters. UEFA (and FIFA) have also been influenced by money and their actions are as much motivated by money as those of the G14 clubs.

Whatever the case, the international and global regulators are increasingly showing their power and this means that clubs who wish to play in their leagues have to do as they are told—whatever the impact on the club and local supporters. For example, FIFA introduced a rule that permits national associations to demand the release of any player they want for international duty. This applies to countries all over the world. There are many African players in the Premier League and they can be asked to play in the African Cup of Nations (which is held every four years). Unlike the European Nations Cup the matches in this tournament are not scheduled to avoid interfering with European club competitions. In 2006 the African Cup of Nations took place in January and February. FIFA argued it is up to national leagues to adapt to the international calendar, and not for the international calendar to adapt to the national leagues. The tail wagging the dog?

Arsène Wenger has had problems with the players from his club, Arsenal, who have been called up to play for their countries. On one notable occasion Wenger wanted two players from the Ivory

Coast to play in an FA Cup match, but two hours after naming his team he was told by FIFA that if Arsenal insisted on playing the two in the cup game, and thus ignoring the objections of the Ivory Coast, the club risked forfeiting the FA Cup game. 'There is no common sense at all,' Wenger insisted. 'We pay the players to play for them, and they can ban the players we pay from playing for us. When they come back they will be dead physically because the tournament is very intense in a different climate.'

FIFA like to portray themselves as a body helping to solve the world's problems, as a force for good.[13] But on some issues they are patently not so good. FIFA certainly speak out against drugs, but they do not want footballers to be treated as severely as competitors involved in other Olympic sports. The World Doping Agency tries to enforces strict rules for all sporting events but FIFA have in the past succeeded in obtaining certain concessions. Footballers found guilty of taking 'recreational' drugs need only be cautioned, and those found guilty of taking performance-enhancing drugs will be able to have their ban from playing reduced or even waived if they can show they were not responsible for taking the drug. Olympic athletes, by contrast, have to take full personal responsibility whatever the mitigating circumstances.

With regard to racism FIFA also talk big, but have done very little. They are attempting to clamp down on racism and whether it is fans, players or management that offend, they say the club involved will be punished. But when the manager of the Spanish club Villarreal made racist remarks about Thierry Henry, very little was done to punish the club. In 2006 UEFA announced a tougher policy against racism. Players making racist remarks or gestures could be banned for up to five matches. (Although the ruling would not apply to the managers of clubs.) If the supporters of a club engage in racist chanting or antagonise players on the grounds of their colour, race or religion, the club would receive a fine.

UEFA — Union of European Football Association

In its simplest form UEFA is an association of national football associations in Europe. In 2005 there were 52 members. It is one of six regional confederations around the world all of whom support and assist FIFA in its self-appointed task of organising football globally. UEFA was formed in 1954 and like FIFA is based in Switzerland. It is responsible for two high profile competitions that are popular with football clubs and the public.

In 2006–07 no fewer than 156 clubs competed for the second of these competitions, the UEFA Cup. The structure of the competition is quite complex, with the 'smaller' clubs needing to compete from the first qualifying round, and the 'larger' clubs entering at a later stage. In 2006–07 the teams who competed in the first qualifying round included clubs from Wales (Rhyl FC and Llanelli FC) and from Ireland (Portadown and Glentoran). Some people argue the competition, in its early stages, is becoming a little silly with four teams qualifying from each of the Faroe Islands, Northern Ireland, Luxembourg and Kazakhstan. For the first round proper, 80 clubs join those who have got through the qualifying stage. In 2006–07 clubs entering at this stage included Blackburn Rovers, Tottenham and West Ham United. For the third round proper the 24 clubs who have so far been successful are joined by the 8 clubs who finished in third place in their UEFA Champions League groups.

The UEFA Champions League has a similar format with three qualifying rounds, a group stage and finally knockout rounds.[14] In the first qualifying round 128 teams are reduced to 64, for the second qualifying round, the 64 are reduced to 32. After the third round the surviving 16 clubs are joined by 16 automatic entrants for the final group stage of the competition. Finally eight teams enter the knockout rounds to produce a winner. The net result of all this is that (with the Intertoto Cup) nearly 300 clubs now take part in European-wide competitions.

As well as organising football competitions UEFA wish to take on a political role. They wish to be seen as the spokesperson for football in Europe. In particular they wish to represent the football industry when matters affecting football are discussed at the European Union level. Decisions are made at European Union level that affect the way football is run, for example the Bosman ruling on player contracts, the rulings on the number of foreign players allowed in a team and the rulings on the collective selling of television rights. Many countries who are members of UEFA are not members of the EU, and so technically they do not have to worry about what the EU says. The major footballing nations are, however, members of the EU and so do have to abide by EU law.

Up until the mid 2000s, the EU had not shown itself willing to regard football as being more or less important in society than any other business. UEFA had been trying to build closer links with EU officials, hoping to change this. One step taken to establish better relations was the setting up of a UEFA office in Brussels, in 2003. This at least made it seem closer to the EU than just an organisation from Switzerland. The retiring Chief executive of UEFA, Gerhard Aigner, in 2005 expressed the view that 'Football is so important in today's society that it is essential we engage more and more in political affairs in order to properly protect the interests of our sport when significant issues are being debated.' UEFA's strategy must be to build a basis of trust with the [European] Commission through constructive dialogue. This is the only way we can ensure that the Commission will give priority to consultation with the official European sports federations regarding sports-related matters, rather than dealing with individual self-appointed representatives of the sports movement.' This is an interesting statement, some people might say that UEFA is as much a self-appointed representative of football as, say, the Premier League, G14 or the Football Supporters Federation.[15]

Ownership Rules

UEFA introduce rules that affect clubs that play, or wish to play, in their competitions. One such rule, which seems from a spectator's point of view to be very sensible, prevents two or more teams owned by the same entity from competing in the same competition. From a spectator's point of view this means that the result of a match is less likely to be fixed; there always being the possibility that if one business owns or controls both teams competing in a match the result could be determined by a management decision. A problem had arisen in 1998 over ENIC's ownership of two clubs competing in the UEFA Cup. ENIC owned 42.8% of the shares of AEK Athens, and 96.7% of the shares of Slavia from Prague. UEFA stated that they would not allow the Athens team to compete in the cup competition. ENIC challenged the UEFA rule in the courts. The Court of Arbitration for Sport in August 1999 found in favour of UEFA, finding their rule was lawful. They said that because of the high social significance of football, the public must be assured that teams allegedly in competition with each other are trying their best to win.

ENIC, of course, did not like this decision. They regarded it as bureaucrats interfering in issues that were best left to self-regulation. But this was not the end of the matter. The European Commissioner did admit that the UEFA rule 'could theoretically be caught by Article 81 of the EU Treaty—that is, the rule did interfere with the free movement of capital. However, he felt that the main purpose of the UEFA rule was to protect the integrity of the competition that was in the interest of the public.

ENIC were still not happy, so they pointed out to UEFA that if a company owning a club or clubs were not free to pursue its business interests, the club or clubs involved would suffer financially. UEFA decided to reconsider the wording of their rule on multiple ownerships. They modified their rules. The fact that some person, persons or organisation may own shares in two clubs was not, they now believed, sufficient to prevent a fair and honest match. Common ownership did not mean sporting integrity was *necessarily* at stake—the key issue was common control. One could not be sure about the integrity (or lack of it) of a match if one company or one person controlled both teams.

The problem of a conflict of interest arose again in 2002, where there arose the possibility of two clubs in which ENIC had a shareholding competing against each other in a European-wide competition. UEFA allowed the two teams that had common ownership to enter the same competition. UEFA turned out to be lucky in that the ENIC-owned clubs did not, in the end, need to play each other. The point of principle remained, however. In the event that the two clubs had met would the result have been decided by the efforts of the players on the field? Whatever the result the spectators (and bookmakers) could not have been sure. UEFA had given in to the interests of big business. In monopoly and antitrust cases there are many judgements made that are based on the definition of control. Control depends on the distribution of the ownership of shares. To own 49% of shares does not give control if someone else owns 51%. Similarly, to own 30% can give effective control, if the other 70% are widely dispersed amongst numerous shareholders, none of whom has the opportunity or the interest to attend meetings and vote on issues. The size of ENIC's shareholding in a club, even though a minority stake, could give them effective control.

Licensing

The last president of UEFA accepted that problems such as corruption, money-laundering, gambling and match-fixing exist— even in Europe. (They accepted this even before the recent scandals in Italy and Germany.) The French government had told UEFA that some players' agents were participating in money-laundering through transfer deals. It was widely known that certain South East Asian betting syndicates had tried to fix matches in Europe. UEFA, with other relevant regulatory bodies, are working together to try to stop such practices. Consequently, at the end of 2005 UEFA attempted to beef up their club licensing arrangements. In future clubs would be required to disclose sensitive information about ownership. However, as mentioned earlier, UEFA rules and regulations only apply to clubs that take part in UEFA-organised competitions. UEFA claim to examine clubs to find out about financial solvency, budgets, corporate governance and the background of their directors. Not an easy thing to do.[16]

As explained in Chapter 2, UEFA have also tried to establish rules relating to the number of foreign players that can play in a team taking part in one of their competitions. Geoff Thompson, the FA's chairman, was the only dissenting voice at the UEFA Executive Committee meeting dealing with the matter. Thompson, in opposing the quota system, was representing the views of the people with power in the Premier League. Apparently all but two of the Premier League clubs were against the quota system. This raises two issues: one is that the FA should be representing the views of English football in general, and should be concerned with developing the strongest England team possible, they should not just be looking after the interests of the owners of the elite clubs; the second issue relates to whether or not the Premier League club were opposing the quota system on financial or football grounds.

The UEFA proposals are quite modest. They would only apply to competitions that they run, not to domestic leagues. UEFA are squeezed between the EU, the national football associations and

140

the big clubs. The internal politics at UEFA reflects this conflict. In 2006 the amount of money paid by UEFA to each of the national football associations to help them with their development of the game was increased. Each of the associations was to receive almost £500,000 spread over two years. Not a lot of money to the associations in England and France, but a lot to the associations in Andorra and Malta. It so happened that in 2007 there was a contested election for the UEFA Presidency, with each of the 52 countries allowed one vote.

The person who ran against Lennart Johansson, the incumbent President, was the respected French footballer Michel Platini. Platini argued that no country should be allowed more than three teams in the UEFA Champions League. He accepted that this policy would upset the likes of England, Italy and Spain but it would appeal to the smaller countries who felt that they had missed out in this competition. They did of course have votes. Platini's proposals could be seen as 'democratic' but could also mean more meaningless games to watch on TV.

Platini would like UEFA to be more like FIFA, who have a similar policy of widening participation in their World Cup competitions. Platini believes that Sepp Blatter has been very good for football. Platini would also like to see football settling its own affairs; he did not like to see UEFA co-operating with the EU on the 2006 'Independent Sports Review'. He has similar ideas to Blatter, seeing of all of football as one happy family, with all parties involved agreeing a charter under which they would operate. One hopes the contents of such a charter would be influenced by the interests of consumers of the game, the football fans. There is a danger that such a charter would be a carve up between the players, the clubs and the organisers of the major competitions.

Johansson, despite being 77 years of age and having already been president of UEFA for 17 years, wished to continue in office. His old adversary, Sepp Blatter, let it be known that he favoured Platini. There were delegates who thought it was time for a change, and who thought it might be good for the game to have an ex-player, especially one who had been a European Footballer of the Year, in high office. Platini won the election by 27 votes to 23, with the result that there were many worried people in European football. Platini favoured a more equitable distribution of wealth between the big countries and the small countries, and between the big clubs and the smaller clubs. He wanted UEFA to be closer to FIFA in its objectives. Not an approach designed to appeal to G14.

A few days after the election the UEFA chief executive, Lars-Christer Olsson, resigned. This signalled that Michel Platini's role would be a hands-on one as executive president. To many this meant difficult times ahead, with a struggle for power between those governing football.

Other International Organisations

In 1991 Silvio Berlusconi brought together a group of the leading clubs to lobby UEFA to restructure the European competitions. The big clubs did not want to waste their time playing against the clubs from smaller countries, and to run the risk of having their star players injured. If they played only against big clubs they could generate more revenue. This led to the beginning of the Champions League in 1991–92, as well as to clubs that had been involved in the lobbying process forming the G14. The UEFA Cup and quali-fying rounds in the UEFA Champions League were introduced to keep the 'minor' clubs happy. The initial G14 clubs (and the four that later joined them) have done well out of the new structure. It is a safe prediction that ten or so of them will qualify for the group stage of the Champions League, and it is money from this compe-tition that distorts domestic competitions.

In 2006 David Dein, the then Arsenal vice-chairman, became president of G14. He had only a few months earlier failed to keep his position as a Premier League representative on the FA Board. Dein announced that he wished to build bridges between G14 and UEFA and FIFA. 'I would want to bring about change harmoni-ously and constructively. There are issues, such as player release, insurance and the international football calendar, which remain a source of dissatisfaction for many professional football clubs, not just G14 ones. We think these can be resolved if we all work together. I hope that over the next nine months we can achieve this.' Before achieving any of these goals, Dein had to resign from G14, because of boardroom changes at Arsenal.

In 1998 yet another body was formed with the intention of having a voice (perhaps even being the voice) in the governance of the game. This was the Association of European Professional

Football Leagues (EPFL). It was, in 2006, chaired by Dave Richard, the Chairman of the Premier League, and a member of almost every other committee in football. This pressure group, which consists of representatives of the major leagues in Europe, is able to fight (negotiate) with UEFA.

The EPFL are of course political by nature. They did not initially invite representation from the Football League. Naturally the Football League were upset. They could point to the fact that in 2005–06 the Championship attracted more spectators to games than Serie A in Italy, and that it was bigger than many other top domestic leagues in Europe. The chairman of the Football League, Lord Mawhinney, believed that reforming football in Europe has no chance of success unless all with interests in the game were invited to take part in discussions. The EPFL condescendingly offered him a place as an 'observer' at their meetings. Lord Mawhinney is a former Chairman of the Conservative Party and is becoming increasingly influential in the governance of the game. He has done well in promoting the interests of the Football League after its difficulties in the 1990s and the subsequent collapse of the TV deal, for instance.

UEFA, we are told in the 'Arnaut Report', have 'developed a variety of structures to give more direct involvement to stakeholders in the decision-making process.' UEFA and the EFPL produced a 'Memorandum of Understanding' in 1998 (amended in 2005). These two organisations, UEFA and the EFPL, formed a 'Professional Football Committee'. So many bodies and committees, all seeking to co-operate but with each interest group having to be careful that they give nothing away.

UEFA and G14 regularly disagree, so in an attempt to find a more friendly voice for representing football clubs UEFA helped establish, in 2002, the European Club Forum (ECF). The ECF is said, in the 'Arnaut Report', to give 'a direct voice to the members at the base of the football pyramid [the clubs].' Are the clubs the base? Manchester United, Real Madrid and Inter-Milan are surely on a different level to Cheltenham, Walsall and Grimsby. The ECF consists of more than 100 clubs from 52 European national associations. The major football associations have a maximum of 4 clubs as members and the smaller associations just 1 club as a member. What sort of agreement can be reached from discussions amongst such a diverse group of club representatives is uncertain. This body is UEFA's attempt to by-pass G14, who they refer to as an economic interest group. But all the governing bodies are economic interest groups. One cannot imagine the G14 clubs being worried by the formation of ECF.

Governance in England

When Margaret Thatcher left office in 1990 politicians of all parties could not wait to be seen to be enthusiastic about football. Conservative MPs such as John Major and David Mellor were keen to let everybody know that one of their favoured pastimes was watching soccer. David Mellor even remarked that 'Football needs to be reminded of its civic duties as our national game.' In previous statements Mellor had commented on the need for community control in football and on the need to appoint an independent regulator for the sport.

Alastair Campbell, at one time Tony Blair's official spokesman and a person at that time with a great deal of influence, had been a life-long football fan. In 1994 he edited a book with David Bull with the intriguing title *Football and the Commons People*. The book consisted of a collection of confessions by MPs about their devotion to the people's game, and included contributions by such distinguished politicians as Michael Foot, Roy Hattersley and Gordon Brown. Tony Blair and Alastair Campbell had both, at one time or another, expressed the view that the fans were being ripped off and said that they supported the idea of an independent regulator. Senior government officials referred to greed at the top of the game and said it was necessary to find ways of ending the scandals that kept occurring in the game.

When the Labour Party came to power in 1997 it was claimed they would introduce a 'charter' for football. They did not believe the game was moving in the right direction, and would try to prevent market forces destroying the soul of the game. They even set up a Football Task Force that was charged with the job of coming up with recommendations. The man appointed to head the task force was David Mellor, a supporter of the free market system.

The wish to 'redress the balance between the moneymen and the fans' may have existed, and the appointment of a regulator would perhaps have been a reasonable way of achieving this, but the means were not equal to the task. Not surprisingly the FA and Premier League, and most of the club chairmen, were against the idea of the Task Force. The FA tried to discredit it and began to court the government directly. (The FA were also at the time working with the government on plans for the new Wembley Stadium.) The Premier League representative on the Task Force was Sir Roland Smith, a Director of Manchester United and of many other companies besides—another champion of the free market system very much opposed to outside regulation.

Tony Banks, the Labour Government Sports Minister was unsure whether Downing Street had the stomach to take on the football establishment. At one point Tony Blair even stated that it was 'not the job of government to interfere in the daily running of football.' He thought that football should regulate itself, but that if club owners and sports administrators ignored the warnings or were not able to act decisively then the Labour Government would impose an independent regulator.

There are good arguments as to why self-regulation is better than outside independent regulation. Those opposed to outside regulators interfering in markets believe that outsiders do not have the requisite knowledge and ability to exercise effective control. They believe that better outcomes can be obtained through the threat to the established producers from potential competitors—freedom of entry to the industry must at all costs be retained, they argue. Experience has, however, shown that such conclusions must now be viewed as suspect. In the US a number of new American football and basketball leagues have been established over time and have attempted to compete with the established leagues, but they all have failed. The barriers to entry in sport are now too great.

As it happened, the Labour Government changed its mind over the need to appoint an independent regulator for the football industry. Prior to election it had argued that such an appointment was necessary, but after the election it was 'persuaded', presumably by powerful lobbyists, that self-regulation was best. The government did claim they would do something to prevent the various scandals in football from happening again. If anything they had placed themselves on the side of big business.

Richard Scudamore, who had been appointed chief executive of the Premier League, and Adam Crozier of the FA, worked to persuade the government against the appointment of an 'independent' person. They said the football establishment would only support an independent football commissioner appointed by the Premier League and the FA. In the end they did agree to the establishment of an 'Independent Football Commission', but one with limited terms of reference.[17] The independent regulator debate did rumble on, but the government had lost interest in changing the direction in which football was heading. They had lost interest in appointing an outside regulator. As Tom Bower pointed out 'self-regulation suited the mavericks. Without a regulator, football's aristocracy could behave as in the Wild West.'

The government and the football establishment had moved closer together. They worked together, as it turned out unsuccessfully, on efforts to make England the venue for a future FIFA World Cup. The Government's relationship with English football was becoming a liability to them. Perhaps the Prime Minister should have kept out of the sordid 2006 World Cup affair. In order to strengthen their bid to host the event the FA broke a promise to support Lennart Johansson in the election for President of FIFA. They switched their support to Sepp Blatter. One of the principle reasons for this change was because Blatter had indicated that he supported the England bid to host the World Cup. The FA should have been suspicious of Blatter, he had a history of criticising football in England. Tony Blair met Blatter to assure him of the government's support for the national bid. He told Blatter that the country would spend £1 billion on new stadiums, including a rebuilt Wembley. One of Blatter's reasons for courting England was to obtain their support in his bid for the presidency. Blatter was re-elected. The World Cup was held in Germany.

The Football Task Force set up by the government did produce three reports, one dealing with racism, another with disabled supporters and the third with investing in the community. None of these reports were really controversial. The Task Force members, not surprisingly, could not agree on measures needed to deal with the more controversial issues, such as club finance and governance. The draft report on community investment contained a proposal to redistribute some of the revenue coming into the game. It was suggested that the Premier League should pay a levy of 10% on its revenue from TV and that this would be redistributed, through the Football Trust, amongst the 43,000 clubs affiliated to the FA. This proposal, if accepted, would have meant that not only other professional leagues would have benefited from the increased commercialisation of the game, but also the grass roots. Since the Premier League had come into existence the Football Trust had actually received in the region of £100 million from that league and distributed this to professional clubs. If the 10% levy had been in effect during this period, it would have meant more than double that amount would have been distributed. The Premier League and the rest of the football establishment, not surprisingly, objected to this proposal.

In August 1998, the Office of Fair Trading (OFT) had begun an action against the Premier League, accusing it of acting as a cartel against the public interest. The football establishment, including members of the Task Force, agreed to speak to the OFT on behalf of the Premier League if the Premier League agreed to pay the increased levy based on their TV income. They could not, however, agree on a suitable percentage. The Task Force wanted 10%, the Premier League 5%. In the end the government said it would pay 5% into a new Football Foundation if the Premier League would pay a similar amount. The football establishment agreed on this solution. The OFT case got nowhere.

The Football Association

'The future of Association Football depends, fundamentally, on confirming and strengthening the position of The Football Association as the Government of the game in England. All other Associations, Leagues and Clubs should be subordinate to the Football Association.' This, perhaps not surprisingly, was the view of the FA in 1991.[18] The FA clearly regard (or regarded) themselves as the governing body of the game in England. They are, however, a private organisation and their power only exists at a private level. Although they see themselves as providing leadership, they have, in fact, a history of resisting change. Throughout its history the FA have fought battles against the Football League, and more recently, against the league they helped establish, the Premiership.

The FA came into existence when a group of football enthusiasts came together in order to establish a code of rules for the regulation of the game. At the time one version of football or another was being played throughout the country, including being played at the leading public schools such as Harrow, Eton and Rugby. The problem was that there were many different sets of rules. On the evening of 26 October 1863, representatives from 12 football clubs met at a pub in the Covent Garden area of London. A set of rules were established, and a national cup competition was launched, the FA Cup. Melvyn Bragg referred to the book on the Rules of Football as one of the twelve books that changed the world! (see *12 Books that Changed the World* 2006) The FA was established out of a desire by enthusiasts to play football, not out of a wish to make money. There were those involved with the organisation of football who saw the sport as helping those who played, to build healthy bodies and to have healthy minds. This they believed should be sufficient reward for playing the game. Perhaps surprisingly only one of the twelve clubs that founded the FA play football today at a professional level: Crystal Palace.

From this well-meaning beginning, the FA by the 1890s was attempting to establish 'absolute power over the whole of football' in England. A number of leagues and cup competitions were taking place independently of the FA so the FA Council proposed that no league should be allowed to operate in England without the consent of the FA. In order to introduce teeth to this attempted take-over of football they added that any club affiliated to them would be barred from playing against clubs not authorised by the FA. This proposal, and a later one that all clubs in England should either be members of the FA or of an association affiliated to the FA, was accepted by the FA Council. This FA take-over was, not surprisingly, criticised by many involved with football. Individuals at the FA were forming their own power base and if footballers and football clubs did not accept their authority they were excluded from their competitions. The association had moved on from its modest origins in a pub with a few enthusiasts seeking to agree on rules, to a position of exclusive authority.

The Football League had been formed in 1888 to organise one particular league competition and to look after the interests of the clubs in just that one competition. The FA recognised this league (and also recognised many other leagues). The Football League was an independent body (independent of the FA), which as

William McGregor, the father of the League, explained 'must be a selfish body (whose) interests are wholly bound up in the welfare of its affiliated clubs.'[19] McGregor introduced to football the idea that a League was necessary in order to introduce some structure into competitions between the better teams. From the beginning the relationship between the FA and the Football League was not easy and has not been easy ever since. McGregor was not against the FA, he just had different interests. He and other Football League representatives were continually urging the FA to accept change.

Many of the rules that the FA set up in the nineteenth century showed great foresight. In those early days 'a tight control was kept on the financial activities of the new-type football companies.' In fact, in those early days, many football clubs were in a weak financial position and were only able to keep going by financial help from wealthy supporters. In the early days betting on matches was a subject of concern. In 1892 a rule was introduced that neither officials nor players should make bets on any football matches, and even worse, clubs were required to take all reasonable measures to prevent gambling by spectators. One hundred years later, players and officials can bet on matches (not their own) and we have betting booths at football matches. Other concerns of the FA in the early days were bad language, drunkenness and hooliganism. A Birmingham-based journalist attended an Aston Villa match and reported that he had found no drunkenness, betting or swearing. If he attended a match now he would not be able to say the same.

What exactly does all this mean? What is the precise role of the FA? In their 2002–03 'Handbook' the FA state that they are 'the governing body of the game in England, recognised as such by FIFA and UEFA, the World and European authorities.' This raises the interesting question of who at the 'World' and 'European' levels gave these bodies their authority. The answer is they are all self-appointed bodies who regulate the competitions they run. If an English club wishes to qualify for the UEFA Champions League it has first to be recognised by the FA. The FA represents England on the councils of UEFA and FIFA. The danger faced by those clubs that broke away from the Football League to form the Premier League was that if they did not receive the FA's blessing they could have not competed in UEFA-organised competitions.

The FA controls one other position which gives it power: it has a representative, one of only eight, on the body that decides on the rules of the game, the International Football Association Board.

It is possible that rival national and European championships and cups could emerge, with new governing bodies, but this would now be very difficult. The cost of entry for new competitions would be very high; they would have to compete with a well-established infrastructure. US experience has shown how difficult it is for new leagues to break into the established sports industries.

The FA refers to itself as 'guardian of the English game' and it recognises a 'responsibility to provide leadership', but not every-one, particularly the chairmen of the Premier League clubs, would agree that it does in fact lead. Its history is largely one of reacting to what is happening, not being proactive.

Organisation

One reason why for so many years there was little change is because over a 60-year period only two people had held the post of secretary. The appointment of Stanley Rous as secretary in 1934 was a major step forward. He had been a goalkeeper but injured his wrist and so became a football referee. By profession he was a school teacher. When he moved into his new job at Lancaster Gate it was 'in many ways a quiet backwater. Many matters were ignored in which the Association ought to have been taking an active part.' One of its now recognised failings was that it was not a member of FIFA and as a result England did not compete in the World Cup. Rous was conscious of the fact that the FA was 'giving a more limited service to football than it could and should.' He came up with new ideas, including youth development programmes, promoting training and coaching facilities, and courses for coaches and referees.

For many decades the top decision-making committee at the FA was a large council consisting of representatives from over 40 different county football associations, many life members and only 8 representatives of Football League clubs. This led to tensions with the Football League, with the FA dominated by the grass roots interests of the game and the League acting in the interests of a specific group of clubs.

In the 1990s amongst the 90-plus members of the FA Council were still representatives from the army, navy and air force, as well as from Oxford and Cambridge Universities. There were only five representatives of the Premier League, five from the Football League and another ten divisional representatives, some of whom were from Football League clubs. Clearly the representatives of the amateur game, in terms of numbers, dominated those from the professional game. The so-called football establishment consisted, like rugby, of men in blazers, who enjoyed their status and perks.

In the 1980s the FA began to change its image, it got rid of the stony-faced and much criticised Graham Kelly, and brought in as its new chief executive a modern marketing man. They moved their offices from the stately, but slightly old fashioned Lancaster Gate, to the trendy Soho Square. It increased its annual turnover from £20 million in the mid 1990s to £55 million in 1999. In response to the criticism that the FA was unwieldy and no longer representative of the new realities of football, a new decision-making structure was agreed. The most significant change was the creation of the Main Board 'to provide a focus for taking important and commercial decisions.' The chief executive of the FA was to be answerable to this board. The FA now had a 'strategic vision' (a cross between a mission statement and a strategic plan). Its goal was to use 'the power of football to build a better future.'

Unfortunately the FA still made blunders, and so continued to face criticism. In response they asked Lord Burns to undertake a structural review of the FA. The final report was delivered in August 2005, and the FA said they welcomed it, although it took them a long time to implement some of the more dramatic proposals. A key proposal was for the FA to appoint independent directors to its Main Board. This would mean some of the 'blazers' who enjoy their involvement with the FA having to go, and new respected figures from outside football becoming involved in decision-making. One reason why the representatives of the amateur game were worried about adopting the 'Burns Report' was because they believed it would lead to yet greater power and influence for the Premier League. They were worried that the new non-executive directors would be 'persuaded' to support the interests of the Premier League more than those of the wider game. They also believed that the proposed independent chairman would spend much of his time at Premier League games and could easily come under the influence of the chairmen of these clubs.

Nevertheless, to the surprise of many, at the end of October 2006, the FA Council voted to approve a restructuring of the FA Board and to the appointment of an independent chairman of the Main Board. The vote was close, with 33 votes in favour to 31 against. The Sports Minister had threatened to withdraw from football as much as £20 million of the public money that the government channelled into football if the FA Council voted against Lord Burns' proposal. So after much uncertainty the major recommendations made by Burns to modernise the FA were accepted by the FA Council. There was, however, to be a delay in taking the proposals for final approval to a general meeting of the FA.

Amongst the major changes was a National Game Board (for the England team) as well as a Professional Board to govern beneath the Main Board. Also, the FA Council was to be expanded to include in future supporters' representatives and a representative from women's football. All these moves are a step forward. The FA was 143 years old and in need of change. The FA chief executive, Brian Barwick, had succeeded in steering the proposals through the different factions, but only just.[20]

Commercialism

As well as being the 'regulators' of the game in England, the FA have a commercial side. They have taken on the task of earning money and have increased their commercial activities in recent years. This enables the FA, it argues, to plough back revenue into the development of the game at all levels. This in theory is good, it helps the small clubs as well as the large, but it leads to conflicts of interest. However, because of its governance structure, it has not been possible for the FA to act effectively as both a regulator and as the body responsible for the successful development of the sport at all levels. The most powerful people at the FA are the chairmen of Premier League clubs and when they express an opinion they are influenced by what is good for their clubs. This is not always the same as what is good for the game of football.

According to Stanley Rous the game will have to become more

and more commercialised.[21] He was commenting in 1978. He did not like what was happening to the game at that time and believed it was the duty of the football authorities to 'slow down the development rather than hasten it.' He was happy to see the FA and the Football League drag their feet because 'Commercialism will not solve problems in the long-term.' Its more harmful aspects will prove more lasting than its helpful ones. One of the particularly helpful aspects he was referring to is as a source of finance to help the poorer clubs through difficult years; harmful would be stronger clubs becoming stronger. Rous refers to the commercial pull of teams such as Manchester United, who would find endless 'opportunities to exploit the fascination of their name.' Thirty years ago he was worried about what we now call 'competitive balance'.

For many years the FA tried to resist change, they even opposed the legalisation of football pools. In a 1936 report they stated that 'the evil influence of pools betting on the actual results of matches is probably less obvious but more insidious than that of other forms of betting; it has, however, exerted a greater influence over the attitude of the general public than any other form of footballing betting.' Strong words. One wonders what the FA thought of this evil influence 40 or 50 years later when 'football pools' popularity was at a peak, and the clubs were benefiting from a levy paid by the pools companies. They were particularly concerned that in the public's mind the game would become less of a 'wholesome sport' and more a vehicle for organised gambling. They were still trying to protect the image of the game as a sport.

The FA have found it more and more difficult to regulate the game as big money has entered football. In 1997 they set up an enquiry 'into the manner in which football regulates its financial affairs.' Sir John Smith, former Deputy Commissioner of Scotland Yard, was appointed as the investigator. The enquiry was not a success, it had very narrow terms of reference. Sir Johns' view was that the FA was a 'bad regulator' and that they did not want anyone to rock their very lucrative boat. Sir John felt that many things were not right and urged the FA to put their house in order. His enquiries had been hampered by a lack of evidence—he could not obtain access to documents—and was not provided with adequate finance or support to do his job properly.

Sir John concluded, however, that 'widespread betting is damaging the integrity of professional football.' He found that at some clubs' players and executives were betting on their own teams to lose. A member of the enquiry team, Robert Reid QC, referred to a 'cult of dishonesty connected with the business side of the game.' Sir John proposed the establishment of a 'compliance and monitoring unit' within the FA whose task would be to oversee the game's integrity and reputation, and he proposed the appointment of an 'independent regulator as an ombudsman.' Graham Kelly (chief executive of the FA at the time) claimed that he and others at the FA would soon forget the recommendations, and Keith Wiseman (chairman of the FA's executive committee) personally rejected the proposals. However, a Compliance Unit of sorts was established.

In 1998 Graham Bean, a former detective, was appointed as compliance officer to help clean up the game. He was sacked in 2003, perhaps because he was too good at his job. Despite receiving little official support (he was paid only half of that of marketing executives at the FA) and his unit being under-funded, Bean did find evidence of corruption. However he was never able to produce evidence against the big clubs. He is reported to have said at the time he was removed from his post that the FA was 'riddled with sleaze and that he could have ripped the game apart if he had been allowed to employ half a dozen investigators. The alleged sleaze involved inflating the value of player transfers, bribes, bungs, frauds, and involved a number of current and past Premier League managers. When he was sacked Bean was investigating certain of the transfer deals of John Gregory.[22] Following Bean's departure this investigation was stopped, but the problems did not go away.

For a number of years the FA turned a blind eye to the tales of corruption, they did not want to rock the boat. They also wanted to continue to attract money into the game. The FA lost control of the business side of football. They are now trying to take steps to improve the situation. In 2006 the FA announced that they were introducing their own licensing laws with respect to the overseas agents that operate in England. Up to that time foreign agents who arranged deals in England did not require an FA licence. With some of the biggest transfer deals being arranged by overseas agents, such as Pini Zahavi, this was a loophole. It should not have been, as FIFA are supposed to be responsible for monitoring agents. The intention is that in the future all agents operate that in England will have to satisfy the FA's compliance procedure.

The Compliance Unit were given an unusual task in 2006. The Belgium legal authorities, whilst investigating money-laundering activities, discovered that a small Belgium football club had received £1 million from an anonymous donor. It turned out to be that it was Arsenal that had paid this money to the club. Arsenal had a special relationship with the club which involved, amongst other things, the loan of players. There was a suggestion that the £1 million was an 'irregular payment'. One club is not allowed to own another club. (Arsenal claimed that the financial transaction was a loan, not a purchase of equity shares.) FIFA asked the FA to investigate, so the FA sent in the Compliance Unit. Arsenal were cleared of any wrongdoing.

Wembley Stadium

The construction of the new Wembley Stadium is another disaster for the FA. It cost much more than was ever intended and was completed over two years late. It was decided in 1996 that Wembley would continue to be the home for the national football stadium. Even at that time the decision was controversial. The FA would be a major user of the stadium, and it would be home for England's international matches and for the FA Cup Final. The FA established a wholly owned subsidiary, Wembley National Stadium Limited (WNSL), to develop and operate the venue. Ken Bates was appointed as the first Chairman of WNSL and the new company took on responsibility for placing the contracts for the stadium construction.

An Australian company, Multiplex, was awarded the construction contract on a fixed-price basis. Following negotiations they said they would build the stadium for £445 million and it would take 3 years and 3 months to complete. They started construction in October 2002. It was not finished until 2007. The construction cost was at least £200 million more than expected. Legal cases will determine who pays the additional costs, as well as the financial implications of the late opening. Multiplex claim that many of the extra costs were the result of WNSL altering its design require-

155

ments. WNSL deny this. WNSL claim that they are entitled to £140,000 per day in penalty payments for each day between the planned handover date of 31 January 2006 and when they actually took over the stadium. Multiplex did not pay this because they blamed WNSL for the delays. They claim that it is the FA who will have to pay them because of their additional costs. These issues will have to be settled by the courts.

In fact the contract negotiations were a mess right from the beginning. There were criticisms of the way decisions were made and in the way the contract was awarded. In 1999, Sir Robert McAlpine, of the respected construction company, wrote to WNSL saying that the Wembley contract 'will not deliver a successful project' because it was based on a rigid maximum cost before the design was fully worked out and that more 'team working and partnering were essential.' A subsequent enquiry concluded that the procedures followed 'fell below industry best practice.' Senior figures at WNSL had 'perceived conflicts of interest' and there was a 'failure of corporate governance.'

The FA did attract some private sector bank money to fund the project but was still heavily reliant on the public sector. That is, lottery money (£120 million); government money (£20 million); and the London Development Agency (£21 million) fund. Initially, WNSL had difficulty attracting support from the banks, but the German bank West L.B. came to the rescue with a £433 million loan. This bank provided the initial cash, and then sold this WNSL debt to a consortium of other banks. (WNSL did not have to start repaying the capital element of the loan until the stadium was completed.) Interest was, however, payable from when the money was borrowed and amounted in a full year to about £33 million. With the annual profits of the FA being only in the region of £23 million, this interest charge was an embarrassment.

From when the stadium was handed over to the FA subsidiary the average annual capital repayments plus interest became in excess of £60 million. WNSL will operate the 90,000-seat stadium. A very risky venture for a governing and regulating body. It is doubtful if the venture will ever make a profit. The stadium will of course be used for many events other than football, but there will be much competition for these other events from other venues in North London, including from 2012 a new Olympic stadium.

One problem is the stadium has not been built to satisfy football fans, it has been built to satisfy the need for corporate entertainment. The financial success of the project depends on being able to sell corporate hospitality, but this will do nothing for the atmosphere in the stadium. A spokesman for WNSL has said that 'all England games are highly popular events with fans up and down the country.' This may be so but a limited number of these fans will be present inside the stadium. In the old Wembley the atmosphere inside the stadium when England played was not wonderful. The England players have said that following the closure of the old Wembley they received better support when they had to play England matches in cities such as Manchester and Liverpool. But the powers that be in the game insisted that the new stadium be built in London.

Mismanagement

'The FA exists to run football for the good of football, to establish its rules and practices, and to protect it from abuses.' The FA clearly see themselves as the good people in football, representing the interests of a wide group of stakeholders, including the smaller clubs and non-professional football. The trouble is that the FA have declined in importance; they have been squeezed out by the international associations and by the big clubs. To some extent, with globalisation this was inevitable, but they have not helped their own cause by a number of mistakes.[23]

One article in the finance section of a newspaper commented that the departure of Adam Crozier from the FA in 2002 served to highlight the chaotic state of the management of the football business. The article was concerned with the problems the FA had encountered in obtaining money to fund the construction of the new Wembley Stadium, and with a number of other cases of mismanagement, including an attempt to bribe representatives of the Welsh FA to obtain their support to bring the European Nations Cup tournament to England, the handling of the removal of the England coach following the 2006 World Cup, and the failure to control costs.[24]

Adam Crozier had been appointed as chief executive of the FA in October 1999. He obtained a business degree before entering a career in marketing; he once sold advertising space for the *Daily*

157

Telegraph. Before moving to the FA he had worked at Saatchi & Saatchi for eleven years, where he became joint chief executive. He had had an impressive business career before joining the FA. Upon leaving the FA he was in fact able to continue with his successful business career, becoming chief executive of the Royal Mail in February 2003. Why did things not work out for him at the FA? There is a suggestion that he was removed because of the machinations of certain powerful chairman of Premier League clubs. During his time at the FA he increased its profile, modernised the organisation and increased its turnover by 250%. His critics argued that when he left the finances of the FA were in a mess, and the Association had become involved in high-risk projects. The FA Council decided to replace him.

Mark Palios was appointed as the next chief executive of the FA. It was unfortunate for him that it became known that he was only second choice for the job, the first choice, an executive at the food company Mars, having turned it down. It is also unfortunate that one of his first tasks at the FA was having to cut costs by reducing staff numbers by 20%. Palios was an interesting choice for at least two reasons, one because he once played professional football (307 league games); and two, because he was an expert on business reorganisations. Whilst playing football he studied and became a qualified accountant. He was made a partner in Price Waterhouse Coopers in 1989, only three years after playing in the European Cup Winners Cup.

The FA moved from a marketing man who led the FA into a number of high-profile projects, but who, in the end, fell out with the all powerful FA Board, to a finance man who was useful in raising funds to pay for the FA projects. The new man was also knowledgeable about football at the club level, which should have made club chairmen happy. Unfortunately, he had personal problems whilst at the FA, which gave his critics the chance to have him removed. When he began to enforce FA rules, certain Premier League chairmen reacted badly. Manchester United threatened to take legal action over the way in which the FA had handled the Rio Ferdinand drug-testing fiasco. As is well-known, the player failed to take a drugs test at the time he was supposed to; he had forgotten about the test. But Manchester United thought it was wrong that the player had been named by the FA, and that Ferdinand was dropped from the England team before he had an opportunity to defend himself. This is an example of a major club trying to by-pass the rules, not to mention undermining the authority of the FA. It illustrates the difficulty the FA have in controlling the game.

There has for many years been a disappointing lack of leadership from the FA. On some issues they are limited in what they can do as they have to follow FIFA and UEFA rules, but on the issues where they are solely in charge they have often been weak. On the selection and removal of the managers of the England team they seem in the past to have been a follower rather than a leader. It is, however, interesting that in selecting a new England manager in 2006, they initially went against what the press and many of the Premier League managers wanted. They offered the job to Luiz Scolari but when he turned the offer down, they played safe and appointed Steve McLaren.

The popular press, the England fans, and a number of Premiership managers had argued that the time was right again to have an Englishman as the manager of the national team. The Birmingham City chairman, David Sullivan, had said that the appointment of Scolari (formerly the manager of Brazil) would be 'a betrayal of Englishmen and English fans.' Whether or not an Englishman was to be appointed, the organisational and public relations aspect of the appointment was badly handled. It was said that David Dein, the vice-chairman of the FA, wanted Scolari, whereas the Premier League chairman, David Richards, wanted a British citizen in the post. There was even disagreement as to whether or not Luiz Scolari had actually been offered the job by Brian Barwick, chief executive of the FA. The press enjoyed the FA's embarrassment and helped influence the outcome by frightening off Scolari. After a while Scolari said he was not interested because of the invasion of his privacy by the British press. The FA then said Scolari had not been offered the job, and their first choice amongst the candidates had always been Steve McLaren.

Football League

The first meeting of what became the Football League took place in Manchester in 1888, with a representative present from each of the twelve clubs who were to become members—six clubs were from the Midlands and six from Lancashire. Those present decided that all league matches should be played under the same rules as the cup matches of the FA. They decided that the price of admission to a match should be determined by the home club and that gross gate receipts for a match be divided between the two teams (except for receipts from season ticket sales). They also decided that at the end of the season the four clubs finishing at the bottom of the league would, if they wished to remain in the league, have to seek re-election. League members were making rules not only about the actual competition but about business matters affecting individual clubs. They were in fact implementing a financial policy that encouraged a 'well-balanced competition'.

It was clear that football from the formation of the Football League onwards was seen by those who ran the clubs as a business as well as a sport. There was much criticism at the time about the choice of the twelve clubs who formed the League, they were referred to as 'the ring'. It was generally acknowledged that some clubs excluded from the twelve were better at football than some included. Quite often the names of the first twelve teams in the League are now written about with great reverence, but the teams actually chosen to play in the League were selected as much for their money-making capabilities as for their football prowess. William McGregor admitted that some of the clubs excluded from the initial membership of the League were superior football teams to those chosen, but he went on to say that they did not attract as many spectators to their games and did not have as good transport facilities available. Everton were seen as the weakest football club in the twelve, whereas Crewe Alexandra, a better club, were excluded. Crewe immediately set about organising a 'second ring', a parallel league.

The Football League was designed to maximise the income of those involved. 'The league as at present constituted, is not formed for the purpose of encouraging football. It is formed so that the allied clubs make more money than they already do.' (The same could be said many years later about the Premier League.) Those involved in forming rules for the League not only wished to maximise income, they also wished to minimise risk.[25] One way to achieve this in a football competition is for the clubs involved to pay approximately the same level of wages, and to share revenue. Of course, such a policy, whilst protecting the 'weaker' clubs, also limits the dominance that can be achieved by the 'better' clubs. This policy, which puts a constraint on economic competition, was the one adopted by the businessmen who controlled the Football League at the end of the nineteenth century. The League was able to maintain this policy for nearly 100 years.

The Football League, from the early days, clearly had a strategy. The wage system and the transfer system were designed to protect the weaker clubs. The football establishment wished to create a solid working basis for all the clubs. They wished to make the League, from a sporting point of view, as competitive as possible, and to prevent the best players moving to a small number of elite clubs. By enforcing a maximum wage system there was no incentive for a player to move to improve his income. The clubs had formed a cartel. In all industries there is a history of the directors of the businesses involved seeking to avoid the worst dangers of competition by some kind of sharing arrangement. The effect is to limit the returns that each company earns, but to make the returns more reliable and to minimise the risk of the company failing (and the directors losing their position). The football cartel worked well until the 1960s. At this time the business climate began to change, a different type of director became involved in the game, and the competition in the leisure industry altered dramatically.

It is interesting that although the football authorities wished to introduce some change, they also wished to continue with a policy of a maximum wage level. Alan Hardaker, who was secretary of the League from 1956–79, believed that the ending of the maximum wage would lead to some clubs being able to buy the best players and to other smaller clubs encountering financial problems as they sought to become competitive on the field.[26] Hardaker therefore wanted to maintain a maximum wage level. After a struggle the League lost and players obtained the freedom to negotiate their own wage.

In 1961 the League produced a plan, entitled 'Pattern for Football', which was based on the belief that there was too much football, particularly meaningless matches. The proposal included a 'four-up-four-down' promotion and relegation system and of particular importance was a change in the voting system within the league so that a smaller majority of votes would be needed in order to introduce changes. Not surprisingly, the proposals were turned down by the clubs. There were over 90 clubs in the four divisions

161

of the League and each club had a vote. For many years, in order to change anything connected with the Football League, a three-quarters majority was required, which meant the leading clubs could be easily outvoted. The smaller clubs would not vote for anything that they believed would harm them. There were numerous attempts to change this governance position, with much talk of break away leagues.

Alan Hardaker realised the League needed to change, but as he said 'they were defeated by selfishness and shallow thinking . . . too many clubs could see no further than their own little world . . . They closed their eyes and minds to anything which even remotely threatened their status, and life style.' The 'they' he was referring to were the majority of the chairmen and directors of the League clubs. As Simon Inglis pointed out, had the 1961 plan been accepted 'the course of League football in the following decades would have been quite different.'[27]

Pressure to change the structure of the League continued. There were new plans, new club chairmen and new directors. Eventually changes did take place, much to the detriment of the 'old established' Football League. The Football League in 1990 had tried to save itself with a plan entitled 'One game, One team, One voice.' In this plan it was proposed that a new organisation be formed, which would control all professional football in England. The new organisation would be made up of representatives of the FA and of the Football League. The FA turned down the proposal and supported an alternative plan, in which a number of clubs would form a new Premier League which 'would be independent commercially, but which would acknowledge the authority of the association.' The FA believed that the changes which resulted in the foundation of the FA Premier League in 1992 would benefit them personally, but they did not. As Simon Freeman points out, the FA have a history of making a hash of things.[28]

The Premier League came into existence, which left the Football League to look after itself without the top teams. It did some things well and made some mistakes. One situation that was mishandled was the selling of the television rights to show non-Premier League matches. The Football League web site at the beginning of August 2002 proudly stated that 'The Football League remains at the heart and soul of football and continues to lead the way in the evolution of the beautiful game. League football has continued to improve and evolve and with even greater money coming into the game, thanks to a new £315 television deal with ITV Digital the future looks even brighter.'

This TV money was to benefit the clubs outside the Premier League. There were two things wrong with the Football League web site statement, however. One, it had not led the way in the evolution of the game, it had been against English clubs playing in European competitions, just as it had been against the widespread televising of live matches and had opposed the formation of a Premier League. The second thing wrong with the statement was that the future was not brighter, ITV Digital failed after one year and went into administration owing the Football League (and therefore the clubs) £178.5 million. The Football League were offered compensation but decided not to accept it. They preferred to take to court the two companies (Carlton and Granada) who were the parents of ITV Digital, in an attempt to recoup £131.9 million (the amount owing less the amount to be received in a new television deal). The representatives of the League believed that the two parent companies had during negotiations guaranteed the money. Unfortunately for the League, no such guarantees had been written into the final contract. Somehow the Football League negotiators had overlooked this. The High Court decided that there were no guarantees legally enforceable against the parent companies of ITV Digital.

The Football League negotiators had been outsmarted by the representatives of Carlton and Granada—as can happen when representatives of small businesses negotiate with those from larger businesses. Brian Phillpotts, who was commercial director of the League at the time of the negotiations and the person responsible, had to admit in court that the League did not request a written guarantee from the two television companies. He said in court 'I always took it for granted the deal was backed by Carlton and Granada.' The legal council for the two companies said that things are often said or implied during negotiations and not intended to be binding; in the end it depended what was written into the contract.

This was a disaster for the football clubs outside the Premiership. Even worse was to follow. The Football League representatives negotiated a new deal with BSkyB for £95 million for the right to show matches for the next fours years. This appeared to be a panic

163

reaction to the collapse of ITV Digital. It was selling broadcasting rights for twice as long as the remaining period of the ITV Digital deal for one half of the amount of the original deal. The Football League clubs were furious. There was talk of a dozen clubs being on the edge of liquidation as a result of the mistake. Teams like Coventry City estimated that the outcome for them would be a loss of revenue of over £5 million a year. The problem was that many clubs had committed themselves to spend the expected television revenue.

The outspoken chairman of Millwall, Theo Paphitis, summed up the views of many when in criticising the League executive for their amateurish approach to running the 72-team setup and to their handling of the ITV Digital crisis, 'It's a billion-pound business but if I had a kebab shop I wouldn't let them run it.' Not exactly what one would expect from a body that 'continues to lead the way in the evolution of the game.' Nor a situation in which 'the future looks even brighter.' The Football League later tried and failed to recover the money it had not received from the TV companies when it sued its own former solicitors for negligence and breach of contract during negotiations of the TV deal. They tried to blame the solicitors for what had gone wrong. One other issue over which the League have struggled to be fair, but have been outsmarted, is the treatment of clubs that fail financially.[29]

The Football League did well in re-branding itself in 2004. They did well to lure Coca-Cola to sponsor all three of their divisions. They are able now to say that (taking all three divisions together) they are the best supported League in Europe. Each division is fiercely competitive. They have been able to introduce a salary cap in League One (tier three) and League Two (tier four). From 2006–07 they will have 85 live games per season shown on BSkyB. The initial Coca-Cola deal was for three seasons and it is uncertain who will be their principal sponsors after that. Nevertheless, the Football League administration are confident that a good sponsor will be found.

Premier League

Currently, the key players in the governance of the game are the chairmen of the Premier League clubs. They represent the elite clubs, the clubs that attract the media and bring the big commercial money into the game. Power is, however, always transitory, even great empires come to an end. With the G14 group of clubs continually threatening to set up a new European League it could mean that at least four of the elite teams at present in the Premier League walk away from it. This is what they did to the Football League. If they go, a great deal of the media and commercial income at present earned by the Premier League would go elsewhere.

The chairmen of the Premier League clubs each have a statutory duty to look after the interests of the shareholders of the companies that own their clubs. This clearly brings them into conflict on many issues with the FA, who are supposed to be looking after the game at the wider level, and with FIFA and UEFA, who have their own priorities. Each Premier League club has its own stakeholders to look after. In the US the NFL clubs have been persuaded that it is in the financial interests of each club to act collectively. This has not yet happened in Europe.

It is interesting that Chelsea's chief executive Peter Kenyon said in April 2005 that his club were committed to the Premier League's collective agreement. He referred to the Premier League as a collective asset: 'We've seen the way rights have been split and sold; I thing collectivity is a core, stable part of the Premiership.' He was particularly concerned at the time whether or not the Premier League would be allowed by the EU to continue to sell the TV broadcasting rights to its matches as a collective package. There was also a concern that not all the clubs in the Premier League would want to act collectively. The G14 clubs had indicated that they had considered acting independently. Chelsea have asked if they could join the G14 group, but have been turned down. The club were for one reason or another not accepted by the top 18 clubs. Perhaps the reason was fear of Roman Abramovich's money? No wonder they talk about the Premier League as a collective asset; it is their only option.

The roles and objectives of the FA Premier League include the following: to 'be regarded as the world's best league football competition'; to 'generate increased commercial value'; to 'improve the game in this country and abroad, through partnership with the FA, UEFA and other bodies'; to 'create a quality of competition that provides a platform from which our member clubs can achieve unparalleled success in European or World competitions'; and to 'develop playing talent that will provide for international success with the England teams at all levels — with the stature of World Champions being the realistic goal.'

All of these are laudable objectives. It can even be argued that the Premier League have already succeeded in the first two of these. Whether its success has been achieved through partnership with the FA and UEFA, though, is a debatable point. There are many issues on which the organisations disagree. With respect to the fourth objective, a Premier League club has won the UEFA Champions League only twice in 15 years. It is, however, the failure to achieve the last objective that has been a major cause of criticism. Over half the players in the Premier League are now from outside the UK, this does not help the England team.

Another cause of concern has been the issue of club ownership and leadership. The Premier League now requires all new directors to sign a declaration. The rules were tightened in 2004, largely in response to criticism from the Football Task Force. A Premier League spokesman said 'The fit and proper persons test means that any new director has to declare if he has been convicted of (any) of a number of offences, as well as meeting other requirements. It is part of a range of measures that augment UK company law and demonstrates that the professional game is, and expects to be, run to a high standard of corporate governance.'

The 'Chairman's Charter' for the Premier League clubs contains a commitment to ensure that their clubs will seek to resolve differences between each other without recourse to law. One of the other commitments is to ensure that their clubs behave 'with the utmost good faith and honesty to each other', and to 'not unjustly criticise or disparage one another'.[30] This is very much self-regulation. This is a league that does not want an independent regulator. Disputes between clubs, between clubs and their league authorities, and between clubs and national football associations, should be settled in-house. If such disputes cannot be settled by national associations, then they are taken to the 'Arbitration Panel for Football'.[31] On the odd occasions where a football club has ignored this self-regulatory rule then FIFA have threatened the club involved with suspension from all international competitions. They will be thrown out of the football family.

Of course not all disputes are between clubs, many disputes are between one group of administrators and another, between one group of regulators and another. The 'European Review of Sport', wanted greater power to be given to UEFA; its new President certainly wants this. The Premier League and other major European leagues do not want this.[32] Where will such disputes be settled?

6

Success

How can one judge (measure) objectively the performance of a football club? If the person undertaking the analysis is a shareholder whose primary motive for buying the shares is financial gain, the answer is easy—dividends paid plus share price gain. If the person asking the question is a fan of the football club, again the answer is simple: the success of the team on the pitch. Both the shareholder and the fan do need, however, to take into account the opportunities open to the club in the time period being considered.

In most 'normal' businesses success or failure is measured in terms of profits. Football is not a normal business, its high public profile, its important place in society and in communities, means that success or failure should be judged on more than the financial returns it offers to one group of stakeholders. In this chapter we are interested in success or failure on the football pitch, not on the stock exchange. Of course success on the pitch is often accompanied by financial success, but not always. The statement of objectives that many football clubs now produce usually mention success on the pitch, only occasionally do they mention returns to shareholders. We will discuss success or failure in terms of results achieved on the pitch; we will keep away from the minefield of whether or not the club provides its shareholders (and directors) with what they want out of the sport.

For a supporter of a club it is important that their club provide them with excitement, and that they play good football and achieve success. Some clubs have for long periods performed above what could be reasonably expected of them, others have continued to perform below expectations. The literature on success and failure in business gives some guidance on the factors that will determine how an organisation performs. The literature is particularly good at helping to identify the factors that contribute to failure.

169

What are the factors that contribute to success in business? Clearly such matters as a good product, marketing skills and skilful financial management are in the short-term important. A necessary condition for long-term success, however, is good leadership. In football the leader can be either the team manager, the chairman or one of the other directors.Such people are needed to plan for, and manage, change. They need to be able to take advantage of new opportunities as they come along.

Stefan Szymanski and Tim Kuypers argue that in any industry (not just football) to consistently outperform competitors a company needs distinctive capabilities.[1] They suggest that such distinctive advantages can be classified into four groups: strategic asset, innovation, reputation and architecture. In football a 'strategic asset' can be a manager or player of considerably above average ability. One example from the past was Brian Clough at Derby County and Nottingham Forest. The 'innovation' advantage would be quite rare at a football club. (An example might be Herbert Chapman with the tactics he introduced at Arsenal in the 1930s.) An example of 'reputation' being used as a base to outperform other clubs is Manchester United; they have a successful recent history that is potentially intimidating. 'Architecture' as an advantage is the structure of a club, the organisation and its governance. One thinks of Liverpool in the 1970s and 1980s.

Ultimately it is a mixture of factors that contribute to success. A club that is lucky enough to have on its staff exceptional people has the opportunity to outperform its rivals in the short run. In the same way, if the directors of the club can work well with a skilled manager, the club will enjoy success for a while. There is no guarantee, however, that this success will continue beyond a few years. Derby County and Nottingham Forest fell away when Brian Clough left them. So did Wolverhampton after Stan Cullis left the club. To have a 'strategic asset' at a club—an outstanding player— is exciting, such a person boosts the fortunes of a club, but whether the success continues over a longer period of time depends upon decisions made by those in power at the club. It also, in the post-1990s game, depends upon access to money.

The generic drivers of performance in any business can be summarised as the following: quality of leadership; organisational arrangements; company strategy—including financial strategy; abil-

170

ity of management to execute that strategy; and to achieve targets. Each of these factors (drivers) is a necessary condition for success, without one the others will not work.

Leadership

The current conventional wisdom suggests that the most successful companies are those led by people who head a strong board of directors, who share a vision of where the company is going. The emphasis is on the benefits of a team working together, with talented people in the team. A chairman or CEO does not have to be a person with a 'big ego'—a strong ego, yes, but not one that seeks to dominate the other members of the team. A company needs a leader who can grasp the important issues faced by the company, but who then wishes to work with his team of directors and managers—not someone who just wants to impose his own solutions.

Danny Blanchflower has referred to 'the men in the director box' as the most important men at the club.[2] Brian Clough, when discussing the attempts made by Derby County to get him to return to the club as manger, stated that the then chairman, 'like most chairmen, he felt he could call the shots and get his own way.'[3] Phil Vasili, in a hard-hitting book on football and the attitudes in the game, refers to the chairman as 'the man with the big stick, reflecting the power structure of the world outside the stadium where, essentially, economic wealth determines power.'[4] Exactly. In the hundred plus years history of the professional game it has always been so.

It goes without saying that the long-term success of teams like Manchester United, Liverpool and Arsenal is based on the decisions made by their boards of directors. That is why they have been successful over a long time while clubs like Manchester City, Tottenham and Aston Villa have not. Chelsea have shown that with access to sufficient finance it is possible to bring the necessary ingredients together for success very quickly. However, they still need to demonstrate that they can continue to achieve success in the long-term. In his first two years leading the club Roman Abramovich spent £250 million on new players. Chelsea now have

171

very large debts. Will these debts ever need to be repaid? (Manchester United supporters are also worried about how the Glazer family intend to service the club's debts.)

John Argenti in his study on management failure identifies six possible management defects in a business.[5] These include the chairman or chief executive being too autocratic; the posts of chief executive and chairman not being separated with the result that too much power is in the hands of one person; the board being ineffective; the finance director having little authority at board level; lack of the necessary management skills and lack of management depth below board level; and a lack of stability.

Some studies have shown that what makes a board fail isn't so much the board's structure, procedures or make up, as it is the board's social dynamics. It is suggested that boards that underperform are characterised by poor communications, buck-passing, political posturing, game playing and a lack of transparency. One or more of these characteristics can usually be found in the boards of unsuccessful football teams. By contrast, effective boards have social systems that encourage trust and open debate. This does not mean the directors agree on everything, but at least they respect each other.

A board needs stability and unity. It is necessary for the directors to work together without different factions fighting each other in public. One reason why a board fails is because it is dysfunctional. The term failure does not necessarily mean financial collapse; it could just mean a failure to make the most of opportunities. The members of a board need to have a common purpose, and to agree on the strategies they will follow to achieve their objectives. Conflicts of interest will divert the club. Terry Venables makes the point that 'internal strife' at a club is counter-productive.[6] If the chairman and manager are squabbling and the fans are calling for resignations 'it cannot possibly help the team to concentrate.' As Chelsea demonstrated in 2006–07, a similar difficulty can arise if the manager and the majority shareholders disagree.[7]

Terry Venables believes that one reason for Liverpool's success over the last 20 or so years has been the good corporate governance structure at the club. John Smith and David Moores understood that the chairman's function was 'to provide leadership without telling everyone else how to do their jobs.' The club had an outstanding chief executive in Peter Robinson, who looked after the administrative side of the game. This left the managers to look after the team. Venables refers to the role of Liverpool's various managers (Shankly, Paisley, Fagan, Dalgliesh, Souness and Evans) as somewhere between manager and coach. Chairman, chief executive and manager all worked together. This contrasts with the position at some clubs where the chairman is all-powerful.

It is it is difficult to judge the 'quality' of directors. Different directors have different styles and approaches to running a business. According to Tom Cannon and Sean Hamil 'Football in the UK has a deeply rooted 'amateur' tradition in its governance and management.'[8] Even today the boards of some clubs are 'peopled largely by non-executive, amateur directors.' They also suggest that within the football clubs there have been 'few dedicated or qualified staff in the key business areas. The key business areas being Finance, Marketing, Customer Service and Media Relations.' This position is of course changing over time, as professional football becomes more and more of a global business and more professional managers become involved.

This amateur tradition in the UK with respect to governance and management has not just been confined to football clubs. Until the last one or two decades, most of UK industry was run by those who believed that the best training for management was to work their way up from the shop floor or to have spent time in the military in command of men. There was in most businesses a lack of trust of 'professionals' and 'graduates'. Values and attitudes in football just mirror values that exist in the rest of society.

We could try to judge quality by the decisions made, but all people make good and bad decisions. They key to success is for the bad decisions not to be too dramatic. There are many recent examples in football of bad judgement and bad decision-making. Mark Goldberg, who was cash-rich and a lifelong Crystal Palace supporter, decided in 1997 to buy the club. The existing owner, Ron Noades, sold his shares to Goldberg for £23 million. But what did he sell?—not the freehold of the stadium at Selhurst Park. All Goldberg owned was the brand name of a club that had just been relegated out of the Premier League, the income he could generate from operating the club, plus any transfer fees he could obtain from selling players. Goldberg's only hope of earning a return on his investment was to obtain immediate promotion. He gambled on a high profile, highly expensive manager, Terry Venables (who wanted 75% of his annual salary as an up front payment). Results under Venables were average, and gates fell. Venables obtained his money and the club went into administration eight months after being purchased. As Goldberg said after the club had gone into administration, 'I must have been the biggest mug in the world to pay £23 million for this club. I thought too big, too quickly.'

The question of specific knowledge and skills required of club directors has long been a topic of discussion. Is prior knowledge of football necessary? The Glazer family obviously think not. The view of Len Shackleton in the 1960s (and later the opinion of Brian Clough) was that many (most) directors know nothing about the game of football.[9] This is true, but is it a problem? As long as some members of the board are knowledgeable about the game, that is sufficient. After all different directors can bring different skills to the board.

It is a fact that those with no playing experience at the professional level usually dominate boards of football clubs. This would be acceptable if those directors with no football experience brought useful expertise to the board, for example financial expertise, or marketing expertise. Unfortunately, too often the directors are on the board either because they have some money they are willing to invest or lend to the club, or because they are 'grey' directors. 'Grey' directors are to be found in much of British Industry. They are non-executive directors who are appointed because they are friends of the chairman, and can be relied upon to support him on key matters.

One well-documented reason for the failure of a business is an autocratic leader: a leader who wants to make all the decisions and will not listen to advice. The 'Cadbury Report on Corporate Governance' emphasised the importance of dividing the role of chairman and chief executive.[10] This is important in football. If there is only one powerful person on a board it can lead to reluctance to change. A reluctance to listen to new ideas. Management literature often refers to the problem of those who are employed in an organisation who fear the boss more than they fear the competitors. The problem is that subordinates are, in such situations, afraid to tell their boss the truth. They fear they will lose their jobs. An autocratic leader can give success for a while. The problem is how to get rid of him when he is past his sell-by date. Powerful chairmen often claim they will only leave a club

174

when they have got things right. But in the end they cannot always let go. Often the trouble is that the chairman has his own money invested in the club and protecting this becomes more important than the good of the club. Football has seen the emergence of the executive chairman, who is paid by the club, works on football business for all or most of the week, and seeks to be involved in decisions involving team matters.

Terry Venables believes that 'one reason we find it difficult to make progress [with respect to leadership] in English football is that the chairmen, the people in charge, are unsure about football issues and don't want to make mistakes.'[11] He is not suggesting that we need more ex-footballers as chairmen—he points to the difficulties faced by Francis Lee as chairman of Manchester City. Many ex-footballers have their views but they do not have sufficient experience as coaches or experience of managing a group of players. English football has only recently accepted that managers need coaching knowledge and qualifications. Even now the Premier League try to find ways around the UEFA requirement on this matter.[12]

In his book *The Football Manager* Neil Carter seeks to answer the question of what difference the manager of a team makes to its success.[13] He concludes that there is no secret formula. As is well-known, some managers have the ability to motivate players, to get them to play to the best of their ability, and some managers lack that motivational ability but hopefully have other useful attributes. It is the same with leadership abilities in all walks of life. The good team 'manager' clearly needs interpersonal skills; he needs to be able to not only motivate players but also to be able to work with the club chairman. From a short-term planning point of view he must be able to outwit the managers of most of the teams the club play. Long-term planning is a particular problem (the average tenure of a manager is in the region of two years), which is not a long time to plan for change.

Organisation

The organisation of a football club has changed over time, as has the role of directors. Until the 1930s (and later in the case of a few clubs) directors were involved in team selection and many other aspects of team affairs. This responsibility then moved to the professional 'Team Manager'. Decisions on the purchase and sale of players is another decision area where responsibility changed; the responsibility for such investments and disinvestments has not only varied over time, but also from club to club, and even from manager to manager. The main management functions that have to be covered in any business are: planning, organising, leading, motivating and controlling. The meaning of planning is obvious—a business needs to plan its future. Competition of course makes the future uncertain, which means that the plan should allow for different scenarios. In football this could mean relegation, or, for a few elite clubs, failure to qualify for Europe.

The work of managing a football club is shared between the board of directors, the team manager, a chief executive, possibly a coach and possibly a director of football. How the work is divided varies between clubs and from one team manager to the next. The board (the top executives), along with the manager, have to provide leadership. The board will be there after the individual players have gone. The manager (the boss, the gaffer) leads the players on a day-to-day basis. He should be able to motivate the players, but it is the board (possibly with the club's supporters) that provide continuity. It is the board that has ultimate responsibility for controlling how the club is run and how resources are used. It is the directors of a club that have the power in so far as they appoint the manager of the team and are responsible for managing the finances of the club. When the club is successful they accept the 'glory' that goes with success, but when there is failure their first reaction is to sack the manager. If they appoint a series of unsuccessful managers, this will lead to pressure from the supporters for the directors themselves to change.

There is a long running debate as to what management structure is best for a large football club. There are those that argue that the employment of a director of football and a team manager gives a superior structure to that in which the manager takes charge of all football matters. With both systems it has now become accepted that the chairman (or another director) has responsibility for the purchase and sale of players, but again there is disagreement as to whether or not the chairman (or director responsible) should be responsible for negotiating the level of the transfer fees.

Many managers in the past, including Brian Clough, made it

clear that they could not work with a director of football breathing down their neck, indeed they also made it clear that they did not want a chairman too close. Arsène Wenger has said that he would not be prepared to operate with the dual-role system that Tottenham introduced in the early 2000s. In such a system there has to be a clear definition of responsibilities, but even then for two powerful personalities to work successfully together there has to be, according to Wenger, 'complicity and shared vision.'[14] Even the highly successful partnership of Brian Clough and Peter Taylor at Derby County in the end split up in acrimonious circumstances. Both men were stubborn and proud and after the falling out never spoke to each other again for the rest of their lives.

At Tottenham the club employed seven different managers in an eight-year period. In the last ten years they spent more on transfers than Arsenal. In 2004 they tried to put their house in order. They appointed a sports director and a manager and changed from the dual-role system to one that involved a third powerful figure who shared responsibilities. Similarly, at Portsmouth, the club had an old-fashioned style manager in Harry Redknapp, who did not take kindly to his chairman's suggestion that a director be appointed at boardroom level who would be responsible for overseeing the whole of the club's football activities. Redknapp had hinted that he could not work with a director of football, he was particularly concerned as to who would control transfers. The chairman tried to reassure the manager by saying that the director would not be able to bring players to the club that the manager did not want. Furthermore, the chairman, in a thinly veiled criticism of the manager said that he was keen to stop the comings and goings of players at the club—forty-five players in two and a half years.[15]

One key decision in a club is the level of salaries to be paid to players. Paying too much can lead a club to bankruptcy; on the other hand, paying too little can mean the team does not achieve success on the pitch.[16] At Manchester United, the richest club in the country, the board are very much involved in decisions on wages and transfers. Alex Ferguson states that one reason Eric Cantona left United was because the club (that is the directors) were not ambitious enough in the purchase of new players. 'I understand that there has to be a rational approach to salary arrangements and that the club has to consider the pay structure as a whole. But talent is not democratic. Manchester United policy on salaries gave me no chance of providing the financial packages required to secure great players' contracts. I think the restrictions applied to wages prevented us from being the power in European football that we could have been in the 1990s.' These comments of Sir Alex Ferguson reveal where the real power lies in a top club.[17]

Another aspect of salary policy is the amount paid to the manager. Clubs compete to attract the top managers by offering high salaries. The amount to be paid is, of course, determined by the board—possibly by a sub-committee of the board, namely the remuneration committee. Alex Ferguson describes the difficult discussions he had with the chairman of Manchester United plc (Sir Roland Smith) when he moved to the club. He had been told that 'We'll look after you,' but he found after ten years at the club that these words 'seemed utterly hollow.' Ferguson believed the club did not treat him properly—he also had a difficult time at the end of the 2000–01 season when negotiating a future contract. The power at United at that time, clearly lay with the board.

Implementing Strategy

Leadership style is the way (manner) in which a leader seeks to bring about the accomplishment of an organisation's strategy. A leader can be classified, based on his style, into one of a number of categories. At one extreme is the Dictator (the management authoritarian) and at the other extreme is the Democrat.

The authoritarian leader takes decisions and then tells everyone what he has decided. He decides what should be done, how it should be done and who should do it. The next stop in the move towards a Democrat leader is the person who takes decisions and then tries to sell them to the organisation. He tries to justify his decisions. The next stages are the 'Consult', 'Support' and the 'Delegate' styles. Finally we have the Democrat leader who seeks to gain long-term commitment to his vision by obtaining group support; by consultation with others in the organisation—he is a facilitator.

The management literature is generally critical of the 'Dictator' style, but does admit that when change is needed in an organisation, or when there is a need for continued improvement, then this style may be best at achieving results. The general conclusion in the literature is that the best leaders are those who adapt their style to the environment they face. The business environment is continually changing and new problems are continually arising. The leader needs to be able to adapt his or her style or face being replaced.

How does this apply to football? Cook, in his study on the differing styles of football manager, refers to four different approaches: Dictator, Wheeler-Dealer, Organiser and Democrat.[18] Cook is referring to the style of 'team manager,' but there is no reason why this same classification cannot be used to help classify the directors who are the 'leaders' at their football clubs.

The Dictator is the person who, as described above, wants it all his own way. He may be a bully or just a hard person. He could be logical or illogical, but usually acts on intuition, and can be wrong as easily as right in the conclusions he draws from available information. The Wheeler-Dealer lives off his wits and intuition. He will be shrewd, but likeable. He will take risks, responding to his feelings about a situation. The Organiser treats people who work in the business as human beings and listens to alternative views. He has an orderly and rational mind; he is logical and acts on signals, but he could be a better planner than leader. The Democrat builds up an organisation by teamwork; he works well with other people and seeks advice from experts. He does not like conflict, and is not always good at handling disputes. He is logical and responds to signals. Each of these styles of director can succeed. In football the results they obtain depend on the situation a club is in, and the personalities of the other people at the club.

Certain directors can be easily classified into one or more of the four styles. Doug Ellis was a Dictator (or is said to have been so by his critics). Chelsea's Ken Bates is a clear example of a Wheeler-Dealer. Martin Edwards was an Organiser *and* Democrat. There are obviously many different types of people, and many different types of executives. The science of classifying them is very inexact. The technique for placing people in boxes is crude. Most people have many elements to their character, which means they could be placed in more than one box.

Do Leaders Influence Success?

The answer, surprisingly, appears to be not in all cases. The research on this topic shows that the amount of opportunity to influence outcomes varies from industry to industry and from time to time. 'Depending on how much discretion exists, an organisation's form and fate may lie totally outside the control of its top managers, completely within their control or, more typically, somewhere in between.'

People within an organisation expect the top executives to lead. They expect them to motivate the organisation and obtain results. We know, however, that the executives cannot always influence outcomes—it depends on the level of discretion they have. This depends on such factors as the economic situation, the resources available to a company and the power structure within the board of directors and the organisation.

It is interesting that when a company does well, when a football club does well, the directors claim credit for this. They imply it is a result of good planning, wise investment decisions and appointing the best people. However, when a football club does badly, the directors like to blame somebody else. The team manager is always a good scapegoat. The turnover of managers is rapid in poorly performing clubs. It is conveniently forgotten that it is the directors that appointed the manager.

There are situations in which opportunities exist, and a good leader will take advantage of these to the benefit of the organisation. In football in the 1990s leaders from clubs from small-to-medium-sized towns had less and less of an opportunity to produce successful clubs. In contrast, the directors of a Premier League club from a big city should have been able to achieve at least some success. In between these two extremes, the directors of, say, a Sheffield club in the 1990s, should have managed the club more successfully than they did.

At different times different contributions may be required from a director. In football at the end of the nineteenth and twentieth centuries you needed an entrepreneurial type of director—one able to take advantage of the growth opportunities that were on offer. At a different stage, say, during a downturn in the market, such as in the 1960s and 1970s, a different type of director is required—

one who can control costs and avoid risk. Doug Ellis was a good director for the situation Aston Villa were in when he first became a director of the club, but not a good director for the situation in the 2000s. A good football club director in one period can be a disaster in another. A Wheeler-Dealer in the 1970s would have led a football club to ruin. A safety-first-only spend-what-is-available type of director would, in the 1990s, result in a team surviving but with little playing success. A dictatorial leader could take his club either way, but even if he was to win during one period, with a change in circumstances, he could fail in another.

The third and fourth drivers of performance that were mentioned at the beginning of this chapter were company strategy and the ability of those running the company to execute that strategy. In the case studies at the end of this book we will see how a number of clubs have adopted different strategies to achieve success. Some have been successful, others have not.

What Do Directors Know About Football?

A question that has been asked many times when a club is not successful is: what do the directors know about football? As Leeds United have demonstrated, it is one thing for the directors to have ambitious objectives, it is another thing for them to deliver. In the final section of this chapter on success, we will return to the question of director knowledge and ability.

'Beware of the clever, sharp men creeping into the game. Business acumen can go too far. Give me the honest plodder, the straightforward man. This is the kind of man we want in League football.' This was the opinion of William McGregor, the founder of the Football League, 100 years ago.[19] He thought the game needed 'the honest plodder' in the directorship role. Times have changed. Tom Bower refers to the 'mavericks, tycoons and opportunists attracted to football. United by their egoism and passion.' He is referring to what has happened in recent years.[20]

It is sometimes assumed that the directors of football clubs in the past were not particularly dynamic individuals, and that the increased wealth and interest in the game over the last two decades is the result of a new wave of directors. The true position is much more complicated. The managerial style and governance position in football, in each period, reflects what is happening in society in that period. In recent years, the successful new wave directors have taken advantage of opportunities that have opened up for them — the unsuccessful ones have failed to do so. This is exactly what has happened throughout the history of the game.

Directors of companies are usually not very popular figures. Directors today, in many industries, are seen as being overpaid individuals (fat cats) who in a search for higher profits to benefit shareholders are willing to downsize the business: to make some employees redundant and to make those that remain work harder for less reward. Directors of football clubs have an additional problem: they are usually not valued by their customers (football fans) either. They are seen as being more interested in financial performance than in producing a winning football team. They are seen as being more interested in satisfying the shareholders and creditors of the football club than the supporters. They are of course often substantial shareholders themselves. They are seen as being people who know little about football, who sack managers without having given them a real chance. They are also characterised as people who at times of success seek the glory that should belong to the players and manager. These criticisms are sometimes justified, but that does not mean that the criticisms apply to all directors all of the time.

Successful directors of companies might not be very likeable people. In fact, the characteristics often required in order for a director to be successful, for example ruthlessness and confidence in their own abilities as well as possessing strong opinions, might make them difficult to like. Likeable, easygoing people do not necessarily become good business leaders. Jim Smith, one of the most experienced football club managers in England, found that 'club chairman come in all shapes and sizes.'[21] As a result of his over 30 years experience in football he concludes that there are those he 'wouldn't have changed for the world' but he goes on to say that these are few in number. 'I have come across the odd diamond but more often than not the jewel might sparkle but close scrutiny reveals nothing but paste.' At the time of writing his autobiography he had worked 'with or under' 14 different chairman, and he refers to only 3 of these with respect. He mentions that amongst the others 'include some of the games most notorious personalities.' In this book we encounter both the 'odd diamond' and a number of the 'notorious personalities.'

'Good managers are hard to find but good chairman are almost impossible to find'. This makes things very difficult because perhaps the most important decision a chairman and his fellow directors have to make is the appointment of a manager. The fact that the average period that a manager stays in a post is now less than two years suggests that directors are on many occasions not making the right appointments.[22] Steve Coppell, the ex-footballer, ex-manager and former chairman of the League Managers Association, has expressed the view that 'the number of sackings is a direct derivative of the inability of chairman and directors of football clubs to appoint properly. Decisions are made on the basis of what will please the public rather than who is best for the job.' As David Sheepshanks, chairman of Ipswich said: 'A lot of management candidates are players with good playing records that say nothing about their coaching record.'

Because many football club directors have little knowledge of football they are tempted to appoint ex-players as managers. The danger is that these ex-players know about the game but do not necessarily know about management or coaching. Former players believe that they know all there is to know about football, and believe therefore that they should be able to move into managerial posts without obtaining an education in management or in coaching. Directors are often willing to accept this way of thinking especially if the ex-player is a well-known figure who will appeal to supporters.[23]

Football club directors and appointed administrators are the people who make decisions at the Football Association, the Football League and the Premier League. It was decisions made by such club directors that led to the formation of the Football League in the 1880s and to the establishment of the Premier League just over 100 years later. Decisions made by club directors, acting as part of the establishment, were responsible for players being exploited in the past with a maximum wage level, for example. These days, they are responsible for the very high wages paid by clubs to players. Decisions made by directors were responsible for the shabby football grounds of the 1980s, as well as the more impressive stadiums of the present time. Directors were responsible for the state of the game in the past and for its present position. It is they who decide how the money coming into the game is spent.

It is generally only when a football club is in difficulties or has a long period without success that the supporters of the club take very much notice of the directors. As Bill Kenwright has said, 'The chairman can't really give the fans what they want. The only people who can do that are the managers and the players.' (He was at the time waiting to take over as chairman at Everton (1999), having just forced out the previous chairman.) What he said is of course correct, but he could have added that it is the chairman and the other directors who are responsible for giving the manager and players the financial resources they need in order to allow them to show their abilities.

Probably the most famous reference to football club directors was that by Len Shackleton in his autobiography (published in 1955).[24] On page 78 of the book, underneath the heading for Chapter 9 – 'The Average Director's Knowledge of Football' – the page was deliberately left blank. Len Shackleton was a brilliant footballer, who enjoyed upsetting authority. At various times he criticised the Football League, the FA, referees, managers, as well as directors. He rightly criticised the system that was in existence at the time. Under this system, clubs and the establishment controlled key aspects of players' contracts, transfer fees and wage levels. He was certainly not discreet; his autobiography was entitled *The Clown Prince of Soccer*. There have been many others that have shared Shackleton's view about directors.

Brian Clough, in his 2002 book, expresses even stronger views. He believed that 'The vast majority of them (directors) knew nothing in my days as a player and nothing in my time as a manager and the modern lot still know nothing.' Clough is referring to knowing nothing about football. It is interesting that he makes references to the 'vast majority', recognising that a minority do deserve respect. He hammers home his criticisms: 'Football club chairman and directors are still so barmy, so naïve, so thick and so stubborn yet so full of themselves that they continue to make stupid decisions when it comes to the appointment of a manager.' Brian Clough was well-known for overstating his case, but a similar point is the theme of the book by Chris Green entitled *The Sack Race*.

Tom Cannon and Sean Hamil, writing over 40 years after Len

Shackleton, suggest that a second blank page should be added to football books 'covering what directors know about business, management and strategy.'[25] They were referring to the amateurish way in which most football clubs have been run, to the lack of marketing skills and to the directors' lack of skills in handling relationships with players and supporters. Brian Clough considered directors to be a nuisance, and is said to have despised some of them. He thought they were only useful for their money. He did, however, admit a number of years later that he 'should never have walked out on Derby in 1973 over a fit of pique with the chairman, Sam Longson. This was the biggest mistake I ever made.'

Was Len Shackleton's comment on the average director's knowledge of football correct? The typical board in the 1960s had a majority of directors with a background in small business, either from the service, manufacturing or trading sectors. Some of them might well have played amateur soccer but until becoming football club directors would have had little contact with the professional game. Many would claim they were supporters of the club at which they were directors, but as Shackleton would probably, and rightly, claim such support does not equate to a real knowledge of football. The point of substance that Len Shackleton was making was correct, and probably still is. The vast majority of directors, until they join a club board, only have a limited knowledge of the business of football. They typically learn on the job, some more successfully than others. But does this matter?

A board of directors consists of a collection of individuals, hopefully working together. As in all industries you need a balance of skills on a board. A problem in the 1950s and 1960s was that there were football clubs with some board members who were experts in nothing, or to be fair expert in very little that was of relevance. Anthony King, in *The End of the Terraces*, refers to the directors of the 1970s and 1980s as a 'motley crew of minor entrepreneurs' and as 'provincial backward businessmen.'[26] The comments of King are amusing and probably applied to many club directors and chairmen at the time—but not all. (The same comments could probably have been made about many of the directors of British companies in the 1970s and 1980s.) It is amusing, but not correct, to assume that provincial businessmen are backward.

Undoubtedly in the 1990s the management and administration of football clubs improved. Professional administrators moved into the game and the marketing, financial management and public relations aspects of most clubs progressed. But they progressed more at some clubs than others, and just because modern business methods are adopted it does not mean that success follows: directors can still make big mistakes.

King's view was that 'the time honoured characteristics that have marked the way Europe's great soccer clubs have been run, [as well as] mindless conservatism and pompous megalomania... have been swept away on a tide of money. As a result the motley crew of minor entrepreneurs which controlled these clubs is being squeezed out by the captains of multi-national commerce.' But where are the captains of multi-national commerce leading football?

King overstates his case. As already mentioned not all directors were 'motley', and only a few of the directors who replaced the old directors were leaders of modern multi-nationals. No leaders of top multi-nationals would choose to take on a chief executive's job (or the executive chairman's position) at a football club for, say, a £800,000 salary, when he could earn well over £2 million a year as a 'captain' of a multi-national. Of course some of the elite clubs (Chelsea, Manchester United) are now paying their chief executives over £1 million per year.

Eamon Dunphy, a former player and a respected writer on the subject of football, wrote in 1986 of 'the mediocrities who run most English football league clubs.'[27] His own playing career had mainly been at Millwall. He blamed the chairman of that club for its lack of success. Dunphy, as have other writers, refers to the period from 1945 to the early 1970s as the golden age of English football. He expressed the opinion in 1986 that 'Football is dead in England today for may reasons, not the least of which is the game's failure to find work for intelligent men whose moment in the playing area has passed.'

Many would not agree with all aspects of this opinion. Dunphy's argument about the golden age is partly based on the fact that it was during this period that England produced its best players of the century. This might be correct, for it was during this period that England won the World Cup for the only time. Certainly by the year 2000 non-British players dominated the Premier League. But golden age? From a spectator point of view, the grounds did not offer very much. The game did, as now, offer skill and excitement. From the director's point of view the game did not offer big financial rewards, but did offer 'respect' and 'status'. The players may have enjoyed respect, but they did not get the financial rewards they deserved. What has changed are the values of society. In the 'golden age' there were good directors for the values of that time. Similarly, in the modern game there are good directors for today's values. As in any business, success depends on directors who can identify change and manage the change successfully.

7

The Dark Side of the Game

In earlier chapters we looked at the changes and problems resulting from the impact of market forces in the football business. Of particular concern is the way that the free market system is destroying competitive balance in the game. In this chapter we look at other associated dangers to the future of the game: the behaviour of spectators, the behaviour of the players, greed, match-fixing, drugs, racism, gambling and the notion of integrity (or lack of it).

Ever since football became a professional sport there have been incidents of match-fixing, gambling, violence and a general attitude amongst some players of 'win or lose, on the booze.' As long ago as 1915 there was a scandal involving both the Manchester United and Liverpool teams over match-fixing (In the 1960s an England player even went to prison for match-fixing.) When David O'Leary became manager at Leeds United he tried to stop the drinking culture at the club, but failed to do so and eventually four Leeds players found themselves in court on charges of violence with racist overtones.

Curiously, the fans do not seem to mind. It is all part of the soap opera, something to read about in the press. The fans do not expect their heroes to be perfect. The stars of previous generations, particularly the film stars, were certainly not perfect. Investigative journalists certainly do their best to reveal this dark side of the game; it sells papers. The national and international football authorities do work hard to maintain a respectable image for the game, however. They try to avoid scandal, and attempt to keep their own houses in order. They introduce rules, such as those trying to prevent clubs and players settling disputes in the civil courts, in order to avoid washing their dirty linen in public. The leagues themselves give money to charities, while the clubs become

189

involved in community projects and FIFA supports football in the poorer parts of the world. All this is done in order to show that football does put something back into society.

People are not only interested in matches they are also interested in the personalities involved. They like to know what the 'good' people in the game are doing, but they also like to know what the 'bad' people are doing. Despite their best efforts the establishment cannot hide the darker side of the game.

When a scandal does arise the authorities initiate various damage limitation exercises, so that the football money-making machine can roll on. For instance, in January 2005, the Spanish Football Federation decided that the racial chanting against Roberto Carlos by the Atlético Madrid fans was only a minor misdemeanour and fined the club a paltry £420. This was in a match in which the referee stopped play so that a public appeal could be made to stop the crowd making monkey noises. The lack of sufficient punitive measures in this case hardly gives out a message that such behaviour is to be treated seriously. Furthermore, on the same day Adrian Muto, who had been sacked by Chelsea for drug abuse, and suspended by the FA for seven months, announced that he would be joining Juventus. A club that only months earlier had been found guilty in an Italian court for giving its players performance-enhancing drugs over a four-year period. A period, moreover, in which the club were the best in Europe (with the help of match-fixing). Again, an interesting message.

'Money, they say, is the root of all evil, and without asserting that professional football is an evil, its origin may be ascribed to money. The majority of spectators favour the clubs that are most often on the winning side. Therefore to maintain popular support teams [have] to be victorious. As they found their local talent insufficient for this purpose, so they imported better players from a distance. This example, set by one club, [is] followed in self-defence by others.' The situation being described has applied to football clubs in the last decade or so, but the words were actually written in 1900 by N.L. Jackson.[1] In another instance, when Jackson refers to importing players, he adds 'chiefly from Scotland.' Now it is players from all around the world who 'dominate' the Premier League.

Deloitte and Touche, in their 2002 'Review of Football Finance'[2], discuss whether or not money is ruining the game. They refer to an ex-player who believes that 'football is being ruined by commercial speculation' and that 'team spirit is being replaced by merely mercenary ambitions on the part of the players.' This particular quotation is, they point out, from September 1900. Deloitte and Touche argue, however, that there is little wrong with the present state of football and that there is nothing wrong with the basic football model. They do not share the view of the pessimists, who hark back to what they see as the halcyon days. Jackson described the aim of the Football League, when it was founded in 1888, as selfish. 'Its object was to increase the gates of the clubs belonging to it, and to endeavour to monopolise the cream of players and the larger share of public support.' Exactly the same could be said about the Premier League, it was formed to maximise the income of the clubs involved. Jackson analysed the problems of the game in 1900 under the following headings: alcohol, foreign players, lack of knowledge, the attitude of directors, gambling and the financial state of clubs. All of these problems are still with us to a greater or lesser extent.

Spectators

The behaviour of spectators has been the subject of much criticism because of the hooligan problem and because of the verbal abuse of players. In the 1980s the hooligan problem was so great it was threatening the future, certainly the commercial future, of football. Advertisers were reluctant to be associated with a sport in which a gang of supporters of one club would fight a gang of supporters of another club. Sponsors, advertisers and many spectators began to stay away from football. Since that time, in England, the police and club officials have done a remarkable job in more or less eliminating hooliganism from the domestic game. Occasionally incidents of fighting do break out at Premier League and Football League matches, but not at a level that drives away spectators or commercial sponsors. The situation at each match still, however, needs to be monitored, and when the supporters of certain clubs visit a town, a large police presence is necessary to ensure that violence does not return to the streets around the ground.

The biggest criticism levelled at football crowds now is racism and the verbal abuse of players. It is an issue in England but is even more of a problem in certain other countries. Spain for example is a country in which black players are often the victims of racial abuse. Roy Keane has written that 'Some of the things you hear from the terraces are really sickening. Racist taunts, chants about players' personal lives, filth that makes you wonder about the people who come to football matches.'[3] The language on the terraces is often foul. Football is not the nice clean pastime that the media and the corporate sponsors of the game would like us to believe.

Stan Collymore has written about the racial abuse he suffered, none worse than in a match when he was playing for Aston Villa against Liverpool.[4] A Liverpool defender, Steve Harkness, was insulting Collymore's mother and using terms such as 'nigger' and 'coon'. The referee did nothing to stop it, and there was a fight between the players after the match. Collymore got the Professional Footballers Association involved, but at a meeting of all those involved the PFA tried to get both players to sign a joint apology to all fans. Collymore felt let down, he had done nothing wrong. The PFA are involved in the campaign to 'kick racialism out of sport,' but in this instance it did nothing. (Collymore, for his part, did something in the next match he played against Liverpool; Harkness was carried off and Collymore was shown a yellow card!) Television, radio and print media commentators are usually 'cocooned' from the realities of life on the terraces. It may be in the interests of the game's administrators and corporate sponsors to sell the football experience as good clean fun, but it is far from it.

The FIFA and UEFA record on punishing racial abuse is weak. Sparta Prague, from the Czech Republic, were only fined 60,000 Swiss francs (£25,000) when their home crowd made monkey chants against Lyon players in a Champions League match. Black English players are abused when they play in Poland. FIFA fined the Spanish FA the paltry sum of 100,000 Swiss francs (£41,000) for the racist chanting by fans in Spain's friendly against England in November 2004. Benni McCarthy, a black South African playing in the Spanish league, regularly has bananas thrown at him.[5] The English FA were fined 150,000 Swiss francs (£62,000) for the crowd's racist chanting against Turkey in May 2003. Sepp Blatter came up with a nonsensical suggestion: 'I believe' he said, 'you could stop the game, identify the people involved in this kind of foul situation and then take them to the middle of the field to be booed by the rest of the spectators. In Britain you have video cameras at the matches and you could therefore do this.' In fact, a large number of 'the rest of the spectators' would cheer those taken onto the pitch who would like as not become local heroes.[6]

At the international level hooliganism still does exist. A dangerous group of supporters continue to follow the England football team whenever they play abroad. Whether they are driven by political ideology, nationalism or just the wish to have a fight does not matter, they threaten the image of the game. In Italy a group of right wing supporters (the Ultras) attach themselves to certain clubs and provoke violence at matches in which 'their' team plays. 'Firebomb attacks on opposing fans, assaults on players by their own supporters, referees besieged in their dressing rooms and pitch invasions' are incidents that are not uncommon. Some matches have had to be played in stadiums from which the public are excluded.[7] In 2007 all the matches scheduled for one weekend were cancelled because a policeman had been killed at a riot following a football match. This is in the country whose national team won the 2006 World Cup! In fact, during the 2006–07 season there were crowd problems in many European countries.

Roy Keane believes that one danger to the game is not just the spectators but also the bloated egos of the hangers-on. He refers to some of the people involved in the game as 'spivs, bluffers, bullshitters and media whores.' He emphasises that football at the top level is now a 'savage business'. He is not referring to the game being played at an aggressive physical level, but to what goes on off the pitch, to mental pressure. You can 'be a failure, humiliated, blasted in the media, sneered at by the crowd, or simply left out of the team.' He discusses the way David Beckham was treated in the media and by many football followers after he was sent off whilst playing for England in the 1998 World Cup. 'He had to endure the nation's bile, generated by the scribes in the press box or their pals on the serious pages, many of whom probably never saw a football match.'

The Players

There have been hard footballers in the game since the beginning. The English game used to be known for being low on skill and high on aggression. Foreign managers and players are now changing this reputation. Older fans can tell stories about how it used to be, when full-backs would early in a game let any tricky winger know that he was going to have a hard time. Centre-forwards were allowed to charge goalkeepers into the net. The legendary English team of 1966 and the Leeds team of Don Revie had players such as Nobby Stiles and Norman Hunter who caused much damage to opposing players. If anything, the modern game, with its yellow and red cards and penalty points, is less physically violent than it used to be.

There are of course still violent clashes. Roy Keane in his autobiography shocked many people, including the football authorities, with his account of his feud with Alfie Haaland. Keane felt that in a particular game against Leeds in 1997 Haaland was winding him up. 'The late tackles I could live with, they were a normal part of football. But the other stuff really bugged me.' Late in the game Keane, in attempting to tackle Haaland, seriously injured himself. Haaland accused Keane of cheating; he stood over him shouting 'Get up, stop faking it.' There were doubts following the tackle whether Keane would be able to play football again, but he did recover and when he played against Haaland in a game against Manchester City, three years later, he was out for revenge. Late in the game 'He had the ball on the far touchline. Alfie was taking the piss. I'd waited long enough. I fucking hit him hard. The ball was there (I think).' Keane was shown the red card. There are many examples of violence on the pitch, it is as old as the game itself but it has never seriously threatened the future of football.[8]

Violence by players off the pitch also attracts a great deal of media attention. Each season there are a number of scandals. A notable case occurred in Leeds in 2000 involving a number of the club's players. Late at night, an Asian lad was badly beaten up, having been kicked about the face, head and body. One of the players involved, Jonathan Woodgate, was found guilty of affray; his colleague, Lee Bowyer, was cleared of all charges, but one of their friends was found guilty on the charge of causing grievous bodily harm with intent, and sentenced to six years in prison. It was the fall out from the case that caused the club and the manager problems. The so-called 'racial attack' by rich young players who had represented their country in international matches was a shock to some. The game had been trying to create a clean-cut, middle-of-the-road image. It has been said that the Leeds case 'reveals something much closer to reality than the new 'image'. The reaction to the attack, and to the case, also reveals something about the culture of football. When Bowyer played football during and after the trial he was cheered by many spectators, yet Michael Duberry, another player involved in the incident who at the trial did not seek to protect his two colleagues, was booed by a section of the Leeds fans.

There are tensions in football clubs between those inside the club and those outside. It has been said that players 'feel exposed and do not know who to trust.' 'They do not have the skills to handle being so much in the public eye. It is not surprising they end up back with mates they can relate to, and use drink as an escape and to boost their self confidence.

Integrity

Pat Murphy, the respected Radio 5 football commentator, has accused modern footballers of a lack of integrity. Certainly it is now quite common to see players diving in order to try to persuade the referee to award a foul, in particular a penalty. Sometimes they are successful, sometimes they are not, and sometimes they are given a yellow card. Footballers contest many of the decisions made by referees and it is now not unusual to see a group of players standing around a referee shouting abuse at him. This attitude can be contrasted with that of Rugby Union, where players accept controversial decisions even in World Cup finals. Gamesmanship has always been a part of soccer, but it now seems to be generally accepted that the amount of it has increased. When David Dunn was tripped over in the penalty area in a match between Birmingham City and Middlesbrough at the end of 2004 the papers were full of praise for him, because he got up and continued to play rather than roll on the floor and appeal for a penalty.

Rape

Footballers have become glamorous high profile media figures. One of the perceived rewards (though it can be more of a problem) of celebrity status are groupies. It is claimed George Best had affairs with at least two Miss Worlds, but less famous players than Best also attract willing partners. Sometimes, however, the partners are not willing, or perhaps are unsure whether or not they are willing. In one case four or more footballers were alleged to have gang raped an 18-year old girl in a London hotel in October 2003. The girl claimed she was willing to have sex with the first of the men, but that the others raped her. The alleged rape story was quite skilfully handled, the footballers' names were not at first released and the case did not go to court. Later the names became known, one was a Newcastle player, another a Chelsea player. During 2003 there were a series of other rape claims and charges involving footballers from Manchester United, Leeds and Manchester City.

Often the claims of rape do not result in the player in question being charged because of a lack of evidence. Just as often the girl involved is paid for her story. There is nothing new about sportsmen being involved with groupies. What is new is that the women are now more willing to tell their stories. The girls might not be able to win a case in court, but football clubs, in order to avoid bad publicity, are sometimes willing to pay a girl to keep quiet. The situation in the US is even more serious. Kobe Bryant, a basketball star, was accused of sexually assaulting a hotel concierge in a luxury Colorado resort hotel. The maximum sentence for such an offence would be life imprisonment. The two sides settled out of court, and Bryant lost a number of lucrative advertising contracts.

Alcohol

One hundred years ago N.L. Jackson pointed out the link between alcohol and football. The relationship has continued. This has led to problems for some, but perhaps not as many now as there used to be. The foreign coaches that have entered the English game have introduced a new attitude towards drink. There is now concern about diet, fitness levels and the effects of alcohol.

In the 1970s and 1980s many very popular players including George Best, Rodney March, Stan Bowles, Paul Merson and Tony Adams were well-known drinkers. Even in more recent times there have been players and groups of players who were known to be hard drinkers. Alex Ferguson tried to stop the drinking culture at Manchester United, and got rid of players, such as Paul McGrath, who he could not control.[9]

To drink with one's 'mates' is seen as a bonding experience. Drink, unfortunately, does not help performance. In the 1970s, perhaps the worst period for football and alcohol, the performance of English club teams was not good—a number of players nearly killed themselves by drinking too much. Players such as Malcolm MacDonald were said to drink three bottles of whiskey a day—to stop the pain in his knees. A few years later the very talented player, Paul Gascoigne, ruined his career through drink.[10] Perhaps now with the emphasis on training techniques, as well as food and energy, the culture will change.

There is another side to the relationship between alcohol and football, indeed between alcohol and most sports. Brewing companies have always been willing to sponsor sporting events, they clearly believe that to do so is good for their sales. In an interesting study on the cultural history of sport and alcohol entitled 'Mud, Sweat and Beers', Tony Collins and Wray Vamplew describe how, in the eighteenth century, it was common for pubs to organise sporting contests.[11] (These included cricket matches between one-legged players, and duck hunting.) The brewing industry was very involved with football from the beginning of the Football League. The grounds of many football clubs, including Aston Villa and Wolverhampton Wanderers, were on land leased from breweries. The closeness of the ground to the pub meant that spectators could drink before and after games at their 'local'. Many clubs had a brewer on their board of directors, too. In the early days brewers advertised heavily in football programmes and in more recent times have paid for their brand names to be on football shirts (Liverpool, Newcastle, etc.) Carling were the first sponsors of the Premier League.

Drugs

A particularly worrying aspect of modern sport is the use of performance-enhancing drugs. It is well-known that many Olympic athletes have taken such drugs, what is not known is the extent of the use of such drugs in other sports. It is known that in the US, in sports such as American football, basketball and baseball, performance-enhancing drugs are used. One respected voice in US sport has referred to the period from 1993 to present as 'the steroid era'. In many sports in the US, as in England, there is a reluctance to test players for drugs, the authorities simply do not want to face up to the problem. If it is found that drugs have been used by certain clubs and certain players, it would help destroy the integrity of the sport and raise doubts about the validity of certain match results. The worry to the credibility of a game being that the team that wins may do so because it is using better drugs than the losing team.

In the US the top baseball star for many years has been Barry Bonds, who has been suspected for a long time of taking drugs (he was a client of Victor Conte, notorious for supplying drugs to American Olympic athletes). He was, however, only required to take a random drug test two weeks before the end of the 2004 season. He later admitted to taking substances provided by Conte, but said that he did not know they contained steroids. The drug control system in baseball is that a player is allowed five positive tests before he receives a one-year ban. Bond, even though found guilty of taking steroids, continues to play and to break records. His records will stand even though many of his home runs would have been helped by performing-enhancing substances. Most baseball players see the use of steroids as cheating, but not the use of 'greenies' (amphetamines), which many feel they need to keep them going through a 162-game season.

What about football in Europe? In Italy a long running doping trial came to an end in 2004. The court found that between 1994 and 1998 certain Juventus players had taken performance-enhancing drugs. Juventus were at that time Europe's best club side. The club won the UEFA Champions League in 1996, were runners up in 1997 and 1998 and were Serie A champions five times. At the end of the 1990s, however, Juventus' reputation was threatened by the doping allegation. The club doctor and chief executive were prosecuted when drugs containing banned substances were found at the club's training ground. The doctor was sentenced to 22 months in jail for supplying players with illegal stimulants between 1994 and 1998. The club's former chief executive was acquitted and no action was taken against the club—even though they had won cups and championships during the period when some of the player's performance had benefited from the use of illegal drugs. The coach at the club during this time was Marcello Lippi, who went on to become the manager of the national team and was in charge when they won the 2006 World Cup. Lippi became a national hero.

Following the court findings the football authorities had little to say about the fraud committed by a leading European football club. FIFA and UEFA ignored the implications of the cheating, and allowed Juventus' name to remain on record as European Champions of 1996. The Olympic Committee regularly take away medals from athletes found guilty of drug taking, yet the dark side of football needs to remain hidden. Nothing must be done to disillusion customers and drive away sponsors.[12] Juventus beat Ajax in the 1996 Champions League final and the manager of the Ajax team of that time, when informed of the verdict in the drug case, said 'I think for the sake of the sport they should take the prizes away if doping has been proved, otherwise you do not discourage it.' During the period of time in which, according to the Italian court, certain Juventus players were taking drugs, they beat Manchester United in European competitions three times. They reached three successive European Championship finals. The drugs do seem to have been performance-enhancing!

The most significant recent high profile case in England concerning possible drug abuse was that involving Rio Ferdinand. The FA have a drug testing procedure, and on 23 September 2003 the drug testers arrived at the Manchester United training complex for a routine test of a number of players. Ferdinand's name was on the list of players to be tested; once a player's name is on the list the testing is mandatory. But Ferdinand went missing (he was shopping it was later revealed) and later claimed that he had forgotten about the test. The club defended him saying he was an absentminded sort of person. He even failed to turn up for the test on the next day. As a result of missing the test he was banned by the FA from playing for eight months. Did he miss the test deliberately or had he forgotten?[13]

Manchester United claimed Ferdinand was innocent and that the whole thing was just a misunderstanding. They continued to pay him his £60,000 a week salary plus bonus payments based on the team's performance. As a result of his suspension Ferdinand could not, however, play for England in the 2004 European Championship finals. There were many who though Ferdinand's punishment was not severe enough.

Ferdinand is not the only player with Manchester United connections to be involved in a drug controversy. Jaap Stam left Manchester United to play in Italy, and within a few weeks of playing there was found to be taking Nandrolene. (The Italian football authorities because of past scandals have become far more rigorous in their drug testing than the English.)

Over the course of the 1990s the FA did not conduct tests for the use of EPO.[14] It was only in October 2004 that they announced they would introduce such tests 'in the near future.' It has been known for some time that the use of EPO improves endurance. It has been used illegally in cycle racing for many years. The FA announced that EPO 'was to be on the banned list and accordingly there would be testing for its use in future.' There are two possible reasons why they did not start testing earlier: one is that they did not want to rock the boat; the other is that such testing is expensive. Nevertheless, it appears they only decided to act when Arsene Wenger expressed the view that some of the overseas players that he brought to Arsenal displayed symptoms of EPO use (abnormally high blood cell count).

Recreational drug use is also something to be concerned about. Chelsea terminated Adrian Mutu's contract when he was found to be taking cocaine, but the FA suspended him for only seven months. A spokesman for the club said, 'We are extremely disappointed with the verdict.' We believe it is far too lenient and sends out the wrong message about drugs in football. It is also indicative of a lack of direction within the FA at this time. As a club, we can only take the action we believe is right for Chelsea. However, the FA has a much wider responsibility to look after the interests of the game as a whole and, in this case, we believe it has shown itself to be weak over the issue of drugs.'

Player Power

In 2006 Alex Ferguson cited 'player power and ego' as the biggest problem in football. If Sir Alex makes that comment it is serious, as he is known to take a very tough stance even with his high profile players—his 'hair dryer' treatment has become well-known. He has clashed with David Beckham, Roy Keane, Ruud Van Nistelrooy and others. He has said that the manager must maintain rigid discipline. The players know, however, that after a few bad results a manager can be sacked.

The top Premiership players have their ego massaged by the media and the fans. Ashley Cole, who was nurtured by Arsenal since he was a young player, believed that a salary of £3 million or so per annum was not enough for him, so in controversial circumstances he moved to Chelsea. After the move he criticised Arsenal, the manager, and the players at the club. Cole has player power, he is an England player, with a pop star as a wife.

The top players are now the equivalent of film stars. It is quite common to read criticisms of the £3 million plus annual salaries they command, but presumably the directors and managers of their clubs think they are worth this, otherwise they would be foolish to agree to pay such high wages.[15] The directors must believe that the additional net revenue a top player can bring into the club is greater than the player's cost. The additional revenue can be the result of success on the pitch, media rights, gate receipts or sponsorship. With the present widespread belief in the advantages of the market mechanism, it is not surprising that the players claim their share of the riches.

A particular problem surrounds the players who represent England. The media build up the prospects of the team every time there is an international tournament. The players involved are written and spoken about as being 'world class'; stars from the best league in the world. They are certainly among the best paid players in the world. No wonder the false praise and the hype affects them. This, despite the fact that England have only won an important international competition once, and that was over 40 years ago in a tournament where, because they were the host nation, they did not have to qualify. They also played all their matches at their home stadium of Wembley.[16]

It really shouldn't be all that surprising that players aged around 20, paid £2 million or so a year, invited to write books on their 'life' so far, touted as fashion celebrities, and courted by the media, have inflated egos. The pity is that they do not win anything—for that's what footballers are supposed to do. Unfortunately the England players are not 'as good as the hype makes them out to be.' This was not only the view, in late 2006, of many football supporters, it was the view of John Barnes (who played 89 times for England).

As Barnes points out, hype is 'the lifeblood of how football is marketed.' Barnes' particular concern is that the England supporters and the England players believe the hype. 'If ever England players were affected by the hype it was under Sven-Goran Eriksson.' With regard to supporters, in order for the riches to be maintained, the hype has to continue. We still have to be told that we have some of the best players in the world and the best league in the world.

Health Problems

A different aspect of the dark side of the game is the treatment of players by football clubs. As Stan Collymore points out, clubs are not good at catering for the individual needs of players.[17] They pay millions of pounds for players, then toss them into 'the general pile of players.' They do not always make the best use of their investments. A similar story has been told by Paul Gascoigne, and earlier than that by George Best.

Yet in one respect clubs are now very conscious of health. The modern manager now thinks carefully about the players' dietary needs and the physical condition of players is carefully monitored, but the psychological needs are usually overlooked. Stan Collymore has suffered from a borderline (cognitive) personality disorder since he was young. It is called borderline because those who suffer from it 'live on the edge between psychosis and neurosis.' When he played football his illness was not diagnosed. The unfortunate truth is that football clubs are more likely to recognise physical problems than mental ones. The way most coaches and managers treated Collymore made his problems worse.

Collymore has been particularly critical of his treatment at Aston

Villa, where he refers to the John Gregory regime as 'hell-bent on destroying' him. (Gregory was the manager). Collymore in his youth had been a Villa supporter, but he admits that when he moved to Villa from Liverpool he was already 'mentally shot to pieces.' His struggle with depression had already begun in earnest, but neither he nor the management at the clubs he played for knew what his problem was. Collymore claims that when he became ill 'John Gregory mocked me and tormented me. He ridiculed the idea that I could have a depression. He turned me into a laughing stock.'

Whilst at Villa, Collymore entered a clinic for treatment. Neither the manager nor the chairman, Doug Ellis, were sympathetic. They could not understand how a man in his twenties who was well paid could be depressed (the chairman's advice being 'just pull your socks up and get on with it'). Collymore was told that the club would not pay his hospital bills. Furthermore, the other players at Villa were not sympathetic to his health problems. The manager even criticised the player during press interviews. Collymore was disappointed with his stay at Villa, he even compared their supporters unfavourably with those from Liverpool. The Villa supporters being less passionate, less optimistic and generally less knowledgeable, with many of the crowd being the prawn sandwich brigade who do not 'have a clue about football.'

Conflicts of Interest — Agents

An important corporate governance problem currently attracting attention relates to a possible conflict of interest at the time a player becomes involved in the transfer market. The issue is not new. The use by players of agents has been a problem for the football authorities since the nineteenth century. In 1899 the FA attempted to stop transfers altogether in order to eliminate what were then referred to as 'outside commission agents.' Over 100 years ago such agents were arranging the transfer of players between clubs in return for a percentage of the fee. The proposal by the FA to stop transfers was not accepted by the clubs, even though the clubs did agree that commission agents were harmful (to them).

A hundred years later the position of agents in the game had become so established that Sir Bobby Robson, in his final days as manager of Newcastle United, referred to Paul Stretford (an agent) as the club's chief scout.[18] He was suggesting that it was Stretford rather than himself that was the main influence in bringing certain players to the club. It helped that Stretford had a close relationship with the club's chairman. At least two of the club's big signings in 2003 and 2004 were arguably not players that Robson wanted to add to the club's squad, but were wanted by the chairman Freddie Shepherd.

At the time Stretford was the agent for Wayne Rooney, and for a while it was thought that the player might move to Newcastle, partly because of the £20 million price offered to Everton and partly because of the links between Shepherd and Stretford. This did not happen. Manchester United outbid Newcastle and at any rate were a more attractive club to Rooney.

Paul Stretford need not, however, have been too disappointed. His company received a £1.5 million fee for their involvement in Rooney's move to Manchester United. Nevertheless there were related problems for Stretford, notably the death threats he received from Everton supporters who blamed him for Rooney's move. Stretford also became involved in strange meetings with Rooney's previous agent (a boxing promoter) and with a notorious gangster. Rooney's previous agent wished to retain a financial interest in Rooney's career. What happened at these meetings eventually became the subject of a court case. There were said to have been threats of blackmail and physical violence against Stretford. In the end, however, the court case collapsed because Stretford had misled the court. Whereas Stretford had told the court he became Rooney's agent in December 2002, papers presented at the trial revealed he had poached Rooney from his previous agent in September 2002.

Over the years a number of problems have arisen in connection with the work of agents. These include: an agent acting for both the player and one of the clubs in a transfer deal; touting; the use of unauthorised agents; the agent being the son of the manager of one of the clubs involved in a deal; bungs paid to one of the managers; a club being overcharged for a particular player; and a player being underpaid at his new club because of a deal between an agent and a manager.

An interesting series of transactions came to light in 2002. A leading agency involved with the transfer of footballers at the time was Proactive Sports Management. This was a company with a number of interesting shareholders. The agency represented the famous goalkeeper Peter Schmeichel, a key player at Manchester United in the year they won the treble. After spending a good number of years at Manchester United Schmeichel moved to a Portuguese team. He was then bought by Aston Villa (whose manager was John Gregory) where he only stayed for one year before moving to Manchester City (whose manager was Kevin Keegan). Proactive Sports Management handled all these transfers, presumably acting in the interests of Schmeichel, and of course their own shareholders. Amongst these shareholders were John Gregory (60,000 shares), Kevin Keegan (200,000 shares) and Peter Schmeichel (300,000 shares). Shareholders are of course rewarded with dividends, the size of which depends on the level of activity of the company. Clearly Gregory, Keegan and Schmeichel, as shareholders, will have benefited from agency fees on these transfers. The chief executive of Proactive Sports Management at the time was Paul Stretford, who was also a personal friend of John Gregory.

Kenneth Shepherd, the son of the Newcastle United chairman, at one time worked for Paul Stretford. His job title was 'business development director.' Later Kenneth Shepherd ran his own football business from the Newcastle ground. Other high profile examples of situations in which a son has had business links with a club in which his father is involved, include Darren Dein and David Dein at Arsenal, and Craig and Sam Allardyce at Bolton. Clearly transactions which involve the father having influence on the one side, and the son influence on the other side, are related-party transactions, and as such need to be reported so that all shareholders of the two companies involved are aware of the potential conflict of interest.

Football clubs have not often disclosed details of transactions in which related parties are involved. Alex Ferguson at Manchester United has in the past used the services of an agency with which his son had connections. This led to questions being asked about corporate governance matters at the club. In fact it led to questions being tabled by the two major shareholders of the club at the time, J.P. McManus and John Magnier. This controversy led to much greater openness and accountability at the club on such matters as agent fees. The 2003–04 annual report and accounts of the club revealed that in that year they had paid agent fees of £5.5 million, on total transfer fees of £49.9 million. Few other clubs are as open about the costs of transfers. Manchester United also disclosed the breakdown of costs arising in connection with a typical transfer: Gabriel Heinze moved from Paris Saint-Germain to Manchester, his French club received £5.7 million, a levy of £300,000 was paid to the Premier League (5%) and £525,000 was paid to the agents involved in the transfer of the player and in the negotiation of his new contract.

A notable concern about agent fees is the large amount of money often involved. Another concern is how much work an agent actually undertakes when a player wants to leave his existing club and another club is keen to buy the player. How could Proactive Sports Management justify a fee of £1.5 million on the Rooney transfer to Manchester United, a club he wanted to go to, and a club that wanted him? In July 2004 the Football League produced a report on agent fees (this was a report on agent fees in the Football League clubs as opposed to Premier League clubs.) It showed that in the six-month period from January to July 2004 the chairman of Barnsley sanctioned agent fees of £60,618. Barnsley were the biggest spenders in the then Second Division (now League One). Their chairman was Peter Ridsdale, the same person who helped build up debts of over £80 million at Leeds. Barnsley finished the season in the middle of the league, in twelfth place. Derby County were the biggest spenders (on agents' fees) in the First Division (now the Championship) with an outlay of £279,000. They narrowly escaped relegation from the First Division, finishing in twentieth place.

A legal case, in October 2004, did much to reveal what the judge called the 'murky world' of transfers. Fulham brought an action against their former manager Jean Tigana, alleging that the manager concealed from the club the true value of some of the players the club purchased. The directors of the club believed that as a result of the behaviour of certain players, their agents and of the Fulham manager, they overpaid for certain players. The High Court Judge having heard some of the evidence at the trial said 'This reveals some unsatisfactory facts' about these agency-club relationships and the possible conflicts of interest. 'It seems to be a pretty murky world in which all clubs and agents are lending their name to these rather bizarre transactions.'

The rules of FIFA and of the FA prohibit agents from acting for or receiving money from more than one party in any deal. It is well-known, however, that these rules can easily be circumvented. The transfer of Steve Marlet, a striker, from Auxerre to Lyon (and later to Fulham) revealed how the rules could be by-passed to the benefit of the agents, the players and possibly other parties. The agency, who were Marlet's agents, was BMB, owned by the Boisseau Brothers, Pascal and Sebastian. At the beginning of 2000 Marlet was at Auxerre, but wanted to move to another club and so BMB began the search to find a buyer. One club they spoke to was Lyon. In May 2000 the agents signed a deal with Lyon agreeing to act for the club in seeking to find a striker. Not surprisingly they found one, namely Steve Marlet. The transfer was arranged and Marlet moved to Lyon in June 2000. At one time BMB were agents for Marlet, they then subsequently became agents for the purchasing club (Lyon), they argued in court that they were not Marlet's agent at the time of the transfer.

Less than a year later Marlet wanted to move from Lyon and again he asked BMB to find him a new club. The agency first approached Liverpool, who were not interested, but Fulham were. BMB then followed their normal method of business. In the early meetings with Fulham, the brothers were agents for Marlet (on August 27 2001 BMB were still Marlet's agents). But they then signed a contract with Fulham, agreeing to act for the club. On 28 August 2007, the day BMB became Fulham's agent, the player signed for Fulham. Marlet never did well for Fulham despite the fact that they had paid Lyon £13 million for his services. BMB received a sum from Fulham which is believed to be £600,000. The club also paid Marlet £500,000 as a signing-on fee. What, if anything, Marlet paid to BMB for their services is not known.

The Fulham chairman, Mohamed Al-Fayed, brought a case against his manager, (Jean Tigana) and lost. The manager was then sacked by the club who did not pay him all that he was entitled to under his contract. This case went to court and again Al-Fayed lost. The judge (in 2006) concluded that the manager had 'behaved properly and conscientiously in his dealings with Fulham and did not act dishonourably towards the club. There is no evidence that

Mr Tigana was in general cavalier about the transfer fees for players,' it was 'always finally down to the chairman whether an agreement could be reached or not. He held the purse strings and had a final veto over any proposed transfer.' The judge added that he did not find the evidence of Mohamed Al-Fayed 'reliable.' This was not the end of the story. There were suspicious aspects of both transfers covered by the case and the agents involved were the subject of further investigation.

There are respectable agents, but also disreputable agents, this much is clear. Gordon Strachan refers to the time, whilst he was manager of Coventry City, that he had to sit in on negotiations between the club chairman, Bryan Richardson, and football agents as 'possibly the aspect of the job I found most difficult to come to terms with.' Strachan says that not all agents are bad, but some are 'dishonest and morally bankrupt.'[19] He refers to agents attempting to alter numbers on documents and squabbling one with another over who represents a player.

One English-registered agent who, even in the lax regulation of the past, was fined by the FA was Mark Curtis, who was found guilty of 'improper conduct' and making illicit payments to a player. As of the end of 2006, FIFA were still investigating the role of Curtis in the transfer of Robert Earnshaw to West Bromwich Albion in 2004. The player's agent, Mel Evans, had needed to negotiate with Mark Curtis, who was the agent for the WBA manager Gary Megson. The club were using Curtis to negotiate on their behalf. There were concerns about whose interests Curtis was really representing and how much the two agents involved in the transaction were paid. Curtis and his company, Sports Player Management, had been involved in a number of controversial deals. Curtis sold his company for £1 million, but it was later disclosed that the company had not paid all the taxes that had accrued during the time Curtis owned the company.

Very rarely do agents finish up in prison but such a situation did occur at the end of 2003. Two agents of Ronaldo (arguably the best footballer in the world at the time) were sentenced to an eleven-year prison sentence for money laundering in Brazil. With the help of others, government funds were diverted into secret bank accounts in Switzerland. A whistleblower, the disgruntled wife of one of the agents, alerted the authorities.

Controversy surrounding agents hit the headlines in January

2006 when Mick Newell, at the time manager of Luton Town, mentioned that on two occasions agents had offered him a 'bung' in connection with proposed transfers. He also said that 'a lot of people involved with the agents and doing the deals are getting backhanders. That's without question. What I suspect is that people in high places are also involved.' Later in 2006 a BBC Panorama programme on the subject of bungs even mentioned the names of two managers who they believed either directly or indirectly received financial rewards resulting from player transfers. At the time of the Panorama programme the Premier League were themselves already conducting an inquiry into agents' activities. They had appointed the distinguished Lord Stevens to head their investigation; he had previously been Commissioner of the Metropolitan Police Force.

There have of course been enquiries on agents and bungs in the past. Brian Clough had been said by Alan Sugar to 'like a bung'. It took an FA-appointed enquiry five years to report on that case. Their findings were inconclusive. The FA did, however, setup a Compliance Unit to, amongst other things, monitor transfers, but unfortunately they did not give the unit enough money to do its job properly.

From a financial point of view the most serious issue surrounding bungs is that managers, and possibly the directors of a company, may have been receiving secret payments that have not been disclosed to the shareholders of the company. If the company is listed on a stock exchange such secret payments are in breach of stock exchange rules. If, on the other hand, the company is private it is principally a matter between the owner of the club and the officials involved. Of course, the Inland Revenue are always interested in any financial rewards individuals receive that have avoided taxation. One related problem is that even if the FA (and Premier League) were to require that all the details of the transfer dealings of agents that are on their register be disclosed, this would not be sufficient. A registered agent can 'negotiate' a transfer, receive a proper fee, disclose it, pay tax on it and then quietly pay an unregistered agent any amount he wants.

One case that illustrates the sleazy world of transfers is that of David Abu, a person whom the authorities call an unlicensed agent, but who prefers to call himself a 'contact man'. Abu is an Israeli who has been active in the transfer of Israeli players to

Premier League clubs. He claims he is just a go-between who receives money from a player when he finds a club interested in the player. He makes the initial contact. Abu has been involved with the transfer of two players to Bolton Wanderers. One of the actual 'licensed agents' who officially handled these transfers, and whose name appeared on official documents, was the manager's son Craig Allardyce. The previous 'licensed agent' of one of the players was Ronen Katsan, who was furious that he had been excluded from the transfer deal. He expressed the opinion that it was not proper for a son of a manager to bring players to his father. Craig Allardyce, who received unfavourable publicity on the Panorama programme on bungs, gave up being an agent following all the criticism. The Israeli Football Association warned clubs not to deal with David Abu, but they could do little to control him as he was not a registered FIFA agent.

'Touting' is a practice that football clubs say they dislike—nevertheless for it to take place it requires at least one club to break with convention. It occurs when one club, or an agent, talks to a player already under contract about a possible move to another club. In other walks of life this is normal practice, a company will identify who is good at another company and approach that person in the hope that they will move. Head-hunters do this job. The football 'establishment' condemns it. A player cannot even discuss a move to another club without his existing employers authorisation. Such restrictions would seem bizarre to other highly paid workers. In fact the existing system is not working in football.

It is well-known that Ashley Cole had discussions with Chelsea whilst still under contract at Arsenal, and that Pini Zahavi, the Israeli-registered agent with close contacts at Chelsea, attended the meeting between the club and player. The FA could not take action against Zahavi because they only have jurisdiction over English-registered agents. The FA appealed to FIFA.

Football is now a global business and the regulation of global markets needs to be carried out at an international level. As the activities of the World Trade Organisation demonstrate this is not easy in any cross border transaction. FIFA do have a code of conduct for agents but it needs to be strengthened. FIFA publishes a list of its registered agents, and it is a vast list: as of July 2006, there were 292 from England, 333 from Spain and 369 from Italy.

These were the largest numbers by country. Among the more surprising were 43 from Israel, 54 from Bosnia-Herzegovina, 52 from Russia, 71 from Nigeria and 75 from Serbia and Montenegro—no wonder when some of these countries produce a good footballer that there are 3 or 4 agents fighting over who represents them. One wonders, too, how discriminating the FIFA regulators are when so many agents meet their criteria.

Many of the biggest transfer deals are arranged by overseas agents and domestic football associations such as the FA have in the past had no control over them. Even agents registered in Scotland have not been subject to FA control. From 2007 it is proposed that the FA will have the power to satisfy itself that all agents that operate in England, wherever they are registered, are of good character and that each transfer is conducted according to the FA's own rules. This could lead to problems with some of the FIFA-licensed agents.

Lord Stevens' enquiry investigated all 362 Premier League transfers that took place between January 2004 and January 2006. During this time it was the FA that were responsible for ensuring that these transfers were conducted properly. In December 2006 the first report was published. Even though the enquiry was in a way incomplete (they had identified 17 suspicious transactions that they wished to investigate further) they found enough evidence to enable them to be very critical of the FA in its monitoring role. They claim that the FA failed to detect numerous breaches of its own regulations, that 3 clubs (out of 29 interviewed) paid agents without an invoice being raised, 6 clubs failed to identify the name of the agent involved in a transfer, at 7 clubs there was concern over the influence of particular agents, and at 15 clubs the transfers involved failed to disclose all the payments that had been made to agents.[20]

Lord Stevens' report confirmed what most people suspected, that there was a dirty side to the transfer business. The report came up with predictable, but nevertheless worthwhile, recommendations (39 in total). These include: only the player concerned in a transfer should be allowed to remunerate his agent; the clubs involved should not influence the fee to be paid; any agent who is a close relative of a club official cannot be the player's agent and there must be a clear separation in the appointment of a player's agent and the utilisation by a club of the services of a person taking on the role of a scout, or an agent for the club. A clear set of rules is one thing, another is who is going to enforce the rules. Stevens was very critical of the work of the FA's Compliance Unit and believes that if it is to continue to take responsibility for transfers that its performance needs to be regularly reviewed.

The FA's reaction to the report was that it was not too critical of them, and that they were, in any case, planning to strengthen their own Compliance Unit (or as it was now to be called the Regulation and Compliance Unit) and to increase the resources available to the Unit to enable it to do its job professionally. They also pointed out that the 'overwhelming majority' of the recommendations of Stevens 'had already been formulated by the FA prior to the enquiry', indeed some had already been implemented and others were to be implemented from the summer 2007.

The Premier League funded Lord Stevens' enquiry, which cost in the region of £1 million. It was a report to the Premier League, who had an opportunity to discuss the report before it was released to the public. It was not really a surprise therefore that the report was critical of the FA, and that there were suggestions that the monitoring of transfers role be taken away from them. Clearly there was a conflict as to who was to be the most important governance body, but this time the battle was between the FA and the Premier League.

The role of agents will continue to be a controversial issue. Agents have an important role. They are able to argue on a player's behalf more effectively than the player. In return for this service, it is right that players should pay the agent a commission. Agents can also claim that they know the players who want to move from one country to another, or from one club to another. They can therefore provide a service to a club in helping that club find the most suitable player available in the market place. The problems arise when bungs and kickbacks are paid to distort the process (for example to keep down the salary a player is offered or to help one club to overcharge another club). Decisions made by managers, their sons, by agents and sub-agents can lead to suspicion because of the possibility that a 'related-party transaction' will result in a distorted price. Sport has proved as corrupt as any other business activity over the years.

The football industry benefits from controversies and scandals. It is all part of the entertainment. The football establishment

212

promise to do something to clean up the game, but they, as with most others involved in the game, benefit from it. The old adage 'All publicity is good publicity' applies. The simple truth is that football fans like players and managers to be interesting characters, certainly to be more interesting than the average. The television companies also like controversy in the form of disputed goals, fouls, sendings-off and grudge matches. It gives the experts something to talk about at half-time. Stories about managers receiving bungs and crooked agents are interesting. It is useful to have goodies and baddies in the entertainment business. It would be boring if everything was perfect. Certainly there are serious governance issues surrounding 'dubious and crooked agents' and managers receiving bungs, but in the grand scheme of things these are not major issues. The amount of money involved in total is not that great. The customer is being overcharged because of costs in the industry being greater than they need to be—but compared with match-fixing scandals it is not such a serious problem.

In 2006 the FA began to tighten up its rules on the employment of agents. One thing that is surprising is why it took them so long to come forward with rules which are obviously sensible and necessary. The new rules will ban members of a manager's family from acting as agents in transfers involving the manager's club. They will also ban an agent from acting for more than one party in a transfer, while foreign-registered agents will in future, if they wish to operate in England and Wales, be accountable to the FA and thus subject to the disciplinary procedure of the FA.

It is doubtful whether any set of rules will eliminate entirely the conflicts of interest in dealings with agents. For this to happen requires the honesty of, and full disclosure by, the interested parties in the transfer negotiations. There will always be those that are able to find their way around the regulations.

Match-Fixing

In order for the public to obtain satisfaction from watching football matches it is necessary for them to believe that the result is determined by the skills and effort of the players on the pitch, not by deals that have been completed before the game started. When the match-fixing scandals in Serie A in Italy became known it was

213

necessary for the football authorities in Italy and at the international level to engage in a damage limitation exercise.

This book is primarily about football in England, but what happened in Italy has lessons for the English game. To be fair to Italy, they are not the only country to be concerned about match-fixing. In Germany it has already been proven that at least one referee was accepting bribes to influence the result of matches. In 2006 match-fixing scandals were being investigated in Belgium, Finland, Russia and Portugal. The difference is that in Italy a number of the very top clubs are involved.

As John Foot explains in his entertaining book on Italian football, *Calico*[21], winning is everything in that country and it does not really matter what methods or tactics a club uses in order to win. The end justifies the means. It has been said that match-fixing is quite common in Italy. 'Eighty percent of the games in Italy are fixed' said Luciano Gaucci, the president of one club. This is widely understood and in certain situations seen as a natural part of the game. One common method of match-fixing is what is called 'settling for a draw', which could happen if it was in the interests of both clubs in a match to avoid defeat. The players would decide on the result they wanted before the kick-off, and then play out a draw. Another situation in which it is understood match-fixing might well take place is where one club has little to play for, but the win is vital to the other club. Fortunately situations in which the fixing of a particular score or result purely for betting purposes are, it is believed, much rarer.

Foot gives examples of numerous recent match-fixing incidents in Italy. In 1980 there was a major betting scandal, where a number of players were found to have been betting on the results of matches in which there were taking part. Thirty-eight people were charged with fraud (thirty-three of these were footballers.) The players had been fixing matches and betting on there own teams to lose. All the accused were let off, as Italian law did not recognise at the time 'sporting fraud' as a crime. The law was changed in 1986, but this did not prevent betting scandals occurring again in 1986, 1990 and then again in 2004. These scandals harmed the reputation of Italian football.

Italian football has had so many scandals and yet the fans still support their team and the country continues to produce great footballers. In June 2005 the authorities found Genoa guilty of fixing the result of a crucial promotion match against Venezia, and the club were sent down to Serie C1. Foot makes the comment that the Genoa scandal meant that 'for the fifth time in 24 years, betting, match-fixing and financial scandals had brought the Italian football championship into question. The system was rotten.' In fact, the biggest scandal occurred twelve months later.

Accusations about this particular match-fixing 'arrangement' had first been made in 2004. It was said that Luciano Moggi, the General Manager of AC Milan, had been requesting specific referees for matches involving his club. He had not only made such requests for Serie A matches, but also for at least one UEFA Champions League match (against a Swedish team in 2004). One of the officials involved with allocating referees to matches in Italy, Pierluigi Pairetto, was also vice president of the UEFA refereeing commission. The subsequent Italian investigators found evidence to support these claims of match-fixing involving at least four clubs.

Italian investigators engaged in monitoring phone calls had recorded conversations between officials at certain leading Italian clubs and officials at the body responsible for allocating referees to particular matches. In Italy the mechanism for the selection of referees is 'fiendishly complicated and ever in flux' and is the subject of much debate. After scandals in the 1980s a very fair system was introduced—a ballot to determine who refereed a particular match—but the big clubs did not like it, as their psychological 'power' was reduced They succeeded in ending the ballot and introducing a system in which a 'technical committee' decided which referees would look after which matches. The members of the committee were ex-referees, and were called 'designators'. Further changes led to the re-introduction, in July 2005, of an old version of the 'designated' system, in which there was now only one designator, an ex-referee—Maurizio Mattes. This was the mechanism that led to the problems in 2006. Juventus, AC Milan and two other clubs were found guilty of persuading the officials responsible for allocating referees to be favourable to their cause.[22]

Although only four clubs were found guilty, there are many people involved with the game who say that what was discovered is only the tip of the iceberg. In fact there is a long history of referees favouring one side or the other in Italian football. John Foot in his book has a chapter on dodgy refereeing. In one section of the chapter entitled 'The Great Robberies', he gives three cases of 'thievery', where the referee decided the result of matches through either awarding or not awarding penalty decisions—all involved Juventus. As Foot explains, 'for the Italian football fan, the referee is always corrupt, unless proven otherwise.' What has to be discovered is how he is corrupt, in favour of whom, and why.

In Italy there is a strong conviction that the government, its rules and regulations, are flexible entities, ready to be flouted and challenged. This helps explain a related scandal, namely the relatively light sentences handed out for cheating. In July 2006 the clubs involved appealed against their original sentences, with the result that Juventus still had the title of Serie A champions for 2005–6 taken from them, and were still relegated to Serie B, but their starting points deduction was cut from 30 to 17. Of the other clubs AC Milan remained in Serie A (with their point deduction reduced from 15 to 8) and Fiorentina and Lazio were reprieved of the relegation to Serie B, and were deducted 19 and 11 points respectively. The official final league positions for 2005–06 were altered to reflect the outcome of the fixed matches. It was a whitewash, with sporting interests secondary to monetary ones.[23]

The Serie A clubs are all big earners with sizeable TV contracts and powerful owners. The moral is 'if you are big enough you can get away with cheating'. The Italian magistrate in charge of the investigation did later widen his enquiries to include a number of other clubs, including three more from Serie A, as well as 26 officials, referees and linesmen who were required to appear before the Sports Tribunal.

In Italy the 2006 cheating incident rumbled on. Silvio Berlusconi criticised the process through which punishments were being decided. He said 'We can't penalise the fans. The individuals should be punished, not the clubs. We cannot accept quick and summary verdicts. They would only damage the fans and people working for TV.' The TV comment was interesting, for as well as owning AC Milan, Berlusconi owns TV stations. Guido Rossi, head of the Italian FA, did not agree, 'I don't care what Berlusconi says. Clubs can be considered as responsible for the situation we found since starting the investigation. Those who enter the world of football have to accept its rules. This is the biggest crisis Italian football has ever faced. The biggest problem is that people who were supposed to control the whole system were controlled by those people they were supposed to control.'

An even worse case of spineless behaviour by regulators was the reaction of UEFA to the match-fixing. The question they had to consider was whether AC Milan would be allowed to participate in the 2006–07 Champions League. Even though UEFA accepted that the Italian club had caused damage to the reputation of European football, they allowed them to take part in the Champions League. UEFA's explanation was that they could not legally bar AC Milan from the competition. Their statement said that AC Milan had taken 'advantage of the fact that UEFA lacks the legal grounds to refuse the club's admission. In this respect, AC Milan is herewith informed that the necessary adaptation will be made to the regulations concerned. The UEFA Emergency Panel is deeply concerned that AC Milan has created the impression of being involved in the improper influencing of the regular course of matches in the Italian football championship.'[24]

The only punishment UEFA imposed was that Milan had to enter at the beginning of the competition, in other words the third qualifying round. So UEFA, after talking big about the competition being 'theirs', and about being the top regulators of European football, had to admit that the only option open to them was to decide at what stage a team entered the competition. AC Milan went on to win the 2006–07 Champions Leage.[25]

The wire tapping of football clubs in Italy revealed a sinister side of the club Lazio. In October 2006 Italian police issued arrest warrants on certain individuals connected with the club for alleged extortion and insider dealing in the club's shares. Four individuals had threatened to kill the club's president, Claudio Lotito, and his wife. Many fans were not happy with the club's performance and they and certain businessmen wanted to take the club over. It was unclear whether the four thugs were connected with any of these businessmen. One consortium trying to take over Lazio was fronted by Giorgio Chinaglia, a former Italian footballer. It was thought, however, that the 'Mr Big' behind his consortium was a leading member of the Mafia. Chinaglia was a colourful figure who had played for Lazio in the 1970s. The players in that 1970s team were self-declared fascists and gun-toting parachute enthusiasts. They were armed and dangerous. They fought opposing teams on and off the field. Chinaglia said 'I used to carry a pistol ... it could have been useful. But I didn't buy it for self-defence. With Lazio we were nearly all armed. It was fun, a game.' Chinaglia did say that he was not involved with the threat to kill the club's president. 'I have never been involved in extortion.' Lazio had experienced many previous scandals. In 1980 the club were relegated from Serie A as a result of a number of their players being involved in match-fixing.

The 2006 Italian match-fixing scandal had unexpected implications for football in England. UEFA was seeking to ensure that similar match-fixing did not occur elsewhere, and so examined the system whereby referees were allocated to matches in other countries. They criticised the system in use in England, in particular the fact that both the Premier League and the Football League have a one third share in the body that regulates referees in England, the Professional Game Match Officials (PGMO). The other one third is held by the FA. UEFA are correct in pointing out that in terms of risk management this is dangerous; either the Premier League or the Football League could use their influence within the PGMO to affect the appointment of referees to particular games. It was precisely this situation that led to the corruption in Italy. UEFA pointed out that the approach adopted in England was a breach of UEFA and FIFA statutes. UEFA want only the FA to be responsible for appointing referees. They first pointed out this problem in 2003, but nothing was done to change it.

Other domestic leagues also have dubious reputations when it comes to footballing improprieties. In China, the football governing body (CFA) has been accused of complicity in match-fixing, bribe taking and gambling. In games that have involved some of the top clubs the players have walked off the pitch in protest at dubious refereeing decisions. The manager of the top Beijing club stated that the league competition is ruined by 'faked matches, black whistles, illegal betting on games and other ugly phenomena.' Supporters often vote with their feet, staying away from matches they believe are fixed.

Every year there are one or two stories about corruption and betting somewhere in the world.[26] A UEFA Cup match (Group D) in December 2004 between a Greek side, Panionios, and the Georgian club Dinamo Tbilsi, was alleged to have been fixed. The Greek side won by the unusual score of 5–2, and there had been an unusual pattern of betting before the match on that precise score. Even more remarkable was that the Greek side had been losing 1–0 at half time, and many of the winning bets had also correctly forecast the half time score. A number of bookmakers who had been receiving bets on this match from all over the world became suspicious and stopped taking bets on the result. One bookmaker said the betting 'stank to high heaven.'

Towards the end of the 2004, cases of match-fixing in Germany came to light. Fourteen players and at least four referees were accused. The suspects were under investigation for manipulating the results of at least ten matches in the first, second and third divisions as well as the German Cup. The scandal came to light when one of the four referees involved, Robert Hoyzer, admitted that he had rigged matches. His refereeing came under suspicion following one particular cup match between second division Hamburg and a minor regional side Paderborn. The hot favourites Hamburg lost 4–2. The bribery and betting coup associated with this match was thought to have been organised by Croatian gamblers. Robert Hoyzer, the referee, was given a lifetime ban by the German Football Association and jailed for two years five months. The German FA filed a £1.2 million claim against him. Undoubtedly there has been match-fixing in Germany, what is not known is the extent of the problem.

There are even suggestions of corruption involving the club that were the 2004 European Champions, namely Porto. At the end of 2004 the chairman of the club was bailed after being accused of two cases of influencing referees, and two cases of sports corruption. The Portuguese domestic league is being investigated by the police.

In England there have been proven and alleged instances of match-fixing by players, but there has never been the suggestion that referees were involved in such activities. It has often been noticed that referees rarely give penalties against Manchester United at Old Trafford, but that is put down to intimidation. (This was nothing compared with the great Inter-Milan team of the 1960s that went 100 league games without conceding a penalty.) In Italy it seems to be accepted that referees favour the big clubs. The match-fixing cases that have been discovered in England involve individual players that have been associated with betting. Even as long ago as 1882 the then Birmingham Football Association was being told that betting was the greatest evil it faced. The FA ruled that 'neither officials nor players shall make bets on any football match, and clubs are required to take reasonable measures to prevent gambling by spectators.' The rule was not consistently enforced. It was not possible to stop players and officials betting on 'any' match.

One hundred years later Harry Redknapp, at the time manager of West Ham United, writing in the *Racing Post* on the subject of the match-fixing trial of Bruce Grobbelaar, expressed the view that 'I can't believe they're considering stopping players and managers from betting, where's the harm in it? It's not as if I am betting against my own side, which is definitely not on.' Graham Sharpe in his review of over a century of betting in football in England has found numerous examples of officials and players quite openly discussing bets they have placed on football matches in which they or their teams were involved.'[27] Steve Claridge, a colourful footballer who has played for a number of clubs and scored many important goals, confesses in the first chapter of his autobiography entitled *A Gambling Man* that he has lost over £300,000 as a result of gambling. Claridge even relates that sometimes he needed to move from one club to another so that he could obtain a share of the transfer fee to pay off his gambling debts. There are a number of well-known English club managers who it is known bet on football matches and the results of competitions, but hopefully not matches involving their own club.

Between 1993–94 Bruce Grobbelaar, John Fashanu and Hans Segars, all Premier League players, are alleged to have thrown games involving either Liverpool, Southampton or Wimbledon. In January 1997 Grobbelaar was tried on a charge of corruption and of conspiring with Fashanu and a Malaysian businessman to fix the results of certain football matches. Grobbelaar was also charged with accepting a £2,000 bribe to throw a match. It was the *Sun* newspaper that first obtained evidence that they claim revealed Grobbelaar accepting a bribe, as well as talking about deliberately losing at least three matches. The jury at the first trial could not agree on a verdict, and so a second trial took place. In this second trial the jury found the defendants not guilty on the corruption charge, but could not agree on the Bruce Grobbelaar bribery charge. The case was therefore dismissed.

Reaction to this verdict was mixed. Grobbelaar sued the *Sun* for libel over the match-fixing charges. He was worried about his reputation. He won the case and was awarded £85,000. The *Sun* then appealed and the Court of Appeal overturned the libel verdict.

The case then went to the House of Lords, which reinstated the guilty libel verdict. The Law Lords agreed that Grobbelaar had taken money from gamblers, but did not believe that it had been proven that he had been involved in corruption, in fixing matches. The judges, however, regarded Grobbelaar's reputation as more or less 'worthless' and awarded him damages of only £1. The Law Lords said that Grobbelaar had acted in a way that, if not exposed and stamped on, would undermine the integrity of the game.

It seems now to be accepted that Grobbelaar talked about throwing matches and that he accepted money to do so. No evidence could be produced, however, to prove that he actually did deliberately let in goals in order to throw matches. He was therefore either so good at hiding the fact that he was deliberately letting in goals that he could mislead the experts, or he planned to throw matches but did not actually want to do so when the time came.

The Law Lords were of the opinion that the player had undermined the integrity of the game by 'acting in a way which no decent or honest footballer would act.' The Lords decided that Grobbelaar should pay the £500,000 legal costs of the *Sun*, but he was unable to do so and was officially declared bankrupt. Whatever the truth, the publicity was not good for football.

Of course, match-fixing in England is not new, but the scale and international aspects of the money involved has changed. In the 1960s there were a number of match-fixing scandals. Eamon Dunphy, a retired player and journalist, claimed 'Manchester United players did conspire to fix the result of at least three games during the 1960–63 period.'[28] In 1965 ten players were jailed for conspiracy to rig matches. The three high-profile players, all from Sheffield Wednesday, were Tony Kay, Peter Swan (both England internationals) and and David Layne. Each of these three were jailed for four months for attempting to prevent their own team winning so that they could pull off a betting coup.[29] They each made a gain of £100 as a result of their team losing a match. Apparently at the time a network of players existed who were willing to throw matches.

Football and Gangsters is the title of a book by Graham Johnson.[30] The book deals with how gangsters have, on occasion, represented, blackmailed or been associates of certain players. In a way, such connections are bound to develop, the top footballers (and many gangsters) are high living, glamorous figures, very interested in money. They are bound to come together. The issue of gangsters controlling football, as opposed to controlling certain players, is a bigger and more important issue.[31] Ultimate control is of course at boardroom level, at ownership level, at FIFA, FA and Premier League level. The term 'gangsters' is also a misleading expression these days, as many criminals who break the law are now more likely to be businessmen than members of a gang. These criminals can do more harm controlling or influencing the game at boardroom or committee room level than the gangsters can working through players and their agents. We know that some agents are criminals. We also know that some players and some referees accept bribes to throw matches. We know that in some countries executives of clubs have been known to attempt to fix the result of games. What we are not so aware of is corruption at boardroom and committee room level, or the details of how dirty money is being used to purchase clubs.

Football and Politics

It is not only gamblers that have influenced the results of games, it is also politicians. Football has in the past been used by politicians to help boost their popularity, or to help promote an ideology. When in 2006 Italy won the World Cup it was correctly reported that this was the fourth time they had done so. What was forgotten was that on the first two occasions, in 1934 and 1938, they were helped greatly by favourable decisions by referees. Benito Mussolini, who was Prime Minister, wanted Italy to win to help show the world the superiority of his fascist regime. He was able to influence the decisions as to who would referee Italy's crucial games. The referee was bought.

A fact that football fans are well aware of is that Real Madrid won the European Cup in the first five years in which the tournament was held (starting 1955–56). What few are aware of is that they would probably not have been so successful without the support of General Francisco Franco. Franco manipulated football competitions and used Real's success to help his own personal ambitions. At the end of the Second World War, Spain was a poor country, it was fascist, and was not well respected internationally.

222

Franco saw football as a means of improving Spain's image in the world and increasing his popularity at home. Not only did he promote the Spanish national team, he promoted his chosen team. In 1955 he awarded all of the Real Madrid players the Imperial Order of Merit, a very distinguished honour. No such award was given to the team from the socialist city of Barcelona even though they had also won the cup. The president of Barcelona football club had been murdered in 1936, and it was said Franco and the fascists were responsible for this. When it became known that the great footballer De Stafano was willing to move from Columbia to play in Spain, Franco became involved. He worked behind the scenes to make sure that the player was transferred to his club Real Madrid rather than the club identified with his political opposition, Barcelona. He welcomed refugees from the communist countries of Central and Eastern Europe, particularly quality footballers who wanted to play for Real Madrid. The success of Real Madrid in European competitions is therefore due partly to political factors. Similar stories can be told about football in a number of countries.

At times the dark side of football is hidden away, over time it is soon forgotten.

8

Why Manchester United?

It is often assumed that Manchester United have a long and distinguished history and that Manchester City have always been the 'junior' team in that city. This is not the case. In the inter-war period, City were far more successful than United. In the 20 seasons between 1919–1939 Manchester United finished the season in a higher place in the league than Manchester City on only 3 occasions. In fact United spent nine of these seasons in the then Second Division. In one season, 1936–1937, Manchester City were First Division champions and in other seasons they finished second, third, fourth and fifth. The highest position Manchester United achieved during this time was ninth in the First Division. Clearly Manchester City during this period were the top team in the city while Manchester United were a below average team.

In terms of support Manchester City were also more successful. In most seasons City attracted a larger average gate than United. In 1936–37, when both clubs played in the top division, there was not a big difference in the size of the gates of the two teams. Manchester City attracted an average of 35,000, and Manchester United an average of 32,000. Remarkably, in 1938–39, a season when City were in the Second Division, they had higher average attendance figures than United, who were in the First Division. (It should be appreciated that at that time neither Manchester teams were attracting the largest crowds in the country. In the years just before the Second World War it was Arsenal and Aston Villa that attracted the largest gates—with Everton and Chelsea not far behind. Manchester was not a leading football centre.)

City fans have argued for a long time that their club is the true club of Manchester. In 2005 an advertising campaign involving City revolved around the notion of the club as 'pure' Manchester and 'real' Manchester. Historically, City were Manchester's big club.

Why, after the Second World War, did Manchester City drift? And what did Manchester United do that led to them becoming one of the top three or four clubs in the world?

Manchester City

In the 1880s, in the pioneering days of football clubs, a group of enthusiasts formed a team that became Gorton AFC. In 1887 the name was changed to Ardwick FC. In 1892 the club was admitted to the Second Division of the Football League and in 1894 they changed their name to Manchester City FC. In their early days they were successful. They attracted to the club an outstanding young footballer, William Meredith. On home match days Meredith would travel the 60 or so miles from his home in Wales to play for Manchester City and then return home after the match. As well as playing football, Meredith would work 75 hours each week down a coalmine.

Manchester City built up a good team and they won the FA Cup in 1904. They were the first Manchester team to win the cup. Unfortunately, in 1906 all the players, some of the club's directors and the club secretary, were banned from football after the FA found that certain players had been receiving illegal payments as bonuses. The specific game that caused the problems was the final match of the 1904–05 season. If Manchester City had won at Aston Villa they would have been First Division champions. The game turned out to be a dirty affair, with a number of fights breaking out between players. Aston Villa won 3–2. Rumours circulated that Aston Villa players had been offered money to throw the game. Meredith was suspended—he denied the accusation—but later changed his story. He admitted to offering an Aston Villa player £10, but he claimed to only do this on instructions from his manager. An investigation found that in addition to paying players bonuses, the directors had also paid senior players above the agreed maximum weekly wage and that they had paid 'amateurs' a wage. Money was important in the sport even at that time. Manchester City were not the only team to make such payments but they were the first club who were caught.

In 1914 one of the directors of the club was Albert Alexander, whose son 50 years later became chairman. The club moved to

Maine Road in 1923 to what was one of the first really big provincial football grounds. In 1925–26 the team were without a manager so Albert Alexander took on the job—he did so well that the team got to the FA Cup Final. In 1934 they attracted a record crowd of over 84,000 to their cup-tie against Stoke City. They were a wealthy club and signed a number of top players. Unfortunately for them, they were relegated at the end of the 1937–38 season, and so started the first season after the 1939–45 War in the Second Division.

When City moved to their impressive new Maine Road stadium, gypsies were moved off the land to make way for the stadium and it is said they put a curse on the club. Perhaps the curse worked because after the Second World War, apart from a brief period in the late 1960s and early 1970s, the club has not been successful. Gypsies also cursed Birmingham City's ground and they too have under-performed. At both Manchester City and Birmingham City, however, the gypsies have had more than a little help from club directors.

Manchester City have been an up-and-down team over the last 50 years, being relegated from the top division on 6 occasions. They have, however, had periods of success; they won the FA Cup in 1956 and 1969, and were First Division champions in 1967–68 (with Manchester United in second place). In 1976–77 they finished second in the First Division and fourth the following season. The success City did enjoy in the late 1960s was based on a very successful partnership at manager level. The flamboyant Malcolm Allison and the reliable Joe Mercer had a board of directors that supported them. When Joe Mercer was appointed manager in 1965, the chairman was Albert Alexander's son. He was bringing to an end 'the Alexander regime'; a period during which the club had enjoyed some success but one in which towards the end the success was overshadowed by that of Manchester United.[1]

During the 1971–72 season, Allison and Mercer fell out with each other. The board were divided. When Peter Swales joined the board he acted as arbitrator between the two battling groups and shortly afterwards became chairman, with Allison the sole manager. Joe Mercer moved to Coventry City to be manager of that club.

Since that time the club has had over 15 managers with an average stay of only 2 years. (Allison was soon unhappy, partly because of politics at board level. He left the club.) Swales appointed a new manager, Ron Saunders (later of Aston Villa and Birmingham City). Peter Swales now controlled the club, he had purchased 30% of the company's shares and a friend, Stephen Boler, owned another 30%, with a brewery, Greenalls, owning 20%. Soon Ron Saunders left and Howard Kendall became the manager. At first the club under Kendall was moderately success-ful, but then their performance fell away. One team manager soon followed another. With Peter Reid as manager the club finished in fifth place in the Premier League in 1990–91 and 1991–92 (their highest placed finish for many years). In 1993 Swales appointed John Maddock, a tabloid journalist, as general manager and this led to the removal of Reid.

Swales worked hard to make Manchester City a successful club, but he did not make himself popular. One decision with which he was involved, which would eventually lead to his departure from the club, was the sale of one of the club's players, Francis Lee. Lee was very popular with the fans and did not want to leave the club. There are many who believe that it was Swales, and not the manager, who was responsible for the decision to sell the player. Francis Lee is alleged to have told Swales, 'You will regret the day you sold me.' He did.

Manchester City went through a period in which they were 'badly run by a succession of boards, more concerned with feuding and sacking managers than winning football matches.' They con-tinued to under-perform and to adopt the standard solution to overcome this problem: change managers.

When Francis Lee ended his football career he became a very successful businessman with wealthy friends. He did not like to see Manchester City in difficulties and he did not like Swales. In 1993 he launched a take-over bid for control of the club. Swales was defeated, but not before a nasty and wasteful battle. Lee became chairman and the largest shareholder, owning just over 13% of the shares. When Lee took over the club, his first priority was to stay in the Premiership. This they achieved but only for a short period. There were many who believed that now the 15 wasted years of Swales were finally over, but this was not the case. The club were relegated in 1995–96. In 1998 the power at the club changed once again when John Wardle and David Melkin became major shareholders. Francis Lee was replaced as chairman by David Bernstein, who had been the club's financial advisor. The club were promoted back to the Premiership in 1999–2000 but relegated again the following year. They then appointed Kevin Keegan as manager, and in the 2001–02 season were promoted back to the Premiership.

In 2003 Bernstein resigned as chairman following a dispute with the manager and with other key directors. Keegan thought that Bernstein was too conservative, that he would not spend enough in the transfer market, and that he was not ambitious enough. This despite the fact that the club had spent £46 million to purchase 17 players in the short period between the time Keegan became manager and Bernstein's resignation. The annual wage bill rose from £24 million to £35 million. Manchester City in fact needed to be careful for they had taken out a long-term loan with a US bank for an amount in the region of £59 million.

With the club moving to an impressive new stadium (built for the Commonwealth Games) in 2003–04, once again many supporters believed the dark days were now at last over, but unfortunately they were not. Keegan spent a lot of money on new players, but the club were still not successful. It was thought that the extra revenue the club would generate when they moved into their new 'large' stadium would cover the cost of borrowing. The actual revenue they could generate depended, however, upon football success. Unfortunately, Keegan did not bring them success and he resigned in 2005.

The quotes from some of those involved in the boardroom squabbles throughout the 1990s give a feeling of the depth of the emotions of those involved, and of the problems of the club: 'I lost a 30-year friendship with Peter Swales because I believed the time had come for a change.' 'I now think that Peter was worth twenty Francis Lees.' 'Lee was supposed to be coming into the club on a white charger. He is riding around on a donkey now.' (Freddie Pye in 1996.) 'I've played in the World Cup, sweated out multi-million-pound business deals. I've trained some good horses and I'm a father. Yet 90 minutes at Maine Road can make me feel like an old dish-rag.' (Francis Lee, on being chairman of Manchester City, 1997.) Joe Royle said, on becoming Manchester City's seventeenth manager in 25 years, 'It is a massive club. It is just a bit sickly.' Frank Clarke expressed stronger views just before he resigned as manager in 1998, 'It will take a very, very long time to sort things out. It's a rat infested place.'[2] In such a business situation it is not surprising the club were underachievers.

In 2006 John Wardle and David Melkin (who together founded the sports goods company J.D. Sports, but sold their interest in that company in 2005) owned 29.95% of the club's shares, but Francis Lee still owned 7.13%. BSkyB owned 9.9% of the shares. In 2005 the club had the fourth highest level of net debt in the league, with £64 million of loans plus £35 million of financial lease obligations relating to the City of Manchester Stadium. The club have a 250-year lease on the stadium, but do not own it. They will be able to play at the stadium for a long time, and the cost of doing so is not high, the annual lease payments being only in the region of £1.7 million. If the club can become successful they will be able to generate high levels of match day revenue. In 2004–05 the average home crowd was 45,192, the third highest in the Premiership. Nevertheless this figure is still far behind the attendance figures of their local rival. With Stuart Pearce having been appointed manager, and with some stability at boardroom level, 2005–06 looked promising, but unfortunately once again the club underachieved. 2006–07 was another disappointing season, at the end of which Pearce was sacked.[3]

The 'story' of the City of Manchester Stadium is notable in itself. It shows how a local authority using public sector money can work in partnership with its local football club to the benefit of both parties. It is a story familiar in the US. When in 2002 the Commonwealth Games were held in Manchester a new sports stadium suitable for athletics was built. It was paid for entirely with public money, the largest contribution towards the cost being £77 million of lottery money that was made available through Sport England. The city of Manchester initially claimed that if allowed to host the Commonwealth Games they would break even financially, but they failed to achieve this goal. The Games were not a financial success and the organisers needed to be bailed out with an additional £100 million of public money. The City Council put in £50 million of this additional money, Sport England another £30 million and the UK Government £20 million.

There was always a question as to what would happen to the new stadium after the event. Manchester City Council approached Manchester City FC to see if they were prepared to make use of it;

the club said that they were, subject to certain quite demanding conditions. They wanted the stadium to be adapted so that it would be suitable for football, they wanted it to be recognised as the permanent home for the club, and they made it clear that they were only prepared to pay a comparatively small amount of money for its use. The club argued that they already had a perfectly good ground at Maine Road that seated 34,000 and that if they stayed at their present home all the revenue they generated belonged to them. The 'Commonwealth Stadium' had a capacity of 48,000 and so they argued it was only the additional net income resulting from the extra 14,000 seats that should be shared with Sports England and the City Council. They were arguing that they should pay no rent at all for the use of the new ground until crowds were above the Maine Road capacity. Sports England and the City Council were in a weak bargaining position with no other tenants for the new stadium and so they agreed the terms. Therefore in 2003 Manchester City moved into a large new stadium paid for with lottery and public sector money.[4]

This case illustrates the difficulty of valuing a sports stadium. As a stadium, it could be hard or impossible to sell; nobody wanted to buy it off the City Council. It is basically the land that has a market value, and that value depends upon location. The old ground at Maine Road was valued in the football club's accounts at £28 million, but it turned out that nobody would pay the club that amount for the asset. The City Council took over the Maine Road property and made it available to a rugby club, who attracted crowds of only about 3,000.

Although in the US it is quite common for a city to build and pay for a new stadium in order to attract a club, the financial arrangements are rarely as generous as that enjoyed by Manchester City. The new stadium was paid for entirely from public money. There were aspects of the financial arrangement that were disturbing. A number of other football clubs moved into new stadiums at about the same time as Manchester City, including Southampton, Leicester and Derby County. None of these other clubs received such large amounts of public money. They were required to spend their own money to finance their developments. Only Manchester City received what is in effect a huge public subsidy, with the result that they will be able to spend a higher percentage of the revenue they generate each year on buying new players and paying high wages. The other clubs, by contrast, will be forced to spend their money on loan interest payments. In the US, the NFL have been worried for some time about the move by certain big cities to finance new stadiums in order to either tempt a new football franchise to the city, or to give extra support to an existing franchise. The NFL banned football clubs from moving into new stadiums that were entirely publicly financed, and now require at least half the costs to be paid for by the football club. The NFL, as has been stated previously, are an organisation interested in creating conditions that result in balanced competition and would not have allowed a club in their league to have been treated so favourably as have Manchester City. Nevertheless, the club was still not in a good position from a financial point of view, with debts in 2006 of over £50 million, plus hire purchase liabilities of a similar amount. Not surprisingly there were rumours in 2006 that the owners were willing to sell the club.[5] In 2007 they did sell, to the ex-Prime Minister of Thailand.

Manchester United

Much has been written about Manchester United; more, certainly, than any other English club. Most of what is written is just 'bland' material for the fans, but the literature does include some serious pieces of work on the club, its history and the people involved. It is interesting that, within the more scholarly work, there is strong disagreement on the contribution of the directors of the club to the team's success.[6] Everyone agrees that much of the success is due to the two outstanding managers, Matt Busby and Alex Ferguson, but there is disagreement over whether or not the two most prominent chairmen of the club, Louis Edwards and his son, Martin Edwards, are heroes or villains. (A further area of disagreement is over whether or not the relationship between the chairmen and their managers has helped or hindered the club.) Most people outside the debate, and aware of the success of the club since the 1950s, would find it hard to believe that the two chairmen were not key contributors to this success, but there are those who disagree with this interpretation of events.

Louis Edwards is sometimes described as the dynamic force

behind the post-war development of United, but he is seen by others as a dishonest operator. Martin Edwards is seen by some as a wise chairman who attracted a group of directors to the board who were able to help the club take advantage of the opportunities opening up in football. 'If United has been in the right place at the right time, it has also had men at the helm who have been able to exploit the opportunities created by others.' Others see Martin Edwards as lucky. His father, after all, obtained a place for him on the board.

Manchester United were not founder-members of the Football League. In the early 1900s the club then known as Newton Heath was nearly bankrupt. An autocratic local businessman, J.H. Davies, saved them. He changed the name of the club and moved them to Old Trafford. In 1915 the club were faced with relegation to the Second Division, (second tier). At that time a group of Manchester United players bribed some Liverpool players in order to make sure United won a crucial match. Manchester won the game, but the FA investigated and nine players, some from each side, were suspended.

In the 1919–1939 period, the club were relegated to the Second Division on three occasions, and in 1934 nearly relegated to the Third Division. Manchester United were, at that time, a second rate club. In October 1930, over 3,000 fans held a meeting and passed a motion of no confidence in the board of the club. In 1931, with the team floundering in the Second Division, the club's bank refused to advance them money so that they could pay the players' wages. The club had debts of £30,000 (a comparatively large sum at the time). This is not the distinguished history one would expect of the club that by the year 2000 was the 'biggest' in the world.

In 1931, for a second time, a local businessman saved them. This time it was James Gibson, who was the director of a local clothing firm. He paid the wages that were due to the players, arranged for new shares to be issued and initiated a public appeal for money. In fact Manchester City helped raise funds to save Manchester United. James Gibson became chairman and helped build up a solid base for United. When Gibson died Harold Hardman, who had a reputation for being tough but honest, became the next chairman. He had been a footballer, which meant he had an opinion on most footballing matters and because of this Matt

233

Busby, who became manager of the club in 1945, did not find it easy to get on with him. 'Hardman never succumbed to Matt's charm.'

What made Manchester United a cult team? It must be remembered that in the 1919–39 period they were a poor team, both from a playing and financial point of view. By 1938, however, they had benevolent owners, an efficient secretary, and a farsighted management team. All of which are necessary ingredients for success in any industry. They established a junior football club in 1938 in order to produce good young players. This turned out to be an extremely significant decision in helping them produce outstanding teams. But perhaps most important of all, the directors appointed an outstanding manager.

The Busby Era

During the period that Matt Busby had been a player for Liverpool, before the Second World War, Manchester United's directors recognised his outstanding teaching and coaching ability, not to mention his strength of character. Initially they wanted to sign him as their football coach, but Busby wanted to be the team manager. This led to some disagreement at board level, but the decision James Gibson and his fellow directors eventually made resulted in a turning point for Manchester United. If Busby had remained at Liverpool or even returned to his old club Manchester City, football history in the second half of the twentieth century would have looked very different.

The Busby era, which began when he was appointed manager in 1945, turned out to be remarkable. With Busby in charge Manchester United immediately began to win trophies. They won the FA Cup in 1948. In the first five post-war seasons, they finished as runner up of the First division on four occasions. Busby had inherited a number of good players, but he also purchased wisely and soon had begun to develop his own young 'Babes'. The club were champions of the First Division in 1951–52, 1955–56 and in 1956–57. In 1957, at a time when the average age of the team was only 22, they took part in the then new European Cup competition (now the UEFA Champions League) against the wishes of the English football establishment. The champions of the previous season, Chelsea, had been instructed by the FA not to take part in the European competition.

Manchester United was one of the few clubs to realise the opportunities offered by European football. When they played their first match in the European Cup, in September 1956, they played on the Manchester City ground; their own ground did not have floodlights. There were many who did not think the game would attract much attention, but 43,635 people attended. For their next match in the tournament, again taking place at Maine Road, the attendance was 75,598. Manchester United lost in the semi-finals of the cup to Real Madrid, who were the dominant team in Europe at the time.

The club were again involved in European competition in 1958 but this time tragedy struck. The plane in which they were returning home from a fixture in the former-Yugoslavia, crashed in Münich. This disaster destroyed the so-called 'Busby Babes'—eight of the team were killed and Matt Busby was badly injured, but recovered. The sympathies of the nation were with Manchester United after the crash. The tragedy in Münich affected United in many ways. If the 'Busby Babes' had been able to stay together as a team they would probably have dominated English football, and possibly Europe, for a decade. Partly because of the deaths of so many talented players they did not dominate, but the disaster did have an unexpected consequence. As Mihir Bose points out, 'Manchester United were a well respected club before Münich, but the air crash elevated them on to a different level.' Bose was referring in particular to Manchester United's international reputation, which has meant so much to the value of their brand.

It is true that Manchester United became known around the world, but in order to maintain and build on that recognition it was necessary for the club to be well managed and to take advantage of any opportunities that arose. To maintain the value of the brand name it was necessary to have continuing success. In 1964–65 and, again in 1966–67, the club were the First Division champions, and in 1968 they won the European Cup—the first English club to do so. This brought the Busby era to a glorious end.

Szymanski and Kuypers believe that a period of consistent above average performance of a football club derives 'from the possession of a distinctive capability.' One type of distinctive capability they identify is a strategic asset.[7] An example of a strategic asset, in

Manchester United's case, would be Matt Busby. He took a 'middling' club and turned it into a world class one. During his period as manager Busby built up three outstanding championship teams. Szymanski and Kuypers point out that Busby had from the beginning made it clear to the club directors that he was in charge, although he did need the support of the directors in order to purchase players in the transfer market, and to develop the stadium. After Busby retired the club went through 20 lean years, with a succession of managers who spent money on transfers and wages but did not achieve success.

There was, however, a darker side to Manchester United's success story under Busby. In the 1950s and 1960s the players at Manchester United were not treated well. Jackie Blanchflower, who had been injured in the 1958 Münich crash, believed that the club were mean to the players that had been injured. The players who survived the crash but could not play football anymore received only £5,000 each (less any tax liability) from an insurance policy. Those who could continue to play received no compensation. The club did not provide any of the widows of the deceased players with a pension. The players who lived in clubhouses, but were not able to continue with their football careers after the crash, were required within a short period of time to move out of these houses. This was particularly hard on players such as Johnny Berry, who suffered very bad injuries as a result of the crash. Berry wanted to continue playing football, but his injuries were so bad he was not able to do so. The club officials soon phoned to tell him the clubhouse in which he lived had to be vacated.[8]

Another criticism of Manchester United, and of Matt Busby in particular, was that the club had been involved in making payments to the parents of talented youngsters in order to encourage them to sign forms to join United rather than another club. Such payments fell foul of the FA's rules. The club, in order to make such payments and in order to keep them 'secret', made adjustments in their annual financial accounts. In their defence, United could argue that many other clubs were doing the same thing, and that they needed to do so in order to compete.

Another aspect of the dark side to the club was that in the 1960s and 1970s Manchester United had the worst behaved fans in the country. They 'pioneered' the hooligan movement in English football. In 1968, when they were competing in the European Cup semi-final, a brick was thrown at the opposing team's goalkeeper. Ten years later the fans were still at it: in 1977–78 the fans rioted at a game in France and the club were banned from European competition (later changed to a fine).

The Edwards Contribution

Busby was clearly an outstanding manager, but to be successful he needed the support of the directors of the club. Immediately after the Münich crash, a new director, Louis Edwards, joined the board. He would have a profound influence on the future of the club.

Matt Busby was manager from 1945–1969 and he worked with a number of directors to build up attractive and successful teams. When Harold Hardman died in 1965 Louis Edwards, a very different type of personality, succeeded him as chairman. Busby has said that he was happier with directors such as Louis Edwards who knew less about the game than he was with Hardman. Busby also said that Louis Edwards 'did as he was told.' Louis Edwards had inherited a relatively small family food and grocery business and successfully built up the butchers side of that business. When he sold shares in the family business to the public in 1962 it had a turnover of £5 million and over 80 retail outlets (including meat counters at Woolworths and Littlewoods stores). In order to appreciate the size of Edwards' 'other' business it is interesting to note that it was not until 1984 that Manchester United's turnover exceeded £5 million.

It is often suggested that Edwards built up his meat business using unfair and underhand practices. It is claimed, for instance, that he bribed Manchester City Councilors in order to obtain contracts to supply meat to local schools and other Council-controlled outlets. Having a brother, Douglas Edwards, as a City Councillor—later to become Lord Mayor—would have helped him obtain Council contracts. The meat supplied to schools was, it is said, not always good quality. This earned him a reputation for supplying second-class meat at first-class prices.

Louis Edwards had, in the 1950s, wished to join the Manchester United board, but there were at that time directors who were opposed to him. A key opponent, George Whittaker, died five days before the Münich plane crash. Matt Busby moved in the same

237

social circle as Louis Edwards; they were both Catholics, they both enjoyed the theatres in Manchester. Busby by then had become a respected figure at the club and supported the appointment of Edwards to the board. One reason why was because 'he saw the need for people of business' to be involved with the club. Another factor was that the existing directors were not young. In the 1950s four of the directors of Manchester United were beyond retirement age. The chairman, Harold Hardman, was over 70. Alan Gibson, who was a major shareholder, was younger, but had never been particularly healthy and did not want to take on the position of chairman. After the Münich crash, Louis Edwards was invited to become a director of the club. He saw his opportunity and he took it.

How one interprets what happened in the 1960s with respect to ownership of the club is a matter of opinion. Manchester United were at the time a private company, which meant that there was no organised market through which an interested party could buy the company's shares and no simple way to identify people who wished to sell their shares. In such a situation it was not easy for an individual who wished to buy shares to find somebody who wished to sell. Edwards, to find shareholders who wished to sell, made use of the Register of Shareholders. All companies (in the UK) are required to keep such a register. Many of the shares of the company were held in small batches by supporters of the club who had held them in the family for a long time. One way in which Edwards built up his holding of shares was for a friend to knock on the door of a shareholder's home and make them an offer. Many of the shareholders did not appreciate their true value. In addition to this face-to-face approach, Edwards would write letters to shareholders making them an offer.

At the same time as building up his shareholding, Edwards became immersed in club affairs. He was the director most active in running the football club. In 1961 he helped establish a sub-committee of three directors, with himself as chairman, to look after financial matters (Alan Gibson was another member). Finance clearly was a key factor if the club was to be a success in the future. Although Edwards would eventually be the subject of much criticism, one important management skill he did have was the ability to appreciate the contribution that others could make to his business. He was always willing to make use of the knowledge and abilities of others. In his meat company he brought in as a consultant and as vice-chairman, the respected businessman Roland Smith. He later used Roland Smith's abilities to benefit his football club.

In 1962, the Gibson family were the largest shareholders in the club, owning 41.8% of the equity. Edwards purchased a large block of these shares. At that time the football club was a private company and all share transfers had to be agreed by the members of the board of directors. As Edwards continued to build up his holdings, the other directors became concerned and so decided that no transfers would be registered if to do so would change the existing balance of holdings. To overcome this problem Louis Edwards persuaded his brother, Douglas, and another relative, Denzil Haroun, to buy the club's shares. In May 1963 Haroun purchased the largest remaining shareholding, outside those of the Gibson's family. Louis Edwards finally obtained control of the club when Alan Gibson agreed to sell him most of his holdings.

Louis Edwards did well for himself—estimates suggest that he paid somewhere between £31,000 and £41,000 to acquire his majority shareholding. He had acquired approximately one half of the club for somewhere in the region of £36,000. This valued the club at £72,000 (one million by today's values). But the financial state of the game was very different in 1964 to what it is now. In the 1960s Manchester United were not particularly profitable, they desperately needed money for ground improvements and to buy new players. Gates were falling across the country—football matches were only just beginning to be shown on television—and the difficult years of the 1970s and 1980s were still to come. In the 1960s buying shares in a football club did not seem to be (to most people) an attractive investment opportunity. Louis Edwards has been accused of bullying and of badgering people, but he actually paid a price for his shares that was not out of line with the value of other clubs at the time. Everton, who were, after Tottenham, the largest club in the country at the time, were then valued at £75,000. It is easy to be wise 40 years later and see the acquisition as a bargain, but there were not many other people at the time wishing to buy shares in football clubs.

A further criticism of the Edwards' business methods arose a number of years later in connection with the rights issue of shares in 1978. At that time the Edwards family owned 74% of Manchester United shares. In 1978 the company had made a loss and, equally worrying, its turnover was falling. (In 1977 its turnover was over £2 million; in 1978 it was £1.77 million.) The club needed money. At the time, in such a situation, all a club could do was either borrow more or ask existing shareholders for more. Manchester United did the latter. They offered all existing shareholders the right to buy additional shares at £1 each. This could be interpreted as allowing existing shareholders, in particular the Edwards family, to buy additional shares at below their market value. Over ten years earlier Louis Edwards had paid Alan Gibson £5 per share. But a rights issue at below the current market price is not unusual. If new shares are sold at below their existing market value it pulls down the market value of all the existing shares. An existing shareholder does not automatically become richer as a result of buying the new shares at below the pre-rights market price. This method of financing and the price set for exercising the rights was not a trick. The Edwards were, however, accused of exploiting the position. They in fact took a risk by investing more money in the club. Most people thought football clubs were in a mess.

Louis Edwards was never popular with United fans and he also had his critics within the club. The mounting criticism of him culminated in a Granada TV (a Manchester-based company) programme called 'World in Action' in which all the bad things Louis Edwards was alleged to have done were revealed and discussed. A month after the programme was broadcast Louis Edwards had a heart attack and died.

Louis Edwards, during his term as chairman, had built up United. Whether or not the leading person behind the achievements of Manchester United was Louis Edwards or Matt Busby does not really matter. They needed each other—that is what good corporate governance is about. Unfortunately, by the end of Busby's period as manager the two had fallen out, one of the disagreements being over the issue of Busby's son becoming a United director. Eamon Dunphy now a respected journalist, but once a Manchester United player, speaks well of Edwards. He refers to Louis Edwards as generous; he always 'bought the lads a drink, and he wasn't a snob.' This, he said, was different to the previous chairman. 'Louis was no villain. He was a nice man.' Dunphy refers to him as a classic Billy Bunter type.

It is often forgotten that the Manchester United went through troubled times in the 1970s and 1980s. They had won the First Division under Busby in 1966–67, were second in 1967–68, and won the European Cup in 1968, but there were then 20 years in which their performance was relatively poor. They finished eighteenth in 1972–73 and were then relegated from the First Division, having finished twenty-first (out of twenty-two) in 1973–74. They were promoted back to the top division the next season, but it was 1992–93 before they were again champions. During the decade from 1969 they had seven different managers. Not exactly a recipe for success. The board was restless and there was concern amongst many followers of the club about the limited time the board was prepared to give each of their new managers to prove themselves.

One remarkable fact about these troubled years for Manchester United was the loyalty shown to the club by their fans. The club's lowest average home crowd was 33,490 in 1961–62, a season in which they finished fifteenth in the First Division. In the year they were relegated, 1973–74, the average was 43,000. Throughout the difficult years of the 1960s and 1970s the average home crowd dipped below 40,000 in only two seasons.

Alex Ferguson was appointed as manager in 1986, and in his first three years at the club they achieved nothing. At one point, in the 1989–90 season, there was even a danger that they would be relegated (they finished in fourteenth place). The team lost 5–1 to Manchester City at Maine Road. A large number of fans wanted Ferguson removed. The board had shown they were willing to remove unsuccessful managers very quickly, but they continued to support Ferguson and the results did begin to improve. They went on under Ferguson's leadership to be one of the top teams in Europe.

Louis Edwards was clearly a true supporter of Manchester United, and his involvement with the club was not just based on money or social prestige. By contrast, neither Doug Ellis or Ken Bates were fans of the teams they owned; both had been directors of small clubs before settling at two of the larger clubs in the country. It has been suggested that directors like Ellis and Bates (and later Johnson of Everton) put their heads before their hearts. It is easy to be critical of this first wave of new directors in football, but modern business methods needed to be introduced in order for clubs to survive and to prosper.[9] When they entered the sport, not only were gates declining but grounds were in a disgusting condition, and the hooligan problem was leading politicians to make outrageous statements and proposals. These 'new wave' directors wanted financial returns but they were not in a hurry. Jason Tomas, who interviewed Ellis and Johnson towards the end of the 1990s, reports that they saw their large financial gains as just 'an accident.' Luck is one aspect of being a successful entrepreneur. Success can depend on being in the right business at the right time—it is not always the result of a brilliant business plan or outstanding ability. Luck, Yes, but the person involved has to be able to take advantage of the opportunities.

In his 1997 book *The Football Business*, David Conn refers to the new entrepreneurs, who would buy a football club 'in the certainty of future profits.' Conn quotes Ellis, 'It was similar in the package holiday business after the war. You try to be in the right place at the right time and then you cash in.' If this is what Ellis believed when he bought control of Villa, he had remarkable foresight, because at the time he first invested in Villa in 1968, the club were in a mess, football was in a mess, and the game was declining in popularity; nobody had yet floated football club shares on the markets.

It is well-documented that Edwards, Bates, Ellis and others all made a lot of money out of football, but that does not necessarily mean that profit was their main motive for becoming football club directors. At the time they invested the risks were great—they obviously did not want to lose money, but their gains were partly a result of their own actions and partly a result of changes that took place in the game that were outside their control. The profitability of an investment depends on future returns. In football the prospects for the future have varied from one decade to the next.

One thing the Manchester United case shows is that chairmen and directors can be unpopular with fans irrespective of whether they bring to success or failure to a club. Few directors have been as unpopular amongst supporters as Martin Edwards. He was seen as the person who had inherited the family wealth and at the age of only 24 had been found a position on the board at Manchester United. In fact, when his father Louis Edwards died in 1980, he left him only 16% of the club's shares (his brother also inherited 16%). Martin Edwards built up most of what became the majority holding by purchasing shares.

In 1983 Martin Edwards nearly sold control of Manchester United, and as much as the supporters disliked him, they disliked the possible alternative owner even more. Football was at a low point, and Martin Edwards was told that someone wanted to buy the club for £10 million (a five-fold increase in value over three years). The interested purchaser was Robert Maxwell. Martin Edwards decided to turn the offer down, a popular decision because Robert Maxwell was a controversial figure.

Following Matt Busby's retirement as manager the club appointed a succession of people to this post, none of whom achieved success or brought glamour to the club. Wilf McGuinness, a former United player, was Busby's first replacement (1969–70). He was followed by Frank O'Farrell (1970–72), an experienced manager and well respected in football circles, but he had problems with Busby (who had been made president of the club) from both a financial and football tactics point of view. O'Farrell believed that Busby was undermining his authority. In 1972 O'Farrell was sacked when the club were third from bottom in the First Division. The next manager appointed was the outspoken, and much travelled, Tommy Docherty (1972–77). The club were relegated to the Second division at the end of the 1973–74 season. They were promoted back to the First division one season later. Docherty was later sacked, not for footballing reasons, but because he had an affair with the wife of the club's physiotherapist.

The years with Dave Sexton as manager (1977–81) turned out to be 'dour'. The teams he selected did not excite the spectators (or the directors). Sexton was a calm, thoughtful and articulate person who had achieved success at Chelsea, but he achieved little at United, just one Cup Final appearance. In 1981 Ron Atkinson was appointed manager. He was seen as a flamboyant character who would bring life back to Old Trafford. Atkinson, in his five seasons at United, achieved a third place in the First Division, and two FA Cup final wins (1983 and 1985). At one point in the 1985–86 season the club looked as if they would be First Division champions but faded towards the end of the season. When they started the 1986–87 season badly Atkinson was dismissed. The Ferguson dynasty began in November 1986.

Ferguson quickly made himself unpopular by criticising some of the established players at the club and then selling them. (Norman Whiteside, Paul McGrath, Gordon Strachan and Remi Moses.) He

243

believed that many players in the squad were unfit, that they drank too much and that there were too few young players at the club.

Martin Edwards was not popular with the fans. The club had achieved nothing in his first nine years as chairman. He, along with the board, realised that there was an urgent need to develop the Old Trafford stadium, and that there was a need to spend money on new players. The club, however, had no money; football in the 1980s was in trouble, spectators were staying away, and the game was being criticised by politicians and journalists. In April 1989 there was the Hillsborough stadium disaster in which 95 spectators were killed—many of them young people. The tragedy was widely shown on TV, and certain newspapers were misrepresenting the reasons for the disaster, all of which added to the public criticism of the game and its fans.

Writing in 1989, Michael Crick and David Smith were highly critical of the Manchester United directors.[10] They believed that the fortunes of the club could be restored if control was passed to directors prepared to represent the wishes of the fans. Over the next sixteen years (1990–2006) the club remained in the control of businessmen who had varying interests in the game of football but all of whom had a big interest in money. During this time the club were Premier League champions eight times, and UEFA Champion League winners once. The directors must have been doing something right. Would a board who better represented the fans have done any better?

Club For Sale

In 1989 Martin Edwards told Alex Ferguson: 'I'm going to sell the club, if you know anyone prepared to pay £10 million for my shares and [willing to] spend another £10 million on the Stretford End.' Edwards was prepared to sell because he felt he had tried to revive the club, but that he could not win over the fans. Alex Ferguson felt sorry for him, and 'appreciated the patience he had shown over two and a half years. The chairman provided good backing without ever interfering with the running of the team.'[11]

Just a few weeks after the disaster at the Hillsborough stadium Martin Edwards received an offer to buy his shares. This was from

Michael Knighton, who had made money through property development. Edwards was offered somewhere between £10 and £11 million for his 50.2% of the company's shares. Edwards was in debt, his home was mortgaged. The popularity of football was at a low, with deaths on the terraces, hooliganism, grounds in poor condition and low crowds. Manchester United had not been champions for over 20 years, and were making losses. Edwards was tempted, and agreed to give Knighton an option to buy his shares — not having consulted the other directors. However, Knighton had difficulty in putting the money for the deal together, so Manchester United escaped from this take-over attempt.

The club did, however, need money, and so the directors decided to float the company. This would enable the club to raise funds, as well as enable those directors that wanted to, to sell some of their shares and raise cash for themselves. The company was restructured with the football club becoming a subsidiary of the listed plc. At the time of its launch the equity in the plc was valued at only £42 million. This was a time before the very lucrative TV broadcasting contracts came into existence.

In June 1991, Manchester United offered 38% of the plc's shares to the public. Some of these were new shares and the proceeds from this sale of these would go to the club. The rest were existing shares, owned by existing shareholders who would personally receive the proceeds of the sale. Martin Edwards, as a result of the sale of his shares at the time of flotation, reduced his holding from just over 50% to 32%. He received in the region of £6 million from the sale of the shares he owned. The 1991 float of United shares was a mixed success. One thing that went wrong was that the Maxwell family, who had over time accumulated 4.25% of the club's shares, 'dumped' the shares they held onto the market as soon as they were listed with the result that the price of the shares quickly fell by 35% from the floatation price.

In 1991 there was not a big demand by investors or by fans for the shares of Manchester United; football was still in the doldrums. However by June 1999, as a result of a general stock market bubble, and a belief that football was now a 'licence to print money', the market value of Manchester United had risen to £517 million. (For comparative purposes the market capitalisation of Aston Villa in 1999 was only £50.4 million, Spurs' was £64.6 million, while Newcastle's was £116.7 million.) Martin Edwards had made gains by selling at the time of the flotation, but he would have done a lot better if he had hung on to the shares for a few more years.

One disappointing aspect of the listing was that it only resulted in the football club receiving £6.7 million. Hardly enough to finance the purchase of three or four good players, and a small sum when compared with the amount the club began to invest in Old Trafford. In 1992–93 the club completed the rebuilding of the Stretford End at a cost of £10.3 million, only partly financed by money raised by the new issue. (In 1997 Newcastle United went to the market and raised over £50 million for the club.)

Was the flotation worthwhile? With the benefit of hindsight the answer is probably No. When the football club became a part of a publicly listed company it became vulnerable to take-over. The amount of money it raised was trivial. At the time they were listed they were only the third club to do so (after Spurs and Millwall). There were those around the club who did warn of the dangers of such listings. In the US the NFL explicitly prohibits clubs in their league from being listed companies—they appreciate what a jungle stock markets can be.

Martin Edwards decided to reduce his financial investment in the club. In 1995 he sold a tranche of shares for £1.5 million; in 1996 he and his family sold further shares for £4.4 million, and then in 1997 he sold another tranche for £5.57 million. This gave him, at that time, total receipts from the sale of his shares of approximately £18 million and he still owned 14% of the club's shares. In October 1999 he sold a further 19.5 million shares, which reduced his holding to just under 7% of the total. It should be remembered that in 1989 Martin Edwards had been worried about his one million pound borrowing from the bank, and as a result nearly sold his 51% holding for £10 million.

Opinions on Martin Edwards differ. Undoubtedly, his family links got him started but at times he showed himself to be a good businessman. When he became chairman of the club football was in a mess and so was Manchester United. He became a director of the plc in 1991 and was chief executive of the plc until he retired in August 2000. He helped turn the club from one that was struggling in the early 1980s to one that, 15 years later, was one of the top 3 or 4 in Europe. As Alex Ferguson explained, Edwards carefully looks after the finances of his business: 'Conversations

246

with Martin Edwards are usually straightforward and pleasant until you ask him for more money. Then you have a problem.' The club in fact spent large sums of money buying top international players. 'No manager could have had better treatment than I have had from my chairman when it comes to running the playing side of the club. He has never interfered in the slightest with my decisions about players.'[12]

A major problem (or opportunity) arose in 1998 when BSkyB decided that they wanted to buy the most successful club in the country. By this time institutional shareholders owned over 60% of the shares in the plc. Secret meetings took place with BSkyB. The Manchester United plc board held an 'unusual' meeting on 6 July 1998 at which three of the directors present knew of the BSkyB interest in buying the club while the other directors, including Peter Kenyon, who was deputy chief executive, and David Gill, who was finance director, did not. The three directors who knew kept quiet about the possible take-over bid; not exactly openness and harmony at board level. In fact, some of the club's directors were at the time engaged in other secret negotiations, namely plans to form a European Super League.

BSkyB made a bid, offering 217.5p for each United share. The United board unanimously recommended rejection. It was the price they were rejecting, not the principle of the take-over. Merrill Lynch, the respected merchant bankers, estimated that the shares were worth at least 240p, which was a very high price, as the price before the BSkyB interest was 160p. BSkyB raised their offer to 230p. Martin Edwards was happy to accept the 230p price for his shares and was annoyed that one of the directors, Greg Dyke, was holding out for more. Bose reports that Edwards lost his cool and said to Dyke: 'if we lose this deal because of you then I shall sue you.'[13]

The United board finally agreed, they would recommend acceptance of a raised bid of 240p cash. BSkyB were happy, it looked as if the £623 million acquisition of the club would go ahead. Unfortunately for the directors of the two companies it did not go ahead. The supporters of Manchester United fought a brilliant battle to save the club. Despite the arguments of Martin Edwards, the *Sun* newspaper and allegedly Alex Ferguson, that the take-over would be good for Manchester United, the Monopolies and Mergers Commission decided (in March 1999) that it would not be good for the game of football in England. They decided that if the acquisition went ahead it would damage competition between broadcasters. In other words, one company would be involved on both sides of negotiations about future broadcasting rights. A further worry was that this acquisition could result in a number of retaliatory mergers between media groups and other top football clubs, and that this would increase the financial gap between the top Premier League clubs and the less glamorous clubs in the league. The government accepted these arguments and blocked the take-over.

Alex Ferguson

A key appointment at the club has of course been Alex Ferguson. The manager himself is an astute businessman, both in looking after his own financial interests as well as those of the club. The three-year contract he signed with Manchester United in 2003 was said to be worth in total £11 million, which may seem a lot, but when compared to the salaries of some of his players it can be justified. Sir Alex is a proven winner who has been loyal to the club.

Alex Ferguson has a well-known interest in horseracing. Through this hobby he met the two very successful Irish racehorse owners, John Magnier and J.P. McManus. Ferguson invested in racehorses. In 2001 the two Irishmen, through a specially created company, Cubic Expression, began investing heavily in the shares of Manchester United. There was an attempt to portray the two as fans of the club, although Michael Crick believes that at the time 'it would probably be more accurate to describe them as Ferguson supporters.' They were, however, shrewd investors, they purchased BSkyB's 9.9% stake in the club for about £62 million (which valued each share at £2.55). There was concern amongst the directors of the club that the two would make a take-over bid.

Surprisingly, early in 2004, Alex Ferguson fell out with the two major Manchester United shareholders over the division of the breeding rights to a racehorse in which Ferguson had an interest. Alex Ferguson threatened to issue a writ against John Magnier. The two unhappy racehorse owners used their power as major shareholders in Manchester United to ask a number of embarrassing questions about the governance of the club. They sent a letter to the club that contained 63 questions relating to financial matters including questions about transfer dealings and the use of agents at the club. They would not agree to Manchester United offering a new contract to Sir Alex until these questions were answered to their satisfaction. The two shareholders won the dispute, Ferguson did not receive the income from the breeding rights that he thought he was entitled to, but his contract at the club was renewed. The club did improve its level of financial disclosure as the two shareholders wanted, including giving details of the amount paid as agent fees on all transfers of over £5 million.

Alex Ferguson has been successful but some of his methods have been criticised. In particular, there is resentment at the way he frequently tries to bully and intimidate referees. It is thought by many important people in the game that Manchester United benefit from so many of the marginal decisions going their way because Ferguson whinges at, and verbally abuses, referees. (He is not the only manager to do this.) In hearings before FA disciplinary panels he is usually supported by a top barrister. Because the elite clubs have power it is believed that they can influence the outcome of disciplinary enquires and that they can harm a referees future in the game through their public and private criticisms. Jeff Winters, who was a top referee and who retired in 2004, has said that 'I always smiled at Sam Allardyce moaning about the perceived small club/big club imbalance but, having seen some non-sending offs and surprising penalty decisions, I'm starting to give a bit more credence to that idea.'

The most important relationship in the running of a club is that between the chairman and the manager. Although Sir Alex Ferguson in general has a good working relationship with the directors of the club, the relationship has at times become strained. It is said that Ferguson became upset that the directors would agree to pay the star players large wages but they would not reward him equally well. He has also at times complained about the amount of money he was given to buy new players.

Manchester United has been well run for a number of years. The ground has been developed to be the best and largest in the country. There have been disagreements but compared to most other clubs there has been stability both at board level and in the chairman's relationship with the manager. Martin Edwards recognised he needed marketing and financial expertise on the board and brought in respected figures in these areas. A necessary condition for success is a stable board—so many teams have failed to achieve their potential because of boardroom squabbles (including Manchester City). Martin Edwards supported Ferguson, even though in Ferguson's early years there was little success and the fans wanted him removed.

Louis and Martin Edwards brought onto the board quality directors when they were needed. They recognised the need to run the football club as a business despite this leading to their unpopularity with fans. The directors made decisions which in retrospect were wrong—this is of course the case with all businesses—but somehow, perhaps because of good luck, the poor decisions made by the United directors turned out to be not of major importance. That is until 2005, when their policy of not borrowing resulted in them being the victims in another game.

The Glazers Era?

Take-over battles for corporate control are a danger for any company that has its shares listed on a stock exchange. Only companies whose shares are closely controlled, for example Arsenal, are in the short-term safe from predators. Predators are wealthy investors who buy a stake in a company that they think is undervalued, either with their own money or with borrowed money. Their objective is either to sell their investment within a short period of time and make a quick profit, or to obtain control of the company and then either engage in asset stripping or to mortgage the companies assets in order to raise funds to pay off the debts they incurred while buying the company. This is the danger of listing the shares of a football club, or any other company, on a capital market. The wider issue has already been discussed in the chapter on globalisation, but here we will briefly add a few more facts about the new owners of Manchester United.

Malcolm Glazer is the owner of the Tampa Bay Buccaneers, a club in the NFL. He paid $192 million in 1995 for his controlling interest in that club. In 2004 the investment was said to be worth $780 million. In 2004 he was not a popular figure in the Tampa Bay region, despite the fact that his club won the Super Bowl in January 2003. In the months following this success, Glazer had allowed the winning squad to break up; he was not prepared to pay top wages and so many players left. He was also not popular with the local community in Florida because he threatened to take the club franchise to another city unless the municipality of Tampa Bay helped finance a new stadium for his club.

Malcolm Glazer has his roots in Russia. His father, who fled that country for a new life in the US, died tragically whilst Glazer was a young man. The son then unfortunately became involved in a ten-year legal battle with his relations over the distribution of the family estate. Glazer built up his fortune starting with watchmaking, before moving into property development, including trailer and mobile home parks and shopping malls. He has at various times been involved in legal battles with residents of the trailer parks and estates he owns, and with directors of companies he has taken over. In 1991 he unsuccessfully attempted to take over the famous motorcycle company Harley Davidson, and at a court hearing at that time the judge referred to Glazer as 'a snake in sheep's clothing.' In the 1990s he attempted to take over a number of sports franchises in the US, eventually acquiring Tampa Bay. This is the person who, with his family, acquired the largest football club in the world.[14] Wealthy men have acquired football clubs in the past but they appeared to care about football, and were knowledgeable about the game. It is said that Malcolm Glazer had at the time of the acquisition only seen one soccer game when Manchester United played in the US.

Malcolm Glazer claims that he will be able to manage the assets of Manchester United more efficiently than the previous directors of the club. His public relations spokesman claims that Glazer is a 'true sportsman who will run [the] franchise like it should be run and win championships.' Glazer's qualifications for the leadership of one of the wealthiest sports businesses in the world are in fact quite limited. His publicists have made much of the fact that he was the owner of the Tampa Bay Buccaneers when they were the Super Bowl champions, but the Buccaneers are an organisation only just over one half the size of Manchester United (it had revenue in 2002–03 of approximately $146 million as opposed to Manchester United's $250 million). Winning the US championship in 2003 was the club's only achievement; before that they were a below average club. This compares unfavourably with the United's sporting achievements over the last three decades.

Malcolm Glazer has claimed that the supporters of Manchester

251

United are xenophobic, but these are fans of a club where over half the players are not British, and where over half of the shares before the take-over were owned by non-British. As fans at other Premier League clubs have shown, English football fans are prepared to welcome money from anyone as long as it promises success; nobody accuses Chelsea fans of being xenophobic. The worry to Manchester United fans about Malcolm Glazer and his sons is that they have incurred huge amounts of debt to acquire the club, and that they will have to take large amounts of money out of the club to pay off these debts. The one certain thing Glazier did was to provide an immediate financial gain to holders of United's shares, for as is usual with a contested take-over, the shareholders of the victim company make good gains.

The directors of Manchester United were against the take-over, one reason being that it would burden the club with having to service a high level of debt. Glazer needed to borrow in the region of £600 million to buy the club, and the cost of servicing the debt would be very high. The fans organised a protest campaign, and called themselves the 'Manchester Education Committee'. Their goal was to keep the club out of the hands of 'parasitic, profit-minded individuals.' They arranged demonstrations in Florida as well as in Manchester. They were keen to point out that Glazer was unpopular with the Tampa Bay Buccaneers' supporters largely because of the fact that having steered them to a Super Bowl win in 2003 he then fell out with players and officials.

Alex Ferguson was manager before the Glazers came to the club, and has continued in that role afterwards. He, to the surprise of many supporters of the club, speaks with enthusiasm about the new owners, describing Malcolm Glazer as excellent for Manchester United: 'I can only speak from my own perspective and I've been more than happy with the new owners. They've supported me 100% and there has never been one bit of a problem. They've given me the money I wanted to buy two new players so what am I supposed to do? Tell lies? It certainly works better for me than when we were a plc, I can tell you that. If we wanted to sign a player back then we had to run it through the football club board, then the plc board, and then go through the stock exchange procedures, all that nonsense. We don't have to bother with that now. It's much quicker. We just pick up the phone and get a straightforward Yes or No. The new owners have been great.'

Such views did not make Ferguson popular with the many supporters who opposed the take-over and who were taking action to try to ensure the Glazers were unsuccessful. The 'United We Stand' view was that Ferguson's 'toadying comments smack of a struggling employee attempting to ingratiate himself with his new bosses.' Ferguson, however, was not on his way out, in 2006–07 the team were very successful and Ferguson was able to silence his critics.

David Gill, the chief executive of the club, tried in 2006 to defend the financial deal that the new owners of the club had arranged in order to enable them to acquire the assets of Manchester United. He said (as an employee of the Glazer-owned club) that the financial package was 'sensible' and 'serviceable'. He said the cost of servicing the interest on the debt 'is not in excess of what we were previously paying in dividends and corporation tax as a publicly quoted company.' This is in fact not correct. In the year 2004–05, dividends paid were £3.4 million and tax £4.2 million, which together are only one third of the annual interest now being paid by the club on the borrowings from banks, and only in the region of one quarter of the annual interest being paid on the hedge fund debt.[15]

In April 2005 the then Manchester United board, and the club's chief executive, the same David Gill, were saying that the level of debt being taken on to finance the take-over would put a 'significant financial strain on the business.' This is what happens with leveraged buy-outs or acquisitions financed with a large amount of debt. To succeed with this approach, the acquirer of the business often resorts to asset stripping, cost cutting, and short-term growth strategies. It is doubtful if such policies can work with a football club.

The Glazer's take-over of Manchester United was definitely a hostile take-over bid. It illustrates one of the dangers to companies of the global financial markets. Football clubs are of course not the only part of the English 'heritage' to be sold to foreigners, other 'assets' that have been sold including Rolls Royce, Jaguar, Harrods, Harvey Nichols, The Savoy Hotel, HP Sauce, Tetley Tea, Roundtrees, Thames Water, London Electricity, Abbey National and Barings Bank.

What of the future? Are the Glazer family interested in the long-term interests of the club, or in short-term financial gain? We will have to wait to find the answer. No empire lasts forever, but it is too early to write about the fall of Manchester United. Although to many loyal supporters of the club who live in England the Glazer take-over appears to be a disaster, to their army of supporters around the world whether or not the club are owned by an Edwards, a McManus or a Glazer does not matter. What does matter is that the club maintain its tradition of success. One major worry for the club will be finding a replacement for Alex Ferguson when he retires. When Matt Busby left the club there were problems in replacing such a powerful personality. Could the same thing happen again?

Manchester United were very successful in the 1990s because they had the best players, the best manager and a team of executives and directors who knew what they were doing. They attracted the largest crowds, big sponsorship deals, were successful in European competitions and had a brand name known around the world. They invested most of the money they earned in new players and in physical assets. In the ten seasons between 1992–93 and 2001–02, they spent over £150 million on improving their Old Trafford stadium and associated facilities. They continue to invest in their ground, and in the 2006–07 season increased the capacity to 76,000. Capital investment decisions are made by boards of directors. The directors of Manchester United, by spending so much on their ground, have showed their ambition and hopes for the future of the club. The only other clubs spending anywhere near £100 million on their stadiums over this period were Arsenal, Newcastle and Chelsea. Whilst spending money on their ground, however, Manchester United were not cutting back on investment in players.

The club are not well liked by supporters of other clubs, partly because of their success, partly because of their arrogance. Perhaps surprisingly, the directors of the club have not been that popular with the supporters of Manchester United. They have been seen as too commercial, as looking after the shareholders' interests more than the fans. Martin Edwards' comment that 'This is the crazy thing about supporters, they want the best players, and they want the best stadium ... If you want all these things you must be commercial. We do not make an apology for that, as long as we don't charge ridiculous prices or rip off people.' (At that time their admission prices were the sixth cheapest in the Premier League.) Edwards made these comments in 1999, but as Bose writes 'such words and facts do little to appease fans' anger and frustration.' Bose believes that the supporters' resentment reflects a distrust of change and a sense of bewilderment that their football club was being so transformed so completely.

The directors of Manchester United did, however, make mistakes. Some would say that the decision to go public was a mistake, although at the time they made this decision it was conventional wisdom that this was what football clubs needed to do in order to raise finance. It was a good decision for the existing shareholders, as it gave them an 'exit route' for their investments. The directors decided that they would not use borrowed money. This was a mistake. They argued that they did not need to take on debt, as they could, in the new prosperous world of football, generate themselves all the finance they needed. But a certain level of borrowing is good for equity shareholders. If you can borrow cheaply and earn a return on the money greater than its costs, then shareholders benefit. Manchester United could have done this, the directors simply decided not to. The club paid the price of ignoring the rules of sound financial management.

If Manchester United fans are upset by what has been happening to them, what about the fans of lesser teams? Fans of many clubs at one time thought their clubs could win something, but they now realise that they have been 'excluded'. Manchester United fans have been the lucky ones, the spoilt ones. If they were angry that their club had become a plc—'the triumph of money men over men of football'—they have now learnt that there are evils other than plcs. They are now once again privately owned, with potentially damaging 'hedge fund' money needing to be repaid. The fans should have realised that it was not the Manchester United directors and the plc status that were the greatest danger to them, it was the unregulated global financial markets that was and is the problem. Manchester United's success made them a target in a world where it is economic forces that are in charge, not the 'people' or the so-called regulators of the people's game.

The Glazer family paid in the region of £800 million for the club, with each share being worth in the region of £3. The club was delisted from the stock exchange in June 2005, at which time its market capitalisation was £924 million, each share being traded at 348½ pence. This was valuing the club at over four times annual revenue, a high ratio of value to revenue for a football club.

The profits and revenue of the club fell in the year ending 31 July 2005 (which covered three months under the ownership of the Glazers). The profits of £46 million showed a 20% reduction. Media revenue was down by £40 million. Included amongst costs were the £6.6 million spent in legal and banking fees in the unsuccessful fight against the Glazer take-over. The costs also included £2.2 million on agent fees, of which £1.5 million went to the Formation Group in connection with the purchase of Wayne Rooney.

The plan of the new owners is to increase club revenue by 50% over five years and to treble operating profits over this time. Things did not start off well for them, the 2005–06 season proved to be difficult. For their European Cup matches there were empty seats in the ground, the fans were showing their unhappiness with the take-over. Their 'fans' booed the team off the pitch twice following defeats. There was disagreement amongst the players: Roy Keane criticised certain players for not trying in matches, and left the club at the end of 2005. The manager was verbally abused at one match, and in the club's fanzine he was heavily criticised. The club were eliminated from the knock-out stages of the UEFA Champions League after finishing bottom of their qualifying group. The Glazer family must have had worries as they need success in order to be able to service the expensive borrowings. As a result of not reaching the group stage of the UEFA Champions League, the club missed out on £10 million or so. But the situation did improve.

The Glazer control of Manchester United increased in October 2006 when two of the three non-Glazer family directors resigned from the board. The two who resigned were the finance director and the commercial director. This left David Gill, the chief executive, as the only non-Glazer on the board. The resignations meant that Malcolm Glazer's five sons and one daughter filled six of the seven directorship positions.

Nevertheless, at the end of the 2006–07 season the club finished as Premier League Champions, and their local rivals, Manchester City, had yet another poor season. The future certainly looked better for United than for City. Manchester United had survived an ownership crisis; City were soon to have a new owner with a history.

9

Whatever Happened to Football in the Midlands?

In the not too distant past the Midlands produced winning teams. Nottingham Forest were European Champions twice (1979 and 1980) — Aston Villa once (1982). Since that time only two other English clubs have been European Champions. At various times since the Second World War, the best teams in the country have been Wolverhampton Wanderers, West Bromwich Albion, Nottingham Forest and Derby County. One hundred years earlier when the Football League was founded half the teams in the league were from the Midlands. Aston Villa were for a long time the best team in the country. It is a very different picture now.

In 2005–06 two of the three clubs relegated from the Premier League were from the Midlands. Aston Villa were in the 2006–07 season the only Premiership club from the region. In 2007–08 Derby County and Birmingham City returned to the Premiership.

Why did the Midland clubs stop winning? There are two reasons. Firstly, in the crucial period when football evolved from being local entertainment to being a global business, the people leading and directing the Midland clubs did not have the vision to be able to take advantage of the new opportunities. The second reason is that with the way the game is now organised, with the way the revenue coming into the game is distributed, the gap between the successful and the less successful clubs is increasing each year with the result that once a club is unsuccessful, it becomes increasingly difficult to catch up.

On one Saturday in December 2005, Aston Villa played Manchester United and Birmingham City played Manchester City. The two Birmingham teams were not only beaten, they were humiliated. The *Sunday Times* match reporters referred to the Villa midfield players as 'plodding, once-paced clones' and to the Birmingham City display as 'gutless.' Birmingham's manager, Steve Bruce,

257

described his team's performance as 'totally inept' and 'ridiculous.' The Villa manager, David O'Leary, admitted his team was 'outplayed and outclassed.' Neither manager was exaggerating. It could be said that this was just the outcome on one weekend, but unfortunately it demonstrated the gap between the teams. For most football supporters in the Midlands the game is rarely beautiful.

In the 2004–05 season Aston Villa and Birmingham City had finished in the middle of the Premier League and West Bromwich Albion escaped relegation only on the last day of the season. Nottingham Forest were relegated from the Championship, a fate Coventry City only narrowly avoided. By January 2005 five of the big eight Midland clubs had removed their managers, they had either been sacked or resigned by mutual agreement. Not a sign of a successful season. Peter Reid had left Coventry, Joe Kinnear had departed from Nottingham Forest, Micky Adams from Leicester City, Dave Jones from Wolves and Gary Megson from West Bromwich Albion.

For Peter Reid it was his fourth departure from the position of manager of a club. In 1993 he was required to leave Manchester City, in 2002 Sunderland, 2003 Leeds United and 2005 Coventry City. The last two appointments were from his point of view far from ideal, he was expected to save the clubs involved without any money to spend. When he left Coventry they were in twentieth place in the Championship, the lowest position they had been in for 41 years. As is well-known, managers take the blame for failure, although the chairman of Coventry, Bryan Richardson, was kind enough to say that 'We as a club were underachieving, but don't put all the blame on Peter Reid. The players have to be accountable as well.' He should have added: so do the directors. In December 2005, the directors of Coventry City appointed Micky Adams as their new manager, their fourth manager in 18 months. (Adams was sacked in January 2007.) The club were £20 million in debt, and were only 3 points clear of the relegation zone. Adams had said, 'We are in a precarious position, and the players' fate plus that of the club this season rests in their own hands.' The decline in the fortunes of the club over a six-year period, however, is the result of decisions made by the clubs directors; the fate of the club has been in the hands of the directors.

As part of the game of musical chairs (or rather musical man-

258

agers) Gary Megson became the new manager of Nottingham Forest in 2005. He had been in competition for the post with Micky Adams and Dave Jones. His immediate task was to save his new club from relegation to the third tier (League One). Nottingham Forest, a club who have twice won the European Cup, had not played at that level since 1951. Megson had experience of fighting relegation, he had saved West Bromwich Albion from relegation to League One (and twice had led them into the Premier League) on a shoestring budget. Unfortunately, Megson was not successful at Nottingham Forest, the club were relegated and after 13 months as manager he left the club by mutual consent.

At the end of the 2005–6 season there was further talk of management changes at the Midlands clubs. The manager whose job was most under threat was David O'Leary at Aston Villa. He survived for a few months, but then left the club 'by mutual agreement.' Wolverhampton and Walsall had appointed new managers for the 2006–07 season, while a few weeks into the season West Bromwich Albion dismissed their manager Bryan Robson. Steve Bruce at Birmingham City was at the end of 2006 only just hanging on to his managerial position.[1]

At the beginning of the twenty-first century Aston Villa, who had a brief period of success in the 1980s, had moved to a situation in which the directors seemed to be satisfied if the club achieved a comfortable position in the middle of the Premier League. West Bromwich and Wolves were pleased to be yo-yo clubs moving up and down between the top two divisions. Birmingham City were, by their standards, reasonably successful.[2] Coventry City, after an exceptionally long period in the top division, were disappearing and the East Midland clubs still had governance problems.

The Midlands clubs had developed a reputation not for success at football, but for being financially prudent, which was good for bankers and some shareholders but not for supporters. In the 2004–05 season only five Premiership clubs finished the season with net funds rather than net debts—the clubs were Manchester United, Aston Villa, Charlton, West Bromwich Albion and Birmingham City. Very good for these clubs, except that in the following season four of these clubs finished in four of the bottom five places in the Premiership. The East Midland clubs were not so prudent, Leicester went into administration in 2002 and Derby in 2003.

The Past

In the first 14 years of the Premier League, 1992–2006, the most successful club from the Midlands was Aston Villa. Based on a points score, allocated according to a club's final league position in each season, Leicester City were, perhaps surprisingly, second best (ranked eighteenth amongst all the clubs who have played in the Premier League). Third best were Coventry City (ranked nineteenth overall) followed by Derby County (ranked twenty-first), Nottingham Forest (twenty-fifth), Birmingham City (twenty-sixth), West Bromwich Albion (thirty-first) and finally Wolverhampton (thirty-ninth). This is not a very impressive record. The best Midlands club, Aston Villa, were ranked sixth overall, which is perhaps satisfactory, but they have not been good enough to win a major competition. It is, however, often forgotten that in the first year of the Premier League they finished in second place, that they won the League Cup in 1994 and in 1996, and were finalists in the FA Cup in 2000. By way of comparison with other big city teams, Liverpool were ranked third and Everton tenth, Manchester United were first and Manchester City seventeenth, Arsenal were second, Chelsea fourth and Tottenham seventh.

When the Premier League started (1992) only three of the Midland clubs were good enough to be in that league. If we go back a further ten years, the position was very different. The final league position of teams in the First Division (the top division) in the 1980–81 season shows Aston Villa as champions, Ipswich second, Arsenal third, West Bromwich Albion fourth and Liverpool fifth. In that season Nottingham Forest were seventh, Birmingham City were thirteenth, Coventry sixteenth and Leicester were relegated. Not a bad performance by the Midland teams.

At a time when the inequality between clubs is increasing is it now too late for any one of the clubs outside the present elite group to ever be good enough to become one of the top teams nationally and globally? Is the gap now too great? In the 2002–03 season the annual revenue (turnover) of Manchester United was £173 million and the annual revenue of Aston Villa was £45 million, which amounts to 3.8 times greater. In the 1992–93 season, a decade earlier, the annual revenue of Manchester United was £25 million, while Aston Villa's was £10 million, or 2.5 times greater. The gap is clearly getting greater.

If we go back to the 1950s and 1960s the Midlands provided some of the best football teams in the country. In terms of playing success, over a 20-year period (1947–67) Aston Villa, West Bromwich Albion and Wolverhampton were amongst the 10 most successful clubs (success again being measured in terms of final league position in each season). Wolverhampton were particularly consistent, finishing in a top 10 position in the top league 13 times, West Bromwich Albion finished in the top 10 positions on 9 occasions and Aston Villa on 7 occasions. In the eight-year period from 1953–61 Wolverhampton were the most successful team in the country, winning the First Division three times, coming second on two occasions and third twice. They were an enterprising club who demonstrated the commercial possibilities of playing floodlit games against top European opposition. The Midland clubs were amongst the soccer elite.[3]

What has gone wrong over the last decade or so, and why have the Midland clubs become minor players in the prosperous new world of football? Is there some regional difference that can account for this lack of success? The Midland football fans have had to put up with a lack of success and with mediocre football teams. They have had to learn to live with football supporters from Liverpool, Manchester and London who now behave as if their teams had some 'right' to success.

Does the lack of success for a region matter? The answer is clearly Yes, because if over time teams from a region do not achieve some success then within that region interest in the local teams, and possibly in the sport, will decline, and around the world an opportunity to promote the name of the city and region will be missed. 'Football clubs are an essential part of the social and economic fabric of the West Midlands and surrounding area.' But as Malcolm Boyden explains the West Midlands is an 'area where the people still lived for the game, yet they'd been starved of success for so long that everybody had forgotten they existed at all.'[4]

The success of a football team can bring a feel-good factor to a town or city, it can give it pride. Liverpool, in making its successful case to be the European City of Culture in 2008, were able to refer to their football success. Birmingham, in making their unsuccessful case, were not able to refer to football. To be home to one of the elite football clubs can be a massive boost to a region, it brings direct financial returns through the extra income that is brought into the region and it can also add to the 'brand' value of the city's name. In the US, cities compete to have the top sports clubs located in their area. It is not being suggested that the US franchise system be adopted for soccer, however. It is mentioned only to emphasise the importance sporting success can be to the image of the city.

The Region

Midlands is a region without a strong sense of identity. In the book *Sport and Identity in the North of England* the difficulty of deciding on a boundary for a North–South divide is discussed. The authors regard the Midlands as the North. As Tony Mason points out football as a game was not invented in the North but he concludes 'football as a spectator sport was.'[5] He refers to the grip of the North on the elite end of the game being assured in 1888 by the organisation of the twelve clubs into the Football League. Six of these clubs were in fact from the Midlands, not from the North. Mason states that 'Professional football was a Northern innovation at which Northerners were top dogs. Not only did they play it better than Southerners, they also watched it with more knowledge and intensity.' The Midlands was again being included in the North.

Over time, as Mason and others point out, regional differences in terms of passion, intensity and knowledge began to disappear, and by the 1930s, with Arsenal the top club, loyalties and passions did not depend on geography. 'The North is an imagined territory with no fixed boundaries and the range of qualities which have been seen as characteristics of Northerners are so diverse as to defy neat definitions.'

It is surprising when travelling overseas to, say, Singapore, Hong Kong or Southern Africa, to encounter the belief, amongst even well read people, that Birmingham is a smaller city than Manchester or Liverpool. This belief is based on the reputation of the football teams from the three cities. It is not widely known outside

262

the UK that the home of Aston Villa is in Birmingham (or that Everton are from Liverpool).

There are numerous organisations, funded by local or regional government initiatives, designed to promote Birmingham and the Midlands. In October 2004 two promotional events took place: 'Birmingham Forward' set up a London office and 'Advantage West Midlands' the regional, development agency, launched a new promotional campaign. At the former event, the leader of the city council said 'I am determined that Birmingham's European and International reputation and its achievements [should be] fully appreciated.' Unfortunately its football teams do not add to this reputation.

It has been said that Birmingham and the Midlands should love itself more than it does. It is also said the citizens of Birmingham are self-deprecating. Part of this problem is that the region suffers from the North-South polarisation. Southerners think of Birmingham as the North but Northerners think of it as the South. Whichever category Birmingham is placed in it is usually to its disadvantage. When the government wish to support a sporting or cultural event in the North, the Midlands are seen as in the South. When large companies wish to move their headquarters to London or to the south, the Midlands are seen as the North.

It is often said that Birmingham does not have a strong 'self image'. It is true that compared to cities such as Liverpool it does not appear to have as much character. It has in recent times been seen by many as the centre of a large sprawling conurbation dominated by motorways and cars, with no easily defined or distinguished centre. In the 1970s it was said to be a dump, but then so were Liverpool, Manchester and Newcastle at that time.

The Midlands region is now ethnically diverse. The traditional 'Brummie' and the man from the 'Black Country' are still known for pragmatism, inhibition, hard headedness and a 'dull' accent. He is not known for his passion, sense of humour or cockiness. With the decline of engineering, particularly the motor industry, the region was, in the 1970s and 1980s, going backwards. But things have changed. Birmingham and the Black Country has become a region of canals, exhibition centres and Balti food. It has also become an entertainment centre. Unfortunately, the revival in the fortunes of the region does not include a revival in the fortunes of its football teams.

By way of contrast, Liverpool is a city self-conscious of its own importance, of its own exceptional identity.[6] This is based perhaps on history, on hardships, on characteristics such as humour, aggression and music, and probably on a mixture of all these factors. A dean of history at Liverpool University has said 'There's a Liverpool thing, in a way I don't think there's a Leicester thing, or a Birmingham thing.' He is probably right. Nobody would ever say that Liverpudlians suffer from low self-esteem. However, if Merseysiders love themselves because of their perceived characteristics, they are loved in far off places because of their football. In China young people know of Liverpool because of the football team not because of the 'culture' of the people or because of the city's architecture.

History and the Regional Economy

In the eighteenth century Birmingham was a place for a man to make a fortune. Even in the 1870s a local saying held that 'Any fool can make a fortune in Birmingham.'[7] Industrialists, scientists and bankers came to live in or near the city and did well for themselves and the community around then. 'A city of makers and traders. Its citizens boasted of its industry, its independence, its bustle and its power.' One reason for its success was its freedom from rules and regulations. In reality Birmingham was noisy, dirty and chaotic, but it was exuberant, individualist and inventive. The manufacturers and traders were global in outlook, they saw their market as not just national, but also as the countries on the continent and in the empire.

Birmingham in the late 1800s was an important city from a political as well as an industrial point of view. The Chamberlain family were leading national politicians, while Quaker industrialists such as the Cadbury family were demonstrating new ways of providing welfare for workers and the local authority were pioneering new ways to improve the quality of life in a city. It was not surprising therefore that reformist ideas about organising sport in the community should come from Birmingham. William McGregor of Aston Villa was the driving force behind the establishment of the Football League. The region had a long football history going back to before the founding of the League in 1888. In the early professional days Aston Villa were the most successful team in the country, in the 1890s they won the League five times and the FA Cup twice. West Bromwich Albion were finalists in the FA Cup on five occasions in the years up to 1914.

Unfortunately, from the beginning the Midlands teams have not been as successful financially as their rivals from other parts of the country. Everton only failed to make a profit in one year between 1891–1914. Liverpool made a profit in every year between 1900 and 1914. By contrast West Bromwich Albion 'were continually in financial difficulties.'[8] The club were forced to hold grand fêtes, military tournaments and prize draws, in an effort to raise funds. One year the directors of the club paid the summer wages of the players out of their own pockets. The *Birmingham Evening Dispatch* launched a shilling fund to help save the club. However it should not be assumed that because the town of West Bromwich is relatively small that the club is destined to be poor. The directors of the club decided to locate their ground 'between the densely populated districts of Handsworth (Birmingham) and Smethwick and within comparatively easy reach of the Northwest side of Birmingham.' This decision was made in order to be able to attract large numbers of spectators to matches. West Bromwich Albion have the same catchment area as Aston Villa.

Although Aston Villa were successful on the pitch, the club's directors were keen to emphasise that they were not in favour of running the club as a 'source of profit to the members.' They argued that to do so would be 'against the sport.' When the directors did turn the club into a limited liability company in 1896, the shares were distributed widely. There were over 700 individual shareholders, the largest shareholder being a tramway company located next to the ground but they only owned 50 shares. This major shareholder, the Birmingham and Aston Tramway Company, 'had a stake in Aston Villa's success not just through its shareholding.' It was the company's trams that transported the huge crowds from the centre of the city to Villa Park and back again. An early example of how shareholders could benefit financially from their involvement with football without receiving dividends.

By the 1960s when the Chester Committee reported on the financial state of football at that time, they found a 'generally gloomy financial picture' with markedly declining attendances and overall losses. There were, however, exceptions, with one half of the First Division clubs showing a profit over the 1964–66 period (the West Midland teams were not in this group). Even as long ago as 1967–68, the average-size crowd watching Manchester United was over twice that watching any one of the five top Midlands teams. The ranking of clubs in that season by size of average home attendance shows that behind Manchester United came Everton, Liverpool, Tottenham, Newcastle, Manchester City, Leeds and Chelsea. Even 40 years ago Midlands clubs were falling financially behind their rivals. What is perhaps a surprise is that ranking the West Midlands clubs by size of home gates in that year shows Coventry as top, followed by Wolverhampton, Birmingham, West Bromwich Albion and finally Aston Villa. In the mid-1960s Aston Villa were in trouble, they were short of money and playing staff, with many key players asking for transfers. In 1968, in their first season back in the then Second Division, they finished sixteenth with an average gate of only 19,783, compared with an average gate at Birmingham City of 28,155.

To be fair, many clubs right across the country were in financial difficulties during the 1960s, 1970s and 1980s. There was a need to bring new funds into the clubs just to enable them to survive. There were some directors who did inject funds into their clubs, even though at that time it would have been difficult for them to see how the clubs would ever be in a position to repay the loans. It was only from the mid-1980s that new sources of income began to emerge and that investment in football as a financial transaction (as opposed to one that boosted one's status, or as a social investment) appeared to be attractive.

In 1968 Doug Ellis (at the time seen as a saviour) loaned Aston Villa £100,000 with the option to convert the loan into equity shares. He became a director of the club. At that time it would have been difficult for him to see the shares rising in value in the future. Three years earlier Clifford Coombs had lent Birmingham City £80,000. Such people were investing desperately needed money into the clubs. They were buying themselves directorships, which in the short-term, was good for the club. It did not necessarily mean, however, that the people involved would turn out to be good directors of the clubs over the longer term.

By the late 1980s 'football was gradually crawling out of its slump and slowly investing in itself. The clubs in the Midlands were however still reigning in their expenditure, cutting costs.'[9] It was at this time that the constraints on competition between football clubs in terms of wage levels, dividends, payments and transfer fees, were coming to an end. It was also at this time that new opportunities were arising, including a new Premier League. It was also at this time that the Midlands clubs needed modern leadership.

There was conservatism in the management of the Midlands football teams, and conservatism in the management of Midlands businesses. Historically, directors of Midlands companies have been reluctant to invest in new technology with the result that the region lost the machine tool industry, the motorcycle industry and most of the automobile industry—all industries in which the Midlands had once led the world. A region that was once famous for its engineering skills and ingenuity suffered a decline in its fortunes as a result of weak leadership and poor quality management. Names such as Austin's, Lucas, Alfred Herberts, GEC, Rover and Rootes disappeared. There was underinvestment in Midlands industry in general and underinvestment particularly in the local football teams.

The conservatism of businessmen running Midlands companies has in certain cases persisted. The chairman and chief executive of Aston Villa in the club's 2003 annual report emphasises that the club 'continues to operate within its resources' and points out that 'this has made the challenge of competing regularly for honours but remaining financially stable extremely difficult.' But what are the clubs resources? Whereas some clubs had borrowed too much, Aston Villa had borrowed too little. Their balance sheet in 2005 showed total assets of £60 million, £36 of which million was financed by shareholder funds, and £24 million by liabilities. Even conventional (prudent) levels of financial gearing would allow for an additional £12 million of borrowing. To be successful the club needed a more 'aggressive' financial strategy.

It is interesting and of relevance to note that Aston Villa in their 2003 annual report make reference to the club's 'distinguished footballing tradition' and state that this 'is the strong foundation upon which we continue to build our brand.' The value of a brand name depends on recent success, not on success over three generations ago!

One question often raised is whether or not the level of economic prosperity in a region has an influence on the success of the local football teams. In the past a high percentage of the revenue generated by a club was from local sources. The Midlands, the North, the North West and the North East were mainly working class areas and the support of the local football club was based on working class people. Was the failure of the Midlands teams, particularly in the 1980s, the result of the general economic decline in the region?

Gavin McOwen, in his history of West Bromwich Albion, is quite clear about the link. He makes the comment that 'All elements of society, including football clubs, reflect the area they inhabit and by the mid-1980s the West Midlands was a wasteland. Like the local economy, the local football clubs were on their knees.' The second sentence is correct, not not necessarily the first.

If we go back to a slightly earlier period, to that immediately following the Second World War and through to the 1970s, the region that enjoyed the most striking economic success was the West Midlands. The region boomed, based on the growth in manufacturing industry, in particular the motor industry. There was a drift of population towards the Midlands in these years. Birmingham and Coventry were boom towns in the 1950s and 1960s. The success of the region was mirrored in the success of Wolverhampton in the 1950s, and later by West Bromwich Albion, Derby and Nottingham Forest.

But things began to go wrong with the Midlands economy in the late 1970s and 1980s. In 1978 the unemployment rate in the region was 7.5%, but by 1982 it was 12.2%. The decline of the motor industry was a catastrophe for the region. But the Midlands was not the only region in decline. The Northern region of England, which includes Tyneside and Newcastle, had the highest levels of unemployment throughout the 1980s. The success team of the 1960s and for some of the 1970s and 1980s was Manchester United, but the region around Manchester was also suffering economic decline. The dominant team of the 1980s was Liverpool, a city with the surrounding region of Merseyside that suffered very bad economic decline.

On the face of it, it is not easy to link the success of a local football team with the prosperity of a region. London and the South East of England are clearly the most prosperous regions. Arsenal have enjoyed success for a number of decades, but a team only a few miles from them, Tottenham Hotspur, have done badly.

There are a number of important factors accounting for football success other than regional economic success.

Expenditure

One of the themes of this book is that it is the directors who are responsible for the long-term success or failure of a football club; it is they who steer the club. *The Economist*, in a 'Survey of Football', argued 'that in the longer run you can generally buy success.' This is only the case if you have directors who can take advantage of the opportunities available to a club, but as Leeds United and a number of other clubs have shown financial resources do not guarantee success. To have money is a necessary condition for success but not a sufficient condition. Some teams have more opportunities than others to earn money. Whether they do so depends on leadership—on the clubs directors.

Stefan Szymanski and Tim Kuypers have shown that the annual wage bill of a club is 'a fairly accurate predictor of average league position.'[10] By 'average' is meant over a period of time. The better players have to be paid the highest wages, particularly at a time when players' agents are continually trying to take advantage of the highly competitive market for footballers. The better players can command higher wages, for the better the players at a club the more likely are the club to achieve success. Successful teams attract supporters, sponsors, and broadcasting income, and the financial rewards for success increase every year. In the newly rich football markets of the world—Japan, China, South East Asia and the Middle East—the demand is for the successful brand names not for the also-rans. More money brings more success; the formula is very simple.

The close correlation between success and relative wage and salary spending applies not only to football in Europe but also to American football, basketball, baseball and ice hockey. Given a club's wage bill it is possible with a fair degree of accuracy to predict their final league position. It is possible to do so with greater accuracy in the European football leagues than in the US sports leagues.[11] The studies show that in recent years there has been a trend towards increasing predictability. The Midlands clubs are relatively poor spenders in terms of wage levels.

If we look at the size of the total wage and salary bill of each of the five West Midlands clubs over the five seasons from 1997–98 to 2001–02, the ranking of the teams is as follows: Aston Villa (twelfth highest), Coventry City (fourteenth), Birmingham City (twenty-second), Wolverhampton (twenty-third) and West Bromwich Albion (twenty-eighth). This is the ranking in the list of 37 Premier League and First Division (as it was then) clubs for which data is available. Of the East Midlands teams (for the five-year period) figures are available only for Nottingham Forest who rank twenty-fourth. These are not wage levels that would suggest that the clubs involved would achieve success. If one looks at a slightly later period, 2000–01 to 2004–05, Aston Villa's ranking is seventh, Birmingham City's eighteenth, Wolverhampton twentieth, Coventry twenty-first and West Bromwich Albion twenty-second.

It might be argued that it is the lack of success that means the clubs cannot afford to pay high wages, rather than the payment of high wages that leads to success. In other words, the causality is success leading to higher wages. There have in fact been studies that looked into the direction of the relationship and they all found that for football in Europe it is access to funds that leads to high wages that leads to success, rather than the other way around. The studies of Szymanski and Kuypers have been based on the period since the mid-1980s, but there is evidence that even before that for a decade or so a similar relationship between access to finance, leadership and success existed. Further back in the past, wage levels were controlled, revenue was shared and there was not the wide financial gap between the revenue earned by clubs in the different leagues.

It is true that in the past there have been cases where exceptional leadership has led to success, without access to money being a key factor. This has not led to success over more than a short period of time, however. There have been clubs where for a particular period of time the interaction of manager, player, club and director have achieved outstanding playing success. (Nottingham Forest, Derby, Ipswich.) This short-term success has not, however, resulted in the clubs being able to accumulate sufficient wealth to enable them to remain amongst the 'elite' clubs.

Deloitte and Touche note in their survey for the first season of the Premier League (1992–93) that 'playing success on the field in any individual season does not necessarily translate to financial success in that financial year ... however the clubs which enjoy consistent playing success do generally translate this to financial success ... in the medium term.' But playing success maintained over a long period depends on sound financial management. This has become very apparent over recent years. It is relatively easy to pay high wages over one or two seasons.

It has been said that in US sport 'the relative strength of a team depends on the financial strength of the team and owner.' But it is not quite as simple as that. The financial strength of an individual football club depends on the total amount of funds coming into the sport, and is also dependent on the opportunities and ability of the directors and managers of that club to attract a share of the finance and to control how it is used. In 2002 when Peter Ridsdale was Chief Executive of Leeds United and discussing his club's strategy and its resulting financial plan, he noted that 'the next five years could be very good or disastrous—that will depend on management.' Unfortunately for Ridsdale within the next 12 months it turned out to be disastrous. Leeds United's board of directors adopted a high risk strategy involving high levels of borrowing which could only be justified if the club qualified for one of the European competitions. The disastrous performances on the pitch for a few crucial months could be blamed on the players and the team management, but the cause of the financial failure of the club was poor decision-making by the board.

Although Szymanski and Kuypers have shown that the size of the wage bill is a fairly accurate predictor of average league position, they also show, perhaps surprisingly, that 'the transfer spending of the top clubs bears almost no relationship to league position.' They were, however, reporting on the period 1991–92 to 1997–98 (the first seven years of the Premier League), and in that period Manchester United spent very little in the transfer market as they had a very successful group of home-produced players. Nevertheless, they did spend very heavily on transfers in the next eight seasons. This was also the period before Chelsea were able to 'buy' their way to success.

The case of Chelsea appears to indicate that expenditure on new players, if large enough, can buy success. Certainly many boards of directors do act as though they do now believe this to be the case. A key factor, however, is the ability of the management of a club to identify good players and the ability of the directors to negotiate

271

a satisfactory transfer fee. It is easy to waste money on expensive purchases and to bring 'star' players to a club that do not perform well. High levels of investment do not bring automatic success. This is not surprising as it is the leadership in a club at all levels that mould talent into a successful team.

Having acknowledged this fact, it has to be accepted that the management of a club does operate at a disadvantage if it cannot buy 'good' players. The Midlands clubs have not been big spenders in the transfer market. The ranking by net transfer expenditure (fees paid less fees received) over the 1998–99 to 2002–03 period showed Aston Villa as tenth highest, Birmingham City as fourteenth, Derby nineteenth, Wolves twentieth and West Bromwich Albion twenty-fourth. A similar pattern to that revealed for wage rankings and league positions. Manchester United were top with net expenditure of £87 million. Aston Villa's net expenditure was £37 million, and West Bromwich Albion's £2 million. Coventry City are interesting because whereas the above figures are for net expenditure, Coventry showed net receipts over the period of £3 million; no wonder they were relegated.

The reason that Manchester United can now afford to spend more on salaries than all other clubs (except Chelsea) is because it generates high income. The fact that it generates the highest income in the league is mainly the result of decisions made by directors over the last 50 years. Factors such as population and tradition have clearly been important, but there are other clubs that have had the potential to be as successful as Manchester United and have failed to be so. Business success is more likely to be achieved if there is harmony amongst the top management team, and in football that means harmony at boardroom level and between directors and managers. At clubs like Aston Villa, Manchester City, Everton, Tottenham and Chelsea there have over the years been frequent stories of disagreements between directors, between directors and managers and between managers and players. In the period that covers the important formative years leading up to the establishment of the Premier League, as well as the first years of that league (from 1959 to 1995), Manchester City had 16 managers, Chelsea had 14 and Aston Villa had 13. In contrast Liverpool had six and Arsenal and Manchester United each had seven. It is directors who make decisions on the appointment of managers. It was the Sunderland directors who in 2003 appointed

Howard Wilkinson to be manager but only kept him for a few weeks. It was the Leeds directors who appointed Terry Venables to be manager in their disastrous 2002–03 season and then appointed Peter Reid in the next season. The boards of the Midlands clubs do not have a good corporate governance record, there have been frequent disputes at boardroom level, and frequent changes of managers.

Passion

It is sometimes claimed that people in the Midlands are not as passionate about their sport as, say, those in the North East or North West regions of England. This is an easy statement to make, but one that is difficult to prove (or disprove). There was certainly a 'passion' about football in the Midlands in the early days of the League and Cup. In the 1882–83 season, when West Bromwich Albion played Aston Villa at Perry Barr, in Birmingham, it was reported that the rival groups of supporters were throwing sods of turf and stones at each other. In 1886 when West Bromwich Albion beat Small Heath in the FA Cup semi-final, the Small Heath goalkeeper was pelted with snowballs. In 1892 when Aston Villa lost to West Bromwich Albion in the FA Cup Final, the Aston Villa fans blamed their own goalkeeper for the defeat, and proceeded to smash the windows of his pub. The strong local rivalries in football in the Birmingham area has a long history, as does crowd trouble.

One problem is that supporters of football clubs in the Midlands have in recent years had little to be passionate about. Given something to become excited about they could offer a level of support as good, if not better, than supporters in any other part of the country. This was proven in cricket in the 2005 Test Match that took place in Birmingham between England and Australia. England won by two runs and many regard this match as one of the most exciting ever. The England players were full of praise for the support they received. The *Sunday Times* reported that 'The game has been played out in an electric atmosphere at Edgbaston, which routinely produces the most vociferous support for England.' Reference was made to the 'raucous patriotism of Edgbaston' that brings out the best in the English players. The hero of the match,

273

Freddie Flintoff, referred to the great atmosphere at the cricket ground in Birmingham, with the crowd being 'like a twelfth man.' Edgbaston is apparently the favourite ground of the English cricket team.[12] There is no reason why a similar level of emotion would not exist at the Midlands football grounds if the directors of the clubs provided the supporters with teams worth getting excited about.

The Scottish footballer Gary McAllister who after leaving Liverpool played for Coventry for a number of years commented that 'Coventry isn't a great crowd, none of them in the Midlands [are], except maybe Wolves. It's not really a football area. Football is most popular in economically depressed areas, in the North and in Scotland. It cheers up people's lives and lets them feel like winners for once. They really identify with their teams, and get behind them.'[13] He expressed this opinion when writing about the advantage a team obtains from having a good home crowd—how such a crowd benefits the team. He believes such a crowd 'intimidates opponents and puts an extra yard on you.'

McAllister argues that football is more popular in economically depressed areas. A similar point was made many years ago by that famous old footballer and sports journalist Charles Buchan. 'Up in the North East the crowd takes its football very seriously ... I think they know more about the game than Southern crowds.' There is a belief by some in the game that fans in the North of England are more loyal to their team than fans in other parts of the country. The evidence is, however, that this is not so. Stephen Dobson and John Goddard have shown that the short run response in terms of attendance to a team's performance is indeed strong, but that the scale of the response is 'remarkably consistent across regions.'[14]

Another explanation for the lack of success in the region is that offered by Bobby Gould, who played for Coventry and West Bromwich Albion for a number of years. He argued that the Midlands lacks glamour. David Bowler and Jas Bains quote Bobby Gould: 'It's not a glamorous area, there is apathy there and the Midlands clubs never took off like Liverpool did, or United have done recently. We didn't have the flamboyancy as an area ... when players reach a certain level, they outgrow the area. It's unfortunate, but it's a fact of life.'[15] Perhaps the top players avoid the

Midland clubs because they want success, they want to play in winning teams.[16]

One would have to agree with Gould in respect of comparing Birmingham as a city with London, but is glamour an expression one can use when describing Liverpool? Birmingham has recreated itself over the last 20 years, but it is true it was certainly not glamorous in the 1970s and 1980s. There is no reason to believe however, that towns like Newcastle and Middlesbrough are now or ever were more glamorous than Birmingham, and these and all Northern cities are further away than Birmingham from the real glamour of London.

Fans like to support a successful club, and in this respect significant changes have taken place in respect of an individual's identification with a club. At one time the vast majority of those who followed football became fans of the local team. They would support the team whether or not it was successful—they had little choice, this was the only team they could watch on a regular basis. The players in that team were the only ones they could identify with. But some teams were more successful than others, and with the increase in the marketing of the game, and the increased exposure of teams through the media, some clubs developed a 'brand' name that was respected nationally. They developed a national image. Young people now have a choice, they do not need to support the local team; through TV and media coverage they can easily follow the fortunes of a club with a glamorous image, a team that is capable of being champions. Over half the people who watch Liverpool and Manchester United home games travel over 50 miles to be there, so it is not the passions of a region that are important.

After developing a local brand name, then a nationally identified brand name, the next step for a club is an internationally known brand name. Promoting a brand name was what business in the 1990s was all about. It was easier to market a club's name if it had a history of recent success and if the playing squad included glamorous players. This is where teams like Arsenal, Manchester United and Liverpool have excelled—it is where teams like Aston Villa, West Bromwich Albion and Nottingham Forest have failed.

In the 1990s the marketing aspect of business grew in import-ance. It became not so much the selling of a product, as the selling

275

of an image. In all markets, consumers were led to believe they would obtain more satisfaction if they were associated with the best product being offered, and one could tell the best product because of the 'brand' name. The Premiership was sold as the best league in the world.

All major clubs are trying to create a global brand. Newcastle United in their 2002 annual report in a section on overseas brand development state that 'The club is taking measures to establish Newcastle United on the international stage principally through new contacts in China, Hong Kong and Australia. We expect current negotiations to establish firm links, particularly with the Chinese market, in the next two to three years.' Aston Villa have also written about trying to build up the value of their brand name. They state that 'the power of our brand is rooted in a track record of success that dates back decades and attracts recognition world-wide.' Who are they kidding—it is only those who are interested in the history of football that know of the club's successes.

Local Demand

In the pre-Second World War period and right up to the 1980s, gate receipts accounted for up to 90% of a club's revenue; attracting large crowds was therefore important for a club. Against this advantage for a club of a good size catchment area was the fact that gate receipts until 1983 had to be divided between the home and away teams. With this revenue sharing arrangement and the control on wage costs it might have been thought the size of the local population was not so important to a team, but not so. If a club had a big ground it had high gate receipts for one half of its games in a season whereas most visiting teams only had a share of a large gate occasionally. The teams that showed continuing success were from the bigger conurbations. The position now is that each year gate receipts account for a smaller and smaller percentage of a club's revenue. (In 2004–05 in the Premier League match day receipts accounted for 31% of revenue; Ten years earlier it was 47%.) The important thing now is to have a good 'brand' name.

Yet the reason the Midlands teams consistently fail to join the current elite clubs is not because they are from a region with a relatively sparse population. Szymanski and Kuypers have analysed the statistical relationship between location and league position. The hypothesis they examined was that certain teams enjoy a natural advantage because they have large populations living near their grounds. The population living within ten miles of the ground was used to a measure the size of the catchment area. The results of the study show that there is some relationship but that it is 'quite weak and cannot explain why clubs such as Liverpool and Manchester United have enjoyed such a high degree of success.' The fact that the relationship is weak can be seen from the fact that the ten teams with the largest populations within ten miles of their grounds, in descending order are Arsenal, West Ham, Brentford, Spurs, West Bromwich Albion, Aston Villa, Manchester United, Manchester City, Birmingham and Oldham. Only two of what we now regard as the elite clubs are in this top ten.

From a population point of view the Midlands region should have one club amongst the elite group. In the 1990s the male population of the West Midlands region was 1.3 million, in Manchester and its surroundings it was approximately the same, while in Merseyside it was 680,000. The male population of Birmingham was 500,000. In terms of population size therefore the clubs in the West Midlands region have had the opportunity to be financially successful. Szymanski and Kuypers refer to the fact that West Bromwich Albion and Aston Villa have populations of over 500,000 within ten miles of their grounds (fifth highest and sixth highest catchment areas amongst clubs), while Birmingham City has a population of 450,000 within ten miles, eight highest, and only just below that of Manchester United.

A comprehensive study into the demand to watch English League Football was conducted by Dobson and Goddard. They studied the period from 1947 to 1997 in an attempt to identify the factors that could explain differences in attendance figures between clubs. They found that in the long-term the base attendance figures for a club depends upon a number of factors, some being the socio-economic and demographic characteristics of the 'home' venue of the club; others being football related characteristics (i.e. the club's age and past success). Factors that influenced changes in the short-term demand to watch a club were the loyalty of fans, the success of the team, admission prices and the entertainment value of the team (measured by goals scored).

Is it the fact that the grounds in the Midlands are smaller than those of Manchester United, Newcastle and Arsenal that explains the lower level of demand? Could it be that the demand is greater than is reflected in attendance figures? Sadly, the answer is No, because (except for Birmingham and West Bromwich Albion in 2002–03 and 2003–04) the Midlands clubs very rarely fill their grounds. Undoubtedly for a few matches the size of the crowd is limited by ground capacity, and so if the clubs had larger grounds the annual average attendance figures would be higher, but not that much more. Villa Park has a capacity of 42,600, but their average Premier League crowd in 2002–03 was only 35,081. This is an occupancy rate of 82%, the lowest occupancy rate in the Premier League, and the position has been similar for a number of seasons (in 2004–05 it was 87%). In their 2003 annual report Aston Villa refer to the loyalty of supporters as being 'beyond question' and to the 'upward trend in attendances over the last five years.' Attendance figures were then and still are below what one would expect for the biggest club in the second city. Birmingham and West Bromwich Albion, with capacities of only 30,000 and 28,000 respectively, whilst in the Premier League had occupancy rates of around 95%. In 2004–05, whilst in the Championship, Derby County and Nottingham Forest had occupancy rates of about 75%.

Leadership and the Midlands Clubs

The 'Chester Report' as long ago as 1968 pointed out that 'variation in the quality of club management will affect playing success, whatever the club's effective population area. It also pointed out that there were 'two aspects of the management of a league club.' One is the management of a business enterprise—the financial aspects and the hiring and firing of key staff (such as the team manager). The other is the playing side—the coaching, tactics and selection of players. The final responsibility for the good business management of clubs lies with their boards.

Coventry City exemplify what can be achieved when a good manager is backed by a supportive board of directors. They were in the top division for 34 years, not bad for a club from a medium-sized town. The success started with an innovative manager, Jimmy Hill, and a dynamic chairman, Derrick Robins. Hill had been chairman of the Professional Football Association, and had been very instrumental in ending the maximum-wage system. He introduced change into the way the club was run, and introduced many of the marketing ideas coming into the sport from the US.

In contrast, Birmingham City demonstrated where poor leadership can take a club. Karen Brady in her autobiography provides a very clear picture of Birmingham City Football Club in 1992. An advertisement had appeared in the *Financial Times* in that year offering a football club for sale. Karen Brady visited St. Andrews on behalf of David Sullivan, who was interested in expanding his investments. He was apparently at the time more interested in buying a racehorse than a football club, but was persuaded that Birmingham City Football Club had potential.

Karen Brady reports when she first saw St. Andrews she was not so much disappointed as disgusted. It was dirty, lacking paint and the boardroom was furnished in a 1960s style. The club was in the hands of liquidators. The then chairman, Jack Wiseman, admitted to Karen Brady that he did not know how long the club could stay afloat, since the books were not available to him. He made the point that he was 70 years old, he was 'all on his own at the club, and he was doing his best.'

The club clearly had been run into the ground. Karen Brady makes the point that the existing directors had been running the club at only a fraction of its potential. She was being kind; for over 40 years the directors had been running the club at only a fraction of its potential.

Ten year later, in 2002, on the day before Birmingham City took part in the play-off finals for a place in the Premiership, one respectable broadsheet newspaper reminded its readers that 'this was the club once owned by a scrap-metal merchant (Ken Whelan) who, when answering the telephone, pretended to be a caretaker in case a creditor was calling. Ownership then passed to a pair of rag-trade kings (the Kumar Brothers) before a trio of multi-millionaires, who had made their fortunes from publishing raunchy magazines, rescued the club from bankruptcy. They appointed a glamorous but capable 23-year old as managing director, who went on to marry the club's star striker.' This reads like the storyline for a TV soap opera about a fictional football club.

Before Ken Whelan bought the club in 1986 it had been owned for over 20 years by a family who ran a wholesale clothing business.

279

This family, the Coombs family, were also involved in politics at a local and national level. The club had been in financial difficulties when the Coombs took it over.

Danny Blanchflower, one of the most interesting and successful players in the second half of the twentieth century, made some challenging comments about the condition of Aston Villa in the 1960s and 1970s. 'The whole place (Villa Park) was crying out for soccer leadership and guidance and I eventually tired of the complacency there. Villa had a tremendous potential and still has but I am not sure how it can be realised.' This was before the Doug Ellis era. At the time Bruce Normansell was chairman.

Clearly Aston Villa have still not reached their potential. Blanchflower expressed doubts as to whether they ever would do so. He believed 'that a club, like a human being, has a maximum vitality which it reaches for a spell once in its lifetime, and Villa passed that period of destiny back in the days when its name was famous throughout the whole world of soccer.' Not all would agree with Blanchflower's assessment. The big three clubs—Liverpool, Manchester United and Arsenal—have managed to stay at the top for many, many decades. A football club is a business, not a human being. It can keep re-inventing itself if it has leadership that can adapt to changing conditions. It is of course true that human beings do have a maximum vitality, but for a company this is not necessarily the case. If the individuals who manage and direct a company are prepared to step aside as society changes, and they age, then clubs, organisations and companies can stay at the top.

What happened to Aston Villa? Thirty years after Blanchflower's comments another successful footballer who played for a time at Villa expressed his views on the club. Paul Merson said, 'I don't like the idea of always coming seventh, eighth or ninth. It is not good enough. We have had bad runs but it's four years on the trot now.' Four years for Paul Merson, but much longer for the fans. Villa, despite for many years being the only Premier League team in a conurbation of over 3 million people, still only attract gates of 30,000 (except against Manchester United, Liverpool and Arsenal). 'We're not playing good football. If we were, people would come flooding back.'

Michael Walker, who interviewed Merson, pointed out that 'People do mind mediocrity, particularly when it is disguised by ambitions that amount to little more than an allegation.' Villa talks big, but do not play big. 'Villa are meant to be a club of national significance' but they are not.

Who is to blame? The chairman? The manager? Or can it be explained by Blanchflower's hypothesis that Villa are past their period of 'maximum vitality'? The managers blame the board (the chairman) and say that all they need is a few more players. The club had in fact been buying players, but every time they buy one good player, they sell another. It has emerged that there might be more than one reason why during John Gregory's time as manager the club were so busy trading players. With every transaction agents obtain generous fees and in the end this fact worried Doug Ellis. In Gregory's few years as manager of Aston Villa the club spent £66 million on new players but recouped £51 million from the sale of players. Although this amounts to a remarkably small net expenditure, just under £4 million a year, the total value of transactions is high and provides considerable opportunities for agents to take commission.

Doug Ellis had been a hands-on chairman. The 'Cadbury Report on Corporate Governance' recommends that in every company the role of chairman and CEO should be divided, but not everyone would agree with this. Ellis made 'no apologies for being a six days a week, hands-on chief executive' with sensible, prudent house-keeping his primary concern. 'Not a single cheque leaves Villa Park without my personal signature on it.' This signing of cheques is an unusual role for a chairman of a £50 million plus company. Prudent is a lovely word, it was popular in the accounting profession before the days of creative accounting. The business philosophy of Ellis at Aston Villa was that one should 'generate income before you spend it.' As Ellis explains, such an approach does avoid disaster, but it does limit growth opportunities.

Nevertheless, Doug Ellis had difficulties in working effectively with the managers he appointed. When he removed David O'Leary in 2006, this was the thirteenth manager to leave the club during Ellis' 40 year period as chairman.

There are lessons to be learned from this case. One is that a divided board does not work in the interests of a business, but also an absence of disagreement amongst directors because of one dominant person, does not necessarily produce favourable results. Perhaps what is best is a healthy discussion at boardroom level of controversial issues, but a discussion which does not lead to directors falling out with each other. A second lesson from this case, as from many others in corporate governance, is that the person in charge should not be allowed to continue past a certain age. As people get older, they become more set in their ways and less willing to change. Doug Ellis was 82 before he sold his major shareholding and gave up control of the club.

Similar stories could be told about other Midlands clubs. Bryan Jones comments that 'Clubs are run by business people and West Midlands business has tended to be backward, traditionalist, resistant to new ideas. There was complacency, a resistance to change and they lost out. 'Clubs were becoming big business and some clubs were too slow to see it. 'There was not the business orientation at the clubs at the time it was needed and so they couldn't generate the money they need to be successful.'[17]

West Bromwich Albion had for many years a 'Board largely composed of solicitors.' Solicitors have a reputation for being inherently conservative; certainly they don't have a reputation for entrepreneurial flair. Larry Canning believes that 'there have been too many times when the clubs here (the Midlands) have been run or managed by people who don't know the game, who are in it for prestige.' The support for the clubs has been good even though the performances have been bad. The directors 'probably don't even think there is anything wrong as long as fifteen or twenty thousand people are coming in.'[18]

Why has the management of Midlands clubs been worse than that of clubs in other regions? Canning believes 'we attract abysmal chairmen because the Midlands is full of business people who have sprung up through hard work, mainly in industry. They're up there and have to do something with their money to get some glory and power, so they take over a club. You get a guy like Doug Ellis who thinks he knows the game, but he doesn't.'

Whilst Aston Villa were in the top division, Canning (an ex-Villa player) asked the Aston Villa manager: 'If you keep buying third division players and putting them in your team, where do you think you will end up?' Villa did drop into the then Third Division in 1971. Canning's reference is to Third Division players, but to that could be added buying poor First and Second Division players, and more recently buying Premier League players who are past their best. Also buying foreign players who are not capable of adjusting to the style of the Premier League. These comments were made about the management of Midlands clubs a decade or so ago. Unfortunately this was a crucial time because errors made then were to have unfortunate long-term consequences. The situation had improved in the last decade but there had still been boardroom disputes at many of the Midland clubs, including West Bromwich Albion and Derby County.[19]

Lessons

In modern times any self-respecting business needs to be able to produce a business plan. Such a plan in management circles is thought to be a useful tool which can be used to give some guidance to external providers of finance (banks and shareholders), as well as being useful inside the business to set targets (or as they are now called benchmarks). The existence of an objective, strategy or plan gives the impression that the directors of a company are in control and know what they are doing. The fact that the goal of every business is to do better than the average for their own industry means that approximately one half of businesses will fail to achieve their targets.

This is the position in football, as it is in other industries. The fact is that all of the 'leading' football clubs have similar objectives — at first maintaining a place in the Premier League and then qualifying for a place in Europe. Leeds United, in their 1999 annual report, explained that they had a five-year strategy (1999–2004) with the goal 'to make Leeds United one of the top football clubs not only in English football but also in Europe.'

Liverpool not surprisingly expressed a similar goal in their three-year strategy (1999–2002) document: 'to achieve a level of success on the football pitch that will allow continual participation in the Champions League.' Aston Villa have had a similar goal. Referring to the team's performance in 2001–02, the chairman commented that the club had fallen 'short of our Champions League goal.' They finished eighth in the league.

There are in fact only four or five clubs who can realistically expect over the next few seasons to qualify for a Champions league place. There are a second group of Premier League teams who do not have the financial resources to be able to compete for a Champions League place in the near future but who believe they

283

are too good to be fighting relegation. There are a third group of Premier League teams whose goal, realistically, should be just to remain in that league. Karen Brady's comment that Birmingham City's objective for the 2002–03 season (their first season in the Premier League) was to finish 4th from bottom was refreshingly honest.

All the above relates to football success. Football companies now have to think of financial success, those owned by 'outside' investors more so than those owned and controlled by their directors. Leeds made it clear that they saw European football success as linked to delivering shareholder value. Because they failed to qualify for the Champion League in the 2002–03 season, and because it became obvious they would not qualify in the next season, they began to sell their top players in order to reduce the level of debt. They acted quickly to try to protect shareholder value. What happened to the five-year strategic plan? It was soon forgotten. Unfortunately, for all concerned at Leeds, the decisions made by a small group of executives at the club in fact destroyed shareholder value. The club went into administration in 2007.

Liverpool, on the other hand, and with a similar objective to Leeds but with different people involved and a different ownership structure, did not cut back when they failed to qualify for the top European competition in 2002–03. They were prepared to continue to take risks in order to qualify for the Champions League, which if achieved 'provides the financial resource to compete at the highest level.' They won the UEFA Champions League in 2005.

For many years Aston Villa were like Liverpool, a company in which one director was a dominant shareholder, but at Aston Villa that shareholder wanted control. Aston Villa talked about European competition but they were not prepared to invest enough to make their goal a realistic one. In their 2002 accounts they noted that clubs are 'beginning to be forced to follow a more prudent stance' and that it will become easier for Aston Villa to manage salary and transfer costs in a very competitive industry when more of the industry is having to manage with similar disciplines. In other words, the financial policy of Aston Villa was to be prudent, their hope being that when other clubs become forced to adopt the same financial policy then the Villa will be able to achieve playing success.

Three clubs, three similar objectives, but three different strategies. Leeds, because of their divorce of ownership and control, might have been thought to be the club that could not afford to take too many risks. Liverpool and Villa, both with chairmen who were major shareholders, the clubs that could invest and afford to take a long-term view about returns. One of these two clubs invested heavily for playing success, which they achieved. The other was more concerned with financial success and adopting a more prudent approach. The three clubs, all having enjoyed success at some point in the past, and all with recent plans to make money in Europe. Leeds a disaster; Villa safe, into property development, modest in football; and Liverpool a team seeking to recapture the glory of the 1980s, and in need of money. The three cases demonstrate the importance of directors to the success, or otherwise, of the clubs. We see differences in constraints and difference in attitudes that are mainly the result of differences in people, in the values and managerial abilities of directors. It was, in other words, the people at the top who determined what happened and what is happening to these three clubs.

Two of these three clubs now have American owners. All connected with these two clubs, particularly their supporters, hope that the new owners will bring in additional funds and that good times lay ahead. But not all American businessmen are successful. The new owners of Aston Villa and Liverpool have not run particularly successful clubs in North America. As for Leeds they are still seeking good leadership and additional finance.

The reason the Midland clubs have not been successful is not because of lack of support, nor is it due to lack of passion, it is because of poor leadership at the time when football was moving from being a small business to being a global business. What of the future?[20]

10

The Beautiful Game? The Future

There are two kinds of power—money power and people power. In football, money power has taken over the game. In the past football has been referred to as 'the people's game'; in a way it still is, it is just that the power now lies with different people. The power is now in the hands of only those with big money. There are some who like what has happened; others do not.

One, perhaps surprising, critic of what has happened to football in general is Günter Grass, Germany's most famous writer. In 2006 (the year the FIFA World Cup was held in Germany), he attacked the commercialism of football. He criticised FIFA in particular: 'Its behaviour has been cowardly. It has ensured that football is no longer a sport for the people but is merely a big business.' Grass also pointed out that in Germany, much like in England, 'there is no fair competition any more in Germany's first and second division. This makes the competition for the championship boring.' There is no balanced competition.

Even more surprisingly, though, is that the professional game brings in great wealth and power for a few and those who are the winners are still not satisfied. There is forever talk of new leagues and new competitions, all designed to generate more wealth for the chosen few. The organisations who represent the fans express their views but their opinions are not as important as those of the people representing the money. Unfortunately we cannot rely on those who have control of the game to make changes that take into account the interests of all stakeholders.

Football is not like other businesses, it has a social relevance, and it is an important part of the life of many people. David Conn wrote in *The Football Business* in 1997 that 'if nothing changes, the future of football is entirely predictable. The future of football will follow the course of every *industry* which has been subjected to the divisive effect of *market forces*; guided by no more human force.' Every decision will be made solely on the basis of whether it will make money for the already rich. Decisions made would be 'entirely based on making money for the top clubs.' Nothing has changed over the last few years and Conn's prediction that 'Three, four or five football companies will dominate English football' turned out to be correct.

Furthermore in the ten years since Conn wrote his book the position has become worse, the special interest groups have increased their power. Conn discussed the possibility of the UK Government intervening and one specific possibility he considered was a windfall tax on football companies who made excess profits out of monopoly positions. This of course has not happened. One reason why it has not is that the elite clubs do not show excess profits, another reason is due to the fact that the UK Government are not prepared to face up to the problems of football—once the Task Force they established got nowhere they lost interest. Conn would have also liked to see football companies become more democratic, with wider share ownership and supporters and fans represented on boards of directors. In fact we have gone the other way, with more and more rich individuals with unusual business backgrounds becoming owners of clubs, with football companies becoming private, with more and more clubs becoming owned by foreigners, with even less public accountability.

The game will of course survive although we cannot be sure with what structure. We know there have been changes in the past. In the early years of its professional existence the game was successful, although even then a few clubs did struggle. In the 1920s and 1930s football suffered financially, in common with most other industries. There was even talk of whether or not it could survive in competition with other leisure activities. After the Second World War the game boomed, before entering a long decline to its low point in the mid-1980s. The period from the early 1970s to the late 1980s was one of almost continual crisis with even the Football League producing a report entitled 'Fight for Survival'. Another earlier report on the problems of football, the 'Chester Report', drew attention to clubs' lack of commercial awareness and to the fact that many clubs failed to respond to consumer demands. Fortunately for football, television helped them become more commercially aware and to find a huge new market, with a new type of consumer. Commercially the game has changed but not necessarily in the right way.

Things will change again. We have in the past had periods when from an economic point of view free trade and globalisation were in vogue, only for it to be followed by periods of protectionism and regionalism.[1] Football faces competition from other parts of the entertainment business. Who in the 1950s would have thought that the 'grubby' footballers would one day replace the stars of cinema as glamour figures? New technology will almost certainly come along. Perhaps football will ruin itself because of its own mistakes? Perhaps football in England at the top level will be owned and controlled exclusively by foreigners? This has already happened to those managing and directing a number of other industries, for example cars and machine tools.

There are now individual clubs that have financial problems, but this is often not because of the state of the game, but because of management who have not responded correctly to changes taking place. Simon Banks, in his book *Going Down, Football in Crisis*, expresses the belief that the crisis will be overcome. He must be right because the social returns for many, and the financial returns for a few, will mean that the professional game continues, but its future would be better if those leading the sport saw football clubs and international teams as not just brand names to exploit financially but as having an important social role.

If we follow the path of increased commercialism there will always be problems. We have already witnessed many clubs in financial difficulties and some have moved into the hands of administrators, with the most high profile case in England being Leeds United. The problem at Leeds was bad management, with marketing people living in a dream world, certainly not one based on financial realities. But the occasional high profile collapse is what one would expect in any competitive industry. It is market forces that act as a discipline on clubs and therefore we must expect casualties.

As Sean Hamil and many others have pointed out, football is not just a business it is also a social and cultural activity, and as such 'it is inappropriate to use conventional governance techniques' to control and regulate the game.[2] The trouble is those running the game are happy with the present system. The FA stumbles along moving from one problem to another. Various UK governments have, at times, taken an interest in the game, particularly when they have thought it could lead to their own increased popularity. The European Commission are keen to support a policy of free market competition in all industries, and are reluctant to treat sport as a special case. Those who control FIFA look after their own interests and the interests of those close to them.

Simon Banks prefers not to name the individuals who have contributed to the present crisis, but he does point out that in his analysis 'some names appear more than others.' Most of the problems of the game are the result of a failure of corporate governance and weak regulations. In recent years the regulation of the football industry has been abysmal at both the national and international level. Within England we have a system of self-regulation in place, but it should not be possible for the FA to be a regulator and also an income generator for the national team. It is not possible for them to control those who run the Premier League.

Where do we go from here? We are now in a situation where the results of a competition depend increasingly on the wealth of the owners of the clubs and the abilities of the boards of directors. If a team from, say, London, is richer than a team from, say, Southampton, and the directors of the London club are reasonably sensible, then over time the London club will be more successful than the Southampton club. In the US and Australia this problem has been recognised by their governments with the consequence that sport is recognised as a special case and is exempt from certain aspects of anti-trust legislation and competition policy. These countries have adopted this approach partly in the interests of consumers, of fans.

Without change the so-called pyramid structure which has developed in football means that there will be a declining interest in the lower league teams, and in order to survive they will require 'exceptional leadership'. The new generation of football fans will choose to support the big name clubs and to follow with interest the lifestyles and activities of the glamorous players hyped by the media. They would rather watch Beckham or Rooney on TV than watch, say, Hull FC play a live game. Meanwhile, in China they would rather watch Henry or Lampard on TV than watch their own league football live.

Jonathan Michie, Christine Oughton and others have argued that we are faced with two possibilities. One is increased commercialisation, with super leagues, world club championships and friendly internationals. The other is a wider public interest in the game, with fans becoming more involved in the governance process, either through football trusts, share ownership, seats on boards or through local government involvement. There is, however, a third route, namely for the structure of the leagues and the financial arrangements to be changed in an attempt to achieve more competitive balance in the game. From the point of view of the non-elite teams, such as those in the Midlands and the North East, the third option would be most beneficial, though the second option could help. The first option would simply mean greater inequality and an increasing number of clubs left behind.

Professional football is at a crossroads. Will it continue along its present path whereby what happens at the national level is determined by a few people in powerful organisations? Will football in Europe be played in each of the twelve months in a year, with mismatches occurring in international competitions and friendly matches arranged in order to earn more money for the organisers and the clubs fortunate enough to be involved?[3] Will domestic competitions be dominated by two or three teams, with more and more clubs struggling to survive? Will television and the marketing people continue to decide the time and day when matches are played, where they are played, and how the structure of competitions best suits them? Will the self-regulatory bodies continue to turn a blind eye to the problems of the game and allow greed to flourish?

Stefan Szymanski states that 'with the model of football currently in place in Europe the main issue is whether the existing structures are stable or whether the growing commercialisation of the sport will lead to restructuring.'[4] FIFA, UEFA and the leading clubs each want a form of restructuring that will benefit them. Change, led by one of these groups, will happen unless it can be stopped. One way to prevent this is to try to achieve greater democracy in decision-making in the existing league system. Another way is through greater supporter involvement through such organisations as Supporters Trusts. Another way is for the government to start taking the national interest into account. It has been argued in this book, however, that the best way to prevent commercialism from ruining the sport is to adopt another model and to allow certain of the restrictive practices that exist in sport in the US to be introduced into football in Europe. It is only if this happens that a club from the Midlands or from the North East will be able to break into the elite group, as well as help England to start producing a winning team.

In 1999, at the time when he was the Minister for Sport, Chris Smith said 'Professional football is in danger of losing touch with its roots.' He was very critical of those running the game, and called for a return to 'community values' and 'social responsibility.' This is the type of statement often made by politicians, good rhetoric, not strictly accurate, and not helpful. By the time football became a professional sport 100 years earlier it had already lost touch with its roots. In recent years a number of governments have had the opportunity to do something about what has happened yet have done nothing.

The game has always been part of the entertainment industry and now, as a result of clever marketing and new communication techniques, an increasingly wealthy population is prepared to spend large sums of money on football and on products associated with the game. The game has been taken away from its traditional support base, its sporting roots, and become part of the global entertainment business. Simon Freeman argues in his book *Own Goal* that 'the show rolls on, louder, richer and more arrogant than ever. Only the fans can force the industry that is football today to come to its senses. It is up to them.' Unfortunately, to change what is now happening is not that easy. The 'traditional' local-based fans are no longer important to the larger clubs, their fans are now spread around the world, and they do not communicate with each other, are not united, and often have different interests (i.e. the time matches are played).

The 1990s was a period of irrationality in business. The boom in the economy and in many industries, including football, was based on 'irrational exuberance'. It was a period when it was forgotten that the bubble in the economy would one day burst. The incentives available to some, including football players and club owners, became distorted. Everything was decided by short-term market forces and the role of regulators, including the government, declined in importance. Those who could prosper did so and ignored the effect on those around them. But in such boom periods are planted the 'seeds of destruction'. History shows us that economies are subject to change, as are industries, as is football.

Brian Clough believed football has become 'too big for its own good.' He claimed to have been 'the first one to use the word *industry* to describe professional football' and was of the opinion that in the early years of the 1990s commercial interests took over the sport. In 1997 David Conn recommended that the issue of ownership of clubs should be looked at closely by the authorities. This has been suggested many times since. What will happen in future to individual clubs depends to a great extent on what changes, if any, take place within the football industry. At the present time most people expect the commercialisation of the game to increase and the demand for the game to continue to grow. But nothing should be taken for granted.

At present most politicians believe, or say they believe, in the beneficial supremacy of the free market, and are willing to go along with those who state that globalisation is the best for all. But this could change. In football, many associations and many individuals clearly benefit from this ideology, as do the elite clubs. But on the supply side rival football competitions could be established, and on the demand side consumers might want more say in what is happening or they might reduce the amount they spend on football and its related products. The amount of money coming into the game from corporate sponsorship and television rights could decline too. Each of these occurrences would affect the individual football clubs in different ways.

We will now consider the alternative paths that professional football might follow in the future.

Increased Commercialism With Modest Change

This scenario is based on the fact that the most powerful bodies and organisations in the game want change, but they do not want to rock the boat. Organisations such as FIFA, UEFA and the various national football associations are powerful, but they do have to allow for the fact that a number of other interest groups are each trying to introduce some element of change; in effect each is trying to improve its own position. The top European clubs—the G14 group—state that they are unhappy with FIFA and UEFA. It is these associations that organise the World Cup, the European Nations Cup and the many 'friendly', and frankly, pointless international games. But it is the clubs that employ the players, pay them large salaries and suffer financially if a player is injured in an international match. It is true that clubs receive some financial compensation when their players are involved in international matches, but the amount of money involved is comparatively small and the risks great. The G14 group believe FIFA and UEFA have been abusing their dominant position, and they are in dispute over the principle of who should have final control over the services of players. They have taken FIFA to court.

There are already cosmetic changes taking place such as the football establishment in England introducing rules as to who are 'fit and proper' persons to own football clubs. However, if a club is short of money, or an owner looking for an exit route is offered a large sum of money, one cannot imagine that the real origins of where a 'saviour's' money comes from will be looked at too closely. In any case, with many offshore financial centres offering secrecy to owners of wealth, it is extremely difficult to find out who exactly is the beneficial owner of a trust fund or an offshore account.

Other structural changes are taking place at the FA where, following a number of ridiculous scandals that were harming the image of the game, it was agreed to set up an enquiry into the way the association was operating. Reluctantly the FA succumbed to pressure to have an independent enquiry. (It had hoped to be able to get away with just an internal review.) The resulting 'Burns Report' came up with a number of recommendations. The FA did in the end reluctantly accept most of the major changes recommended. These are, from the point of view of the FA, significant changes. With the globalisation of the game, however, the importance of national football associations has declined markedly.

The FA suffer in part because of the democratic structure of FIFA: one country one vote. It is ironic that one of the reasons why the FA Premier League was formed was because the big clubs did not like the one club one vote system in the Football League. The FA would probably like to alter the voting system at FIFA, but that would require very radical change. The most likely change will be towards greater power for the global governors and less power for national governing bodies, along with less power for local clubs and local supporters. We have already seen evidence of this, with FIFA and UEFA putting pressure on the national football associations to reduce the number of clubs in their top divisions, as well as their call to play more international matches and to arrange a domestic football calendar to fit into international needs.

Within this scenario of little change much posturing between the powerful interest groups will continue, with the stand taken by the different protagonists being based not so much on what is good for football but more on what is good for their individual financial positions. Lip service will be paid to the social importance of the football club to many individuals and to the community. Lip service will continue to be paid to the importance to the club of its fans, but if BSkyB request that the date of a scheduled match be changed the club will accept this in return for a modest sum of money. They will ignore the inconvenience to the fans. As one football club chairman has said, 'he who pays the piper calls the tune.'

FIFA would like to see football as even more important than it is now. FIFA presidents now talk to world leaders. The status of the game has changed remarkably in 20 years. In the 1980s football spectators were enclosed in cages, and the Prime Minister wanted them to carry ID cards. In 2006 the Secretary General of the UN, Kofi Annan, visited FIFA headquarters and discussed with Sepp Blatter such issues as the role that the values of sport and football can have in bringing about human development, world peace and tolerance. They discussed 'the role of sport in general and football in particular in world development.' Blatter said 'Our long standing partnership has helped to take football to the world and make it a better place.'

All this sounds grand, but it is rather sanctimonious stuff. Particularly considering that FIFA were at the time of these discussions having to deal with the growing problem of racism at matches in Europe. Racism has been said to be endemic in Spanish football yet in 2007 the authorities in that country overturned a fine against a national team manager. The fine had been levied because he made racist remarks about a footballer. The Spanish courts found that the committee for sporting discipline in that country had in their view incorrectly evaluated the evidence. FIFA find it hard to enforce their anti-racism policy. If Kofi Annan believes that playing a football match brings countries closer together he has obviously been to few international matches. FIFA were worried about the behaviour of English fans in Germany in the 2006 World Cup. They were worried that the singing of 'The

Dam Busters March' by the England fans would provoke German fans—precisely why the England fans would sing the song. Football does not always make the world 'a better place'—it also affords an opportunity to bring back old hatreds. (England versus Scotland is bad enough, what about Serbia versus Croatia!) Still, FIFA does try. It uses a part of its great wealth to encourage football in poorer parts of the world.

In response to the many 'challenges' faced by football around the world, in 2006 FIFA set up a brand new 'ethics committee'. They already had a 'Committee for Ethics and Fair Play' but the duties of that committee were limited and so its remit was enlarged and it was renamed the 'Committee for Fair Play and Social Responsibility'. The FIFA executive who coined that name certainly came up with all the politically correct words, the problem is whether or not the re-branding will lead to change. It is unclear whether the new ethics committee will be independent enough to criticise its masters.

In January 2007, Richard Scudamore, the chief executive of the Premier League, was claiming that 'the Premier League is pretty much now the world's domestic league, with players from all over the world, particularly from Africa.' This may be not far from the truth. But if it is, who decided this was the way the league would develop? What about a domestic league for football fans in England?

Richard Scudamore's claim was made at the same time as he was announcing that countries in Africa were being given the right to show on television, live, those Premier League games that were played on Saturdays and on Monday evenings. They could broadcast these matches free because the Premier League were already earning enough from the sale of television rights around the rest of the world.[5] As Gordon Brown said, this act of giving 390 million Africans the opportunity to watch Premier League football at no cost is 'part of our cultural diplomacy. Our message to the world is that we want to be friends and help.' Mr Brown believes that such acts could help prevent the growth of anti-western sentiment in Muslim countries. Times have certainly changed. At one time the British took the Bible to Africa, at another time they provided monetary 'Aid', now they offer Premier League matches.

Although the elite clubs in the Premier League might be attracted by the idea of a Super League, there is no doubt that the majority of the clubs in the Premier League are satisfied with the way the game is progressing. The owners, the managers and the players in the majority of clubs will be well rewarded as a result of the television broadcasting deals signed in 2006 and 2007.

The broadcasting deals for Premier League matches from domestic and foreign television, from internet companies and from mobile phone companies mean that the league will receive £2.7 billion over the three years from 2007–08. This amounts to £0.9 billion per season, which is an average of £45 million a season for the Premier League clubs. In fact the club that are champions in a season will receive in excess of £50 million and the bottom team in that league will receive (as a share of media revenues) £30 million. By contrast the average Championship League team will receive just over £1 million of media income. This gap is significant and is increasing over time. The majority of the players in the Premier League will be satisfied with the changes at present taking place. As a result of the extra television revenue, quite modest players in the Premiership will be receiving salaries in 2007 and beyond of at least £3 million a year. This is three or four times higher than a reasonably good player in the Championship will receive. The result is that the better players in the Championship will be lured to Premier League clubs.[6] Revenue determines salaries, and salaries determine success. Inequality is increasing. Not surprisingly those clubs that are promoted to the Premier League find it hard to survive in their early years in the top division, while those that are relegated, with the aid of parachute payments, have a good chance of bouncing back. If no, or little change, is made to the way the game is organised financially competitive balance will continue to decline.

One other major concern with the way the game in England is progressing is the fact that ownership and control of more and more clubs is passing into foreign hands. As of October 2007 nine of the Premier League have passed into foreign ownership. Arsenal has announced that they are building strong links with a US club but have a Ukranian predator upsetting their plans. Birmingham City and Blackburn Rovers were having discussions with foreign investors. There is a strong possibility that by the end of 2007 over one half of Premier League clubs will be owned by people who are not British.

This is globalisation. At the beginning of 2007 a British company purchased Greyhound Bus Lines (who also operate the iconic

297

yellow buses that transport American schoolchildren). The head of the UK company said, 'we own US buses, they own English football clubs.'

It is one thing for a foreign company to take over a British hotel company or a British engineering company, but there are other interests to take into account in the taking over of a football club. The government cannot stop a company registered in the European Union from taking over a British company. It might be possible, however, to prevent a non-EU company from doing so. There are provisions in the Competition Act.[7]

Continuing Growth With a New Super League

There has for many years been talk and much written on the subject of a Super League. Sir Stanley Rous, writing in 1978, expressed the belief that a Super League of only a dozen or so major clubs would one day be formed. One form of Super League has of course come into existence, not the Premier League, which clearly contains teams that are far from super, but the UEFA Champions League (which is not really made up just of champions).

There are those who support the idea of a European Super League. With such a league, it is argued by Hoehn and Szymanski, the 'big clubs will be able to focus on the competition that generates the greater proportion of their income.'[8] Although the small and medium-sized clubs would lose by no longer competing in the same league as the big clubs, the impact of this 'is likely to be offset by the improvements in competitive balance in the domestic competition.' The argument against this is that many people would not really be interested in following what happens in the more competitive lower level competition. The media, the advertisers and the younger generation, all of whom are interested in superstars, would all concentrate on the over-hyped Super League. Television would determine the popularity and ultimately the financial success of the football clubs competing for the same space.[9]

Nevertheless, the structure of the domestic and international club competitions could change at any time. Silvio Berlusconi, at the time Prime Minister of Italy and owner of AC Milan as well as a number of TV stations, suggested in 1998 that a European Super League should be formed. He had of course a personal interest; the restructuring of European football leagues would bring financial rewards to his business empire. It was partly as a result of this threat that UEFA restructured their own Champions competition into a league structure; this enabled the top teams to earn money.

In 2000 Rupert Murdoch proposed a new breakaway European Super League to be run by pay-TV operators including Kirch Group of Germany, Canal Plus of France and Telephonica of Spain. Sixteen clubs were to be invited to join. In 2000, 14 European clubs had established a central organisation to coordinate activities and, possibly, form a breakaway European League. This organisation, the G14, were also talking about establishing a new league.

A few years later Stefan Szymanski and Andrew Zimbalist proposed a version of a Super League based on the model that exists in the US with the NFL.[10] It has a 'local interest' element, combined with a play-off system that would produce the 'Champions of Europe.' It is designed to overcome the decline in competitive balance but also to safeguard the financial position of the clubs involved in the League.

Szymanski and Zimbalist are concerned that the present 'dual' system that exists in Europe leads to financial instability. Clubs first compete in national domestic leagues, and then just a few qualify for European competition. Those who do qualify generate much larger revenue than those that do not. They believe that the methods that could restore competitive balance in a domestic competition, such as salary capping and revenue sharing, would put some of the clubs that do qualify for European competition at a disadvantage. Clubs from the smaller countries such as Portugal would not be able to generate as much revenue from their domestic competition as those from Spain and England. Their lower expenditure on salaries would put them at a disadvantage, while the Spanish and English clubs, though forced to limit their salary bill to, say, 60%, would still have a much larger revenue base. This argument is based on one version of salary capping.

Szymanski and Zimbalist propose six regional divisions in Europe: the North West (comprising England and Scotland), the South West (Spain and Portugal), South (Italy, Greece and the Balkans), the North East, West Central and East Central. Each division would comprise ten teams. The North West would include eight English teams, plus two from Scotland.

Each team would play participants from their own division on a home and away basis, and also three teams from each of the other divisions, again on a home and away basis. This would mean a total of 48 games per club. This formula is designed to please fans by combining traditional rivalries with international exposure. As in the US at the end of the season, the leading teams from each division would play a knock out competition to determine an overall European champion.

It is an interesting idea. It could work with a closed or open structure. Additional measures could be introduced to further improve competitive balance.[11] A limited amount of promotion and relegation could be allowed. The downside is that large numbers of clubs would be disenfranchised. The medium-sized clubs, such as Derby County and Sunderland, and the less successful big city clubs (Birmingham City, West Ham United and Manchester City), would be more or less be permanently relegated to lower level competitions. This would not worry the eight England clubs in the Super League, it would not worry TV companies, it would not worry sponsors and it would not worry football fans in China, Africa and Scandinavia, however.

If this structure was introduced it would be good for the owners of the top clubs (as it is in the NFL with the same structure) but thousands of people who enjoy watching live quality football would be deprived of the pleasure. It would be harder for the Lord Coe's of the future to introduce their sons (and daughters) to the pleasures of a live match. They would of course have plenty of opportunity to listen to the 'experts' comments before, during and after televised games. No doubt clubs who are excluded would continue to play in competitions but the leading players would not be in these divisions. The standard of football would be inferior, while the owners of the top clubs, the best players and the top administrators, would have gained.

Sport in the US has shown that new leagues can be formed to compete with the established leagues. If the new leagues can attract enough money they can lure profit-seeking clubs and players away from the existing structure.[12] Nothing stays as it is forever. The top English clubs were able to obtain FA support when breaking away from the Football League to form the FA Premier League. Other new leagues could be formed in England, but it is doubtful if they would be recognised by the FA. These new leagues would therefore come at a cost to those who played in them. In particular, they would not be able to play in FIFA-organised international matches.

At the present time proposals for new competitions are driven by money. Many traditionalists feel that domestic leagues should be seen as the main club competitions, not new competitions often dreamt up by marketing people to attract TV income. Competitions such as the UEFA Champions League should, in other words, be seen as the icing on the cake, not the cake. The Confederation Cup, for instance, is a phoney new competition pushed by FIFA because of TV money. There could well be new super leagues in future at club and international level, but it is to be hoped they are driven by sporting interests not TV money.

Market Led Growth, But With Intervention

With this scenario it is required by those responsible for regulating economic competition that football clubs be seen as more than just business enterprises. It would need to be accepted that in order to obtain competitive balance in a competition some form of intervention in the market is needed and should be allowed.

One form of intervention is some type of control on costs. UEFA have examined the possibility of introducing a limit on the amount players can be paid. Their concern is, however, less with the competitive balance in the game and more with the clubs paying more to players than they can afford and thus getting into financial difficulties. UEFA would like to license clubs, and a key factor in deciding whether a licence would be granted would be the financial health of the club. Their idea of salary control is to limit the percentage of a club's revenue spent on wages, but this form of control would help the richer clubs to be even more successful.

In an article in the popular football magazine *FourFourTwo* on the subject of reclaiming the game, one recommendation was the introduction of a 'reasonable' wage cap.[13] What is reasonable depends on what one is trying to achieve (and reasonable to whom). Manchester United and the other elite clubs in the G14 group have indicated that what they regard as reasonable is a salary cap where no more than 50% of revenue is spent on salaries.

This seems more like an attempt to keep down salary levels at each of the clubs in the elite group than an attempt to move towards competitive balance. In fact, it is not even a real attempt to keep down wages, it is window dressing. In 2005, Manchester United revenue was £160 million, and its total wage and salary cost was £77 million (less than 50%). The players at Manchester United need not be disturbed. This form of salary cap would hurt players more at the smaller clubs than at the large.

In fact in England some clubs have already accepted the idea of a salary cap. The clubs in League One and League Two of the Football League have accepted a 'Salary Cost Management Protocol' in which they agree to limit the wage bill at each club to 60% of the club's revenue. This is a voluntary salary cap. It is of course easier to agree to this in the lower divisions because there is not a great difference between the revenue of one club and that of another. The problem of obtaining agreement when the rewards are very high is much greater. A possible form of salary capping was discussed in Chapter 3.

Amongst those who benefit from football being a global business are the officials that have been elected or appointed to direct football at the national and international level. These officials, and those elected to be council members of the various national and international associations, have their own agenda. They appoint the executives to run the associations. The officials and the executives usually initially resist change and then when either the law or powerful economic forces bring about change, they seek to make the best that they can out of the new situation. A century ago the FA opposed professionalism, and not so many decades ago the FA and the Football League were arguing in favour of a maximum wage and a transfer system that kept players in servitude. More recently the FA tried to prevent the television of football matches, and a decade ago the Football League tried to prevent the formation of a rival league. Not a glorious record of leadership by the self-appointed governing bodies of the English game.

For this third scenario to come about certain interest groups would need to persuade politicians and outside regulators that football is a special case. This of course is what happened in the US where collective agreements between sports club owners and players have been allowed. These have been justified on the grounds of maintaining competitive balance. It is a fact that a greater equality of playing strength ensures a greater uncertainty of outcome, and so the competitiveness of smaller clubs is crucial to maintaining uncertainty. With the NFL model, gate receipts, licensing revenue and national television revenue are shared between the different clubs. Salary capping is also allowed.

The 'Arnaut Report' recommended that certain changes be made. It called for a more effective system of cost control to promote greater competitive balance and also wanted the EU and member states to provide greater legal certainty over what could and could not be done in sport to achieve this objective. It also called for clarification of the rights of sports governing bodies.

The 'Arnaut Report' did not ask for more intervention from government, just for clarification of the position and for greater cooperation. It recognised that co-operation was necessary if problems were to be solved. The conclusion and recommendations of the Report were fed into a EU White Paper on Sport.

Commercialism, But With a More Equal Division of Revenue

When ITV and the BBC started broadcasting football matches the money they paid was divided between the leagues. In 1988, for instance, 50% of the TV revenue went to Division One (the top division), 25% to Division Two and the other 25% to Divisions Three and Four. It was only when BSkyB entered the picture that the big differences began to appear. In the 2002–03 season 95% of the money went to the Premier League.

In February 2004 an 'All Party Parliamentary Football Group' recommended that a more equitable distribution of TV money be introduced, but the Premier League were not interested. Amongst the recommendations was one that would have involved the Premier League redistributing an additional 5% of its broadcasting revenue to clubs in lower divisions. There were also recommendations on a more equitable distribution of the TV money between the 20 clubs in the Premier League, on reintroducing the sharing of gate receipts between the two teams in a match, and on a levy on all agent fees from transfers. Any one of these recommendations, if adopted, would improve the competitive balance in the game. The chairman of the 'All Party Parliamentary Football Group' said 'Football flourishes on competition and uncertainty and that is why we have to look at the way the finances of the game are redistributed to ensure that this continues.' The report also called for the FA to introduce a 'fit and proper' person test for anyone who wanted to become a club director or who became involved in the running of a club. A licensing system was also proposed so that clubs would be allowed to compete in competitions only if they could meet certain standards on how they were run, and their finances were fully transparent.

The chairman of the 'All Party Parliamentary Football Group', however, would not support the idea that if those running football rejected the recommendations contained in the report, that an independent statutory regulator be appointed to look after the industry. 'We have got powers behind us but we don't want to use them,' he said. 'There should be no need for government to get involved in football.'

Football in England is allowed to collectively sell the rights to its matches, although in 2004 there was a threat to this policy from the EU. A form of revenue sharing is in use in England with respect to TV income. This question is whether or not it can be applied more effectively. A redistribution of TV revenue is something the clubs could decide on themselves, it has nothing to do with European economic policy or the UK Government's attitude towards industrial intervention. In fact the Premier League in 2007 decided that the £625 million they would receive from overseas broadcasters for the rights to show matches for the three seasons from 2007–08 would be shared equally between the 20 teams in the Premier League. This is revenue sharing, but it only relates to a minor part of the television revenue received—nevertheless it is a start.

Commercialism Slows Down

One possibility is that the commercialisation process will slow down possibly because the local supporters of clubs will become of greater importance.[14] Historically, football clubs have been tied to their communities in an emotional sense, but also because the club was financially dependent on gate receipts. The club therefore had its roots in the local community. Television and mass marketing have worked against this historical link.[15] There are many who lament the commercialisation and globalisation of the modern game, but it is not possible to change what has happened. The big clubs are no longer dependent on local communities. They have been taken over by the mass media. Smaller clubs and clubs in financial difficulties do, however, need local support. It is here where supporters' organisations have been found to be useful.

'Supporters Direct' are a pressure group that is trying very hard to bring about more supporter involvement in the running of clubs. They believe that it is important for the corporate governance of football clubs to have a degree of local share ownership in the local football team. One way of achieving this is for individual fans to own shares in their club, another possibility is the establishment of 'Supporters Trusts' that purchase as many shares in their club as they can afford. The ownership of shares by the trust, together with the pooling of votes by supporters who are also shareholders, would give power to local people. 'Supporters Direct' have had success, particularly with smaller clubs in financial difficulty.

The Football League, after some difficult years when the top teams broke away from them, have done a good job creating a 'niche' for themselves. It is the Football League, rather than the Premier League, who claim to provide 'Real Football for Real Fans'. Judging by the number of people who watch matches, and the results of surveys, they have been successful. The support for a Football League club usually comes from its local population, and with one or two exceptions the clubs are not trying to sell themselves globally. The clubs seek to make a significant contribution to their local community.

The Football League have done well for themselves in attracting sponsorship. The Coca-Cola involvement was obviously a big help. Those now running the Football League are imaginative and have been being willing to experiment with such issues as the disclosure of agents fees, salary capping and even talking about a 'sin bin' to punish wayward players. Football at the Premier League level is a 'show'. It is a business and it needs access to large sums of money to succeed. At a lower level, a club's success can depend on attracting local hometown supporters. The major interest in the FA Cup competition now is when small town clubs, like Burton Albion, play matches against teams from the top two leagues.

Teams like Carlisle United and Northampton Town have a role in professional football and it is different from that of Arsenal and

Chelsea. Unfortunately they do not now have a voice at the top table. In the past, perhaps they had two much of a voice, which was an argument used to justify the formation of the Premier League. But now there is evidence that interest in the lower leagues is growing. This interest would become even greater if a new European-wide Super League was formed, for it would be only the games in the lower leagues that most football fans could watch live. Football can succeed even if commercialism slows down, although it is doubtful if the excesses of the Premiership would survive.

Disillusionment Amongst Supporters

The vast majority of football fans seem at present quite prepared to sit back and accept what has happened. In England, they are quite prepared to accept that only four clubs have a realistic chance of winning the top domestic competitions. But the power of the consumer should not be underestimated. The collapse of the Carlton-Granada TV deal to show Football League games occurred because not enough people wanted to watch such games on television. A number of mid-table Premier League teams are now experiencing falling attendances.[16]

In the future, and it is becoming evident already, power will move towards consumers of the media. Rupert Murdoch has said the consumer can now obtain 'what they want, when they want it, how they want it and very much as they want it.' This is because of the new ways available to the consumer to access information and entertainment via the internet, mobile phones and TV. What does this mean for football? It means the elite clubs will increasingly seek to break away from the collective selling of Premier League matches. They will want to show their matches directly to their fans around the world. Unfortunately, those interested in football in the Far East and Africa do not want to watch clubs such as Wigan, Bolton and Aston Villa (they want to watch Arsenal, Chelsea and Manchester United). At the moment companies such as BSkyB and the BBC, and of course the Premier League, control what the consumer can watch. This will change.

At Premier League matches lack of success means that stadiums are not full. Already some supporters are rebelling at the rising ticket prices. There are signs that the demand for football will not continue to grow in all its markets. A number of English clubs are finding it difficult to fill their ground week after week. Aston Villa, which has a capacity of 42,000, now fill the ground for less than two or three matches a season. In 2005–06 they did not even fill the ground for a match against an attractive Chelsea side. The lack of success of Everton has led to a dramatic fall in season ticket sales.[17] Even the fanatical Newcastle United fans do not now turn up in large enough numbers to regularly fill their ground. Nevertheless, Leeds United, in the year following their relegation, raised the price of some season tickets by 27%. (The seats were to be leather covered.) In February 2007, the chairman of Birmingham City, in a match day programme, criticised the fans of the club for staying away from games. He commented on the number of empty seats at matches and said that perhaps the supporters of the team did not deserve Premiership football. This criticism was made following a match which the club rearranged at short notice so that the kick-off moved from a Saturday to 11:30 a.m. on the Sunday. The club did this because they were offered money by BSkyB. The resulting attendance was 10,000 below what the club might have expected. Some businesses add to their own problems.

Some supporters organise in an attempt to influence what is going on at clubs while many just stay away. William Buckley, a football writer for 15 years who once loved the game, expressed the view when discussing his comic novel *The Man who Hated Football* that the game is becoming 'boringly predictable.' At the moment it is only the minority who turn away from the game, however. It is Buckley's belief that 'Football will continue to be a placebo for the masses. Phone-ins will be log jammed, analysts will proliferate.' He would like to see us 'take football a mite less seriously.' This will only happen when commercialism ceases to drive the game: money is not something to be light hearted about.

When, in 2003, the FA came to re-negotiate the TV deal for the right to show the England games for the three years from August 2004, they found that they could only obtain a fee of £230 million. This was a fee of £115 million less than the previous deal. People only want to watch winning teams. Around the world people want to watch Premier League football, but not necessarily the England team.

The market is changing. Football is competing for consumers' time and money with many other forms of entertainment. Fans do not want to pay £40 or more to watch inferior entertainment. Unless something is done to change the direction in which the game is going, there will be less and less games worth watching. It cannot be claimed that Watford versus Charlton, one week, followed by Aston Villa versus Wigan, the next, offer the prospect of exciting entertainment. (A match between Aston Villa and Birmingham City shown on TV in an Irish bar in Suzhou, China, attracted an audience of three. A match involving either Arsenal, Manchester United or Chelsea would have filled the same bar.)

There is no guarantee that the boom in sports business in general and football in particular will continue. There are even indications that a decline has already begun. In 2002 the giant German media business, Kirch Group, which owned television rights to the German Bündesliga matches, nearly collapsed. The near bankruptcy was said to be due to the failure to attract sufficient advertisers and TV subscribers. This was a management failure—a flawed business strategy, based on a desire for too fast growth and on overestimates of market trends.

Similarly, a Swiss marketing agency, which was the main commercial partner of FIFA, collapsed in 2001 after paying too much for the rights to sell the 2002 and 2006 FIFA World Cup matches. ITV Digital also paid too much for the rights to the English Football League games.

In 2002 Robert Murdoch's Fox Entertainment Group, in the US, wrote $387 million off the balance sheet value of the company's $4.5 billion eight-year NFL deal. They also wrote down the value of their motor-racing and baseball rights. They blamed it on the fall in the advertising revenue that they could attract from selling time on the sports programmes they broadcast. By themselves, such write-downs are not significant and could just be the result of a well-known creative accounting technique known as the 'Big Bath', where the write-down is timed to take advantage of a notable event, for example the World Trade Center disaster in 2001. By reporting all the bad news about a company's performance in a year in which it is possible to blame it on somebody else (i.e. not the company's management) it is possible to show very good performance in the next year.

Against these examples of a decline in commercial interest one must take into account the record TV deal signed by the Premier

League for the three seasons starting in 2007–08. For the UK, a rise of 66% was achieved, while the foreign rights figure was double the amount of the previous deal. This is evidence of the success of the Premier League and the global appeal of that League.

Football has been described as the beautiful game—or more accurately football in Brazil has been called beautiful. But look at what has happened to football in that country. Many of those leading the game are corrupt, sometimes players are not paid and many are forced to play in foreign countries to earn a living. Supporters stay away from domestic matches but despite these problems the national team are good enough to consistently win the World Cup.

Is football in England beautiful? Well, it has never been as attractive as the game in Brazil. Only very infrequently can an actual game in England be described as beautiful. Exciting, Yes, but the media would like us to believe that the modern game is one of skill, artistry and excitement. The reality is the modern game is fast, tough, aggressive and occasionally exciting—but not always.

Advertising hype regularly attempts to sell a particular game as one where something exciting will happen because of the presence of so many international stars, but that does not guarantee excitement or beauty. The fans know all this, but those involved in promoting and selling the game cannot admit it. They need to attract large TV audiences in order to sell products—their worry is that viewers will switch to another channel if they are not persuaded that something exciting is about to happen.

Blackburn, one of the Premier League clubs worried about falling attendance figures, announced in January 2007 that they would use some of the extra revenue coming to the club as a result of the larger than expected television broadcasting rights settlement to cut admission prices. Blackburn supporters had cited high admission prices as one of the reasons why they were staying away from games.[18] Other reasons included the difficulties resulting from the club changing the day and time of match kick-offs in order to satisfy TV and the increasing predictability of final league placements.

309

Less Globalisation

A further scenario is one in which the globalisation process slows down, either because in general globalisation becomes less popular, or because football itself becomes disturbed by where the process is leading the game. Apart from problems that arise in football there are general problems associated with globalisation. The rich countries are getting richer and the poor countries relatively poorer. There are disputes at the World Trading Organisation about countries imposing tariffs and quotas. There could be a backlash against free trade, and a move to trading blocks. This would affect football. In football there are already a number of national associations seeking to obtain permission to introduce quotas on the number of foreign players allowed in any one club.

The free movement of labour causes problems. The European Commission, with its role of promoting a community-wide approach to such issues, might not like the idea of a home-grown quota. It needs to be recognised, however, that there is a problem. Most football followers like to identify with a club and with their own national side. If their national side performs badly all the time they will lose interest in international competitions. This is reducing the pleasure of consumers and could lead to a reduction in interest in the game at all levels.

For some reason most local supporters of clubs have continued to be loyal to their local team, even though it might be owned by foreigners, managed by foreigners, and, on occasion, all the players are foreigners. Why? Is this the power of globalisation, or is it the power of traditional loyalty, of clinging to one's 'roots', of tribalism? The 'people' who are traditional supporters of, say, Chelsea, Liverpool or Manchester United, are happy to see their clubs owned by rich foreigners. They are happy to see their clubs managed by educated French, Spanish and Italians, and they are happy to see their team made up of skilled players from anywhere in the world, and of any religion or race. Yet many of these people are xenophobic when it comes to supporting the English national team. They are willing to hurl abuse—to even demonstrate hatred—against foreign teams.

A Rival League

One radical possibility, possibly a fantasy, is the creation of a new football league outside the control of the FA, UEFA and FIFA. If the European Commission means what they say, that in the name of consumer interest they wish to encourage economic competition, then they would be pleased if a new league was established to break the present monopoly.

One possibility is that a new league could be formed and given the name of, say, the 'Soccer League of Britain and Ireland'. Teams from the five (four) countries could compete; a game between Dublin Rovers and Birmingham Athletic would have appeal. Sponsors could be secured, possibly Guinness or HSBC. It would give the BBC or ITV a chance to show live league football. The games could be played at stadiums used by other sports, a ground-sharing arrangement. The players could come from those in the lower leagues, from out-of-contract Premier League players and from overseas. As the league became established it could tempt some of the better players from the present leagues. Of course those who play in this 'rebel' league would not be able to play for the present international teams, given that with the present monopoly structure a club has to be recognised by the FA before a player from that club can play for his country. The answer would be that rival soccer leagues could be formed in other countries, and the rebel clubs could feed players into rival international teams. They could then compete every four years for, say, the 'Global Cup'.

To show independence the new 'Soccer League of Britain and Ireland' could even slightly change the rules, for example no offsides. Another change could be that if after 80 minutes the game is a draw, 2 players from each team could be withdrawn, and then every 5 minutes another two players from each side be withdrawn, and this would continue until a winning goal is scored. These changes would make the game more exciting. Cricket has been experimenting with different versions of the game. A change to make football fairer would be to use TV evidence at the time of controversial decisions. To prevent managers from slowing the game down too much, each club would not be allowed to challenge more than two decisions (as in US football). A 'sin bin' could be introduced for players who foul too often or commit serious offences. The above are only suggestions. The serious point is that the football community does not have to lie back and let FIFA and the globalisation process take over the game. Clearly the people benefiting from the present structure would fight any change, but they should at least be challenged.

The Way Forward

In this book the case has been made for a more equal distribution of the wealth coming into the game. It is appreciated that this will not happen without what has been described as a 'change in the mind-set of those running the game'. The commercial policies of the European Union limit the 'restrictive practices' that can be introduced into the game, but some changes are still possible. Match gate receipts could be divided in some way between the two teams taking part in the game. It was those people with power in the Football League a few years ago that abandoned this policy. The huge amounts received by the Premier League for selling broadcasting rights could be divided more equitably. A percentage of this money could be put in a fund to plough back into football in one way or another. 'Supporters Trusts' should be further encouraged and supported by the government through the tax system. The salary bill of a club could be controlled.

Will this happen? Stephen Morrow points out that the main conflict faced by football is the prioritisation of sporting outcomes versus the prioritisation of economic or market solutions. It is Morrow's belief that all recent trends suggest that there is little or no likelihood of the policies that would improve competitive balance 'being implemented in practice.' In the short run, unfortunately, Morrow is almost certainly right. The best hope for the long run is that there will be a sea change in economic thinking about sport.[19]

Morrow has argued that if football is to be changed by some form of restructuring of the reward system, then in order to do this properly it is necessary to take into account the interests of all those affected by the outcomes, including 'shareholders, supporters, employees, governing bodies and the community.' Any changes that take place will result in one group gaining but another group losing. At the moment any decisions on change are based on the financial interests of a small number of powerful parties. There is much that has been written about attaching more importance to the social and societal aspects of the game, but as Morrow points out, at the moment we have no way of measuring the benefits that would result from attaching more importance to the interests of supporters and the community.

Morrow argues further that any change that is introduced should be based on the results of research into 'the preferences of as many of football's constituents as possible.' This is correct. The problem is that we do not have ways of measuring the preferences and are unlikely to develop such ways in the near future, and whilst we do nothing, the inequality in the game is increasing year by year. By the time major decisions are made to reverse what is happening it might be too late. Change is driven by those who hold the power. It could be argued that some communities, such as the supporters of certain clubs in Manchester, London, Milan and Madrid, have already benefited from the changes that have taken place in the game. This is, however, no compensation to the citizens of, say, the Midlands or Yorkshire. Football is a selfish game. The supporters of Aston Villa or Sheffield Wednesday get no pleasure from the success of other teams (particularly if the other teams are Manchester United and Chelsea).[20]

Economists argue that optimality can be increased if, as a result of a decision, the benefits that flow to one group are greater than the loss of benefits to another group. In other words, if the increase in social welfare of one group is greater than the sum of the decline in social welfare of another group. This might be the position from the overall point of view of society, but football involves passion, emotion and heritage, and to supporters of the average or failing club there is simply no compensation in seeing the success of others. It is being argued here that the game needs restructuring so that competitions give a reasonable level of sporting balance, rather than one that results in self-perpetuation. Those making the decisions now, whether they are at the level of the European Community, FIFA, UEFA, the FA or at one of the top clubs, are ignoring the interests of many of football's constituencies. A great many clubs, supporters and communities are losing the game.

When Lord Coe became chairman of FIFA's watchdog committee he said, 'I decided to take this important role because I want to help ensure the integrity of the sport is guaranteed so my children and, hopefully, their children, can get as much pleasure out of it as I have.' Seb Coe is a long time season-ticket holder at Chelsea. 'Football has been at the centre of my life for nearly 40 years, since the first time I travelled down from Sheffield to watch Chelsea at Stamford Bridge as a young boy, and has continued to provide me with so much fun, and more than the odd moment of heartbreak, in that period. It may now have turned into a multi-billion-pound industry but at its core it remains a game for the supporters and without them it would mean nothing. I hope in this new role I can play some small part in trying to ensure this continues.' Lord Coe was expressing his belief that football is, or should be, a game for the supporters. Good emotional stuff, but unfortunately not the whole picture.

Szymanski and Zimbalist express the belief that soccer 'possesses a governmental structure that enables the long-term interests of the fans to be articulated and supported.' But which fans? They argue that 'defending these interests . . . does not mean preserving exactly the same competitive structure that suited the interests of the game 25 or 50 years ago. Unless some means is found to offer a minimum of prosperity for the clubs and their owners, the entire system is in danger of collapse.'[21]

Change is necessary, but not because the system is in danger of collapse. The Premier League clubs are far from collapsing. More TV money is coming into the game than ever before; there is no shortage of 'businessmen' wanting to buy football clubs and the directors of the marginal clubs now seem to be managing their clubs in a prudent manner. The system is not in danger of collapse. The proposals to restructure football so as to create some form of Super League are finance driven, and if adopted would move the game away from the supporters Lord Coe seeks to protect.

Case Studies

One of the themes of this book is that the success of a football club depends, in the long run, upon the abilities of the top directors of that club. This has always been the case, but since football has now moved away from being a sport with a business side to it to being an all-out global business selling a sport, the leadership of a club has become of even greater importance.

There are many specific cases that demonstrate the truth of this proposition. The failure of leadership at some clubs has been well-documented. The mistakes made by Leeds United's directors in the late 1990s and early 2000s, for example, are well-known. The reasons why Manchester United succeeded and Manchester City did not, have been discussed above. The cases of Everton and Liverpool and of Arsenal and Tottenham are dealt with below.

Newcastle United

One colourful case that illustrates the importance of directors is Newcastle United. Despite being one of the best supported clubs in the country they have not been champions of the top division since 1927.

Despite the lack of success there has been an arrogance about Newcastle United, or at least about the leadership of the club. They are quite a successful business, but are not a successful football team, and yet Freddie Shepherd, their chairman for many years, behaved as if the club were among the football elite. At the 2004 'International Football Business Forum' (Soccerex) he argued against the top clubs sharing their revenue (income) more evenly with the poorer clubs. He believes that in England only the Premier League matters and within that League only the top clubs matter.

315

He said: 'I think it is dog-eat-dog. The big fight will be for the Premier League to take over the running of the other leagues. The others can't hold us back, the time will come, I think, when it is the Premier League running the whole show. Many of these other clubs will have to go part-time. When we have got 52,000 fans at each home game the last thing we are worried about is clubs in the third division.'

He is clearly not worried about the grassroots of the game. It is the big clubs that are marketable and so bring the money into the game, and that is what Shepherd is interested in. He obviously believes that if a new European Super League were to be formed that Newcastle United would be invited to join. They are not, however, members of the prestigious G14.

Freddie Shepherd emphasises that the directors run Newcastle like a business. 'We are not ashamed to say we take a dividend out of it.' In 2004 Shepherd received £1.66 million from Newcastle United plc in the form of directors' fees, salary, bonuses and dividends. Douglas Hall received £2.35 million from the plc, which covered his remuneration as a non-executive director, as well as payment for his executive director position at a subsidiary company registered and operating from Gibraltar. (This figure also included dividends on his shareholding.) In 2005, despite the company making a loss after tax, the plc maintained its dividend payments of £3.95 million. Newcastle's directors continued to make decisions that surprised and disappointed their supporters. In 2007 the club was taken over by Mike Ashley.[1]

The club has a history of corporate governance disasters (despite being run like a business). In 1998 the *Financial Times* said that the club had 'given a master class in how not to run a publicly owned football club.' This comment followed what became known as the 'Toongate' scandal which resulted from comments made by Douglas Hall and Freddie Shepherd in a Spanish brothel about what they thought of Newcastle women, as well as their thoughts on the club's fans who purchased overpriced replica shirts. The conversation was recorded by a journalist from a newspaper that was carrying out a 'sting' operation on the directors. *Investors Chronicle* then published a strong recommendation to investors to sell the club's shares 'while the Halls remain dominant.'

Shepherd and Hall resigned. This was heralded in the press as evidence of good corporate governance. The *Guardian* said that the three non-executive directors at the club had 'struck a real blow for corporate governance with the removal of Freddie Shepherd and Douglas Hall.' The *Financial Times* believed that the credit for their removal should go to the company's customers, the fans. 'Rarely have a company's customers forced such a drastic change in the boardroom in so little time.' The *Independent* agreed that it was the club's supporters who forced the two disgraced directors to resign.

The real lesson on corporate governance that eventually emerged from this fiasco is that at Newcastle United neither the supporters or the non-executive directors matter. Shepherd and Hall were soon back at the club as directors for they were major shareholders, and they had real power. Lip service had to be paid to supporters and to the non-executive directors looking after minority shareholders' interests, but in the end their views could be ignored. So much for good governance at Newcastle.

Although the two directors had resigned in March 1998, Shepherd became chairman of the football club in July 1998 and was made a non-executive director of the plc in December 1998. He became the full-time executive director of the plc in August 2001. So three years after his comments in a brothel were said to have harmed the plc, he became an executive director. Hall followed a similar path. He became deputy chairman in July 1998, and a non-executive director in December 1998.

No wonder Newcastle shares were not popular in the City, for they quite rightly believed that good corporate governance is a condition that contributes to success. With the then power structure at Newcastle, one would almost certainly predict a lack of football success. At the annual general meeting in 1998 following Hall and Shepherd's 'sleaze' scandal, the small shareholders tried to keep Shepherd off the board—they voted overwhelmingly against his re-appointment but not surprisingly proxy votes were enough to keep him on the board. The *Investors Chronicle* commented, 'It's a complete joke. It's not the way a plc should behave and I don't see what future Newcastle has as a public company ... It just shows how family interests can ride roughshod over the interests of small shareholders.' The *Financial Times* referred to 'the damage that family fiefdoms can do to corporate values.'

The City has not been comfortable with the way the club has been run. The *Investors Chronicle* refers to the 'mistrust of the management.' One problem was that Newcastle United was run like a private business. In their annual report they state that 'the size and structure of the Board ... results in a number of areas of non-compliance with the Combined Code [on the Principles of Good Governance].' These include the role of chairman and chief executive being combined, the remuneration committee not consisting exclusively of independent, non-executive directors, and the board not consisting of the recommended number of independent non-executive directors. As it was, the minority shareholders would have had difficulty in making any changes to the governance of the club.

Questions were also raised about Newcastle United's subsidiary company, Newcastle United Football Club (International). The club has said that this subsidiary is involved in expanding the club's brand overseas, especially in China and the Far East, but the reasons why this has to be done through Gibraltar (where the company is registered) are not convincing. Work done for this Gibraltar based-company has, nevertheless, resulted in a payment of £524,427 to Douglas Hall, who lives in Gibraltar as a tax exile.

The supporters of Newcastle United might not be happy with the performance of the club on the pitch, but the directors of the club have had no reason to feel disappointed. The directors of this company prior to its takeover owned (directly or indirectly) more than two thirds of the shares of the company. The two 'leading' directors, Shepherd and Hall, did not need to worry about their future. They each had a contract that 'specifies retirement at age 70.' Douglas Hall was aged 44 when this contract was signed. These contracts required two years notice before they could be terminated. Both directors enjoyed generous salary and pension arrangements.

In earlier years the club also experienced corporate governance problems. The 1930s were particularly difficult, but in 1938 Stan Seymour came along and saved the club. The club also had a reputation for meanness. The Newcastle players were each paid only £12 for playing in the 1951 Cup Final, a game that raised £40,000 in gate money. The club's attitude can be gauged from the fact that the club did provide tickets for the players' wives to watch the match, but they initially only provided standing tickets—after protests these were exchanged for seat tickets. Newcastle beat Blackpool in the final. At a celebration dance after the final, the directors told the players to bring their wives as a special presentation would be made to them. This turned out to be a handbag for each wife, which the club had bought at a job-lot-cut-price for £17. The bags were of poor quality but were bulging. The players initially thought the handbags were bulging with money, but they were in fact bulging with old newspapers.

Willie McKeag, a solicitor, former Lord Mayor of Newcastle, as well as a former Member of Parliament, became chairman of the club in 1957–58. His family had long had a connection with the club, and he had been a director for a number of years. He did not get on with Stan Seymour and wanted him removed as director-manager of the club. There were those who thought that McKeag wanted to become the new 'Mr Newcastle'. In a sense, they were 'born to hate each other.' Seymour, a former miner, footballer and shopkeeper, spoke Geordie out of the side of his mouth, while McKeag had 'a grand style of affected oratory.' The one knew about football, the other did not.

Once again problems at board level resulted in a lack of success on the pitch. McKeag believed that Seymour meddled too much in the affairs of the club and should move aside and let a younger, more energetic manager take over.

Stan Seymour retired from the board in 1976 and died in 1978 but his son Stan Seymour junior maintained the family presence on the board. The Seymour family's old rival, Willie McKeag, also retired and was replaced by his son Gorgod McKeag—so the dynasties continued – but fortunately the sons got on better together than the fathers. Gordon Lee, who had been appointed as manager in 1975, left the club early in 1977. There was then another dispute over the appointment of a new manager, during which the players issued a statement informing the people of Newcastle 'that they had no confidence in the board of directors.'

Manager followed manager. In 1991, the respected Jim Smith left the club because he had had enough of the ferocious infighting. In that same year John Hall, who had been investing in the club for a few years, took over as chairman. He was the new saviour, and also, through his company, the majority shareholder. He brought Kevin Keegan to the club as manager and the future looked promising for Newcastle, just at the time when large amounts of television and sponsorship money were coming into the game. However, it was not to be, the club still did not have the right leadership. John Hall's son Douglas took over the chairmanship from him.[3] (Freddie Shepherd took over from him.) In the three seasons from 2001–02 the club finished fourth, third and fifth in the Premiership, but did not succeed in breaking through into the elite group. In 2006–07 they finished a disappointing thirteenth.

The City of Liverpool

Liverpool is the third largest city in England with a population of just under half a million. Each of the two Liverpool clubs have populations of approximately 320,000 living within ten miles of their grounds. This contrasts with the two Manchester teams, each of which has a population of just under 500,000 within ten miles. (Each of the central London teams have a population of 1 million within 10 miles, while Aston Villa, Birmingham City and West Bromwich Albion each have a population of just over 500,000 within 10 miles.) The city's two teams have performed above what could be expected based on their immediate catchment areas. Liverpool FC have been champions of the top league in the country on 18 occasions and Everton on 9 occasions. On the basis of their league performances over time they are, respectively, the first and fourth most successful teams in the country.

In the 1980s when discussions were taking place about the formation of a breakaway league—the key clubs in these discussions were referred to as the 'Big Five' and these included both Liverpool and Everton. By 2000 Everton were certainly not one of the 'Big Five'. Why? At a time when big money was flowing into football, why did Everton fade away? They only narrowly escaped relegation from the Premier League on more than one occasion.

The two clubs had a colourful beginning. Both were influenced by a controversial director named John Houlding, who was yet another brewer who became involved with the ownership of football clubs. He was also a leading Conservative on Liverpool City Council. He owned part of the land on which Everton played and acted as agent for the person who owned the remainder of the land on which the ground was sited. He had the sole right to sell refreshments within the ground, and also owned a hotel (with a bar) that was near to the entrance to the ground. The Everton

320

supporters of course needed to pass the bar on the way to and from the ground. In addition to being landlord to the club and selling spectators food and drink, he also lent the club money.

Everton were financially successful. Houlding asked the club to pay a higher rent for the ground and higher interest on his loan. Houlding did not, however, have a proper lease agreement with the club, and so there occurred a long dispute over the issue. This resulted in the directors of the club moving the Everton football team away from Anfield.

Houlding did not, however, give up his interest in football. He founded a new club, Liverpool FC, who played on the land previously used by Everton. He appointed his friends and his staff from the brewery as directors of his new club—a good way to avoid future disputes with the other directors, and of ensuring he could continue to make money out of the game. One person appointed as an early director of Liverpool was 'Honest John' McKenna. 'Honest John' was a humble man, who lived modestly in a terraced house, but he was one of the driving forces behind Liverpool football club, and went on to become the third President of the Football League.

The Everton directors who fell out with Houlding were not financial innocents purely interested in football as just a sport. The *Liverpool Review*, a local newspaper, when reporting about the dispute, made the comment that 'there would seem to be more beer than anything else mixed up with the row.' There was talk of 'King Houlding' obtaining 'incalculable' wealth from his hotel outside the Anfield ground. However, the directors who moved Everton were able to find brewers in the vicinity of their new ground (Goodison Park) to help finance its development. Goodison Park, which was opened in 1892, was the first major football stadium in England. The financial and marketing link between beer and football has a long history.

Both the Liverpool teams have a successful history. Both teams achieved reasonable success in the inter-war years, Everton winning the championship three times and Liverpool winning it twice. It was in the 1980s when the fortunes of the two clubs began to diverge. Everton went from being one of the 'Big Five' to a team regularly fighting against relegation. Not surprisingly, one club had problems at boardroom level, the other did not.

Everton

Everton were members of the First Division from the 1888–89 season, and three years later they were champions. They were one of the last of the big clubs to appoint a manager. Up until 1939 the team selection was decided by the senior coaches, by the leading directors and by the captain of the team. One would have thought it hard to get agreement amongst such a diverse group, but the method seemed to work. When at last they did decide to appoint a manager all they did was move the club secretary into the position.

The club started badly after the Second World War, being relegated from the First Division at the end of the 1950–51 season (and promoted back in 1953–54). They then struggled to maintain their status in the top division and did not achieve success until John Moores became involved in the club and Harry Catterick became its manager (1961–73). They then entered a very successful period, being First Division champions in 1962–63 and 1969–70, finishing third in 1963–64 and 1968–69, and fourth in 1961–62 and 1964–65.

As a benefactor John Moores enabled the club to become one of the best in the country. Moores had created and built up the famous Littlewoods. Betting on the results of football matches had of course been taking place since the beginning of the organised game, as it had in all sports. The idea of 'football pools' as such was not in fact that of the Moores family but that of a man from Birmingham named John Jervis Barnard. John Moores, with two friends (one of them was named Littlewoods), started their own pools business in 1924 by selling football coupons outside the grounds at Goodison and Anfield. After early losses the friends dropped out of the business but John Moores kept going. He made a huge success of his pools company and expanded the business into mail order and retailing. His business went from strength to strength and became a major employer in the Liverpool area.

In the 1950s and 1960s Liverpool was a city facing economic difficulties. John Moores appreciated the importance of football to the people of the city. As mentioned, in the late 1950s Everton were struggling, finishing sixteenth in each of the years 1958, 1959 and 1960. It was at this point that John Moores purchased a controlling interest in Everton. He had supported the team from his childhood. He had been an amateur footballer. He put money into the club, and the club in turn invested in good players and made a series of good managerial appointments. Because of the amount of money the club had available to spend on transfer fees they became known as the 'millionaires'.

The first year of their big buying policy took place in 1960. There were criticisms of this policy, partly caused by jealousy, and partly because some of the big name signings came and went very quickly. But as Brian Labone, an ex-Everton player pointed out, spending money does not guarantee success—'there were teams who were even bigger spenders without getting the same results.'

By 1963 the club could 'virtually' field a team with an international player filling every position. This was of course unusual in the 1960s, partly because clubs did not have large numbers of foreign internationals (from outside Wales, Scotland and Ireland) on their books. Moores saw this big spending as a short-term policy to overcome the position in which he found the club, with his longer-term policy to be based on patience and developing a nursery system.

Everton were successful again in the 1970s, finishing at the top of the First Division in 1970, third in 1978 and fourth in 1975. They had considerable success in the 1980s, winning the league again in 1985 and 1987 (with Howard Kendall as manager), finishing second in 1986 and winning the FA Cup once (as well as being losing finalists three times). Unfortunately for Everton, they were not able to repeat this success in the 1990s—they finished twelfth, thirteenth and, disastrously, seventeenth, in the Premier League in 1992, 1993 and 1994 respectively.

Philip Carter was chairman of Everton from 1978 to 1991, and again from 1998 to June 2004. In the first of these periods he led the board in the most successful period in the club's history. He was a widely respected figure throughout the game. He received a knighthood for his services to football. The club made him Life President.

Before taking on the leadership of Everton, Carter had been employed by Littlewoods, whose principal shareholders, the Moores family, were of course the major shareholders at Everton. The Moores family knew they were appointing a man of ability to look after their interests in the club. Carter was a key player in the restructuring of the leagues (he hosted an early meeting on such matters in 1981), and was important in bringing about change. He believed that sponsors, advertisers and TV companies were only interested in backing those aspects of football that involved the big clubs (which at the time included Everton). There was of course much opposition to the proposals from 'traditional' directors, as well as from directors of smaller clubs, and the rebel breakaway group initially backed down.

But then in 1985 the 'Big Five' (which at the time included Everton) announced that they had plans for a Super League. The various factions continued to argue. Terry Neil, who had experience of being manager of both Tottenham and Arsenal, said of the negotiators from the big clubs, that they 'look out for their own selfish interests. It's purely a selfish thing. Top clubs are entitled to their share of the cake but it's the secrecy, the way it's being done, without regard for their lesser brethren. I know it dismays the public. Fragmentation will lead down the road to ruin.' Carter believed the Premier League would be good for Everton.

Ironically, Everton have not benefited as much from the Premier League as have its other big club rivals. The team did not perform well on the pitch, and they only escaped relegation on the last day of the 1993–94 season. At the beginning of the next season, they only won one of their opening 14 matches and the manager Michael Walker was sacked. The club's former striker, Joe Royle, became manager, but he only lasted two seasons. In 1997–98 Howard Kendall returned for a third spell as manager, but he was not successful this time, and once again the club only avoided relegation as a result of the outcome of matches played on the last day of the season.

The situation in the boardroom was no better than on the pitch. The future ownership and the future funding of the club was a major concern. John Moores was ageing and the club was short of money.

At the time John Moores first became involved he was just what the club needed, but by the 1990s the game had changed. A number of the top clubs had floated their shares on the stock market and raised large amounts of debt finance. They raised the equity finance they needed by going public. But John Moores did not believe in selling shares on the stock market; to do so could mean losing control of the business he regarded as his own. He kept Littlewoods as a private company (it was the largest private company in the country) and did the same for Everton. John Moores believed, as did many entrepreneurs of his generation, that once financial institutions began to own shares in a company they would begin to interfere in the management of the company in the interest of generating short-term profits.

When John Moores died in 1993 he left his shares to his children, but they did not wish to continue as the major investors in Everton. John Moores' instructions were that his Everton shares should be left in a 'safe pair of hands.' In other words, they should be left to a person who would not 'use the club for speculative purposes.' He asked the family to make sure the shares were sold to owners who had Everton's best interests at heart. The family asked the directors for guidance on who would be the most suitable purchaser. Events did not turn out well. The outcome was a take-over battle for the club. This is never good, even for large corporate bodies. Comments are made in the heat of a take-over battle that can cause difficulties within the company for years after the change in ownership. Take-overs benefit lawyers and accountants, and to be fair they also benefit those shareholders who wish to dispose of their financial interests in the business. Take-over battles can also take time, which can mean a long period of uncertainty, with decisions not being made.

In 1995, after an 18-month battle, Peter Johnson became the new majority share-owner of Everton. Peter Johnson was a successful local entrepreneur. But not all entrepreneurs are equal. His father had been a shopkeeper in Liverpool and Birkenhead. Peter Johnson saw an opportunity to make money. His idea was to sell Christmas food hampers to people who could only afford to make small payments each week. The cash would be collected throughout the year, and those involved could be sure they would have a good Christmas. The business prospered and Johnson floated his company, Park Foods, on the Stock Exchange in 1983.

Not only had Johnson done well with his packaging company, he had in 1987 purchased a one-third stake in a freight company which, when floated on the stock market, resulted in a capital gain to Johnson of around £15 million. He clearly had the financial resources needed to buy control of Everton, and football clubs appeared at the time to be a profitable avenue for investing funds.

Johnson had always been a Liverpool supporter, and when Sir

John Moores died, Johnson saw the opportunity to take control of a major club even though it was not the team he supported. He offered to buy a majority stake in Everton. Unfortunately for Johnson, his offer was not the only one received. A consortium of five investors, led by a builder named Arthur Abercromby and the theatre impresario Bill Kenwright. A number of the consortium members were Everton supporters and they emphasised this fact when comparing their offer to that of Johnson's. They also emphasised that they could bring a broad range of skills (public relations, advertising, management, property development and entertainment promotion) to the running of the club.

Johnson made a revised offer, which included a proposal for a rights issue, which if it took place, would result in £10 million being available for the club. This bid divided the members of the consortium making the counteroffer. Three of the consortium were now advising existing shareholders (including the Moores family) to accept the Johnson offer. Johnson was successful and it cost him only in the region of £10 million to purchase control. This was a good investment at the time, with the Premier League proving successful and with TV companies paying large sums for the right to show football matches.

Why did Johnson buy? He would enjoy the prestige and status that came with ownership and control, but there was more to it than that. He referred to owning a football club as 'a rich man's hobby', but by the 1990s it was more than that. It was by this time thought possible to make money out of the ownership of a football club. Others were doing so. BSkyB was paying large sums for TV rights.

Both Sir John Moores and Peter Johnson purchased control of Everton in order to raise their status in the local community—to be seen as acting to benefit the people of Liverpool. It is doubtful if John Moores expected to benefit financially from his ownership, although his family did benefit considerably. Peter Johnson would not have expected in the 'golden days' of the mid-1990s to lose money from his investment in Everton. He did, however, lose money because of a divided board of directors. Johnson was a Liverpool supporter and made himself unpopular with fans during the take-over battle. If the club had been successful on the pitch during his time as chairman all might have been forgiven. But they did not do well and Johnson was criticised by supporters and other directors. He agreed to step down as chairman in November 1998. It was, however, another 16 months before he eventually found a buyer for his 68% controlling shareholding in the club.

During Johnson's reign there were troubles at board level. Even though Johnson bought control of the club in 1994, and became chairman, two members of the losing consortium, Abercromby and Kenwright, were on the board. The relationship between the directors was so bad that on one occasion the police were called into the directors' box at a home game in order to break up a squabble.

The club were soon short of money, and forced to sell good players. They talked about building a new stadium but did not do so. By the end of the 1990s their revenue was only one-third of that of Manchester United and their ground was old-fashioned. They could no longer compete with the elite teams. They had been interested for some time in purchasing a prime piece of land in the centre of Liverpool on the King's Dock site, but this proposal had to be abandoned.

In order to raise additional finance for the club, a further rights issue of six new shares for every one existing share (the total shares issue by the club now being 35,000 shares) was conducted. This meant Johnson, in order to maintain his percentage holding, had to buy an additional 20,000 shares at a total cost of £10 million. The total cost of his by now (68%) holding in Everton was just over £20 million.

Everton's share price was very volatile. At one point in 1997 the club was valued at about £147 million. This meant Johnson's holding was worth about £100 million, a very good return on a three-year investment. Johnson refers to the gain as an accident. Nevertheless, in 1998 the value fell to £79 million. When Johnson agreed to step down as chairman, he said he was willing to sell his shares at a price that valued the club at about £42 million. Nobody would pay this price. (He sold just over a year later at a price that valued the club at £30 million.) Johnson sold his share holding for £20.3 million, resulting in a small loss on his investment.

What had gone wrong during Johnson's time at the club? When he became chairman he described himself as a 'hands-on' owner. 'One of the things I believe football clubs need is one man with the power to make decisions—a club owner.' This may have been his belief, but one could be unkind and say that judging by results the decisions he made were not good. Indeed it was his autocratic decision to sell Duncan Ferguson (a favourite with the fans) without agreeing with the manager that was a key issue leading to his resignation as chairman of the club.

The Everton board were divided during Johnson's period as chairman. One well-known recipe for disaster at corporate governance level is a divided board. Another lesson to be learned from this case is that you cannot be successful as an autocrat unless you either prove to be a winner or you carry your board with you. Most chairmen only want to have people on a board if they know these people are going to agree with them.

Johnson failed as chairman. Eventually the 'True Blue Consortium' (consisting of Kenwright, Woods, Abercromby and Gregg) bought Johnson's 68% shareholding. In the period of disagreement at board level, and the period during which Johnson was trying to sell his shares, the club stagnated. Johnson was blamed for this 'paralysis'. At this time Everton also entered into a 'media partnership' with a NTL subsidiary, 'Premium TV Ltd'. This meant that the media company purchased shares in Everton.

In 1997–98 Everton finished seventeenth but would have been relegated had not results in certain other matches worked in their favour. In the company's annual report for that year the chairman stated: 'For a club of our size and aspirations it was totally unacceptable to end the season seventeenth.' But he added 'whilst success on the pitch is central to our activities, even during troubled times we were able to report an improved and therefore encouraging financial result.' What was meant by this was that the club was able to show an operating profit, before amortisation of players, of £1.9 million in that year, and a profit of £2.3 million after taking into account 'profit on disposal of players and the amortisation of players.' This was in fact quite a turnaround because the loss in 1994–95 was £9.4 million, and this was followed by losses of £8.0 million and £2.9 million in the next two years.

From a financial point of view 1997–98 might have been encouraging, but the better financial times did not last. The operating loss (before amortisation of players) was in 1998–99 £1.1 million, and in 1999–2000 it was £500,000. After amortising players, and allowing for profit and losses on the sale of players, the losses amounted to £11.1 million and £10.8 million. The club was in a bad way financially at the end of the 1999–2000 season.

The new owners brought in the respected manager Walter Smith in an attempt to revive the fortunes of the club. This appointment did not, unfortunately, lead to success and Smith left the club in March 2002. This was at a time when the team were in danger of being relegated. As usual in such situations, the fans were also pressing for Walter Smith to be dismissed. It was claimed by his critics that he had brought to Everton certain celebrity, older players, who were paid high wages, but who failed to deliver. There were those, however, who thought that it was the board were to blame for the team's poor performance, not the manager.

The board had not made money available to Smith to enable him to increase the quality of the playing squad. In his period as manager (starting July 1998) he had spent £58 million on new players, but had sold players worth £57 million. His net expenditure was less than £1 million over three and a half seasons. A respected ex-Everton player, Neville Southall, said: 'To me it's a miracle Everton are still a Premier League side given what Walter has been able to spend.'

The club have been in decline since the mid-1980s. However, despite the fact that the club have been consistently fighting against relegation, the crowds still average over 35,000.

In March 2002 the directors replaced Smith with David Moyes, who had a reputation for being one of the best young managers in the country. He had enjoyed success at Preston North End with only limited funds to spend on quality players. There were no changes made at board level, however. The club remained short of money. They were £40 million in debt. They remained the poorer relations on Merseyside, not having the funds to compete in the transfer market with their neighbours. They did, however, have one of the most promising young players in the country in their team, Wayne Rooney, who began to attract attention. The press, looking for heroes, turned the spotlight on Rooney. The player, then aged 17, dropped his local agent, and moved to Proactive Sports Management, one of the leading agencies in the country. He started to make demands on Everton with regard to his future at the club. It was rumoured he was seeking a three-year contract that would give him £2 million a year. The outcome of these negotiations would indicate whether or not Everton had the financial resources to re-establish themselves as one of the top teams in the country. If Everton were not able to retain the services of one of the best young players in the country it would not be a good sign. They were not able to keep him.

In July 2004 Everton had experienced yet another boardroom crisis. One of the directors, Paul Gregg, a member of the 'True Blue Consortium' was not satisfied with the progress the club was making. He came up with new plans and the offer of new money for the club, but the chairman, Bill Kenwright, was against the plans and he had the support of a majority of the directors. This split the board and certain directors resigned. Trevor Birch, the chief executive, who had only moved to the club from Leeds in June 2004, resigned six weeks after joining; he had seen enough.

Gregg offered the club £15 million, which he said he and a third-party consortium could produce, and challenged Kenwright to match this offer. Paul Gregg is in fact very wealthy (ranked the twenty-fifth richest person in football). He was at one time Britain's biggest theatre owner (Apollo Leisure) but sold his interests in 1999 for £129 million. He has had a number of other business interests. Many thought that it was his wealth that would be the key to Everton's future success. Kenwright is wealthy but nowhere near as wealthy as Gregg. Gregg claimed he had financial backers from the Far East but they did not materialise. A power struggle erupted at the club between Gregg and Kenwright.

The club was clearly in financial difficulties. Philip Green, the very successful owner of a number of retail chains (wealth estimated at £3.6 billion), stepped in to help his friend Bill Kenwright secure a £15 million cash credit; Green provided the guarantee. Green made it clear, however, that he was not interested in a long-term involvement with the club (he is a Spurs supporter). He was simply helping the club overcome a short-term crisis.

In September 2004 the financiers behind the Fortress Sports Fund expressed an interest in taking over Everton. The founder of the fund was an Everton supporter, Christopher Samuelson, who lived in Switzerland. The other individuals involved included wealthy bankers and business people from across Europe.

The plan was for the fund to initially take over responsibility for the £15 million debt that had been guaranteed by Philip Green. This debt would be guaranteed or repaid, and the investors receive equity, which would enable Fortress Sports Fund to build up a 29.9% holding in the club. Fortress Sports Fund would then be given an option to enlarge its holding at a later date to 50.1%. It was reported that this additional holding would cost £17.2 million. These dealings were valuing the company at somewhere between £65 million and £85 million, which was at the time a high value for a company that had not enjoyed recent success. Samuelson, the financier behind the bid, believed that the club could attract regular crowds of between 55,000 and 60,000. To attract such crowds the club would need a new stadium and to be successful, however. This would require Fortress to invest considerable sums directly into the club, as opposed to spending money to buy shares off existing shareholders, and repaying or guaranteeing debt.

In the end, Bill Kenwright survived the challenge from Paul Gregg and remained as chairman. The club, however, was still heavily in debt and had to sell Wayne Rooney (for over £20 million) to help its financial position. They also had to abandon their plans for a new 55,000-seat stadium. Neither of these moves were popular with fans or with Bill Kenwright.

In December 2004 the 'True Blue Consortium' (which had owned 71.4% of the club's shares) was voluntarily wound up and its holdings distributed at par value, to its members. The result of this restructuring was that in May 2005 Bill Kenwright owned 25% of the club's shares; Jon Woods, 18.9%; Anita Gregg (who was appointed to the board in August 1994), 11.6%; Paul Gregg, 10.8%; and Arthur Abercromby (who had resigned from the board in July 2004), 5.5%.

Unfortunately, selling your best players is not the best way to assure continuing success. In 2005–06 the club were quickly eliminated from the European competitions and finished in eleventh place in the Premiership. The move to a new stadium at Kirby was still being discussed.

All clubs except one (Chelsea) would argue that they are short of money, but Everton in particular does seem to have problems. They have had high levels of borrowing, with a low level of shareholders' funds. The chairman, in his statement in the 2005 annual report, makes a point of thanking Barclays Bank. The major borrowing of the club is £30 million of loan notes; this is a securitised loan, repayable in annual instalments over a 25-year period.

The finance to service the loan is secured against future season ticket sales and match day ticket sales. The problem with such loans is that the club have already received and invested the money and there is not a great deal to show for it. What it means is that out of future revenue, somewhere in the region of £2 million per season will have to be paid out as interest on the loan, and a further £1 million per season on repayments of the loan. It is true that the loan does not have to be repaid quickly and that the funds obtained have helped the club survive as a Premier League club, however. There is continuing talk of new equity coming into the club from a foreign investor.

After a difficult recent history, the club does now seem to have a more settled governance structure. It is owned by people who are loyal Everton supporters, even if they do seem to have a propensity for squabbling. The club finished in sixth place in the Premiership in 2006–07, good, but they need money if they are to break through into the top group.

Liverpool

Liverpool FC like to be thought of as a friendly club, one in which people matter. Everton, however, have actually given themselves the title of 'The People's Club' and emphasise the importance they attach to efforts to support football in the community. A cynic would point out that it is clearly good public relations for highly paid players to be seen to be trying to put something back into the community. Furthermore, clubs benefit from the strengthening of links with young fans. Nearly all clubs are now involved in such community programmes.

Manchester United is sometimes referred to as a 'supermarket club' while Liverpool is the 'cosy corner shop club.' This is one point of view; another is that both are now global businesses not local sports clubs. Liverpool once boasted they had only a few executive boxes, in other words that Anfield belonged to its loyal supporters. The planned new stadium, however, includes many executive boxes.

The marketing of the club is now not just within the local community or even just at a national level—it is now international. The Liverpool team make regular post-season tours to Asia to promote their brand name, for instance. The club's sponsors put money into the club because it has an international brand name. Approximately half of their season ticket holders live more than

50 miles from the ground. In fact, Liverpool is no longer the 'cosy corner shop club'. The club is now owned by Americans.

Liverpool FC give the impression of being a well-managed business. Managers and players are treated well and the supporters (the customers) are valued. Terry Venables has argued that Liverpool's success for 25 years has been not just the result of the way they play the game on the pitch, it is also the way they structure the game off the pitch.[4] The late Sir John Smith, and his successor David Moores, both understood that it is the chairman's function to provide leadership without telling everyone else how to do their job.[5]

The club dominated English football in the 1980s, but were disappointing in the 1990s. They returned to the 'elite' group in the 2000s, winning the European Champions League in 2005. They have, however, still not been able to win the Premier League, very few clubs have, but Liverpool have greater expectations than most.

Liverpool has a great history, having been champions of the First Division on 18 occasions. As Peter Robinson, their then chief executive said in 1996, 'We are here for one reason: to win trophies. We are an old-fashioned football club, not a quoted plc and we don't pay dividends to shareholders. Any money we generate is ploughed back into the team and stadium.' The non-payment of dividends does not mean shareholders do not gain from the club's success. The share price of Liverpool climbed for many years, with or without dividends.

In the early years of the 2000s, however, Liverpool were beginning to suffer in that they did not have access to such large amounts of money as their three, big, English rivals. They needed access to more money in order to build a new ground and to increase their playing squad. There are disadvantages in being a 'cosy corner shop club'. In 2007 two American sports entrepreneurs, George Gillett Jr. and Tom Hicks, came to the rescue.

History

Although Liverpool were the most successful team in the country in the 1970s and 1980s, being champions on eleven occasions in those twenty years, they do not have a history of unbroken success. They were First Division champions twice before the First World War, and twice in the inter-war period. They won the championship again in 1946–47, but then experienced a very bad period. They were relegated in 1954 and stayed in the second division until 1962.

In the 1950s Liverpool were a disappointing club. At the beginning of that decade they had been defeated in the FA Cup final. They then had a bad period, during which one of their biggest humiliations was to lose to non-league Worcester City in the FA Cup. The chairman at the end of the 1950s was T.V. Williams and he was under pressure to introduce change particularly because Everton (and their supporters) were enjoying success. Everton were certainly the top team in the city.

In 1959 Williams managed to persuade Bill Shankly to move to Liverpool to become the manager. A great deal of the future success of Liverpool was due to this one appointment. In Shankly's early days at the club it was not easy for him, he soon discovered what had been holding Liverpool back.[6] He had to change what was referred to as the 'defeatist' approach of the then directors and 'turn the boardroom into a dynamic environment geared towards success.' Like all managers Shankly needed the directors' support in order to make these changes and he also needed their money, but he did not want them interfering in football matters. According to Tommy Docherty, 'Bill hated to see amateurs running a professional sport. People who'd never played, didn't understand the game, didn't know what it means to the people, the loyalty to the supporters.' Shankly identified more with the supporters than the directors.

In his early years at Liverpool Shankly did have to battle to obtain the changes he wanted—he did need the co-operation of directors. Shankly certainly did raise standards at Liverpool, but the so-called 'genuine football men' did not raise standards in football generally. If one looks at what happened to football over the next 25 years (1960–1985) it finished up in a mess.

The Liverpool FC were suffering when Shankly inherited the club. The ground was a disgrace, as was the training ground. Shankly began to establish what became known as 'The Boot Room' in which he worked closely with a small group of people, including Bob Paisley and Ronnie Moran, who were to go on to be future managers of the club. He built up an organisation not just a football team.

The directors did not find the new manager easy to deal with and did not like all the credit for the club's revival going to Shankly.

In his early days at the club the directors did not give him the money he wanted to buy new players. (For example, he wished to buy Jack Charlton, but was not given the funds to do so.) In 1961 Shankly made it clear that he would resign if the directors continued to decide who the club would buy and sell.

A change in their working relationship came with the appointment of a new director, Eric Sawyer (who was a top executive at Littlewoods). He was introduced to the club by John Moores who, although on the Everton board, had an affection for the Liverpool club as well as a financial interest. Although the new director knew little about football he understood business and became a big supporter of Shankly at the boardroom level. Sawyer was a hard-headed businessman who was not afraid of Shankly or in competition with him: he simply recognised his managerial abilities. Sawyer told Shankly, 'If you can get the players, I'll get the money.'

Shankly contributed so much to the rise of Liverpool, yet the rewards he received were modest. He admitted he had been single-minded in his pursuit of football success, and had not asked for money. Money may not have been too important to him, but years later he regretted that he had not accumulated more for his family. At the time he retired he was still living in the same house he had moved into when he first became the Liverpool manager.

John Smith became chairman of Liverpool in 1973, and he did not have an easy relationship with Shankly. Smith had first watched Liverpool when he was four years old, and was a committed supporter. His enthusiasm meant that he wanted to be involved in all aspects of running the club. He introduced a policy that all directors had to watch a player before the club bought him. John Smith began to handle all the transfers. Shankly resented this, and retired a short time later. 'As Smith made his presence felt, Bill no longer had the energy to break in the new man.' This was the view of Emlyn Hughes, a former Liverpool player and distinguished captain of the team.

Peter Robinson and the chairman 'tried all sorts of ways to persuade him to stay.' Shankly was offered the position of general manager at the club, on generous terms, but turned it down. (Busby had upon retirement accepted a similar position at Manchester United). Shankly said: 'You fight on the field to win but you've other battles to fight inside the club too, political battles. Candidly it was a shambles here when I came, not good enough for the people here. I'd fought the battles inside and outside and I was only in it to win the games for the people.'

Shankly felt that the Liverpool board had not been generous with him. He became bitter about the meagre financial rewards he had received. He did not enjoy retirement. 'He took umbrage and a lot of people were sad it came to that.' There were many that thought he should have been made a director. Shankly did 'not want to sever his links with the club' but he was too proud to ask for such links. One problem was of course that with one or two exceptions he did not like directors and had at various times upset them.

Shankly was clearly unhappy with the trend towards chairmen taking on increasing powers. John Smith found it easier to get on with Shankly's successor, Bob Paisley, who was easier to work with. Paisley was much more relaxed at board meetings.

John Smith was chairman at Liverpool for 17 years, during which time the club won 22 major trophies. No chairman has, in terms of trophies won, been more successful. His professional approach to being chairman of a board won him praise throughout football. He was widely respected (if not by Bill Shankly). He was appointed chairman of the Sports Council in 1985.

In the 1970s and 1980s Liverpool had an unusual ownership structure. Sir John Moores had purchased a substantial shareholding in both Everton and Liverpool before the rules on shareholding in more than one club came into existence. He was not, however, allowed to be a director of both clubs. Even though he was the largest single shareholder in the Liverpool club he was not on the board and 'never questioned or interfered with board decisions.' He did, however, have a nominee on the board, namely John Smith.

Towards the end of the 1980s, with Sir John Moores approaching his ninetieth birthday, Liverpool became concerned about who would inherit his shareholding. They were naturally worried they would fall into unfriendly hands. (This was a similar problem to that faced by Everton.) One Liverpool director for over 15 years, Sydney Moss, suggested that David Moores (a Liverpool City Councillor) would be a natural heir for Sir John Moores' Liverpool holding. David Moores was a lifelong Liverpool supporter and was the only member of the family with Sir John Moores' love of the game. In fact, John Moores divested himself of the shares before his death by spreading them amongst 32 members of his family. Ownership of the shares was therefore well dispersed both within the family and amongst outside shareholders.

David Moores was invited to join the board, and to bring funds into the club. As Sir John Smith said, 'The Moores family have been great benefactors to Merseyside football. David's appointment will keep the predators at bay.'

David Moores was a character, he had long hair despite being in his mid-40s, he was into heavy rock music and he was a 'Kopite' (the number plate on his Mercedes was KOP 1). There were those that doubted his potential as a director of a club known for its sound approach. The club had steered clear of flamboyant characters, in contrast to many other football clubs. 'It was not the style Liverpool fans had grown used to from their directors.'

At the beginning of the 1990s Liverpool not only faced a corporate governance problem but also a financial problem. They were short of funds and it was necessary for them to convert their ground to an all-seater stadium. (This meant removing the world famous 'Kop'.) A problem was that as with other clubs this change would reduce the ground capacity and consequently reduce match revenue unless changes could be made elsewhere in the ground. The club needed £7 million to alter the 'Kop' and £8 million to add a new tier to another stand (including executive boxes and dining suites). They also needed money to acquire new players and strengthen their existing squad. By Liverpool standards they had a playing crisis: they only finished sixth in the League in 1992 and 1993, and eighth in 1994—it had been over 20 years earlier (1963) that they had finished this low! It was estimated they needed to spend at least £10 million on new players.

The board decided that in order to raise the £25 million or so they needed it would help if they increased their equity base. To do this they would make a rights issue (a similar decision to that made by Everton a few years later). The advantage of a rights issue is that it enables the existing shareholders of a company to maintain their control. It meant in Liverpool's case that the company did not need to have their shares listed and therefore could avoid the need to satisfy institutional investors who would at that time have been attracted by a public offering of shares. A possible disadvantage of a rights issue is that there is no guarantee the existing shareholders will be able to produce all the funds needed to buy the new shares. This problem was overcome by David Moores agreeing to underwrite the issue. This meant that if an existing Liverpool shareholder did not take up their 'right' to purchase additional shares then David Moores would buy the shares. Surprisingly (in view of the boom years for football in the early 1990s), hardly any of the rights were exercised—the existing shareholders did not want to buy additional shares at a price of £700 per share. They were being offered one new share for every four they held. This increased the total number of shares to 15,000, and by May 1992 David Moores owned 3,101, that is 20% of the total. This meant his holding in the club was worth over £2 million. He became chairman. With all the euphoria that now surrounds football it is surprising that people with a financial stake in Liverpool declined the opportunity to buy more shares.

David Moores became chairman because the existing directors wanted him to. He did not, however, take on an executive role. It was not a boardroom coup as has been seen at so many other clubs. There was continuity in the boardroom—stability and unity. By 1994 David Moores had acquired half of his uncle's (Sir John Moores') shareholding, increasing his total holding to nearly 40%. In June 1994 Liverpool announced they would make yet another 'rights' issue. It was planned that this would raise an additional £10 million, with most of the issue again being underwritten by David Moores.

David Moores was similar in age to his new manager, Graham Souness, and they had many interests in common. Moores was a big admirer of Souness and the policies he wished to pursue. He argued Souness' case at board meetings, sometimes being his only supporter. He was instrumental in keeping Souness in his job 'on more than one occasion.' One of Souness' policies that caused difficulties at board level was his wish to buy and sell players at a rapid rate; another cause for concern was the quality of the players he purchased.

There was much criticism of Souness' transfer dealings. Tommy Smith (an ex-player who had become an influential local journalist) could make no sense of his transfer dealings, and unusual for Liverpool there was public criticism of the manager. Souness in fact wished to sell the old guard of players at Liverpool and replace them with his own team. The problem was that he spent large amounts to bring in quite average players. Liverpool did have very good young players in their squad but these had been brought to the club by Souness' predecessor, the popular Kenny Dalglish, who had unexpectedly resigned in 1991.

The board were becoming fed up with supporting Souness' purchasing policy; it was not achieving results. The manager did not endear himself to supporters either, partly because of his extravagant lifestyle and partly because of the lack of judgement he showed in 1992 in giving the story of his heart by-pass operation exclusively to the hated *Sun* newspaper. It was the *Sun* who had incorrectly claimed that many of the Liverpool supporters who had been killed in the crowd crush at Hillsborough had been drunk.

In April 1993 the board decided they would sack the manager at the end of the season. The last time a Liverpool manager had been sacked was before Bill Shankly came to the club. Unfortunately, before Souness was informed of the decision the information was leaked and appeared in the press. Souness and his legal advisers then became involved in discussion with the club—he still had three years of his contract remaining. Souness said he wished to remain at Liverpool. A compromise settlement was agreed upon. Souness remained, but with Roy Evans as assistant manager. It was hoped this arrangement would settle the concerns of some of the more experienced players at the club.

On 9 May 1993 the club held a press conference that turned out to be highly embarrassing for all concerned. The directors had made a U-turn. David Moores began by saying that 'The past few days at Anfield have probably been the most difficult in the club's history.' Then he announced that the difficulties had been sorted out and that Souness would be continuing as manager of the club for the remainder of his contract, and 'I hope for much longer than that.' He then announced that Tony Ensor, a director of the club, was resigning. Ensor said at the press conference that 'There were a number of matters relating to the way in which the club is being run with which I do not agree.'

Unfortunately this was not the end of the matter. The team did not perform well in the 1993–94 season and by Christmas pressure was mounting yet again for the removal of Souness. David Moores made the usual chairman's statement that Souness' position was secure but the players Souness had purchased were not playing well. When the manager tried to sell players other clubs were not prepared to pay high transfer prices for them. Furthermore, the players did not want to leave Liverpool because they were being 'overpaid'. The board again decided Souness had to go. On 18 January 1994, at a press conference, David Moores read a statement to the effect that Souness had offered his resignation and that the board had accepted it.

Moore was very sad and said so. He added, however, that the results achieved in the two years and nine months of the period with Souness as manager were 'well below what is expected by the club and its supporters.' Tony Ensor was not sorry to see Souness go. He believed the sacking was 'always inevitable . . . Personally I regret that it has taken him so long to see that his confrontational style of management has not been in accordance with Liverpool's tradition.'

In this case we have an interesting example of where the disagreement was not between the chairman and the manager, but between the manager and the majority of the directors, as well as between the manager and the fans. Liverpool may have taken time but they did in the end demonstrate the way in which a board of directors is supposed to work. The chairman, even though he had effective control of the club, did not behave in an autocratic manner (which is unusual in football). The board in the end came out of the crisis quite well.

The board acted quickly to cover any damage the confrontation may have caused the club and company. They quickly appointed a new, safe manager, Roy Evans, who was in the Liverpool tradition. They raised new equity funds through the 1994 rights issue, borrowed money, bought new players and succeeded in getting back into Europe.

On 13 July 1999 the Granada Media Group purchased 9.9% of the club's shares for £22 million. The money they paid went to the club (not to another investor). This purchase valued the club at £220 million, which was a value of over £6,000 per share. By now David Moores owned just over 50% of the total shares, with Granada the second largest shareholders.

A Division of Opinion

Historically, Liverpool has a reputation for appointing directors who are businessmen and professionals rather than entrepreneurs. These directors have also tended to be very loyal to the club. The

340

club have a reputation for good corporate governance. The directors leave the running of the club to the chief executives. David Moores in particular has been very well liked. In his autobiography Michael Owen writes that 'Everyone I have played with at Liverpool has passed comment on David Moores. They all say "What a great chairman he is. He's a supporter who loves the club. He's not in it for the business or the money, he just wants Liverpool to do well."'

One problem was faced by Liverpool was that their ground only had capacity for 45,362 people. This put them at a comparative disadvantage with Manchester United and Arsenal. But Liverpool are to build a new stadium in Stanley Park that will help the social and economic regeneration of the Anfield area. The planned 60,000-seat football stadium would be able to retain its emotional link with the Anfield neighbourhood as one perimeter of the new site is only 500 yards from the existing stadium. The problem the club faced was how to pay for it. The football club, together with Liverpool City Council, were at one time hoping to raise a large amount of money for the overall project from the public sector but most of the money will have to be provided by the football club.

Liverpool has made a profit in most years and managed at the same time to keep down their level of borrowing. As at 31 July 2005, the club's net debt was only £17.1 million (down from £18.9 million in 2003). With equity funds of £35.6, the company had nothing to worry about from a financial gearing point of view.

With Liverpool's annual turnover being £122 million in 2005, the net debt to turnover ratio was 0.14, one of the lowest in the League, and an easy level of debt to service. By contrast, the ratio for Everton was 0.98, one of the highest in the League. Liverpool clearly have been a well managed club from both a financial and human resource point of view.

The Liverpool board cannot be criticised for failing to provide their managers with money or for not giving them time to deliver results. For example, the directors were very loyal to Gérard Houllier, who became manager of the club in 1998 and who helped modernise the club. Houllier believes that he re-educated the club, but in a book on the subject (*The Red Revolution: Liverpool Under Houllier*) the author, Paul Tomkins, refers to it as a 'revolution'. The changes introduced included ending a drinking culture amongst

341

some of the players, changing coaching methods and introducing a dietary regime.

Unfortunately for Houllier, in his six years at Liverpool he did not deliver the Premier League championship to the club. Houllier did lead Liverpool to six trophies, but the club did not like being behind Manchester United and Arsenal in the League competition. The performance of the club was certainly satisfactory, but that was not good enough for either the fans or the board. He was replaced as manager at the end of the 2003–04 season by Rafael Benitez. Benitez was a well-respected manager who had proven himself. He had twice led teams to the Spanish championship. The Liverpool directors gave him money to spend. In 2004–05 he spent more than £30 million on top foreign international players, and then at the beginning of 2005–06 spent another £19 million on new players including the purchase of Peter Crouch, who had promised much at his earlier clubs but had yet to deliver. Liverpool, in winning the UEFA Champions League in 2005, brought an extra £22 million to the club, helping fund the acquisition of the new players.

Ironically, in Benitez's first season at Liverpool, when they won the Champions League, twelve of the fourteen Liverpool players who took part in the final match had been at the club whilst Houllier was manager. In fact, Houllier had been manager at the club in 2003–04 when they finished fourth in the Premiership and so qualified for that competition. Houllier was at the 2005 final when Liverpool won and so was able to join in the celebrations with the players, the new manager and the chairman. In the club's 2004 annual report the chairman had reported that 'although unanimous, the decision to replace Gerard was one of the most difficult the Board had to face in recent years; he was regarded as a friend by us all.'

Unfortunately for Liverpool, their plans for a new stadium were causing them financial problems. Their total debts in 2006 stood at £73 million. The costs of the new stadium were rising, and by mid-2006 the estimate was £180 million. The regional development agencies were having second thoughts about the project, David Moores was trying to find an investor who would buy all or some of his shares, and the club were trying to find a company willing to pay a substantial sum for the naming rights to the new stadium.

342

The club were becoming very dependent on banks to provide them with funds.

Ownership

At various times there has been talk of a possible change in the ownership at the club. In April 2004 there were rumours that the then Prime Minister of Thailand, Thaksin Shinawatra, was interested in buying an interest in the club, perhaps not with his own money, but with money collected from the national lottery in Thailand. Discussions did take place between the club and the Deputy Commerce Minister of Thailand. It was thought that the people of Thailand would enjoy having links with the famous Liverpool club, and that it would help the image of the politicians who completed the deal. What was less certain was whether the purchase would be good for Liverpool.

Liverpool had been a tightly controlled club, but there had been tensions. The majority shareholder, David Moores, and the third largest shareholder, Steve Morgan (who owned 5% of the shares), had public disagreements. In May 2004 Morgan, not a director himself, discussed with the directors various ways in which the club might strengthen its financial position. He proposed a £73 million rights issue, with part of the money being used to buy new players and the rest used to cover some of the costs of the proposed new stadium. The directors did not like the Morgan proposal, nor did the then manager, Gérard Houllier, like the criticism made by Morgan of his team selection. It was said that Morgan had the support of a large number of the club's fans, but whether that would have been the case twelve months later when in the summer of 2005 Liverpool won the UEFA Champions League, is less certain.

Morgan is a wealthy man, said at the time to be worth over £300 million. He is the founder of a successful home building company. He had offered to invest £70 million in the club in return for a greater role in its management. An issue was how many shares he would receive in return for this investment in the club. In May 2004 the equity value of Liverpool was in the region of £140 million. (In 1999 it had been £220 million.) In 2004 the shares of Liverpool would appear to have been undervalued, which meant it would be a good time for Morgan to buy, but a bad time for the club to sell.[7]

Stories about the future ownership of Liverpool continued to run. In November 2005, it was revealed that the club's chief executive, Rick Parry, had been having discussions with Robert Kraft, who is not only heir to the famous cheese family, but owner of one of the best NFL clubs, the New England Patriots. The Kraft family are quite willing to invest their wealth in sport; in 2002 they provided the Patriots with a £182 million new 68,000-seat stadium—just what Liverpool would have liked. Apparently Robert Kraft made encouraging noises about the two clubs collaborating, but was not interested in a take-over.

In December 2006 the club announced that representatives of a financial institution, a private equity fund with really serious wealth, were scrutinising their financial accounts with a view to purchasing a controlling interest. The possible investors were Dubai International Capital, who were responsible for investing the wealth of one of the richest countries in the world. As a country, Dubai had invested its great oil wealth in arguably the best airline in the world, the best sports facilities in the world, the best hotels and villas in the world—why not the best football club in the world, too?

For a while it appeared to outsiders that the Dubai investors would be the new owners of the club, but then in February 2007 they withdrew from the take-over negotiations. They had apparently been willing to offer £155 million for the equity shares of the club (£4,500 per share) but had heard that two American investors were willing to pay £175 million. They did not wish to enter into a bidding war that could have resulted in them paying more than they thought the club was worth. Both interested parties had been willing, in addition to purchasing the equity shares, to cover the club's £80 million debt and to provide finance for the £180 million stadium.

The two American purchasers were George Gillett Jr, owner of the Canadian ice-hockey club Montreal Canadians, and Tom Hicks, who owned the Texas Rangers baseball team. Both men have experience of running sports clubs. In order to fund their acquisition of the Liverpool club they needed to borrow large sums of money.

David Sullivan, the co-owner of Birmingham City, expressed

astonishment at the amount being paid by foreign investors to take over English clubs. Speaking of the purchase of Liverpool he forecast that there would be 'blood on the carpet in the next five years. If they are not doing it for the money, why are they doing it? They are probably looking at all the money that is made in American football. But over there you can't get relegated.' He also pointed out that in American football there was a salary cap, as well as a more equal sharing of the pot.[8]

Nevertheless, Sullivan and a number of other football club owners let it be known they would be willing to sell if the price was right. David Moores received in the region of £90 million from the sale of his Liverpool shares.

Conclusions

The thesis of this book is that football is now a global business, and in any such business long-term success depends upon those at the top, the 'dominant' directors. Liverpool demonstrate this, as do Everton. Both clubs had the same opportunities. Liverpool became one of the 'overlords' of English clubs. Everton after some success became also-rans. However, it has taken a while for Liverpool to get back amongst the elite. They have not been Premier League champions since 1990. Their success illustrates the importance of good leadership. Turning to Everton, we find the opposite.

Tottenham Verus Arsenal

What does the recent history of these two famous clubs demonstrate? Both clubs have at times been champions and the best team in the country. For a long time there was not a great deal to choose between the clubs in terms of wealth but there was a big difference between them in terms of the style of corporate governance. Tottenham have experienced a number of battles for ownership and control, with disputes at boardroom level. Arsenal have not. The managers at Tottenham have faced job insecurity, those at Arsenal have not. Both clubs have had the same market opportunities; one has taken advantage of these opportunities, the other has not.

At Arsenal there has been remarkable stability at boardroom

level. In contrast, at Tottenham the old guard were forced out at the beginning of the 1980s by one of the so-called new wave of owners. There were high hopes when Irving Scholar took over, but he led the club nowhere. Then came a take-over by the 'Dream Team' in 1993 that led to further disappointments. Alan Sugar has described his time at Spurs as a sad failure.

The boards of both companies were cautious in the early days of the Premier League, but the Arsenal board were confident enough to invest for success. The new owners of Tottenham were still, in 2001, talking about controlling costs and setting up a new organisational structure, but they carried on with the policy of sacking managers. Arsenal meanwhile had, by 2000, twice the annual revenue of their local rivals (and were paying twice the salary level). Roman Abramovich was said to be interested in buying Tottenham at one point, but was turned away. It was then that he went to Chelsea.

As recently as the early 1980s, two of the 'Big Five' clubs in the country were seen to be Arsenal and Tottenham. Why did Arsenal remain as one of the elite teams, and Spurs fade? In 1961 Spurs became the first club in English football to achieve the double. In 1963 they won the European Cup Winners Cup and become the first English team to win a major European football competition. They were known as 'Super Spurs'. How did they become, by the 1970s, a mediocre club? (In 1974–75 they finished nineteenth in the First Division, and were relegated in 1976–77.) The answer is bad leadership.

Tottenham's directors made decisions that resulted in financial difficulties at the club. The construction work on a new stand cost much more than had been expected, and at the end of 1982 the club was on the brink of disaster. Sidney Wale, who had been chairman for many years, was as a result of criticism forced to resign and another member of the board, a local waste paper merchant, Arthur Richardson, took over.

The Scholar Era

The new stand cost £5.25 million to build against estimated costs of £3 million. The executive boxes in the new stand were slow to sell and a hoped-for sponsorship deal failed to materialise. Irving Scholar, who had made his money through property development,

346

offered to help to finance the club, but he was not welcomed by the directors. The peculiar rules of the club (the company) at the time meant that existing directors had the right to refuse to register the ownership of shares in new names. This meant shares in the club could not be sold to a new owner unless the existing directors agreed to the transfer. The take-over of football clubs was almost unknown at the time and Spurs' board, because of this club rule, was thought to be 'impregnable' to outsiders.

What normally happened to the shares of the club was that the father passed them on to his son who passed them on to grandson and so forth. Although this style of governance seems odd by present standards, it must be remembered that it was the normal way in which succession occurred in family-owned companies, and that family companies are the most common form of business ownership.

Scholar's problem was how to break into a family-controlled business. The solution turned out to be comparatively easy. A lawyer, who was a friend, bought shares from existing shareholders, but did not try to register the transfer of the shares. The people who had sold the shares still had them registered under their name, but they signed an irrevocable proxy to appoint Scholar as their nominee on matters that required a vote. This meant Scholar could vote on behalf of the 'names' on the shareholder register. In other words, Scholar was buying the votes and so would be able to influence the club.

Early on in his attempt to take over the club Scholar had taken the unusual step of writing to all female shareholders, assuming that they had inherited the shares from male relatives and so would be happy to sell the shares to him. Scholar also acquired the Wale family holding. Another property developer, Paul Bobroff, a friend of Scholar's, bought a block of shares from the estate of a deceased Tottenham director. Eventually, Scholar and his associates purchased shares that gave them over 50% of the votes and completed what has been described as one of the more remarkable coups in English football history. The purchase of Spurs cost this 'rebel' group only £600,000. This was partly because the club had only issued a few shares (5,000 had been issued in 1905) and partly because many holders of small blocks of shares did not appreciate their true value. Twenty years earlier Tottenham had been one of the top clubs in England.

The first chairman of the club following the Scholar-led take-over was Douglas Alexiou. He was optimistic about the future of the club despite inheriting the largest debt in English football at that time (£5 million). The new directors found when they took over the company that the administration was inefficient and, not surprisingly, old-fashioned. They decided that it would be beneficial for all concerned to have the club's shares listed on the Stock Exchange. They were the first club in England to do so. The 1983 share issue was a big success. The equity finance obtained enabled the club to pay off its debts. The club sold its training ground for £4.5 million, and started to market merchandise linked to the Spurs name. At first everything seemed to be going well: the club won the UEFA Cup in 1984 and came close to winning the League championship in two seasons, 1984–85 and 1986–87.

Scholar was in many ways ahead of the times. He believed in marketing the club's brand name, the public flotation of equity shares and diversification into leisure goods. He also wanted to be involved in all aspects of running the club.[9]

Problems began when the directors had a falling out with the manager. The marketing policies were also having difficulties because at the time football was not an attractive product to sell. The demand for football and its spin-off activities was simply not there. This should have been foreseen. These policies failed also because they were badly executed.

It was not the enormous cost of building yet another new stand (over £9 million) that was the main problem. Rather, it was the financial losses of the club's subsidiaries that was the problem. The football side of the business was actually making a profit, but the non-football business, that is the computer-ticket operation and the sportswear franchise, were making losses. The club had invested £3 million in these subsidiaries. The diversification policy had not worked.

In 1987 Scholar had appointed Terry Venables as manager. Venables had built up his reputation through success as a manager in Barcelona. Immediately, however, there were problems to do with a number of issues, including the club's transfer policy. Scholar wanted young new players, but Venables wanted older, more experienced and therefore more expensive players. There was disagreement even on the extent of the chairman's wish to be involved in decisions regarding players. Scholar commented that

348

he 'was surprised how often he [Venables] would seek my opinion on team matters. I would tell him the job was his, not mine.'

Venables, however, gives a different version of the relationship. He believed that the millionaire-type chairman and directors who have come into the game 'find it extremely difficult to resist interfering in the running of the team.'[10] This he says was certainly the case with Irving Scholar, who would interfere in all aspects of the club. This was, Venables admits, because Scholar 'loved Tottenham so much, he was an absolute Spurs nut.' Venables regarded Scholar as an absolute charmer, who usually got his own way. Venables later experienced another interfering chairman, Alan Sugar, who also wanted to be in charge of everything. The difference was that Sugar did not 'bother too much with the niceties of social intercourse.'

In his early days at Spurs, Venables did not do well in the transfer market, and he cost the club a good deal of money—he was known as 'an extravagant spender'. His early purchases did not bring much success. In 1989, however, the club purchased Gary Lineker and the next season finished third in the First Division (still the top tier). In 1991 they won the FA Cup, and as a result Venables said that given the financial difficulties the club were having 'it was my finest achievement as a manager.'

The club was in need of additional funds. Scholar approached Robert Maxwell in July 1989 to see if he would be prepared to underwrite a rights issue of new equity shares. The plan was that Scholar and some other existing shareholders would not take up the shares that they were entitled to and Maxwell, as underwriter, would purchase these shares, which amounted to 26% of the total. The rights issue would produce £13 million, which would be sufficient to enable them to pay off their debts.

These arrangements were initially kept secret even from Paul Bobroff, the club's chairman. Scholar had to seek approval from the board of directors for the rights issue but he did not disclose the name of the person who would underwrite the issue. When Bobroff found out who it was, he attempted to block the deal. Scholar, in turn, attempted to remove Bobroff from the chairmanship. At a board meeting in September 1989, a vote of no confidence against Bobroff was passed by four votes to one but he refused to resign. In the end it was the Football League who stopped the Maxwell deal.

Although Scholar tried to introduce new business methods at Tottenham he was also responsible for some corrupt business practices at the club. In 1992, a routine check by the Inland Revenue of wage payment records at Tottenham found serious irregularities, including evidence of numerous illegal payments. These included secret payments to players who had joined Spurs. Other problems concerned a football agent effectively being on the club's books. Scholar personally authorised many of these irregular payments. The club were fined heavily as a result. In addition, an FA enquiry found the club guilty of some 40 charges, half of which related to breaches of transfer regulations. The club were fined £600,000 by the football authorities and had points deducted.

In October 1989 the Stock Exchange suspended Tottenham's shares and Scholar, under pressure, resigned from the board. What had happened to the director who entered the game as one of the new wave? Initially there had been such high expectations. By the late 1980s Tottenham had bank debts of £11 million (very high at that time) and there was a real danger that the club would need to go into receivership.

The Manager Who Wanted to be Chairman

It seems to be generally agreed by all that know him that Terry Venables, ex-footballer, ex-director, football manager, businessman and TV pundit, is charming and in possession of a great personality. He is self-confident and full of optimism. He has shown a remarkable ability to bounce back after troubles and is a respected coach. Unfortunately, there is less agreement on his ability as a football manager, director and businessman.

As a footballer he was good—he did play for England. As a manager he has had mixed success—he did quite well whilst in charge of England and as manager (coach) of Barcelona the club won two tournaments. But what about the business side of his life? Mihir Bose refers to him as being different from 'his cheeky chappie public image'; rather, he is 'a figure of intrigue with dark unfathomable secrets.'[11]

Alan Sugar had risen from a working class background (his father was a tailor from Hackney) to be one of the richest people in the UK. He had supported Spurs from childhood, as had his family. Sugar admitted that he knew little about the management

350

side of football, however. But he could see the growth potential of the market for football in the UK, especially if one added TV into the mix.

After a series of protracted and labyrinthine financial negotiations Terry Venables and Alan Sugar purchased control of Tottenham for three million pounds each in 1991. Although Venables had accumulated wealth from his involvement in football (and other ventures) he still needed to borrow money in order to purchase his 17.8% of the clubs shares, however.

Having sold his computer company, Sugar now turned his attention to how the club was being run by Venables. He did not like what he saw. He commented that 'all sorts of cretins are turning up (at the club) saying we owe them money.' One particular concern of Sugar's had been the role of Eddie Ashby in advising Venables about the running of the football club. Ashby was an associate of Venables, but he was also an un-discharged bankrupt who at the time of his involvement with Spurs had been involved in 43 companies, 16 of which were in receivership, 8 in liquidation and 15 struck off the Register of Companies. Venables had developed a reputation as a good football coach, but as a very shoddy businessman.

A key issue at Spurs was the demarcation of responsibilities. Sugar wanted Venables to run the football side of the business, but claimed Venables wanted to be in control of all aspects of the club. Sugar offered to buy Venables' shares, but the offer was rejected. A classic case of a divided board.

Venables had mortgaged almost all he had to be a major Spurs shareholder. He was taking great risks. Scholar revealed in his autobiography that Sugar 'was not overly impressed by Venables' business acumen.' Sugar had by now accumulated ownership of 50.1% of the shares of the company. After yet another acrimonious confrontation Sugar gave Venables a letter telling him he was sacked. Venables then obtained a court injunction, which resulted in him being reinstated as the club's chief executive. Venables' legal appeal was based on the argument that if he was not able to run the club, the club would suffer. He was allowed an interim settlement that permitted him to continue for the time being. At the full hearing a number of months later, large numbers of supporters were in the street supporting Venables and ridiculing Sugar. The court hearing, however, ruled against Venables. Venables left the club and Sugar stayed on even though he was not popular with the fans.

New Ownership

In December 2000 ENIC (English National Investment Company) purchased 20% of Spurs shares from Alan Sugar for a price reported to be of £22 million. Alan Sugar, however, retained ownership of 13% of the company's shares and continued to be a regular attendee of Spurs home games. He said that he missed the 'hustle and bustle' of being involved with running a football club. The chairman of ENIC, Daniel Levy, became chairman of Spurs.

The two businessmen behind ENIC are Daniel Levy and Joseph Lewis. Daniel Levy and his family own 29.41% of Criales Holding Ltd, a company incorporated in the Bahamas. It is this company that own ENIC and so ultimately control Tottenham. The remaining 70.59% of shares in Criales are owned by the family interests of Joseph Lewis. Lewis is a British citizen who is a resident of the Bahamas. He is ranked in the top twenty in *The Times* Rich List, and is described as 'one of the worlds great currency traders'. His major business dealings are in the US where he is involved with a leading foreign currency trading firm and with the ownership of land in Florida. He is reported also to have investments in the Russian oil industry. With his wealth estimated to be £1.8 billion million, his investment in Tottenham Hotspur is not one of his major involvements.

In November 2003, Spurs announced plans to raise additional funds through a convertible bond issue. Shareholders were to be given the opportunity to buy the bonds and would be able to either convert these to equity shares at some time in the future or to take the cash with the bonds being redeemed. One of the non-executive directors at the club, Howard Shore, was very much against this move, and resigned from the board. Shore believed, and he was proved right, that this policy was an attempt by Daniel Levy and ENIC to obtain even more influence at the club. (ENIC were to underwrite the bond issue and so would be able to purchase any shares not taken up on conversion.) The club also announced plans to move from a full market listing to being traded on the AIM. Shore saw all this as a move to eventually make the club a private company. Nevertheless, the club went ahead with a convertible issue, but with preference shares as the base rather than the bonds.

When the club made the £15 million issue of Convertible Redeemable Preference Shares (CRPS), ENIC Sports invested just over £11 million to purchase 73.7% of these Convertible Redeemable Preference Shares and then transferred the ownership of these to Crailes Holding Ltd. This meant that Criales had a 'potential fully diluted interest in Tottenham Hotspur plc of 53.8%', and that they would have full control when conversion took place; the earliest date for conversion being October 2007. In June 2007 Alan Sugar sold his 12% stake in the club for £25 million. This valued the club at over £200 million. ENIC announced they were willing to buy all the remaining shares in the company. They planned to make it a private company.

The chairman of Tottenham Hotspur plc, Daniel Levy, combines this role with the position of chief executive. To combine these two roles is not normally considered to lead to good corporate governance but statements in the company's annual reports seek to reassure minority shareholders by pointing to the presence on the board of independent non-executive directors who 'have the ability and authority to ensure that the combination of roles does not work to the disadvantage of the Group and its shareholders'. One of the so-called independent directors was David Buchler (who had been deputy chairman of the club). He resigned from the board in 2006, however. This left only one independent director, Mervyn Davies. It has also meant that the club was not complying with the City code on corporate governance that requires two independent non-executive directors to sit on its audit and remuneration committees.

Between 1985 and 2005 Tottenham had twelve different managers, an average stay of less than two years. Martin Jol, appointed in 2004, was the fifth manager in five years. Not a way to build up a club. In fact, the highest position achieved by Spurs in the Premiership before Jol took over had been seventh, in 1994–95. In 2005–06, they finished in fifth place and qualified for a place in the UEFA Cup—their best performance for many years. In 2006–07 they again finished in fifth place, and had a very profitable year financially. One feature of the footballers that made up the Spurs team in 2005–06 season was the number of good and promising English players. In October 2005 there were five English international players in the first team squad, with at least three very promising young England players on their books. This was at a time when Arsenal were fielding a team, and a substitute's bench, with no British players. Much of the credit for Tottenham's encouragement of English players must go to David Pleat and Frank Arnesen. It was said that one reason why Chelsea eventually lured Arnesen away from Spurs was so that he could attempt to build up a youth policy based on British players.

By Way of Comparison

In the 1960s Spurs were First Division champions on one occasion, were second once and third on three occasions; their lowest position was eighth. In contrast, Arsenal were a mid-table First Division club, with fourth being their highest final place; fourteenth their lowest. In the 1960s the clubs had similar annual revenue figures but by 1971 Arsenal were showing slightly higher figures, with £653,000 against £512,000.

By the late 1980s Arsenal were very successful (being First Division champions in 1989 and 1991) and Spurs were good, but not outstanding. The annual revenue figures were surprisingly the opposite to what one would expect from their relative league positions. In 1991 Arsenal's revenue was £11.3 million, while that of Spurs was £18.7 million. By 1997, after two good seasons for Arsenal in the Premier League (they came fifth and third) their revenue was £27.1 million, whereas the annual revenue for Spurs, after two modest seasons (eighth and tenth) was £27.8 million. Spurs were able to turn their relatively high revenue figures into profits but not into success on the pitch. Arsenal showed pre-tax losses but were successful on the pitch. Arsenal spent over £10 million in net transfers over these two seasons, whereas Spurs spent £6.5 million. Arsenal were investing for success.

The annual salary figures also present a confusing picture. In 1994–95, those of Arsenal was just above those of Spurs (£8.9 million as opposed to £8.4 million) but the next season Spurs paid the higher amount (£11.5 million against £10 million). It was not until the end of the 1990s that Arsenal began to emerge as one the 'Big Five' clubs, paying salaries of £21.9 million in 1997–98, as against £17.0 million for Spurs. By 2003–04, Arsenal were paying £69.9 million, which was over double the Spurs bill. In June 2000

Spurs spent £11 million to acquire the services of Serhiy Rebrov, a record transfer payment for them. The purchase was not a success. The club were running at a loss in the early years of the 2000s and introduced a policy to cut wage costs, which were just over 50% of turnover.

In the following season, 2004–05, they finished ninth, and the club began to invest. They spent £61.8 million (gross) on new players between July 2003 and July 2005. This, for Spurs, was a large investment; in the six seasons to 2002 they had spent only £53.0 million on new players. The club (and supporters) were expecting the 2005–06 season to be a successful one—it was, they finished fifth in the Premiership.

The club's performance over the first 14 years of the Premier League puts them in seventh place overall. Not a particularly good performance for a club with a good name, a good reputation and from the wealthy South East of the country. It is especially disappointing when compared with that of their local rivals, Arsenal, who were ranked second in terms of overall Premier League performance. Tottenham do, however, now appear to have sorted out their corporate governance problems.

Arsenal

Arsenal moved into their new stadium for the 2006–07 season. They needed to: their 2004 revenue from gate and other match day income was £33.7 million; Manchester United's was £61.2 million. Although the directors of Arsenal agreed a move was necessary, there was apparently disagreement as to the new location. It is said that David Dein would have liked some sort of ground-sharing arrangement at the new Wembley Stadium. Other Arsenal directors, in particular Danny Fiszman, wanted the club to have their own stadium, in the Highbury area. Fiszman and these other directors won the argument. Not surprisingly the club had difficulty putting together the financing arrangements for their new 60,000-seat stadium. There were also hiccups regarding planning permission. The directors showed considerable courage in starting work on the new project with only short-term banking facilities in place. It was not until February 2004 that all the funding plans for the stadium were settled.

The new 60,000-seat Emirates Stadium has the potential to generate the largest match day revenues of any football (soccer) club in the world. This is because of the high ticket prices that can be charged in London. It is also to do with sponsorship deals, and of course the expected success of the club. Arsenal have also kept a financial interest in their old ground by being involved in the property development at that site.

The Good Old Days

In late 1940s and early 1950s Arsenal were one of the most successful teams in the country. They were First Division champions twice (1947–48 and 1952–53), were third on two occasions and fifth on four occasions. They won the FA Cup in 1950. The very successful and popular manager was Tom Whittaker, an ex-Arsenal player. Amongst their star players at the time were such respected and well-known players as Joe Mercer and Denis and Leslie Compton.

The directors had an interesting relationship with the club's players and managers. Tom Whittaker writes about the directors of Arsenal with respect and warmth—not always the way in which managers see the directors. He pays tribute to many of the club's directors of football at that time, who he believed were 'perhaps the most maligned people in football, the men who give plenty but who take nothing out.'

He was of course speaking about the 1950s when directors did not receive a fee, when dividends paid by the club were limited and, perhaps just as important, when the wages of players were not so much controlled by club directors as the league administrators. His experience of directors was also mainly limited to those at Arsenal.

George Graham, who in the 1980s became the manager of the club, referred to the Arsenal of the 1950s and 1960s as the 'Upstairs/Downstairs' club. He did not mean by this the club was being promoted and relegated on a regular basis. Graham was taking this title from a popular TV series at the time, which dealt with the differences in lifestyle and values between those who in Edwardian times lived upstairs in a house, an upper middle class family, and those who lived below stairs, the servants. At Arsenal at that time the directors of the club could be seen as being upstairs, and those below stairs were the managers and the players (one of whom was George Graham).

For a number of years there had been no doubt as to who it was that held power at the club, it was two families: the Bracewell-Smiths and the Hill-Woods. In 1929 Samuel Hill-Wood had become chairman when he took over from Henry Norris, who had very successfully led the club before being been found guilty of making illegal payments to players. This was the start of the new dynasty. In 1953 Guy Bracewell-Smith became the next chairman. These two families were the major shareholders and the power at the club for over 60 years. In 1962 Sir Guy Bracewell-Smith resigned as chairman because of the strain of too much travelling to see his club play. Family and club traditions were maintained, however, with Denis Hill-Wood taking his place. There were, however, now problems at the club. The last time the club had won a trophy was 1953. The directors were being criticised for Arsenal's lack of success. Even worse, in the 1960s the local rivals from Tottenham were the most successful club in the country.

Billy Wright was appointed as manager in 1962. Wright had been a very successful and popular Wolverhampton and England player but he had had no experience of managing a football club. He did not succeed in his new role. In 1966 Wright was quietly sacked and Bertie Mee replaced him. Mee was a surprise appointment, he was not well-known, and was in fact the club's physiotherapist. Bill Shankly made the comment that Arsenal had 'appointed the medicine man.' Mee did not immediately improve the club's position and the directors were still under pressure from supporters. It had been obvious for some time that Arsenal needed to strengthen their playing squad, the only doubt was whether or not the directors could afford to provide additional finance, and if they could, did they want to. In the 1968–69 season the chairman wrote an article in the club programme which said that 'There appears to be a misconception abroad that Arsenal managers, since Tom Whittaker, have been stifled and restricted by the Board of Directors and refused money with which to go into the transfer market. I can deny this absolutely. In the past 12 months alone, we have made approaches for 4 top class players and offered in each case a fee that would have been a British record. In each case the club concerned said it did not want the money and would not part with the player.'

In fact Mee turned out to be a very good appointment, and in his ten years in charge revived the club's fortunes. He made some interesting appointments too, including bringing in two young football coaches, Dave Sexton and Don Howe, and players such as George Graham and Frank McLintock. (All of whom went on to become good managers.) Arsenal were beginning to improve and to achieve good results on the pitch. In 1970–71 everything went right for the club: they achieved the double; they were First Division champions; and they won the FA cup. Particularly satisfying for fans was that they became champions by beating Spurs away from home on the last day of the season.

The coach of the team at the time of the double was Don Howe but he was soon lured away to be manager of West Bromwich Albion. Arsenal did not want him to leave, but Howe wished to take on a position as a manager of a club. Arsenal could not promise him the management post, but the chairman, Denis Hill-Wood was angry anyway. He expressed the view that 'loyalty is a dirty word these days.'

By the middle of the 1970s Arsenal were struggling once again. They had sold most of their double-winning players, and there were criticisms concerning the 'low' level of wages they were paying the players. They finished sixteenth in the First Division in 1974–75 and seventeenth the following season. Bertie Mee announced that he would resign as manager at the end of the 1975–76 season, but that he felt very attached to the club and it was his 'dearest wish' to be allowed to remain at Arsenal in some capacity and to help his successor. The directors had other ideas; they were worried that if they kept Mee at Arsenal the same problems would arise as had happened at Manchester United when that club had kept Matt Busby at the club after he had retired as manager. There was some disagreement as to whether the directors had promised Mee a continuing role at Arsenal, possibly as a director. Mee believed that they had, but the chairman, Dennis Hill-Wood, said they had not. Mee had a reputation for not suffering fools easily and in his long period as manager he, not surprisingly, had disagreements with some of the club's directors. 'He never courted the directors. The only one he really respected was Denis Hill-Wood.' It could well be that it was his reluctance to be friendly with the directors that was the reason why he was not invited to join the board. Liam Brady wrote: 'Bertie was always a fair man and deserved a better farewell.'

In contrast to the position at many clubs Arsenal had a reputation for being very loyal to their managers. In over 60 years they had only had 11 managers and 2 of these died while in office. Arsenal's 'old boy' directors clearly valued continuity and loyalty.

When Bertie Mee left the club he was replaced by Terry Neill, who was to hold the post for seven years. Neill had been an Arsenal player and made a number of good signings—the club had a good squad—but underachieved. In Neill's' time at the club, Arsenal appeared in four FA Cup finals, but won only once in 1979. The board of directors were again criticised for a lack of investment in new players. Neill was replaced by Don Howe. He, unfortunately, was not very successful either and in 1986 was released from his contract.

The New Directors

The balance of power at the club began to shift and the club moved into a new dynamic era. In 1983 David Dein became vice-chairman. He had paid £300,000 to buy shares in the club and this enabled him to join the Arsenal board, but it was not so much the money that he might invest that was important to the club, it was his ideas. When Dein joined the board, professional football was in a disastrous state, it needed to change. Dein was a successful businessman, who had built up his wealth as a commodity trader in the City of London. He started buying shares in Arsenal in the early 1980s, he was a long term supporter of the club and becoming involved with the running of the club would give him pleasure, as well as of course increasing his public exposure and importance. He continued to acquire shares and at one time Dein owned 42% of the 'ordinary' shares of the club, but this percentage holding was reduced when Danny Fiszman bought some of Dein's holding.

Danny Fiszman became a director and the major shareholder. He was said to be worth in the region of £150 million, much of this a result of his interests in the diamond business. (His other business interests included computers and waste recycling, and the latter turned out to be important in helping Arsenal put together a financial package to fund their new Emirates Stadium.)

Although Peter Hill-Wood (son of Denis, grandson of Samuel) was still chairman, the shareholding of the family had been considerably reduced (from 14% to less than 1%). The Bracewell-

Smith family holding (which was once approximately 26%) was inherited by Lady Nina Bracewell-Smith (and by Richard and Clive Carr, a solicitor and a wealthy businessman, respectively). Lady Bracewell-Smith and Richard Carr continued to be directors of Arsenal Holdings plc, and so despite the introduction of new entrepreneurial directors, some stability and continuity was maintained. Lady Nina was, in 2005, still the second largest shareholder in Arsenal, with a 15.9% stake.

The George Graham Years

George Graham became manager in 1986 and the club began to win trophies again. In 1988–89 the club were First Division champions (first tier), they were fourth the next year, they won the First Division again the next year (1990–91), and were fourth the following year. Then came the Premier League. But Arsenal were having problems. Graham as a manager had developed a reputation as a disciplinarian and autocrat. Whilst he was winning it was difficult to criticise his style of management. But when results started to go against the club, criticism began to mount. His style meant that he began to lose control of some of his more senior players and in the 1993–94 season team spirit became very low. Tony Adams refers to the bitterness building up amongst the players at the club. It was felt that the club did not have enough talented players to win further competitions. According to Adams, Arsenal 'had won six trophies but there was no money available.'

The club had a low wage policy. Adams blames the manager George Graham for this, but in his autobiography Graham blames the directors. After Graham had resigned in 1994, Arsenal paid £12.5 million to purchase two players (Dennis Bergkamp and David Platt). Graham comments that if one year earlier he had gone to the managing director and asked for that amount of money to buy players he would have been told the club could not afford it. Graham states that the 'tight, even-handed wage structure' was the policy of the club, not his policy.[13] Because no player was allowed to earn very much more than any other player, it was, Graham believed, difficult to attract big names to the club. Arsenal were competing for the big names against the likes of Manchester United and Blackburn; clubs who were willing to pay high wages.

Graham claims that he tried many times to get directors to change the wage policy 'but my pleas fell on deaf ears.'

Whatever the case, when Graham left Arsenal the wage policy changed. Graham believed that the new players brought into the club were 'earning three or four times what some of their Arsenal team-mates were picking up.' With the change in wage policy 'several of the players were given substantial pay rises to keep the peace.' The case of Arsenal and its wage policy clearly illustrates the importance of directors for the success of a football club. A manager cannot keep a team at the top for long without directors who are willing to pay the level of wages needed to attract the top players.

At the beginning of the 1990s Arsenal had not been spending very much on buying new players, or even on rewarding the players that they already had at the club. In the 1993–94 season their wage bill was £7.7 million (36% of turnover) and only just above that of Tottenham, which was £6.8 million (38% of turnover). The so-called conservative Aston Villa paid £6.2 million (48% of turnover) in wages. Arsenal were paying much less than the other 'Big Five' clubs (Manchester United: £11.1 million; Liverpool: £9.8 million). An interesting illustration of how quickly fortunes can change in football is the fact that in the 1993–94 season, the second year of the Premier League, the wage bill of Nottingham Forest was £8.0 million, and that of Chelsea only £4.9 million.

In the first two years of the Premier League Arsenal's net expenditure on transfers was only in the region of £1 million, less than that of Spurs, and way behind that of Manchester United (just under £5 million) and Liverpool (£6.5 million).

Graham believed that the reason the policy on transfer fees and wages changed was because the balance of power at board level changed. The old guard had served Arsenal well for over 50 years, but times had changed. Tom Whittaker had referred to a good relationship at the club between directors, managers and players—but it was a relationship based on values from a by-gone age. The owners and directors of the club valued the players but saw them as employees who should be paid a good wage—not a wage that would result in them becoming seriously wealthy. The new wave directors, by contrast, were prepared to compete in the transfer market to attract the top players. Their rationale was that winners should be able to accumulate wealth.

At the beginning of the 1990s Arsenal experimented with a new method of raising external finance (new to football at any rate). They offered a type of bond to supporters that guaranteed the bond holder the right to purchase a season ticket, for a specified seat, for a number of years. It was known as a 'Highbury Bond'. The bond issue raised about £14 million, and the money received was used to help fund the costs of a new stand at Highbury.

In 1994 George Graham was sacked by Arsenal not because of poor results or because of his autocratic management style but for receiving payments that were judged to be illegal. It is ironic that Graham, in his autobiography, compared his success at Arsenal to that achieved by the leading manager of the 1930s, Herbert Chapman. Chapman was also sacked by Arsenal (with Henry Norris) for financial irregularities. In 1993 and 1994 a Premier League committee had been investigating what happened to money paid out by clubs in transfer fees. There were stories about missing money involved in transfers at a number of clubs, but George Graham was the only person charged. Graham's difficulties arose in connection with money he received from a Scandinavian agent — Rune Hauge. Hauge did pay Graham £425,000 cash and Graham, in order to avoid tax, put this money into an offshore bank account. Graham later claimed the money was a payment to him personally for advice he had given the agent in connection with the transfer of Peter Schmeichel and Andrei Kanchelskis to Manchester United, and had nothing to do with his work at the Arsenal club. Surprisingly, the money had been handed to Graham in the bar of the Park Lane Hotel, a hotel that was owned by two Arsenal directors, Richard and Clive Carr.

There are many in football who believe that George Graham was unlucky. Tommy Docherty claimed that there were 'half a dozen managers I know who have committed worse offences than Graham yet are going scot free.' Graham in his autobiography refers to the money that was paid to him as 'unsolicited gifts', and comments that 'few people would have found it possible to refuse the offer.' The agent paid the money to Graham in thanks 'for opening up the British transfer market to him.' Graham argued that he had done nothing wrong but he could not convince the directors of Arsenal of this fact. Dein said that Graham had lost the trust of the board. The board were also concerned about possible Inland Revenue problems connected with this payment, and with the question of to whom the money really belonged.

The Premier League threatened to take action against the club unless they acted against the manager. Graham was given legal advice that the money really belonged to Arsenal, and that it should be repaid. George Graham resigned and paid the money to the club. This, unfortunately, was not the end of the story. At the Premier League hearing, the agent involved, Rune Hauge, admitted that it was not unusual for agents to pay managers. He did not, however, give the names of any managers who had been paid. It was decided that the receipt of the payment constituted misconduct by Graham and he was banned from football for one year.

Graham believes that he was made a scapegoat. He admits what he did was 'probably morally wrong ... But if we start analysing morals in the game, I would think come Judgement Day some club chairmen and directors will be perspiring in the queue along with managers.' An interesting comment, but he did not give names as he had no wish to drag others down with him.

Modern Times

Following the departure of George Graham the man who took over as manager was Bruce Rioch, but he did not remain in the job for very long. The board then did extremely well to attract Arsène Wenger to Arsenal as manager. At that time, 1996, Wenger was hardly known in England but was very well respected in informed football circles. With Wenger in charge, a number of very good players were brought to the club. And in Wenger's first full season in charge, 1997–98, the club won the Premier League and the FA Cup. The club then entered a remarkably successful period. They came second in the Premier League in 1998–99, 1999–2000 and 2000–01; were Premier League champions again in 2001–02; second again in 2002–03; Premier League champions again in 2003–04; second yet again in 2004–05; and fourth in 2005–06. They won the FA Cup in 2001–02 and 2002–03, the first of these occasions being yet another season in which they completed the double. However, as outstanding as Arsenal have been in the Premier League, they have not been able to repeat this success in Europe. The best they achieved was reaching the quarterfinals of the Champions League in 2001 and 2004, and being a finalist in the UEFA Cup in 2000.

One aspect of Arsenal's 'modern' wage policy led to problems, namely the use of 'tax havens' to financially reward players. The club had set up a number of 'employee benefit trusts' into which amounts were paid that would benefit players (particularly overseas players), and the payments would avoid UK tax and National Insurance deductions. Income received in a tax haven is either not taxed by that country or taxed at a very low rate. Arsenal also used these offshore accounts to pay agents.

The Inland Revenue had been investigating such payments for some time, and in 2005 they hit Arsenal with a bill for nearly £12 million in unpaid taxes. The club would channel money into the overseas trusts, and these trusts would pay the players. If the club had paid the players directly, the players would have had to pay tax in the UK on the income. Certain payments to agents through these trusts (amounting to more than £4 million) were also judged not to be acceptable business expenses. Peter Hill-Wood, the Arsenal chairman said 'The Revenue are crawling all over us. We thought we acted perfectly legally ... but now maybe the rules have changed. We are not the only people who have been doing this.'

He went on to say that these new rules would make it more difficult in future to attract top foreign players. What he meant by this was either the club would have to pay the players more money, because the player would have to pay taxes in the UK, or the player would have to learn to live with a lower net salary.

The House of Lords ruling on the issue of payments by football clubs into offshore accounts, and the victory in this case by the Inland Revenue, did not attract that much interest or comment in the media or amongst football followers. The fact that players earning somewhere in the region of £3 million or more each year were able to avoid paying tax in the UK did not even lead to criticism. The vast majority of supporters and fans have no chance to avoid tax, but they did not seem concerned that the highly paid players at Arsenal and a number of other clubs were able to escape paying tax.

This is in fact all part of the globalisation process. It is called 'regulation arbitrage'. Multinational companies organise their businesses so as to be able to minimise their own tax bill, as well as the tax bill of their top employees. They also seek to avoid countries with demanding tax regulations. Arsenal must have been using offshore trusts for two or three decades. In 1979 David O'Leary, then an Arsenal player, received money through the SG Hambros Channel Island Trust Corporation. Such payments became quite widely known about as a result of the divorce case of an Arsenal player, Ray Parlour. His wife was claiming a part of his income, and the divorce court was given details of Parlour's 2001–02 salary (and tax payments). The tax payments, as a result of offshore accounts, were less than would have been expected of someone on his income. Parlour is of course English, so it is not just foreign players who have benefited from the schemes.

One can criticise Arsenal for using such schemes, but it is not against the law to attempt to minimise the payment of tax so long as it is done legally. Alternatively one can congratulate the Arsenal directors on being imaginative, of being aware of opportunities, and taking them.

Questions about the future ownership of Arsenal began to be asked in the 2005–06 season. The club was financing the development of its new stadium by a mixture of borrowing and the sale of land. It was a difficult time financially.

It was disclosed that a hedge fund, Lansdowne Partners, had acquired 2.7% of the shares of the club. The hedge fund had started to purchase Arsenal shares in April 2005 using nominee names, so that its identity would remain a secret. Nobody knew their intentions. Were they starting to accumulate a shareholding in the company, so that with other parties they could take over the club, or were they happy to remain as minority shareholders seeing the shares as just a good financial investment? Hedge funds are mysterious (and perhaps dangerous) organisations, and Lansdowne Partners are regarded as one of the shrewdest. Such funds are of course not particularly interested in sport, but they are interested in buying undervalued companies and selling them a few years later at a profit. The managing director of Lansdowne Partners (Keith Edelman), as expected, dismissed the idea of a future take-over, saying 'that is so far from reality. It does not in any way concern us.' The fund of course is unlikely to reveal its true intentions. Edelman has also said that a comparison with what

365

happened at Manchester United is meaningless. 'The shares in Arsenal are held by four different groups that are committed to Arsenal as a belief rather than as an investment.'

In fact the position at Manchester United before Glazer was not so different to the situation at Arsenal. The major Arsenal shareholders may be committed, but if an offer price was attractive enough there are very few investors who would say no to a bargain.

In October 2005, when Lansdowne's interest was first disclosed, an Arsenal share cost £4,525, which valued the equity of the club at £286 million. The debts of the club, largely linked to the new stadium, were at the time £160 million. This gave a total value of the club of about £450 million, still far behind the £790 million value of Manchester United when the Glazers purchased the club. But perhaps the Glazers overvalued their club? When Granada purchased their first tranch of Arsenal shares (5% of the total) they paid £9,100 per share. At that price the total equity of the club was worth £537 million. In 2004 Granada entered into an 'additional subscription agreement' with the club whereby they agreed that they would 'subscribe for an additional 2,947 Ordinary Shares (another 5%) for a consideration of £30 million upon the fulfilment of certain conditions.' This was valuing the equity of the club at £600 million, not far behind Manchester United.

The Future

The future for Arsenal, as of any football club, is uncertain. David Dein's view is that in football 'There will always be change, it's the nature of the industry. And it's healthy.' He points out that now everyone is talking about Chelsea, but they were dormant for 50 years. Arsenal are building up a new team of young players, for a number of the stars of the last decade are no longer with the club. 'We are building for the future.' This applies both to the team and the new stadium. Dein resigned from the Board of Directors in 2007.

In 2005 Arsenal's match day income was £37.4 million; by 2007 this had more than doubled. They expected to be able to generate more gate revenue than any other club in the world. 'Club' level seats on the halfway line require a four-year contract and cost £19,000 (which was payable in May 2006). The executive boxes start at £76,375 a season. All the boxes and the 'club' level seats were quickly sold. This is the advantage of being based in London, and of being in a country where spectators are now used to paying high prices. In Germany football supporters will not pay high prices, and in Spain the football clubs have a membership structure that enables fans to keep prices down.

In order to build the new stadium Arsenal have taken on a large amount of extra debt, but this does not seem to have worried shareholders. The share price rose by nearly 30% between May 2005 and Jan 2006. (At the same time the debts were rising.) The debt service cost in 2005 was £14 million, but this was not a problem: the net debt to market capitalisation of equity was only about 50%. That of Newcastle was over 100%, while Manchester United's comes somewhere between these two figures.

The year 2005–06 in fact began with Tottenham in a higher place in the Premiership than Arsenal, but by the end of the season the situation had returned to normal. Spurs finished in fifth place and Arsenal were fourth. This meant both teams were in European competitions the next season, a big boost for Tottenham, who appeared to have at last got their managerial structure right. It would have been a big blow to Arsenal if they had not qualified for the Champions League competition in the very season they moved into a new stadium. In the 2006–07 season Arsenal again performed better than Tottenham in the Premiership (they finished fourth, with Spurs fifth). They were, however, still below Manchester United and Chelsea.

The future ownership position of both clubs is uncertain. In 2007, Arsenal were able to report record profits, an annual revenue figure in excess of £200 million, but a predator had appeared on the scene.[14]

Notes

Introduction

1 Stanley Rous, *Football World* (1978).
2 When in 2007 new owners George Gillett Jr. and Tom Hicks acquired Liverpool they said, 'There is a strong consciousness within the Liverpool family about the world wide aspects of the sport.' They expressed the belief that Liverpool were the number one brand in Europe and number two brand in the Far East. They talked about 'the possibility of branding [the club] in a different way.'
3 The beautiful game was an expression first used to describe the type of football played by Brazilian teams. It is an expression used less and less to describe Premier League games and UEFA Championship games involving English clubs. The new wave of owners of clubs cannot afford to take risks – they are profit maximisers. They have financed their acquisitions by borrowing large amounts. One way to lower risk is to adopt a style of play that reduces the chances of losing a match. Cut out 'flair and creativity' and play a physical, direct, collective, extremely intense game. This is the way the game is moving in the Premiership according to many people, including Jorge Valdano, the former Real Madrid coach and Argentinean World Cup winner. According to Valdano, the English clubs adopting this approach are ushering in a bleak future for football. (See Sid Lowe, *Guardian*, 8 May 2007.)

   Evidence to support Valdano's claim is the fact that the number of goals scored each season in the Premier League is on its way down. In the 2006–07 season the total was 931 (in a 38-match season). In the first year of the league, 1992–93, it was 1,222 (42-match season). The rate of decline has been particularly dramatic since 2003–04.
4 By way of comparison the annual revenue of Marks and Spencer in 2006 was nearly £8 billion while that of Manchester United was approaching £200 million.
5 He was re-elected and South Africa were named as hosts for the 2010 FIFA World Cup.
6 On the last day of the 2006–07 season West Ham United appeared to have escaped relegation by beating Manchester United at Old Trafford. There was, however, the possibility that a Court of Law would decide

which teams were actually relegated. West Ham United were said by their rival clubs to have used an 'ineligible' player and should have suffered a points penalty deduction, which would have meant that West Ham would have been relegated. The Premier League's Disciplinary Committee only fined the club; this despite the fact that they had found West Ham guilty of 'dishonesty and deceit.'

Sheffield United appealed against the decision. The Arbitration Panel that considered the matter were limited in the conclusions they could reach. They could either say that there was something wrong with the Premier League's disciplinary process or there was not. They could find nothing wrong with the procedure followed. The chairman of the panel, Sir Phillip Otton, did, however, comment that he would have deducted points because of the failure of West Ham to disclose all the details about the ineligible players' contracts. Sheffield United considered taking the matter to the courts. They were not happy with issues concerning the legality of contracts being settled by self-regulation within the sport. There was once again more excitement at the bottom of the table than at the top.

7 See www.footballfunerals.co.uk

8 Unfortunately just over twelve months later more or less the same England cricket team lost the Ashes. They were humiliated by Australia, losing all five test matches in the series.

9 There are many excellent books on the history of football. For a selection see those listed in the Bibliography.

10 See *UEFA Champions Magazine*, December 2005, p32.

11 See Michael MacCambridge, *America's Game* (2004), p422.

12 José Luís Arnaut, 'Independent European Sport Review' (2006).

13 The politics of football hit the headlines in 2007. Richard Scudamore speaking on behalf of the Premier League, and in particular the elite group of clubs, expressed a fear that the European Parliament and the European Commission would seek to introduce a EU-wide Super League under the control of UEFA. The national football leagues and associations opposed the control of football by a European body. They did not want politicians meddling in football matters. The G14 clubs in particular were worried about the EU giving greater power to UEFA. If a Super League was to be formed, the G14 clubs wanted to set it up and control it themselves.

14 Freddie Shepherd, speaking at the Soccerex international football business forum, held in Dubai in November 2004. At the time the Newcastle directors and supporters saw themselves as one of the top teams. Just over two years later Shepherd was replaced as chairman and major shareholder by someone with greater wealth. He was 65 and felt it was time to leave. He came up with the fashionable cliché—'I gave it my best shot.'

1 Present Environment

1 James Hamilton Muir, *Glasgow in 1901*.
2 Peter Beck, *Scoring for Britain: International Football and International Politics*, Frank Cass (1999). See also James Walvin, *The Only Game*, Longman (2001), p273, and *When Saturday Comes – The Half Decent Football Book* (2001), p304.
3 op cit *The Only Game*, p216.
4 Deloitte and Touche, 'Annual Review of Football Finance' (2003), p2.
5 Wayne Rooney, *My Story So Far* (2006).
6 See the 'Burns Report'.
7 For 2005–06 they managed to reduce their loss to £80 million. This made a total loss, over the three years with Roman Abramovich as owner, of £308 million, and a total investment on his part of £500 million. In addition to funding the losses the owner was providing funds for the club to purchase players. The wage bill of the club was in the region of 75% of its revenue. No wonder the club was successful. Arséne Wenger's view was that Chelsea were dependent on 'artificial income'. He believes football clubs should only spend what they can earn.
8 The last eight clubs in the 2006–07 season once again included AC Milan and Chelsea, with Manchester United, Liverpool, Bayern Münich, Valencia, PSV (Eindhoven) and Roma. Only PSV were a surprise.
9 In 2007 the last eight teams competing for the Super Bowl were from Indianapolis, Chicago, New Orleans, Boston (New England Patriots) Baltimore, Seattle, Philadelphia and San Diego. Four of these clubs had been in the final eight the previous season.
10 The top four clubs in the Premiership at the end of the 2006–07 season were the same four as in 2005–06 and 2003–04. The only difference in 2004–05 was that Everton replaced Liverpool in this elite group. The predictability of the final league placings was also evident in the Championship, where two of the clubs promoted at the end of the 2006–07 season had been relegated from the Premiership the previous season. The 'parachute payments' certainly helped. In 2006–07 the Premiership was a two horse race, but one that was not too close: Manchester United finished six points ahead of Chelsea, who finished fifteen points ahead of third place Liverpool. The much-hyped 2007 FA Cup Final in the new Wembley Stadium was a dull affair featuring the two clubs who had finished at the top of the Premiership. What have football fans got to look forward to in the 2007–08 season? The same four clubs finishing in the top places in the newly branded Barclays Premiership, and two of the three newly promoted clubs fighting against relegation.
11 There is an increasing gap between the top four and the remaining clubs in the Premiership, and between the Premiership clubs and those below them. From the beginning of the 2007–08 season the gap between the clubs in the top league and those below became greater than ever. The

371

play-off game in May 2007 was referred to as the £60 million game. The value of the club that won the game would, after the game, be £60 million more than the value of the club that lost. The clubs that were promoted would in the next season receive £30 million more from television rights than the Championship teams. If relegated after their first season in the Premiership the club would receive £22 million over two seasons in 'parachute payments', and the extra income they could earn from match day receipts and sponsorship income over one season should be at least £8 million. So much for balanced competition.

12 UEFA's 'Vision Europe'.

13 FIFA's 'For the Good of the Game'.

14 Jules Tygiel, *Baseball as History*, Oxford (2001).

15 Gerry Boon was editor of Deloitte and Touche's (later just Deliotte's) 'Annual Review of Football Finance' from its beginning in 1992 through to the 2006 edition.

16 See Carter and Capel-Kirby (1935).

17 The *Daily Express*, 3 October 2003.

18 BSkyB needed the rights to Premier League football in order to survive. Prior to the contract they had been making huge losses.

19 In 2006 the UK Government were able to 'persuade' the League to distribute an increased percentage of revenue resulting from the next TV deal to the grassroots. The government had helped the League in their negotiations with the European Union. The amount to be distributed was to be 6% of the first £1.1 billion, 7.5% of the next £0.3 billion and then 10% of the amount beyond £1.4 billion. In addition, 3% of the revenue was to be given to the Professional Footballers Association. In total the amount to be distributed to the 72 football league clubs would be over three years nearly £100 million. This at first seems a lot of money but in fact means that on average a Championship League club would receive just under £1 million (the exact amount depending on final league position), a League One club £103,000 a season and a League Two club £69,000. Not a lot per club.

20 Guardian, 9 August 2003.

21 Guardian, 30 August 2003.

22 See Leo Moynihan's *Gordon Strachan: A Biography*.

23 He did resign from the board, but continued to own a significant number of shares. In 2007 there were stories that he was planning to take-over control of the club once again.

24 The Premier League signed a three-year global (overseas) TV deal, which was worth £625 million. This agreement covered broadcasting matches in 208 countries. It was worth more than double that for the three-year period ending with the 2006–07 season. As Richard Scudamore pointed out, the contract illustrated the 'continuing global appeal' of the League. The new American owners of English clubs seem to believe much more money should result from that appeal.

25 In 2007 the FA also did well. They secured a TV deal with ITV and Setanta (that was worth 42% more than its previous deal) for the

broadcasting rights to international
sold for £425 million (from 2008 to
who needed a financial boost follow
but bad for the BBC who lost t
suggestions that the FA moved the
they were fed up with the criticis
England team by the BBC football
in fact £70 million less than that of

26 Jim Smith and Bob Cass, *Jim Smith*

27 The business of football and the pa
dependent on each other. BSkyB
while footballers, managers, agen
income from television to maintain
very close link has developed betw̶e̶e̶n̶ ̶t̶h̶o̶s̶e̶ ̶p̶e̶o̶p̶l̶e̶ ̶r̶u̶n̶n̶i̶n̶g̶
England and television companies. Brian Barwick, the chief executive of
the FA; David Davies, the FA's executive director; and Simon Johnson,
the FA's director of corporate affairs, all have a TV background.

28 In 2007 the FA accepted the recommendations of the 'Burns Report', and
so football supporters will in future be represented on the FA Board.

2 Globalisation

1 When Liverpool were purchased by George Gillett Jr. and Tom Hicks at
the beginning of 2007 they became the seventh Premiership club to be
foreign-owned. Manchester City became the eighth. In 2007–08 another
foreign-owned club entered the Premier League, namely Sunderland.
(The club is in fact owned by Irish investors.) During 2007 Arsenal and
Birmingham City attracted the interest of wealthy foreign investors.
There were other clubs who had let it be known that they would be
interested in selling a stake in the club if the right purchaser came along.
Blackburn Rovers were talking to an American investor (who had been
born in England) about a possible take-over. There were also Championship clubs attracting interest from foreign investors.

2 Tom Bower believes that the sale of football clubs 'portends disaster for
the national game.' He is concerned that nobody is complaining. When
asked about the effect of the foreign purchasers, Brian Barwick, the FA's
chief executive, is reported to have said: 'We'll only know in ten years.'
(See Tom Bower, *Guardian* 9 February 2007.)

There is, however, an understandingly increasing unease about the
number of foreign take-overs. As David Conn points out, 'In football's
greatest boom all the clubs are up for grabs. A few long-term shareholders, like Martin Edwards, Doug Ellis and now Terry Brown, are cashing
in while fans are pulled along for the ride, feeling in their hearts that
something about it all is not quite right.' (See *Guardian*, 22 November
2006.) However, to be fair to Doug Ellis, he was 82 before he cashed in.

...n the owners and the fans had an emotional attachment ...ow the new foreign owners have no such attachment, they ...terested in financial returns or public acceptance.
...when he was Minister for Sport, Richard Caborn said that he ... worried by the trend in England for foreigners to take-over clubs. ...aid he was more concerned with governance issues. He may not be ...orried but many others are. The problem with foreign ownership is that what happens in another part of the world, with, say, the economy of a foreign country or with the wealth of the overseas owner, might affect what happens to English football clubs.

4 See Peter Dicken, *Global Shift* (1986).

5 See the books written by Joseph Stiglitz on the subject of globalisation (2000, 2002, 2003).

6 See Leslie Sklair, *The Transnational Capitalist Class* (2001).

7 See Deloitte's 'Annual Review of Football Finance 2007'.

8 One reason why Americans have become interested in the ownership of English clubs is 'the Premiership's global reach' (*Time*, 7 May 2007). It is estimated that of Manchester United's 75 million fans, 41 million are in Asia. The major US sports do not have this global appeal. AIG, a US-based insurance company (who few people in England have heard of), pay £15 million a year to have their name on Manchester United's shirts, not to sell themselves to English TV viewers but to those in Asia. Increasingly, a higher proportion of the revenue of the top clubs will come from outside England. The chief executive of the Premier League, Richard Scudamore, believes that it will not be long before overseas television rights will produce one half of the total revenue from television rights. By contrast, in the NFL the revenue from foreign markets contributes less than 5% of total NFL revenues.

9 In 2006, Spanish companies purchased Abbey National, O2 and the British Airport Authority. Pilkington Glass was taken over by a Japanese company, Thames Water was taken over by a German company, and there were even attempts by foreign firms to take over the London Stock Exchange. In total over £75 billion was spent by foreign firms to acquire British companies, and most of the money used to pay for the purchases was borrowed money. The financial risks are increasing and control is passing out of British hands.

10 See *Guardian*, 23 April 2005.

11 See Bose (1999) and Crick and Smith (1989) for interesting and detailed accounts of the attempted purchase of Manchester United.

12 Sir James Goldsmith was a leading industrialist during the 1980s who was also very active in the take-over market.

13 It has been shown that the primary motives of owners of sports franchises in the US are commercial. They are seeking to make money (Zimbalist, 2003). This is the reason they are now acquiring ownership of English football clubs. They can see the amounts that can be earned from exploiting the global appeal of the game. They are building up business

empires, with an English football club just one part of a broad portfolio of investments.

American businessmen, normally big supporters and beneficiaries of globalisation, have missed out on the phenomenal growth in the market for football. They are now trying to cash in on this market. One way is to acquire the top football clubs, the other is to seek to develop the market for football (soccer) in the US. The signing of David Beckham in 2007 by a weak US team was an attempt to create an interest in the sport in the US. American entrepreneurs had tried before and failed.

In the 1970s and early 1980s the North American Soccer League tried to arouse interest in the game. The New York Cosmos were the top team attracting some of the best players from around the world (including the legendary Pelé). The Cosmos attracted crowds of 70,000 plus in New York, but the game did not take off elsewhere in the US. The television rights were sold to ABC, but the viewing figures were poor. There was not enough interest, no competitive balance, and the league collapsed in 1985.

14 But Manchester United continued to be successful and profitable. In 2005–06 they doubled their operating profits of the previous year, and made pre-tax profits of £30 million. The Glazers transferred responsibility for all £559 million of the borrowings to the football club. The club (the family) carried out a refinancing exercise, paid off some of the PIKs, and reduced the rate of interest they had to pay on the other debt. The interest charge on the PIKs remained high, however, at 14.25%. The total annual interest to be paid in 2007–08 was in the region of £62 million; this being on total borrowings which were now £663 million. This is a very heavy interest payment. The total revenue of Manchester City in the 2004–05 season was only £61 million.

However, the club continues to be successful, being Premier League champions in 2006–07 and reaching the semi-final of the UEFA Champions League in the same season. To help pay the borrowing costs the club increased season ticket prices in the 2007–08 season by up to 14%. The club has the brand name, the stars, and play exciting football; they will be able to get away with higher seat prices. In 2006–07 they had 57,000 season ticket holders. In 2007 they spent over £60 million on new players.

(See David Conn, *Guardian*, 16 May 2007.)

15 For further revealing details of the financial aspects of the Glazer purchase of Manchester United see the writings of David Conn in The *Guardian*.

16 Liverpool needed access to additional funds if they were to stay in the elite group and the existing shareholders could not provide the amount of money required. The directors of the club had discussions with a number of potential purchasers. This appears to be the direction in which the ownership of English football clubs is heading: the last generation of owners cashing in on the globalisation of the game, selling to those with cash (or who are willing to borrow) and who promise to look after the

'heritage' of the clubs. We will have to wait to see whether or not they do protect the heritage or whether they are just after the new found profitability of the Premiership.

17 Prior to 1978 the only non-British players allowed to play in the Football League were citizens of Ireland, those from Commonwealth countries, amateurs from Scandinavia and for a brief period foreign servicemen who happened to be based in the UK. The Professional Footballers Association was keen to restrict overseas players, but once the UK entered the European Community the position changed. Not only was football opened up to the free movement of labour within the Community, but clubs were to be allowed to sign two players from outside the Community. Tottenham Hotspur signed two Argentineans, the successful and popular Ossie Ardiles and Ricardo Villa.

18 In 2007 the Premier League began to live up to its hype. Three of the four clubs in the semi-finals of the UEFA Champions League were from that League. Football supporters in England were supposed to feel proud of this achievement. But interestingly only 12 of the 53 players that had been used by these three clubs to get to this stage of the competition were in fact from England. It could be said that for that season the foreign players in England were better than the foreign players in the Italian, Spanish and German leagues.

19 Arsenal and Manchester United have links with feeder teams in Belgium, which they use as Nursery clubs. Young Africans play for these clubs and qualify for passports that allow them to stay in Europe.

20 Not everyone appreciates the influence of foreign players. In March 2007, the Manchester City captain Richard Dunne said, 'When players come from abroad you always give them that settling in period, but its March and we've still not clicked.' He accused some of the foreign players at Manchester City of hiding. (See *Sunday Times*, 11 March 2007.)

21 Football is following the path of other British industries. The clubs started with local owners and local money; the bigger clubs then attracted finance from national capital and money markets and owners who operated on a national scale. Now they are attracting finance from the global markets and attracting foreign owners. Is this the end of the story? Almost certainly not, but it is difficult to predict what the next changes will be and when they will occur.

Globalisation is sometimes called Americanisation. The reason for this is because one of the drivers of globalisation is the spread of US culture. Some sectors of the US economy have benefited from globalisation, but some, for example workers in the motor industry, have lost out. Certainly US investors have spread their money around the world, benefiting from globalisation. Now American money is moving into the global business of football. One advantage of globalisation to many of those involved is what is called regulation arbitrage. For many of those involved it allows them to minimise their worldwide tax bill. This applies in football to players and managers as well as to owners. The United Kingdom has a very generous tax legislation for those who are classed as non-resident or non-domiciled. In 2006–07 non-domiciled status was claimed by 302 people involved in football and non-resident status by 67. Non-domiciled are those who have been born abroad or who have parents abroad. The way the system works is that such players (and mangers) can have more than one contract. What they earn whilst playing matches in the UK is taxed in Britain, and their global image rights (which covers the money earned from merchandising) can be paid to a company in a foreign country (for example a tax haven). The money they earn from playing in foreign countries is also paid into a company in a foreign country.

3 Competitive Balance

1 See Neale (1964).
2 See Andrew Zimbalist and Stefan Szymanski, *National Pastime* (2005).
3 See Michie and Oughton, *Competitive Balance in Football* (2004).
4 See Borland and McDonald, *Demand for Sport* (2003).
5 See Schmidt and Berri, Competitive Balance in Major League Baseball (2001).
6 Two thirds of the money coming into the NFL is from the sale of TV broadcasting rights and all this is shared equally. The money from the sale of licensed products (including club jerseys) is shared equally. The gate receipts are shared 60:40 between the home and the away team.
7 In theory no team can pay above the salary cap. Every player's contract must be approved by the NFL League office. If a proposed contract for a player were to push the total salary bill for the club above the level of the cap, the NFL could reject it.
8 See the regular reports on 'US Sports Clubs Finance' by the international rating agency, Fitch IBCA.
9 See Quirk and Fort, *Pay Dirt* (1997).
10 See Gladden/Irwin/Sutton (2001).
11 See Quirk and Fort.
12 See Michael MacCambridge, *America's Game* (2004).
13 This is one of the worries about Americans taking over ownership of the top English clubs. They will be in a position to influence the future structure of football in Europe.
14 *FourFourTwo* magazine, December 2005, p81.
15 Adam Smith is a famous eighteenth century economist. His book *An Inquiry into the Nature and Causes of the Wealth of Nations* (1776) influenced many people, including politicians of the late twentieth century.
16 Stefan Szymanski points out in his *Economic Design of Sporting Contests* (2003) that at the present time we do not have the knowledge, or the techniques, to obtain the knowledge to enable us to decide whether a completely free market system or a system in which restrictive practices are allowed is best for sport. We cannot measure the consumer benefits or consumer surplus that results from either the free market system or

the 'regulated' system. 'The appropriate welfare function against which the optimality can be measured is not carefully specified.' As Szymanski states: 'more work remains to be done to settle this crucial issue.' This is correct, but from the point of view of those consumers in a region of the country deprived of success (for example the Midlands or Yorkshire) and with little hope that the existing arrangements and governance system will change things, the answer to the question is quite clear. A system that offers competitive balance, in which every well run club has some hope of achieving some success, is infinitely better than a system where all but a very few (four) clubs have to settle for second best.

A 2004 survey (by Sports Nexus) revealed that the fans of most Premier League teams had given up hope that their team could win the title. It was only the fans of the very wealthiest clubs that believed their clubs had a realistic chance of winning the title. The survey showed that at present 38% of football fans were dissatisfied with the lack of competitive balance, and that 57% feel it will get worse. Of those surveyed 82% want a new system of redistributing TV income introduced. The authors of the report point out that in 1993 the big 'five' clubs' share of overall Premier League income was 26.8%, and it is now 47%. They refer to it as 'the virtuous circle of success.'

17 See   Tom Bower, *Broken Dreams* (2003).
18 See Stephen Morrow, *The People's Game? Football Finance and Society* (2003).

4 Finance and Ownership

1 For interesting details about football in Italy, see Foot (2006) and Marcotti and Vialli(*The Italian Job*, 2006).
2 In the pre-First World War period, British business thrived, so did football. The football business, from the late 1800s, was increasingly controlled by the same 'class of men' who directed other concerns and institutions in English society. In this respect, football existed as a microcosm of the larger business environment. It still does.

As Tischler points out, the growth of football along commercial and professional lines was not a spontaneous occurrence. It was the result of entrepreneurs extending to football 'an ethos which touched numerous endeavours outside of sport.' The organisation of the game was designed primarily to protect the interests of the owners of the clubs, not the interests of the players (employees) or football fans (customers).
3 However, with foreign entrepreneurs now taking an interest in English football clubs, we have seen leveraged buyouts with very high levels of borrowings being used to take over ownership of clubs. This has become 'normal' business practice, but it adds to the risks of all those involved in football. The world of finance changes. Whereas in one period companies were rushing to have their shares listed on a stock exchange, in the next

period companies were de-listing and going private. The 'in vogue' method of financing investment and particularly acquisitions was in the first decade of the 2000s private equity funds and hedge funds. The football business was not immune to the fashion.

Private equity firms engage in leveraged buy-outs. There is not necessarily anything wrong with this – it is also not new. It does, however, add to the financial risks. One reason why private equity funds began to attract bad publicity in the 2000s was because of the use they made of tax havens to add to their financial gains. They were able to borrow large amounts, invest that money in UK companies (say football clubs), and use the interest they had to pay on the loans to reduce their tax bill in the UK. The net profits the football clubs made were paid as dividends (with no withholding tax) to companies registered in tax havens. If the new owners were also directors of the clubs they could also be paid directors fees into their tax haven base, and so avoid taxation. The capital gains resulting from their investments could also receive favourable tax treatment.

4 The total debt for the League clubs was £1,035 million, and the total shareholders funds (equity) was £469 million. Deloitte (2007) point out that this debt figure 'excludes the debt of the parent companies of Manchester United.' Distinct from other clubs, this debt originally arose to help finance the acquisition of the club in 2005 by the Glazer family, rather than to provide new financing for the club itself. This is factually correct but the Glazer family have restructured the debt so that it is now the responsibility of the club.

5 The position can quickly change. Tottenham Hotspur had been listed on the AIM for a number of years. In July 2007 the major shareholder, ENIC International, made an offer to purchase all of the shares that they did not own. They had the intention of de-listing the company and making it private.

6 The two Americans paid £171.4 million to purchase the equity shares of Liverpool and took on responsibility for the net liabilities (net debt) of the club. This valued the enterprise at approximately £219 million. Not a lot for a club with annual revenues in the region of £125 million (as already mentioned Manchester United were purchased at four times revenue, and even West Ham United at over twice revenue). David Moores explained in the letter recommending to shareholders that they accept the offer from Gillett and Hicks, that he and the other directors of Liverpool had for a couple of years 'actively sought new investment to enable the club to continue to compete at the highest level.' The club certainly did need funds to enable them to build their new stadium. In August 2006, David Moores and a family trust had lent the club £10 million to enable preliminary work on the new stadium to go ahead. But what was the source of the £219 million, plus the £10 million in fees paid to merchant bankers, lawyers, accountants and financial advisors? Where will the further £200 million needed to construct the stadium come from? Very little will come from the two new owners.

379

As David Conn puts it, the offer document 'thumps away the fantasy that these two men are sugar daddies.' As with most private equity deals it was only possible because bankers were prepared to provide a high percentage of the funds. This was a leveraged buy-out at work, complete with a subsidiary in the infamous tax haven of the Cayman Islands.

Hicks and Gillett borrowed £298 million from the Royal Bank of Scotland. The annual cost of servicing this debt, at the interest rates in existence at the beginning of 2007, was £21.5 million. It has to be assumed that it is money that will be earned by the club that will be used to service this debt. Another £200 million will be borrowed to finance the future costs of constructing the stadium.

The irony is that Americans could not get away with such levels of borrowing in the NFL. That League has rules that prevent clubs and their owners taking on excessive amounts of debt. They also have rules that limit the amount of public sector money that can be used to finance the construction of new stadiums. They require a percentage of the cost to be met by private sector money – and limit the percentage of this that can be debt. Yet North American sports club owners can come to Europe and acquire football clubs using hardly any of their own money.

The two owners were keen to emphasise that they were not the usual type of 'smash and grab' private equity investors. In a way they showed evidence of this by announcing plans for a much improved stadium a few months after they had taken over the club. 'The families' ownership of the club is intended to be a multi-generational family commitment to invest in and develop the club.' One good thing about the ownership of North American sports clubs is that there is a tradition of 'multi-generational' commitment. Many of the leading NFL clubs have seen the ownership pass from father to son. Perhaps that will happen with Liverpool (and Manchester United).

The major criticism of this type of take-over is that it is being funded so heavily by debt. This is risky, if not necessarily expensive. Many who have commented critically on the Liverpool and Manchester take-overs draw attention to the cost of servicing the debt. But if the acquisition had been financed with equity money there would still have been a cost. The providers of any form of finance, debt or equity, want a return on their money, whether the returns are in the form of interest, dividends or capital gains. The trouble with high levels of debt is that the interest has to be paid whether or not the club is profitable, whether or not it performs well – the risks are greater.

Interest is tax deductible (and dividends are not). This is one reason why the football club, Kop Football Ltd, is owned by Kop Football (Holdings) Ltd, which is owned by Kop Football (Cayman) Ltd, which in turn is incorporated in the Cayman Islands. Dividends, interest, management charges and directors' fees can flow to the Cayman Islands with the minimum of interference from the UK tax authorities. The Cayman Island company is in fact owned by Kop Investment LLC, a limited liability company formed in the State of Delaware in the US. It is a state famous for its generous approach to company taxation.

7 In June 2007, Alan Sugar sold his shares (by then 14.7% of the total) for £25 million. He sold them to ENIC, which gave them a 66% holding in the club. The sale valued the total equity of Tottenham at £209.5 million.

8 This was before the news in 2007 that Stan Kroenke, a wealthy American investor, had acquired over 12% of the club's shares.

9 David Moores did well out of the sale of his Liverpool shares, making a profit of £81.6 million. Terry Brown on selling his WHU shares made a profit of £31.4 million and Doug Ellis when he eventually sold his Aston Villa shares made a profit of £22.5 million.

Not all foreign owners have, however, found life in the Premiership easy. Mohamed-Al-Fayed has for many years lost money at Fulham, and Eggert Magnusson and his consortium have not found it easy at West Ham United. Neither of these clubs and their owners stand much of a chance of benefiting from European competition or being able to market their brand name globally. Perhaps the David Sullivan prophecy will be shown to be correct.

In February 2007, David Sullivan, co-owner of Birmingham City, warned that many of the new breed of owners would 'leave with their tails between their legs' when they realise it is not easy to make money from Premiership football. He said that his 14 years involvement with Birmingham City had cost him over £10 million. He was always interested in the ownership position at his local club, West Ham, and purchased some shares in that club for £900,000 towards the end of 2005, and 'I ended up getting £4.25 million for them. So I was glad to see the Icelander arrive. I would love to have bought West Ham myself but the asking price was too much.' He believes West Ham were purchased for well beyond their worth. See Neil Moxley, *Daily Mail*, 15 February 2007. David Sullivan did in fact sell some of his Birmingham City shares in July 2007. He made a profit.

10 See Morrow, *The New Business of Football* (1999).

11 For the 2005–06 season the total Premiership revenue was £1.38 billion (with the big four clubs accounting for 42% of the total). Wages were £854 million, giving a wages/revenue ratio of 62%.

12 Derby County are an interesting corporate governance case. They were promoted back to the Premiership for the 2007–08 season. A review of these recent ownership problems is given in Chapter 9, note 19.

13 Jack Hayward sold Wolverhampton Wanderers in 2007 for £10. He sold to Steve Morgan who had been a keen Liverpool supporter and director of that club for many years. Hayward believed that Morgan would be good for Wolverhampton. He had promised to make funds available for the club to invest.

14 Canon and Hamil, 'Reforming Football's Boardrooms', *Football in the Digital Age* (2000).

15 Most of the financial details about the problems at Oxford, Wrexham,

Darlington, QPR and Chesterfield are obtained from the exposes of the murkier side of football clubs in David Conn's regular Wednesday column in The *Guardian*.

16 For details of the activities of supporters' trusts see the Supporters Direct Newsletter produced by Birkbeck College, London, and various research papers published by Birkbeck College (including one on Northampton Town and one on the West Midlands).

17 See Eamon Dunphy, *A Strange Kind of Glory* (1991).

18 See Peter Lilley, *Dirty Dealing* (2006).

19 A problem concerning the identity of foreign investors arose again in 2007. At the time of the sale of Ken Bates' Leeds United a major creditor of the club was a business with the name of Astor (registered in Guernsey). The business had a significant influence in deciding who would be the new owners following the club's move into administration. Leeds had been relegated to the third tier and were in a financial mess. Astor was said to be owed nearly £13 million by the club and it was their agreement to the proposal that Ken Bates and his unknown associates be allowed to purchase the club that determined the outcome. Astor said that if Bates was allowed to purchase the club they would not ask for their debt to be repaid. A problem was that few people knew who owned Astor. It was said at the time of the club moving into administration that they had no connection with Ken Bates.

20 See *FourFourTwo* magazine, October 2005.

21 Gaydamak's money saved Portsmouth from relegation and enabled the club to purchase players in the January transfer window; without the new players the club would almost certainly have been relegated at the end of the 2005–06 season. Mandaric sold all his shares in Portsmouth to Gaydamak, but did not lose his interest in English football. He purchased Leicester City.

22 Jonathan Wilson in his fascinating book *Behind the Curtain* raises the possibility that there may be a 'network' of clubs across Europe and South America, in which the ownership of the clubs as well as the true relationship between the clubs, is not known. There is circumstantial evidence of this. Indeed with the ownership of one third of the world's wealth being secret and money laundering being one of the top three businesses in the world it would be surprising if there were not secret financial links. There are clearly links between Russia, certain Central and East European countries, Israel and South America. The links involve the movement of money and of players. There are agents and owners who have interests in football in the three continents. Chelsea have strong links with Benfica and PSV Eindhoven. Media Sports Investments are said to have had financial links in Russia, and have owned the Brazilian club, Corinthians, who have had strange dealings with WHU, whose major owner in turn has been a successful businessman in Russia.

23 See Peter Lilley (2006)

24 During 2006 Newcastle United had discussions with a number of possible purchasers, one of whom was an American financial institution, Polygon,

who had the financial support of the United Bank of Switzerland. Another possible purchaser was Belgravia, who were said to have financial backing from Middle East investors. By the end of 2006 the discussions with these two possible purchasers were over. As long as the Hall family and the Shepherd family continued to work together, it seemed that control of the club was secure. Freddie Shepherd had referred to Newcastle as a club that it was impossible for someone to buy. In the mid-2000s, however, signs began to appear which indicated that there were serious disagreements at boardroom level. Then in May 2007, a few days after the club announced that they had sacked one manager and appointed a new one (Sam Allardyce), there was an unexpected takeover bid for the club. Mike Ashley, who had earlier in 2007 obtained £930 million (he is said to be worth twice that amount) from the sale of his shares in the business he founded, Sports Direct, a sporting retail firm, announced that he had agreed to buy 41.6% of the plc's shares that had been held by the Hall family. The Hall family had agreed to sell their holding for £55 million, which valued the club at £133 million. After discussions Freddie Shepherd agreed to sell his shares, and the take-over went ahead.

Newcastle United fans were very pleased that they might have a new owner, who together with the new manager might be able to obtain success. England football fans were also pleased in that at last a British billionaire had purchased one of the top clubs.

Meanwhile at Arsenal, changes were taking place. In February 2007, the club admitted that they had established links with Colorado Rapids, a US Major League soccer club. The objective being to help build up Arsenal's brand name in the US to assist with their marketing and to establish a useful working relationship with the Rapids in order to jointly develop young players. It was said that the owner of the Rapids, Stan Kroenke, was not interested in purchasing Arsenal. But some Arsenal shareholders began to sell their shares.

Stan Kroenke, who is said to be worth just over £1 billion, owns a portfolio of sports clubs. He is co-owner of one of the top NFL clubs, St. Louis Rams; owns the successful basketball club, the Denver Nuggetts; the ice hockey club, the Colorado Avalanche; as well as a lacrosse team. An English football team would fit in well with this stable of clubs. Kroenke has a reputation for making a profit out of his clubs. He purchased the 9.9% stake of ITV in the Arsenal club.

In March 2007, the largest shareholder at the club, Danny Fiszman, sold 659 of his 15,659 shares to an undisclosed buyer. This reduced his shareholding from over 25% to 24.11%, a significant reduction in terms of possible influence on major changes that could take place at the club. He sold each share for £5,975 which taking into account the ITV sale, valued the total equity of the club at close to £400 million. (Twice the value of Liverpool!) By the end of the 2006–07 season Stan Kroenke had acquired 11.26% of Arsenal's shares (which included ITV's 9.9%). The chairman of the club, Peter Hill-Wood, said that the club did not want and did not need a rich foreign investor to take over control of the club. There was disagreement, however, amongst the directors. David Dein, the deputy chairman, resigned as a result of 'irreconcilable differences.' Dein owned 24% of the club's shares and it was uncertain whether he would sell all or some of these shares to Kroenke. The remaining directors, who together owned 45.45% of the club's shares, announced in the April 2007 that they had 'entered into an agreement not to dispose of their shares for at least one year and that they intended to retain their interests on the expiration of this period.' However, there were still rumours that Kroenke would make a bid to take-over the club. Later in 2007 another 'investor' appeared on the scene, a billionaire from Uzbekistan.

Manchester City are another club that has attracted the interest of foreign investors. Thaksin Shinawatra, deposed Prime Minister of Thailand, bought the club in 2007. The club needed additional funds, and appeared to be not too fussy about where the new owners' money came from. Thaksin was charged in Thailand with corruption and a question arose as to whether or not he was a fit and proper person to own a Premier League club.

25 In 2007 Paladini said that he would sell the club if a wealthy investor came along, but until then he had no option but to stay. This is a problem with owning a less successful football club, there are few exit routes. A worry for fans of QPR is that one exit route could involve property developers, and the sale of the club's Loftus Road ground.

Other second tier clubs have also attracted foreign investors. In 2007 Coventry City had discussions with Manhattan Sports Capital Partners who represented certain American investors. The chairman of the football club said at the time that he was not sure whether or not a deal would go ahead. In April 2007 it was revealed that Paul Allen, the world's nineteenth richest man, had made a preliminary approach to Southampton with a view to a possible purchase. Allen was the co-founder of Microsoft, and already owned the successful NFL team Seattle Seahawks, as well as the basketball team Portland Trailblazers. This was yet another American seeking to add to his portfolio of investments in sports clubs.

26 What happened to the Parma Football Club in Italy is an example of what could happen to other football clubs taken-over by 'entrepreneurs'. That club was taken over in 1990 by Parmalet, a very successful Italian company in the food industry. The company had been founded in 1962 by Calisto Tanzi. His son was put in charge of the football club. For various reasons the parent company collapsed in the early 2000s and so did the football club.

27 Italy has had many problems with ownership and financial mismanagement. Naples, once the best team in Europe, twice collapsed with too much debt. In 2002 Fiorentina failed financially and were relegated to Serie C. A new rule was introduced which for established clubs meant that if they failed, a new club could be formed in the same city as the old one, the Mayor of the town could invite bids for ownership and the new club would start one division below the one in which the old club failed.

384

This new rule proved to be very popular amongst clubs with financial problems. Unfortunately this approach has not led to a healthy financial situation in Italian football. See Vialli and Macotti, p340–5.

28 Ownership of clubs in Spain is sometimes held up as an example of what should happen, but even they have their problems. In 2007 it was revealed that votes had been falsified in a recent election for the presidency of the Barcelona club. A secretary who had been involved in the fraud was too frightened to talk to the police because she had been warned she would be killed if she talked about what happened.

5 The Confusing State of Governance

1 Sugden and Tomlinson, Great Balls of Fire: How Big Money is Hijacking World Football (1998).

2 There has been no agreement as to who should regulate the regulators. Those clubs and associations who are in countries who are members of the European Union have to follow the legislation that applies to the EU. The European Commission have shown that they wish to enforce their laws on employment and competition in sport, but have shown a reluctance to interfere in other issues concerning sport. They have left the different sports to regulate themselves. In football they have not (so far) been willing to recognise UEFA as the regulating body for football in EU countries.

3 Andrew Jennings, Foul (2006)

4 See Rob Hughes, 'The stench of corruption', International Herald Tribune, 19 September 2006.

5 It was reported in April 2007 that FIFA had secretly fined Jack Warner's son $1 million for touting World Cup tickets. FIFA's vice president sold the shares in his travel company, but his son continued to run the business. The business continued to overcharge for tickets, which led to the fine.

6 Nobody stood against him. Sepp Blatter received a salary of just over £500,000 in 2006. This might seem a lot, but it has to be compared with that of the best paid director in the Premiership, namely Peter Kenyon, whose salary plus bonuses in the 2005–06 season was in the region of £1.7 million. The annual revenue of Chelsea is one quarter that of FIFA. See Paul Kelso, 'Digger', Guardian, 20 February 2007.

7 See Paul Kelso, 'Digger', Guardian, 20 February 2007.

8 FIFA do of course produce annual financial accounts, but the more meaningful figures are those for the four-year period which conclude with the year in which the World Cup event is held. For the 2003–2006 period the total revenue was approximately £1.32 billion, and the expenses £990 million, showing a very healthy profit. Of the revenue, 52% came from the sale of TV broadcasting rights and 22% from marketing rights.

In fact, the financial position of FIFA has improved, as has the standard of their financial reporting. The financial year ending 31 December 2006 was very successful and as a result of a surplus of 303 million Swiss Francs (£123 million), the positive equity of FIFA at the end of the year stood at 752 million Swiss Francs (£300 million). FIFA have adopted imaginative financing techniques, and to overcome the working capital problem resulting from the uneven flow of revenue, they now securitize future marketing revenues, based, as they point out, on conservative estimates of future revenue.

9 Early in 2007, certain executives of the failed ISL were charged in Switzerland with embezzlement and fraud. FIFA executives may be required to give evidence in the case. At the same time FIFA faced a further embarrassment in the US, a judge had accused FIFA officials of lying whilst negotiating with MasterCard over a sponsorship deal.

10 FIFA is not the body responsible for the laws of football. The International Football Association Board has this role. This board consists of eight members, four of whom are provided by FIFA, and one each from the national football associations of England, Scotland, Wales and Northern Ireland. The reason why the board have this strange membership structure is, of course, historic. The rules of Association Football were first developed in the UK.

11 Sugden and Tomlinson (2002).

12 At one time football authorities, in particular UEFA, were arrogant enough to believe that European Community law did not apply to them because they (along with FIFA) were Associations, that is legal entities registered in Switzerland. They argued that EC law should not apply to associations in countries not members of the Community. In 1988 the president of UEFA, Jacques George, stated that UEFA could 'make up what rules we want as long as they are within Swiss laws, as we have nothing to do with the European Union.'

Of course technically he was correct, UEFA could make up what laws it wanted to, but football clubs and national associations based in countries within the Community had to obey the laws of their lands, and not the rules of a private 'club' that had set itself up in Switzerland to avoid accountability, transparency and tax. UEFA of course had to back down otherwise the leading football clubs in Europe would not have been able to play in their European Championship and the national teams would have been unable to play in the World Cup. They would have established rival competitions.

The Bosman case was settled at the European Court of Justice in 1995. The decision showed that football was not a special case, and that UEFA and the clubs in the EU had to follow the European employment laws. UEFA, who had argued for special treatment, lost the case, and adopted the ruling for all of its then 49 member countries (many of whom were not EU members).

13 FIFA like to see themselves as the centre of a football family. In fact the family analogy moved closer to reality in 2006. Philippe Blatter became the new chief executive of Infront. This is a Swiss-based marketing agency

that controlled a significant part of the 2002 and 2006 World Cup TV rights, and had acquired the Asian rights to the 2010 and 2014 World Cups. Philippe Blatter is Sepp Blatter's nephew. (See *Private Eye*, 15 September 2006.)

14 The UEFA Champions League is a brilliantly marketed competition. During the Tuesday and Wednesday televised games across Europe viewers are exposed to 30 very visible, advertising messages. (The Premier League packs in 60 such messages, and a typical international match has 50.) The competition has six 'blue-chip' sponsors. The marketing revenue rises from one season to the next – in 2006–07 it was about £500 million. About 80% of this goes to the clubs, which is one thing the G14 clubs have to consider should they wish to break away.

15 A Belgian member of the European Parliament (MEP) early in 2007 tabled a motion at that Parliament which contained proposals which he hoped would bring to an end football's present obsession with money. He recommends the familiar package of a more equal distribution of TV money, controls on players' salaries, more home grown players, and a more important role in the clubs for supporters. Many football fans would support these proposals but the European Parliament is reluctant to interfere with the internal running of sport. Sports ministers want the European Commission to allow sports to have exemptions from certain aspects of the EU's free market and open competition policies, but the politician concerned with competition policy in the EU see no reason to treat sport differently from other industries. The UK Sports Minister, Richard Caborn, took a populist stand: 'The political challenge is, is the Commission prepared to give sport back to the people? Are they pre-pared to give powers to sport to carry out better governance and regulation without being threatened by the courts of Europe.' But the real issue the Commission had to consider with respect to football, was who could it give power to? Would it be UEFA, or the chairmen (owners) of the top clubs? It certainly would not be 'the people'. It has not been for over one hundred years. See Roger Blitz, *Financial Times*, 8 May 2007.

16 UEFA require clubs to demonstrate that they are liquid and do not owe money to employees, other clubs or the tax authorities. The financial situation of the club will be monitored over time by UEFA. All this appears to be good, but one wonders how UEFA would react if, say, AC Milan or Juventus were shown to be in financial difficulties during a UEFA Champions League campaign?

17 The Independent Football Commission (IFC) was set up in 2002. It was created as a result of recommendations by the Football Task Force. Its role is to provide independent monitoring of the FA, the Premier League and of the Football League. The government nominate the chairman, but the IFC is not a government body, in fact its funding comes from the three bodies it is supposed to be monitoring – which raises interesting questions about its independence. It is supposed to advise on the best practices in commercial and financial matters in football, in particular

387

with regard to customer service. It has not been very successful, most customers do not even know it exists. It did have success with a report on child abuse in football, however. In 2006 it sent UEFA a set of recommendations on ways to avoid crowd and hooligan problems at matches. The report was not welcomed by UEFA who said that there was a 'strong xenophobic undercurrent' in the IFC report.

Unfortunately, the Independent Football Commission is a toothless body. They would like to be concerned with such issues as vetting owners and directors of clubs, but neither the Premier League or the Football League want them interfering.

18 See the FA's 'Blueprint for the Future of Football'.

19 See Gibon and Pickford, *Association Football and the Men who Made It* (1905); also Inglis, *League Football and the Men Who Made It* (1988).

20 In May 2007, FA shareholders (at last) approved the fundamental changes recommended in the 'Burns report'. This meant that the FA Council would be expanded and would in future include representation from supporter groups and an independent chairman of the board would be appointed. Burns had actually wanted to see two additional independent non-executive directors on the board, but in the end settled for a compromise set of proposals. Sports Minister, Richard Caborn, welcomed the changes, claiming that they would 'at last give English football a governing body capable of making decisions for the good of the game as a whole.' This is a lot to ask for. There was even disagreement on what is meant by 'independent'. The government had in mind somebody from outside the game, but those closer to the governing bodies had in mind somebody who had not been involved in the game for a year!

21 See Stanley Rous, *Football World* (1978)

22 John Gregory has been manager at Aston Villa, Derby County and QPR. He was involved in a number of transfers, some of which had unusual features. In 2003 Graham Bean set up a company that worked for football clubs, defending them against disciplinary charges bought against them by the FA – the opposite to compliance.

23 Michie and Oughton discuss whether the FA is fit for its purpose. They believe that the FA has been failing in its role as the football authority for England, and list what they believe are the 20 worst decisions by the FA in recent years. In their radical proposals to improve the situation, they include the recommendation that the FA should hold a golden share in each member club, so that the FA would have authority over key decisions made by the club. They would also like to see the supporters trust of a club given the option to purchase up to 30% of the equity of that club. Should these two proposals be accepted it would increase the power of the FA and of football fans, and would make ownership of clubs less attractive to financiers. Politically, however, at the present time it is unlikely that such radical proposals would be adopted.

24 The FA showed a lack of judgement when they helped the Division One clubs to break away from the Football League, they weakened their own position. It was the newly formed Premier League that attracted the big

money; they did not need the FA, in fact they found them to be a nuisance. For the first 14 years of the new league the official title was the FA Premier League. In 2007 the League was re-branded, and the FA was dropped in favour of the Barclays Premier League. Money talks.

One other area where the FA has failed is in the lack of a successful youth training programme, but a contributing factor to this has been the lack of co-operation received from Premier League and Football League clubs. Certain countries, particularly France, have excellent youth development programmes.

25 See Inglis (1988).
26 See Hardaker (1977).
27 See Inglis (1988).
28 Freeman, *Own Goal* (2000).
29 The Football League had sensibly introduced a statutory penalty of a 10-point deduction for any club moving into administration. Fine in theory. Leeds suffered a 10-point deduction in the 2006–07 season but it was meaningless, the club had by the time they went into administration effectively been relegated from the Championship. It appeared to be that the points deduction would have no impact on anything. If the club had gone into administration a few weeks later, the points deduction would have applied to the 2007–08 season. Those managing the club had outwitted those managing the League, and had at the same time been able to avoid paying many of their creditors. The League had overlooked the cunning of club owners, such as Ken Bates, who waited until he and his fellow directors knew the points penalty would have no effect before going into administration. As a result of the behaviour of Leeds United, and also Boston United (the club went into administration five minutes before the end of their final game of the season), the League plan to alter their rules. It is proposed that if a club goes into administration when they have four games or less to play, the points deduction penalty will apply to the next season. Leeds United did not however escape punishment.

Another set of League policies, drafted in agreement with the FA, cover the controversy surrounding the arrangements for clubs and players when a club goes into administration. The policies were designed to minimise the risks of those closely involved with football, which had the effect of increasing the risk of all those outside football. The policy is that all money which is owed to 'football creditors' (this includes players and other clubs) by the club that goes into administration has to be paid in full before any other creditors can be paid. This means that all the wages of a club's players and all unpaid transfer fees are, if possible, paid in full, and what is left over out of the failed club's funds is divided between all the remaining creditors.

The unfairness of this policy was brought to light in 2007 with the collapse of Leeds United. At first it was proposed that the club make a voluntary arrangement with its creditors (CVA). This was the policy followed by all the other 41 clubs who had become insolvent since 1992. This would have meant the club paid in full all the players' claims against

389

Leeds (including payments in the region of £700,000 to two players) and the claims of other clubs. These payments were just over £5 million. There was so little money left after these payments that it was possible only to offer one penny in the pound to settle the £35 million of claims of outside creditors. This meant that Her Majesty's Revenue and Customs was offered only £77,000 to settle a tax and VAT bill of £7.7 million. Other outside creditors included the police and hospitals, and three mysterious offshore companies, one registered in the Cayman Islands, another on the island of Nevis and the third in the British Virgin Islands. The three offshore companies claimed to have lent the club £17.7 million. The situation was made even worse by a certain amount of skulduggery. At the meeting of creditors, which required a 75% vote in favour of the proposed voluntary settlement, the vote in favour was 75.2%. The players (expect one) who would benefit handsomely from the settlement not surprisingly voted in favour. See David Conn, *Guardian*, 14 June 2007.

Not surprisingly Her Majesty's Revenue and Customs were not happy with this outcome and challenged legally the CVA. The administrators, KPMG, then surprisingly announced that they wanted a quick sale of the club and abandoned the CVA. They invited offers for the club and then announced they had sold it to a new company, Leeds United 2007. The new company was owned by Forward Sports Fund and chaired by Ken Bates, the same person who had led the old company so disastrously. KPMG acted in a way that does nothing for the reputation of accountants. They claimed that although the new owners had not offered the highest price for the club (they offered £1.8 million whereas another bidder offered £3.5 million) the Bates consortium had offered the best deal for creditors (the offers to creditors increased from 1p in the pound to 8p in the pound to 13p in the pound). KPMG, however, had done little for football. They had sold the club to a company of which little was known.

The Football League was not happy. They had not been kept informed about details of the sale and been given little information about the new owners. They imposed a 15 point deduction on Leeds for the 2007–08 season because the club had not followed the rules on entering administration.

A question that again arose was whether or not the new owners were fit and proper to own a football club. The relationship between the three major creditors of the old club was a cause of concern. Two of the creditors only agreed to waive their claims on the old club as long as the new owners were the Forward Sports Fund. At one time there were business links between one of the creditors and Forward but these were said to have ended before the club went into administration. Little is known about who lies behind these organisations and where their money comes from. The Revenue and Customs decided not to pursue their legal challenge against the club. For more details see Conn and Scott, *Guardian*, 27 July 2007.

30 The solidarity principle was put to the test at the end of the 2006–07 season. West Ham United escaped relegation on the last day of the

390

season at the expense of Sheffield United. But West Ham had made very good use of a player (Carlos Tevez) that many regarded as ineligible to play.

Prior to the end of the season, in April 2007, an independent disciplinary panel had found West Ham United guilty of entering into illegal contracts that allowed a third party to 'influence its policies' relating to two players. They were also found guilty of acting in bad faith in their dealings with the Premier League – they did not disclose the true position with regard to the contracts of those two registered players. The club were fined £5.5 million for breaking the rules.

The problem with this decision by the game's regulators was that it was inconsistent. Other clubs who had been found guilty of playing unregistered players had suffered points deductions, and in the case of Bury thrown out of the FA club. If West Ham had suffered a points deduction they would have been relegated, not Sheffield United.

The lenient decision made by the independent disciplinary panel was justified on dubious grounds. One was that a points deduction would be unfair to the club's fans and players who had not been to blame for the situation. In other disciplinary cases where points were deducted, and in the case of clubs who suffer a points deduction because they move into administration, it was not the fault of the fans, so why were West Ham United fans and players given favourable treatment? Another factor taken into account was that the club had new owners, but the club were guilty and the new owners, if they did not know of the problem, should sue the old owners for compensation. See David Conn, *Guardian*, 2 May 2007.

The regulators were criticised. A fine of £5.5 million is trivial in the context of Premiership versus Championship football. Relegation would cost a club £30 million or more (the amount depending on if and when they were promoted back). It was for this reason that Sheffield United were unhappy and reluctant to let the Premier League settle the matter as a domestic issue.

The League have still to settle the third party ownership problem. In the summer of 2007 Manchester United let it be known that they wished to purchase Carlos Tevez. The question that then arose was who would receive the transfer fee. Would it be West Ham United, the club who owned the registration, or MSI, who owned the economic rights to the player? West Ham said that they would not release the registration unless they received the transfer fee. It was agreed that West Ham had signed a third party agreement with MSI and another company (Just Sports Inc), but they had torn up the agreement following being found guilty of breaching Premier League rules.

The dispute was taken to FIFA, who had no rules governing third parties having an influence in contracts between players and clubs. FIFA recommended that the case be taken to the Court of Arbitration for Sport. Kea Joorabchian, the player's representative and a past official at MSI, was not happy with this proposal and planned to take the matter to the High Courts. He believed that matters as to whether or not contracts were legally enforceable should be settled in a court of law.

When the other controversial Argentine player at West Ham, Javier Mascherano was sold to Liverpool earlier in the season, it was Joorabchian who received the £1.5 fee. The third party arrangement is not so different to the system of acquiring a player on lease. This was the arrangement when Rio Ferdinand moved from West Ham to Leeds. In such situations there is a third party involved in the ownership. If Leeds had not been able to pay all the lease payments, Ferdinand would have been sold and the money raised used to pay back the lessor. See Martin Samuel, *The Times*, 16 May 2007.

31 Another problem arose in the 2006–07 season. The Premier League rules, understandably, do not allow a player 'on loan' to play against the club that owns their registration – this prevents a conflict of interest. When a player is sold, however, the club making the sale is not allowed under the third party league rules to influence whether or not the player is selected for any match. Unfortunately, towards the end of the 2006–07 season some clubs showed once again that they could, and would, outmanoeuvre the League. Manchester United had sold the goalkeeper Tim Howard to Everton, and there was a 'gentleman's agreement' between the clubs that Howard would not play in what turned out to be a crucial match between the two clubs at the end of the season. It was said that the chief executive of the Premier League knew of the agreement.

A similar problem had arisen earlier in the season when Luis Boa Morte was sold by Fulham to West Ham United. Fulham believed they had entered a 'non-contractual agreement' so that Boa Morte would not play against his former club. West Ham United denied such an agreement existed and played Boa Morte in the match against Fulham.

32 The Premier League want as little interference as possible. They want UEFA to be given as little power as possible. They objected to the attempts to limit the number of foreign players allowed in a club's squad, and objected to plans to reform UEFA. The president of UEFA, Michael Platini, claims that no other European League is so opposed to the reforms as the Premiership and even accused the Premier League of a 'knee jerk' response. He was keen to explain that he was not seeking to introduce a European-wide super league: 'European club competitions is the icing on the cake but the European Leagues are the cake,' and it should remain this way. See Roger Blitz, *Financial Times*, 8 May 2007.

6 Success

1 Tim Kuypers and Stefan Szymanski, *Winners and Losers* (1999).
2 Danny Blanchflower, *The Double and Before* (1961).
3 Brian Clough (1994 and 2002).
4 Phil Vasili, *The First Black Footballer* (1998).

5 John Argenti, *Corporate Collapse* (1976).
6 Terry Venables (1996).
7 In May 2007, when it was uncertain whether or not Jose Mourinho would stay as manager of Chelsea, a key player, Frank Lampard, said that if Mourinho did leave, the club would be losing its leader. Tension had arisen in the relationship between Mourinho and Roman Abramovich as a result of players that had been purchased by the club, allegedly because of the wishes of the owner of the club, rather than the wishes of the manager. A number of the players said that the dispute between these two powerful figures had had a destabilising influence in the dressing room. Mourinho remained as manager for the beginning of the 2007–08 season but surprisingly a director of football was appointed. Whether a successful working relationship could be established between the new director, Avram Grant (who had been manager of the Israeli national team) and Jose Mourinho remained to be seen. It could not, Mourinho left the club.
8 Cannon and Hamil (2000).
9 Shackleton (1955).
10 The Cadbury report, 'The Financial Aspect of Corporate Governance' (1992).
11 Terry Venables (1996).
12 As long ago as 1946, the then FA secretary Stanley Rous wished to establish a director of coaching for the sport. He was not successful. The coaching system in England has for many years lagged behind that in other major football countries. Only in the last few years has it been felt necessary for the managers of the leading clubs in the country to hold coaching certificates. But in May 2006 the Premier League were willing to let Glenn Roeder become the new manager at Newcastle even though he had not completed his FIFA Pro Licence. The League Managers Association were critical of the qualifications rule being waived. Unfortunately for Roeder, Newcastle did not have a successful 2006–07 season, and at the end of the season he was sacked.

One reason why the England team has not been successful in international tournaments is the poor quality of coaching. For many decades it was not recognised as a specialist skill for which there is a body of knowledge that can usefully be learned. Until recently we did not differentiate between the role of the manager of the club and the coach. Most managers have been ex-footballers chosen because of their playing ability, not their coaching skills or managerial abilities. To appoint a person who was once a well-known player is a 'safe' decision for directors. It gives the supporters the impression that the directors are doing their best for their club, they are bringing in someone who 'knows' the game. To argue that the club needs a qualified coach, who is not well-known, invites criticism. It requires the directors to be bold, to be courageous, even though from what we now know it could be in the best, long-term interests of the club. For clubs to have made such appointments, and to have required such coaches to be qualified, would have been good for the good of English football.

Chris Green, in his book on football managers (*The Sack Race*), makes a very strong case for the need for education and training for football coaches. He refers to the experience of Danny Bergara who played most of his football in Spain but who then came to England as a manager in the 1970s. Bergara 'came across managers and coaches in England who didn't fully appreciate or understand fitness, psychology or medicine.' He found there was little logic in training, with little emphasis on skill, technique or fitness. This is the fault of the managers but even more so the fault of the directors who appointed those not sufficiently qualified.

13 Neil Carter, *The Football Manager* (2006).

14 Arsène Wenger worked very well with David Dein at Arsenal. Dein was very involved with player recruitment and the negotiation of player transfers. When in 2007 Dein fell out with the other Arsenal directors, it was necessary to find someone with the same skills as Dein to take on that role.

15 Some managers enjoy coaching, but do not enjoy negotiating financial deals. Howard Williamson (before he went to Sunderland) made the comment that 'only a lunatic would enjoy this side of the job' – he was talking about the financial management side of the job. There are, however, many managers who believe that transfer negotiations are part of their work and become annoyed if the club chairman takes on the work.

16 A high payroll does not of course guarantee success. See Berri, et al, *The Wages of Wins* (2006).

17 Ferguson and McKvanney, *Managing My Life* (1999).

18 Tom Reilly, *Science and Soccer* (1996).

19 A statement made by William McGreggor at the FA's annual general meeting – 1909, quoted in Simon Inglis' *Official History of the Football league*.

20 Tom Bower, *Broken Dreams* (2003).

21 Jim Smith, *Jim Smith* (2002).

22 Chris Green, *The Sack Race* (2002).

23 Arsène Wenger and Gianluca Vialli agree on how, given time, one can decide on whether a manager is good at his job. The first criteria for success is whether in the short-term the team achieves good results, and plays quality football. The second is the ability of the manager to help players progress on an individual level, and the third is the impact of the manager in the long-term on the club. Of course few managers have a chance to show their long-term abilities, and to show how good they are at helping build the image of the club. See Marcotti and Vialli(2006).

24 Shackleton (1978).

25 Clough (2002).

26 King (2001).

27 Dunphy (1986).

7 Dark Side of the Game

1 Jackson, *Association Football* (1899).
2 Deloitte and Touche. 'Annual Review of Football Finance' (2002).
3 Roy Keane (2002).
4 Stan Collymore (2004).
5 The manager of the Spanish national team was found guilty by the Spanish Committee for Sporting Discipline of making racist remarks about Thierry Henry, but a court in Madrid later controversially over-turned this verdict. In 2007 the supporters of the Serbian Under-21 team racially abused black players in the England Under-21 team. The referee had to halt the match whilst an announcement was made. FIFA threat-ened to severely penalise the Serbian FA. In fact, the fine amount was trivial.
6 The comment by Samuel Eto'o (a star player with Barcelona) on racism in Spanish football is interesting. He expressed the view that if a black referee was appointed in the Spanish 'La Liga' the fans 'would probably kill him.'
7 For many years it has been known that there have been links in Italy between organised crime and the right wing supporters group, the 'Ultra's'. Lazio are well known to have a hard core of Neo-Fascist supporters. There has also been a mafia boss who owned a football club (see Vialli and Marcotti, p335). This undesirable aspect of football became an issue once again in 2006 when Middlesbrough supporters were attacked with knives whilst in Rome and in 2007 following violence amongst supporters that led to the murder of a policeman at a match in Sicily. The president of the Italian parliament anti-Mafia commission believes the mafia moved into football when they realised that controlling football terraces was a big business opportunity – it provided a major market place for drugs. The 'Ultra' supporter groups who controlled the terraces could help the mafia.

The reaction of the Italian football authorities was to close grounds until minimum safety standards on terraces could be demonstrated, to stop clubs maintaining financial links with supporters groups, and to ban the block sale of tickets to visiting fans. In the past some clubs had provided 'Ultras' with free tickets to matches to stop them causing trouble (*FourFourTwo*, May 2007). New safety requirements (which included the installation of turnstiles and cameras) had been introduced in 2005, but over a year later had not been implemented at most grounds. Stadiums were soon allowed to re-open after the ban. In 2007, two months after the grounds were re-opened Manchester United supporters were attacked by police and rival fans in Rome.
8 Roy Keane was a great admirer of Stuart Pearce who was 'a leader, a real pro. He was an amazing warrior, a man it didn't pay to mess with.' Playing with Pearce at Nottingham Forest taught Keane that 'mental

strength to out-battle the opposition was more important than mere technical ability.' This is the Premier League, not the beautiful game, but a tough and hard game. One reason why Keane became involved in many battles on the pitch was, he explained, because 'You can't allow yourself to be the victim. If they put it up to you, try to intimidate you, to see if you've gone soft, you've got to send the signal back.'

Each period has its own hard men. In 1995 Duncan Ferguson was sent to prison for three months for head butting an opponent during a match. He was at the time on probation following similar assaults. In 2007 Manchester City had had enough of the aggression shown by one of their players, Joey Barton. The violence was off the pitch as well as on. One of the players from his own club was badly disfigured after a fight with Barton on the training ground, another player at the club was deliberately burned with a cigarette by Barton in a fight at a nightclub. The club sold the player to Newcastle United.

9 See Paul McGrath, *Back from the Brink* (2006).

10 Davies and Gascoigne (2004).

11 Collins and Vamplew, *Mud, Sweat and Beer* (2002).

12 In 2004 a survey undertaken by Leicester University, supported by the Professional Footballers Association, found that up to 160 players were taking performance-enhancing drugs. Harry Gregg, who was Manchester United's goalkeeper in the 1960s, has admitted that he took performance-enhancing stimulants before matches (he took speed). He also said that stimulants were being taken by players at other clubs at that time. Random drug testing was not introduced in England until 1994. It has been suggested that clubs routinely take steps to protect their players from being caught. The clubs are warned that a drugs tester will be visiting them and the clubs ensure that certain of their players are not at the ground when the testers arrive. See *When Saturday Comes, the Half Decent Football Book*, p112.

13 Ferdinand admitted that he was told after training he would be required to take a drugs test, but there was no time set for the test. Ferdinand said that 'you (normally) popped along when you were ready.' After training, whilst having a shower, he was reminded he was required to take a test. As he put it: 'twenty minutes later I'd finished getting ready and walked straight out of the door to my car.' He went shopping and his mobile phone was not on. By the time he was contacted, the drug tester had left the training ground. He was, he said, told by the FA that he would be able to take the test two days later. Two days later he took the test and passed it. Ferdinand explains in his autobiography that he did not understand what all the fuss was about. 'I'm thinking, bloody hell, all this fuss over me missing a drugs test. I took one within 48 hours and it was negative.' See Rio Ferdinand's *My Story* (2006).

Unfortunately for Rio Ferdinand, and for anyone else required to take a drugs test, passing the test on one day does not mean that the person would have passed a test taken two days earlier.

14 This is a comparatively recent entry into the list of medical techniques

396

used to boost performance. Erythropoietin is a protein hormone that stimulates the production of red blood cells.

15 In June 2007, Mohamed-al-Fayed, the owner of Fulham, when criticising the Premier League for its unequal distribution of the income from the sale of television rights, said that most clubs were living on the edge financially. He said that the difficulties were added to by the huge wage demands of players. 'It is crazy. Imagine a player who can hardly read and write – he can earn £4 million to £5 million pounds.'

16 An interesting illustration of the attitude of players was that of John Terry in early 2007, at the time he (and his agent) were negotiating a new contract. Terry was the captain of Chelsea (his autobiography had the title 'Captain Marvel' and referred to him as a 'football legend'). John Terry rejected a deal offered to him by the club, which was worth £6 million a year until 2011. Terry felt a sense of injustice because there were three players at the club being paid more than him, including Shevchenko, who despite not being a regular first team player, was paid over 50% more than Terry.

17 See Stan Collymore, *Tackling My Demons* (2004).

18 Brian Robson (2005).

19 See Strachan (2005).

20 The second 'Stevens Report' was released in June 2007. This was the result of further enquiries into unusual transfer deals. Stevens reported that although most transfer deals had been cleared there were still 17 being investigated. He reported that certain agents who were still not co-operating including the super-agent Pini Zahavi, who denied that he was being difficult. Stevens concluded that there were five transfers involving Zahavi that could not be signed off as being above suspicion. The report recommended FIFA investigate Zahavi. This agent had over recent years been involved in many of the events which have had a big impact on English football. He was a key player in the Abramovich take-over of Chelsea and has since been a key person in bringing many of the big name players to that club. He was Rio Ferdinand's agent when the player moved from West Ham to Manchester. He has acted as a consultant to MSI, the company that owned the economic rights to Tevez and Mascherano. He has been immensely successful. Perhaps this is the reason he did not want to show his bank statements to the Stevens inquiry.

The 'Stevens Report' was also critical of Craig Allardyce and a possible conflict of interest at Bolton; of Graeme Souness, a former manager; and of Kenneth Shepherd, at Newcastle. No evidence was found that clubs or club officials had been taking illegal payments, although there was a 'prevalence of slack administration.'

In July 2007 the police raided the grounds of three football clubs. They were undertaking an inquiry into corruption in football. The police raid came as a surprise to many who thought that the 'Stevens Report' had indicated that there was not much wrong with the game. The three clubs being investigated were Newcastle United, Portsmouth and Glasgow Rangers. Records were taken away from the three clubs. The homes of certain individuals were also searched. The results of the police investigation were awaited with much interest. The representatives of the clubs involved, not surprisingly, said they had done nothing wrong.

Two particular transfers that had caused concern were the move of Amby Faye from Portsmouth to Newcastle and the move of Jean-Alin Boumsong from Glasgow to Newcastle. The second of these transfers was particularly mysterious. The player cost Newcastle over £8 million and turned out to be not very good. Glasgow Rangers in fact had obtained his services on a free transfer only six months before they sold him for £8 million. The manager at Newcastle United at the time of the move was Graeme Souness.

21 Foot (2006).

22 A central figure in the scandal at Juventus was the general manager, Fabio Capello. He resigned in May 2006, before the verdict on the match-fixing charges, and moved to Real Madrid.

23 There was an additional controversy. A club that benefited from Juventus being stripped of their title was Inter-Milan. They had finished third in Serie A in 2005–06, but were awarded the title. It has been suggested that they were as guilty of match-fixing as any of the other clubs. The president of Inter-Milan was also president of the telecommunications company involved with the wire tapping which resulted in the match-fixing scandals.

24 In 1992–93 Marseille had beaten AC Milan in the final of the UEFA Champions League. The owner of the club, Bernard Tapia, was then found guilty of being involved in a bribery conspiracy. Marseille were allowed to keep the 1993 title, but were not allowed to enter the competition in the following year. UEFA had had experience of dealing with clubs involved in bribery charges. They did not, however, set up rules that would adequately punish clubs in future that were found guilty of cheating.

25 AC Milan won the UEFA Champions League in 2007, but there were many who believed that they should have been excluded from the competition. AC Milan had been found guilty of match-fixing. The club's refereeing liaison officer had been found to have tried to influence the appointment of match officials at Milan games. Their punishment was initially set at a 44-point deduction for the 2005–06 season (the season just finished) and an advanced deduction of 15-points for the 2006–07 season. Such a deduction for 2005–06 would have meant that they did not qualify for the 2006–07 UEFA Champions League. The club, however, appealed against the decision. The punishment was altered, and they were only deducted 30 points for 2005–06 and 8 points for 2006–07. This meant they finished third in Serie A in 2005–06 and so qualified for the UEFA Championship. The club's name was sent forward by the Italian Football Federation to UEFA as one of the Italian club's qualified for the tournament. According to the then statutes and regulations of UEFA they had to accept the clubs put forward by national football associations. Whatever the individual committee members of UEFA

thought about AC Milan and their involvement in match-fixing there was nothing they could do about it.

In January 2007, UEFA changed their statutes, so that in future they could intervene in such a situation. From that time if UEFA were not happy with the way a club had behaved, for example if the club had tried to fix results, then they could ban that club from their competitions. We will never know whether UEFA would have decided that the AC Milan involvement in match-fixing was so grave that they would have been excluded from the 2006–07 Champions League. Many thought that the Italian authorities' punishment, particularly the reduced sentences following appeal, were far too weak a punishment for what amounted to four years of cheating. Things soon returned to normal. Inter-Milan were Serie A champions in 2006–07, by a good margin, partly because many of their rivals had been punished by points deductions and some had been moved to a lower division. Fiorentina remained in Serie A but with a 15-point deduction, despite which they finished seventh. AC Milan had an eight-point deduction and finished fourth. The other 'big' club, Juventus, were champions of Serie B.

26 Jonathan Wilson in his book *Behind the Curtain* provides a fascinating account of the colourful history of football in Russia and other Central and East European countries since the collapse of the USSR. It involves murder, arms dealing, money laundering and of course match-fixing. One of the more successful clubs, CSKA Moscow, has at different times been owned by a Chechen businessman, by the Russian defence ministry and by a mysterious company registered in Stevenage, England (but with the true owners being secret). Russian football 'is now in the hands of a small group of very rich men.' (English football is moving in the same direction.)

'Where there is football, there is money, and in Russia, generally speaking, where there is money there is corruption.' A 'clean' agent was stabbed to death, a FIFA referee was beaten up and there is evidence of match-fixing. All of this might not matter, but it has to be remembered that the top Russian clubs, the ones that attract big sponsorship deals and big business, compete in UEFA competitions. Indeed CSKA Moscow won the UEFA Cup in the 2004–05 season.

27 Sharpe (1997).

28 Dunphy (1976).

29 Peter Swan was at first banned from playing football again, but this ban was overturned after 8 years, and he returned to play for Sheffield Wednesday.

30 Johnson (2007).

31 The selling of inside information by sportsmen to those involved in the gambling industry has occurred in a number of sports. In cricket it has been particularly bad, as has the even more serious transgression of match-fixing.

The International Cricket Council in response to scandals about betting and bribes in the game set up an anti-corruption unit. A report was produced by a retired Metropolitan police commissioner that concluded that match-fixing was rife throughout the game. But the money making circus of international cricket was allowed to roll on. There is evidence of match-fixing and of players being paid to play below their best for a whole or part of a match. Organised criminals, operating through book-makers in Asia, on occasions bribe players. The large amount of money that is now bet on the outcome of cricket matches means that criminals have become involved with the sport.

It is not so easy to fix the result of a football match as it is a cricket match. Also a cricket match provides many opportunities to bet on an outcome, for example the number of runs or wickets during a time period. In football the safest ways to fix the result of a match seems to be either to bribe the referee or a goalkeeper. Betting syndicates have, however, tried other ways to 'fix' the outcome of games in England. In 1999 three men admitted that they had planned to sabotage the floodlights at a match between Liverpool and Charlton. Two floodlight failures had occurred at matches in 1997, and it was thought that these failures were the result of actions by Far Eastern betting syndicates.

In an attempt to restore confidence in the integrity of the sport, the UK Government in 2007 proposed that sportsmen and women should be jailed for up to two years if they were guilty of passing on inside information.

8 Why Manchester United?

1 For a history of Manchester City Football Club see Garry (2006) and Johnson (2004).
2 There are a number of books that contain football quotations, for example see Shaw (1999).
3 At the end of the 2006–07 season Stuart Pearce was sacked, the club had finished fourteenth in the league, and perhaps even more disappointingly the club had scored only 10 goals in home matches that season. This was the worst performance in terms of scoring goals in home matches in the 119-year history of league football. Pearce, who as well as being manager of Manchester City had been the England Under-21 coach, claimed, in his defence, that the club had not given him enough money to spend. His critics, however, pointed out that he had purchased a number of so-called goal scorers, one of whom had cost £6 million, and they were all disappointing. He was the tenth manager to leave the club in a 14-year period.
4 See David Conn, et al. *Football Confidential 2*, (2003).
5 At first it was said that an American investor would purchase the club. Then in 2007 Ray Ranson, backed by a British consortium, announced that they were interested. Ranson had been interested in acquiring a Premier League club for some time. He bid £45 million for Aston Villa

but was not successful. One other possible purchaser was Thaksin Shina-watra, the ex-Prime Minister of Thailand, and said to be the richest Thai person. He did have a number of problems including corruption and fraud charges against him in Thailand and his assets frozen in that country. He was said to have altered the law whilst Prime Minister so that he and his family could sell a telecommunications company they owned to a foreign investor and in doing so make $2.0 billion profit. He was living in exile in London, where he assured everyone that he had access to enough wealth to be able to acquire Manchester City. The principal owners of the club, Wardle and Makins (who between them owned 29.95% of the shares), had to decide whether to sell to a person who might be convicted of corruption. Also the Premier League had to decide on the suitability of Thaksin as an owner of the club. Was he a 'fit and proper person?' He had not been convicted in court, and it was a military government that were pursuing him.

At the end of April 2007 the market capitalisation of the club was £22.72 but was falling. A purchaser would need not only to purchase the equity shares but also to pay off all or part of the £23 million of loans made to the club by Wardle and Makin. He would also need to take responsibility for the remaining debts of £20 million or so. In June 2007, Shinawatra's formal offer for the club was accepted by the directors. Wardle and Makin were to be paid £7.2 million for their shares (valuing the total equity of the club at approximately £24 million) and £17.5 million for their loan. The club needed to revive its fortunes, attendance figures had been falling, they were losing their traditional supporters, the new ground was said to lack atmosphere, and new players were required. Thaksin said that he would bring in a top, internationally respected manager. He brought in Sven-Goran Eriksson. (See David Conn, *The Guardian*, 28 February 2007 and 23 May 2007.)

6　See in particular Bose (1999) and Crick and Smith (1989).
7　Kuypers and Szymanski (1999).
8　See Anderson and Gregg (2002) and Connor (2006).
9　See Tomas (1996).
10　Crick and Smith (1989).
11　See Ferguson and McKvanney (1999).
12　op cit.
13　Bose (1999).
14　Manchester United were the biggest earning football club in the world until 2005 when they were overtaken by Real Madrid. In 2006 Barcelona and Juventus also overtook them. This is ranking clubs according to their annual revenue.
15　The club was in 2007 attempting to restructure the debt to bring down the costs of borrowing. One possible solution being explored was to securitize match day revenue. This helps meet current costs but means that less money is available in future.

9 Whatever Happened to Football in the Midlands?

1 The Birmingham City directors had shown that they were prepared to allow their manager time, and they continued to support Bruce. They were rewarded: the club finished second in the Championship, and were promoted back to the top division.

2 In *When Saturday Comes, the Half Decent Football Book* (2005) the authors refer to Birmingham City as not so much a sleeping giant, as a dozing middleweight. They refer to the club's performance over time as one of 'mediocre achievement' with a record that is 'probably the least successful of any big city club in English football.'

3 In the six seasons between 1970–71 and 1975–76 Derby County finished each season in a top ten position in Division One (Top tier) and won the division twice. In 1979 and 1980 Nottingham Forest won the European Cup (the major European competition at the time). A key factor linking all these achievements was of course Brian Clough.

4 Malcolm Boyden, *Brum's the Word* (2003).

5 See Tony Mason (1980).

6 Liverpool has more civic pride than Birmingham.

7 Chris Upton, *A History of Birmingham* (1993).

8 See McOwan (2002).

9 See Matthews (2004).

10 Kuypers and Szymanski (1999).

11 Probably because of salary capping in US sports.

12 Sir Ian Botham has referred to Edgbaston, as 'the bull ring of English cricket.' The football grounds could also be bull rings, if there was something to be passionate about!

13 See Clarke and McAllister (1995).

14 Dobson and Goddard (1996).

15 Bains and Bowler (2000).

16 Other managers and directors of Midland clubs have said the same things about the problems of attracting top players to Midland clubs. The outspoken David Sullivan said in 2007 that fans in the Midlands were moaners. He said that top players did not feel appreciated. 'We had players last year we tried to sign who would not come to Birmingham City because they don't like the crowd and the reception they get.' Perhaps the Midland fans get the clubs they deserve. Or perhaps the top players do not come to the Midlands because they do not believe it will lead to playing football at the top level. They want to move to winning teams that might provide an opportunity to play in European competitions.

17 See Bains and Bowler (2000).

18 Larry Canning is an ex-footballer and a respected Midland journalist.

19 Derby County provide an interesting example of the governance problem in football. There had been problems over a long period, but we will consider just the recent situation.

Brian Clough blamed Derby's relegation from the Premier League in 2001 on 'bad judgement at boardroom level.' He was critical of the directors at the time he left the club and critical of the directors 20 years later, in particular of the decision to get rid of the experienced manager Jim Smith, in the 2000–01 season and bring in the local hero Colin Todd. By the time the directors got rid of Todd, having appointed him to do a job he did not have the experience to do well, it was too late for the new manager John Gregory to be able to keep the club in the top league.

In 2002 the club went into administrative receivership; the debts, the loss of revenue, the high wage bill and a compensation battle with a former manager were all too much for the club. A number of potential buyers looked at the club but did not pursue their interests. A consortium of business people stepped in and saved the club. They paid off the £15 million owed to the Co-op Bank, but the way in which they obtained the money to pay the bank was of concern to many and particularly of concern to supporters of the club, if not necessarily to the FA.

The five members of the consortium that took over the club were a barrister, namely, John Sleightholme (who became chairman); Jeremy Keith (who became the chief executive), who referred to himself as a business doctor; Steve Harding, with a marketing and communications background; Murdo Mackay (who became director of football), a former football agent; and Andrew Mackenzie (who became director of finance). Mr Mackenzie had worked with the previous owner, Lionel Pickering. All the members of the consortium appeared to be worthy citizens and to be promising owners of Derby County. Mr Mackay had, however, a chequered business background. He had in the past been 'sequestrated for outstanding debts', and had been made 'bankrupt after his recruitment agency left creditors owing £150,000 in 1993.' In 2001 another of his agencies, 'Inside Soccer Recruitment', went bust owing a number of creditors, including the Inland Revenue, and the former footballer, Terry Butcher. Mr Mackay had in fact been a director of five other companies, all connected with sport and which 'were dissolved between 1999 and 2004.' Perhaps he has just been unlucky! But so have the three other members of the consortium. 'Messrs Keith, Harding and Mackenzie in total have been involved in 17 UK limited companies that were dissolved while they were a director or company secretary.' The members of the consortium certainly have business experience. (See www. ramstrust.org. for details of a letter written to the Minister of State for Culture, Media and Sports, January 2006.)

The Derby supporters were unhappy with the five members of the consortium that took over the club. The new directors removed the popular manager George Burley in June 2005 and replaced him with Phil Brown. They sacked Brown seven months later. In the four and a half years between October 2001 and February 2006, the club had seven different managers. In an attempt to reduce the club's debts, the new directors had sold the better players and had reduced their wage bill. The wage bill had over the first two years with new owners in charge been cut by 25%. It could be said that the club were now paying modest Championship wages (second tier) and this was reflected in their performance. They were fighting against relegation to the third tier with many players obtained on loan from other clubs.

The debts of the club had risen alarmingly. It was estimated that in 2006 the club owed £44 million, which was over twice their annual turnover. It might be argued that the club had assets to cover their debts, but there was a problem. The club had sold their most valuable players and no longer owned Pride Park. The new owners paid off the money the club owed the Co-op bank by mortgaging the stadium. The situation became even more worrying for supporters when it became known that Pride Park had been mortgaged to a Panamanian-registered company. Of all the tax havens in the world Panama is recognised as being about the worst; it is awash with dirty money and is protected by strict secrecy laws.

The name of the Panamanian-registered company was ABC Corporation, but it was not known with certainty who the owners of this business were. Many people believe that the owner was Michael Hunt, a person who was sentenced to eight years in 1993 for his role in the largest tax fraud ever perpetuated in the UK. Because of the secrecy laws in Panama it is not of course known with certainty who owns or owned the ABC Corporation, the same company that have lent money to QPR.

There were attempts to remove Derby County directors. Peter Gadsby, who had been vice chairman at the club under the previous ownership and was the prime 'driver' behind the move by the club to Pride Park, led a consortium wanting to take-over the club.

In April 2006 Sleightholme resigned, and the rest of the board followed him. The Gadsby-led consortium bought the club, helped reduce the debt, and succeeded in returning ownership of Pride Park to the club. The club appointed a new manager and were successful in the play-offs in 2006–07 and so returned to the Premier League. In June 2007 they appointed the respected Trevor Birch as chief executive and member of the board. Birch was a financial specialist, who had done his best at Leeds, and had been chief executive at Chelsea, before the Abramovich take-over.

20 For the 2007–08 season, expectations were high at Aston Villa, with a new owner and a top manager. Derby County and Birmingham City were back in the Premiership but both needed to invest money. A Hong Kong businessman, Carson Yeung, had purchased a 29.9% stake in Birmingham City. It was uncertain whether or not he would make a bid for full control of the club. Yeung had previously tried to buy into Sheffield Wednesday and Reading. He was yet another wealthy foreigner wishing to own an English football club. David Sullivan had said for some time that he would sell his shares in the club if the right offer came along. There were said to be a number of other investors interested in the club, including Ray Ranson. The offers were said to be in the £50 to £70 million price range.

Nottingham Forest had a wealthy British owner, Nigel Doughty, and were talking about building a new 'super' stadium. Wolverhampton also had a wealthy new British owner, Steve Morgan, who had bought the club for only £10 but had promised to invest £30 million in the club in an attempt to get them back into the top division. Leicester City had a wealthy new foreign owner, who had shown his willingness to support a football club with his earlier involvement with Portsmouth. Coventry City were said to be talking to foreign investors. West Bromwich had a new manager, a stable board, narrowly missed promotion in 2006–07, and hoped for better the following season. Even Walsall had been promoted.

The prospects for Midland football looked good, but only in terms of success amongst the also-rans. Globalisation and poor leadership had meant they were too far behind to join the elite.

10 The Beautiful Game: The Future

1 There are signs of resistance at the top political level to free markets and globalisation. At the EU summit meeting in 2007, at which the constitution (treaty) was being amended, the new President of France, Nicolas Sarkozy, tried to introduce a change that would have made it possible to block inconvenient take-overs. The existing treaty stated that the EU shall have 'an internal market where competition is free and undistorted.' The French President wanted the words 'free and undistorted' removed.' He does not believe that all decisions on trade and business should be left to the market to decide. He did not succeed in having the words changed.

There is also growing criticism of some of the results of globalisation. For example, the increasing inequality in income and wealth and the fact that many middle-class workers are finding their jobs under threat.

2 See Hamil, et al. (1999, 2000 and 2001).

3 Germany played San Marino twice in the 2006–07 season to help determine the best national side in Europe.

4 See Szymanski, *Income Inequality* (2001), *Economic Design* (2003) and Szymanski and Zimbalist, *National Pastime* (2005).

5 The income from the sale of foreign TV rights for the three year period from 2007–08 was double that for the previous three years.

6 The 'elite' clubs already have the best youth teams in the country. The two best teams in 2007 being from Liverpool and Manchester United. Arsenal have attracted large numbers of the best players from around the world, and because they cannot provide them all with enough playing experience, they 'loan' them out to other clubs. The elite teams are hoarding the best players.

7 Until the Competition Act of 1998 became effective it was possible for the British government to stop a take-over on the grounds of 'public interest'. The new Act, however, introduced a more substantive test, namely that a proposed take-over would 'substantially lesson compe-

tition'. This is different from the position in the US, where a committee on foreign investment in the US can vet foreign take-overs. The US committee are particularly worried about take-overs that have an impact on national security, infrastructure and communications.

There are signs that the British government is not happy with its present impotence. In particular they are concerned that Russian companies are taking over British energy companies. Could this concern be extended to football? Could we protect our cultural industries? In 2007 Ford announced that they needed to quickly sell Jaguar and Land Rover because Ford's business interests in the US were in a financial mess. The same could happen with English Football clubs that become part of global sports empires. Should we protect our heritage or is everything up for sale?

8 See Hoehn and Szymanski (1998).

9 There are signs that attendance figures for matches involving clubs outside the Premier League fall when a more important match is shown on TV.

10 Szymanski and Zimbalist (2005).

11 A problem with even a Super League is that it too would soon lack competitive balance unless revenue sharing and salary capping arrangements were introduced. The eighteen teams in G14 are not all equal and do not all have equal revenue earnings possibilities.

UEFA does not want a Super League. Its new president, Michel Platini, wants to give the opportunity for more league winners from smaller countries to participate in the Champions League. This would be at the expense of clubs from the larger countries. The result would be a competition with many meaningless matches, with even less competitive balance than with the present structure. (See Martin Samuel, *The Times*, 4 April 2007.)

12 American investors are naturally interested in cashing in on the increasing interest around the world in football. They are also interested in developing the market for football (soccer) in the US. The officials running the world game together with the top clubs and players are also interested in developing this market.

In 2007, the most marketable player in the world, David Beckham, moved to the Los Angeles Galaxy. As mentioned in the chapter on Globalisation, this was not the first attempt to popularise football in the US. An earlier attempt had failed in the 1980s. The new league has been in existence since the 1990s but has not had much impact. Its television deal only produces revenue of £11 million or so per annum and most clubs make losses. There are really two things to consider. One is whether the Beckhams will succeed and the other is whether football will succeed. Many commentators feel David Beckham left top flight football too early. Real Madrid, the best team in Europe, wanted to keep him and he moved to a club where the size of the ground is smaller than that of Darlington, but he moved to a town obsessed with celebrities. Is this the future of football, where money, image and status are more important than quality and respect?

13 *FourFourTwo*, December 2005, p74–89.
14 'The popularity of a sport is not predestined and shouldn't be taken for granted.' (See MaCambridge, *America's Game*, p. 452.) The NFL succeeded in the US because the league was 'better conceived, better organised and better run than its competition.' By competition is meant not only other sports but also other leisure activities. Football, as run by FIFA, UEFA and the national associations, is not well conceived, well organised or well run. In its greed, it forgets the fans.

In football the downward spiral has begun. In the 2006–07 season Birmingham City visited West Bromwich Albion to play in a crucial Champions League promotion match. The crowd was nearly 10,000 below capacity. The police had asked for the game to start at midday, television wanted it at 11.30 am. It started at 11.30; the fans stayed away. This was the third Sunday 11.30 kick-off for Birmingham fans in two months. Aston Villa were at home to Liverpool the same day, television wanted it to start at 1.35pm. It started at 1.35pm. The crowd was nearly double that of the West Bromwich Albion versus Birmingham game. It was one of only two capacity crowds at Aston Villa that season. The lessons: one, crowds will come out to watch the top talent (i.e. Liverpool); two, the needs of television dictate.
15 Jonathan Wilson (2006) expressed the opinion that 'Local football will never wholly die, for certain clubs have an emotional hold, and the market, anyway, requires a nursery of talent'. But many clubs are losing their emotional hold, and the nurseries for players could be in the poorer countries of the world, not European countries.
16 One problem is that football is losing its younger fan base. The average age of those attending Premier League matches in 2005 was 43. In 1992, those watching matches aged between 16 and 20 was 25%, but by 2006 the figure was 9%. One reason for this decline is rising ticket prices. In 1998–99 the average price of a ticket to watch a match at Liverpool was £5.50, and in 2006 it was £34, a six fold increase (600%) over a period when general price levels rose by only 82%. For younger people, watching a match in a pub with friends can be more fun, and certainly cheaper than visiting a stadium. See 'Fan Surveys' produced by the Centre for the Sociology of Sport at the University of Leicester and David Conn, The *Guardian*, 7 March 2007.
17 Delia Smith, the popular director of Norwich City (and author and cook), believes that the modern game is a recipe for disaster. She expressed the views of many when she questioned the motives of the new breed of foreign owners, not believing that they have got involved because they really love English football. She pointed out that it becomes a joke when a team like Norwich has to play against a team that cost £250 million to bring together. She also pointed out that the game was becoming a TV game. See Matt Scott, The *Guardian*, 17 February 2007.
18 In May 2007, having heard of the price of tickets for the first big match to be held at Wembley, the FA Cup Final, Steven Powell, head of development at the Football Supporters Federation, commented: 'Fans

407

are sick and tired of being treated as turnstile fodder. They do not want to be treated as extras on a TV set.' The fans of each club playing in the final had been allocated 25,000 tickets, of which 4,000 were priced at £25, and the remainder had prices of either £60, £80 or £95. The traditional fan was being exploited at special events and at normal Premier League games. The cost of attending matches has been rising by 15% or so per annum.

19 See Morrow (1999 and 2003).

20 A possible outcome is a European Super League, run by the top clubs themselves, and a Premier League in each country. The elite clubs would compete in the Super League but not in the domestic leagues. The Super League would not have salary capping but would have a form of revenue sharing. The elite clubs are doing so well with the present arrangements they would not want to change things too much. They would, however, like to reduce risk, so the European Super League would not have relegation.

   The domestic leagues would operate much as at present with promotion and relegation, but they would introduce salary capping. This would be good for competitive balance, would make the outcome of competitions uncertain, and would attract football fans who were not able to watch the Super League games live. It would encourage those who enjoy football to support their local teams. There would, however, be the danger that the top clubs would hoard the best players.

21 Gianluca Vialli, at one time a very successful footballer and later the popular manger of Chelsea (1998–2000), has expressed concern that the football business will 'gravitate' to where it can make the most money. He believes that the only way to prevent this is to 'find a business model that works and is fair to everyone. And that includes the big clubs.' Unfortunately those with power in the game benefit from the present model. See Marcotti and Vialli (2006).

Case Studies

1 Mike Ashley made his money by developing the Sports Direct empire, which owned a number of well-known sports retailing and sports goods manufacturing businesses. In 2006 he was ranked the twenty-fifth richest person in the UK, with wealth approaching £2 billion. He paid in the region of £133 million for the equity of Newcastle United.

   He first purchased the 41.6% stake of Sir John Hall's family, and this put pressure on Freddie Shepherd. The Halls had been willing to sell for some time but Shepherd was reluctant to sell. After deliberating over the Ashley offer, the chairman sold his interest in the club. The Hall and Shepherd family had made a very healthy return on their investment in the club.

2 For a history of Newcastle United see Hutchinson (1997).
3 Bobbie Robson refers to Douglas Hall as something of a recluse as far as the staff were concerned. Robson comments that 'Hall did not ask to see me during my five years at the club.' He docs say, however, that Hall was immensely powerful within the club. An interesting insight into the relationship between a manager and the major shareholder.
4 See Terry Venables (1996).
5 It remains to be seen whether or not the new owners and new chairman will adopt a similar approach.
6 See Keith (2001).
7 Steve Morgan subsequently bought Wolverhampton Wanders for £10.
8 Those businessmen taking over English clubs obviously know how to obtain access to finance, but do they know how to run a sports business? George Gillett Jr. at the time of acquiring Liverpool was the majority owner of the Montreal Canadians in the National Hockey League. His son was managing director of the club. The club is described in the offer document as 'one of the most successful ice hockey franchises in the NHL,' having 'won the Stanley Cup Championship 24 times.' It would be more accurate to describe the club as once being the most successful. It was a great team up to the 1980s, since then it has won the cup only three times in 1979, 1989 and 1993. The NHL is divided into two conferences; the Montreal team is in the Eastern conference. As at March 2007 it was tenth out of 15 clubs in that conference. In the previous four seasons it had finished seventh, seventh, tenth and eighth out of the fifteen teams in that conference. Not one of the most successful clubs over recent years.

The same picture emerges when one looks at the recent business record of Tom Hicks. The offer document refers to him as an 'experienced operator' whose family interests include 'ownership of the Stanley Cup-winning NHL team, the Dallas Stars and Major League Baseball's Texas Rangers. The Dallas Stars won the Stanley Cup in 1999; a year later they were losing finalists. These were their only appearances in the finals.

The Texas Rangers have never been champions in baseball, but did appear in the play-offs in 1996, 1998 and 1999. Tom Hicks and his fellow investors in June 1998 purchased the Rangers from George W. Bush for $250 million. Since 1999 they have not qualified for the play offs. Major League Baseball is organised into two leagues, with 14 clubs in one league and 16 in the other. The Texas Rangers play in the Western Division of the American League. There are four clubs in the division. In 2002 and 2003 they finished bottom of their division, and in 2004, 2005 and 2006 finished third out of four. In June 2007 they were bottom.

Both gentleman do have considerable experience of running sports clubs in North America, but not as successfully as the 'Offer Document' would suggest. The *Guardian* (7 Feb 2003) tells a story of how in 2000 Tom Hicks nearly ruined the club by paying too much for the then best player in baseball – Alex Rodriquez. He paid more for this one player than he had paid for the club, the player's contract being worth $252 million over 10 years. The result was he had little money left to pay the rest of the squad. In 2003 Hicks had to pay the player $67 million to leave the club. The richest club in baseball, the New York Yankees, were then willing to sign him on, needing only to pay him $16 million a year. Before the club got rid of Rodriquez, the Rangers had one of the highest paid teams in the league, and one of the worst performance records.

9 For a history of Tottenham Hotspur, see Scholar and Bose, *Behind Closed Doors*.

10 See Terry Venables (1996).

11 Scholar and Bose, *Behind Closed Doors*.

12 Adams and Ridley (1998).

13 Graham, *The Glory and the Grief* (1995).

14 At Arsenal over the last few years there has been disagreement at board level as to whether or not the club needed access to a new source of finance. The annual interest bill, as a result of building a new stadium, was approaching £20 million. The club also needed to buy new players. They were only finishing in fourth place in the league. David Dein certainly thought new money was needed. Not all the directors agreed with him. As explained in the chapters on Globalisation, and on Ownership and Finance, Arsenal had begun to build up links with an American sports business. What was uncertain was whether Arsenal were the prime movers in this development, or whether it was the American sports entrepreneur who was seeking to take-over the Arsenal club. The American concerned was Stan Kroenke.

Prior to Kroenke's involvement, there were stories about other investors being interested in acquiring Arsenal. The Arsenal chairman at the annual general meeting which was held in October 2006 had said that the directors as at that time had received no take-over approach. There was, however, a strong rumour at the time that ITV had had talks with representatives of the royal family of Qatar about the possible sale of the television company's strategic 9.9% holding.

There was a division of opinion about the financial strength of Arsenal. There were those who argued that they were falling behind the other elite clubs. They had finished only fourth in the last two seasons. The other argument was that they did not need additional funds because they already had a very talented squad of players and unlike Liverpool they had already financed a new modern stadium.

Stan Kroenke purchased the stake of ITV for £65 million (valuing the total equity at £650 million). At first the Arsenal Supporters Trust (who own 2% of the clubs shares) welcomed Kroenke's involvement as it ended uncertainty about the future ownership of the 9.9% of the club's shares, but there was concern as to whether he wanted to be the new owner. He continued to build up his holding.

Dein believed Arsenal did need new money, he fell out with the other directors and resigned from his position as deputy chairman. Then Thierry

Henry, the club's leading player, announced he was leaving Arsenal and moving to Barcelona. He had earlier criticised the board for not investing in new players. There was uncertainty about the future position of Arsène Wenger, he had only one year of his contract to run and it was uncertain whether he would stay at the club after that (he did). He had worked well with David Dein, they respected each other. The uncertainty about Wenger's position was one reason given for Henry leaving the club.

Just at the time when Arsenal needed stability they began to face problems. They had big debts to repay, high interest charges and a large and expensive stadium to fill. The future was uncertain. Would the old guard continue to run the club? Would the mysterious businessman from Uzbekistan, Alisher Usmanov, seek to take over the club? Would David Dein return? Would Stan Kroenke increase his shareholding? Would Arsène Wenger remain at the club? The drama off the pitch continued.

Bibliography

History

Bellos, A *Futebul: The Brazilian Way of Life* Bloomsbury (2002)

Carter, F W and Capel-Kirby, A W *The Mighty Kick: The History, Romance and Humour of Football* Jarrods (1935)

Connolly, K and MacWilliam, R *Fields of Glory, Paths of Gold – The History of European Football* Mainstream, Edinburgh (2005)

Douglas, P *The Football Industry* Allen and Unwin, London (1973)

Fishwick, N *English Football and Society 1910–1950* Manchester University Press, Manchester (1989)

Giller, N *Football and all that: An Irreverent History* Hodder & Stoughton, London (2004)

Lowndes, W *The Story of Football* Thorsons, London (1952)

Magoun Jnr, F P *History of Football from the beginning to 1871* Boshun-Langendreer, Cologne (1938)

Mason, T *Association Football and English Society 1863–1915* Harvester, Brighton (1980)

Murray, B *Football: A History of the World Game* Scolar Press, Aldershot (1994)

Polley, M *Moving the Goal Posts; History of Sport and Society since 1945* (1998)

Russell, D *Football and the English* Carnegie Publishing (1997)

Shaw, P *The Book of Football Quotations* Mainstream, Edinburgh (1999)

Taylor, R *Football and its Fans: Supporters and their Relations with the Game* Leicester University Press, Leicester (1992)

Taylor, R and Ward, A *Kicking and Screaming: An Oral History of Football in England* Robson, London (1995)

The Rules of Association Football (1863) Oxford University Press

Tischler, S *Footballers and Businessmen: The Origins of Professional Soccer in England* Holmes and Meir, New York (1981)

Upton, C *A History of Birmingham* Biddles (1993)

Walvin, J *The Peoples Game: A Social History of British Football* Allen Lane (1975)

Walvin, J *Football and the Decline of Britain* Macmillan, London (1986)

Walvin, J *The Peoples Game Revisited* Allen Lane (2000)

Winner D *The Feet: A Sensual History of English Football* Bloomsbury, London (2005)

Present – General Economics

Agnew, P *Forza Italia* Ebury Press (2006)

Banks, S *Going Down: Football in Crisis* Mainstream, Edinburgh (2002)

Baroncelli, R and Lago, U 'Italian Football' *Journal of Sports Economics* 7,1 pp. 13–28 (2006)

Binns, S et al *The State of the Game: The Corporate Governance of Foootball Clubs* (2002)

Bower, T *Broken Dreams* Simon and Schuster (2003)

Buraimo, B, Simmons, R and Szymanski, S 'English Football' *Journal of Sports Economics* 7,1 pp. 29–46 (2006)

Chandler, J H *Television and National Sport* University of Illinois Press, Urbana (1988)

Crolley, L and Hand, D (Eds) *Football, Europe and The Press* Frank Cass, London (2002)

Conn, D *The Football Business: Fair Game in the '90s?* Mainstream, Edinburgh (1997)

Conn, D *The Beautiful Game? Searching for the Soul of Football* Yellow Jersey, London (2004)

Canter, D, Comber, M and Uzzell, D *Football in its Place: An Environmental Psychology of Football Grounds* Routledge (1989)

Connelly, C *Spirit High and Passion Pure: A Journey Through European Football* Mainstream, (2000)

Davies, H *The Glory Game* Mainstream, London (1972 and 1996)

Dobson, S and Goddard, J 'The Demand for Football in the Regions of England and Wales' *Regional Studies* Vol 30, No 5 pp. 443–453 (1996)

Dobson, S and Goddard, J *The Economics of Football* Cambridge University Press, Cambridge (2001)

Freeman, S *Own Goal: How Egotism and Greed are Destroying Football* Orion, London (2000)

Flynn, A and Guest, L *Out of Time: Why Football isn't Working* Pocket Books, London (1994)

Flynn, A and Guest, L *For Love or Money: Manchester United and England – The Business of Winning* Andre Deutsch (1998)

Garland, J, Malcolm, D and Rowe, M *The Future of Football: Challenges for the Twenty-First Century* Frank Cass (2000)

Gerrard, B 'The Economics of Football: A Review of the Current State of Play' *European Sport Management Quarterly* Vol 2, No 2 pp. 167–172 (2002)

Giulianotti, R *Football: A Sociology of The Global Game* Polity Press, Cambridge (1999)

Hamil, S, Michie, J, Oughton, C and Warby S *Football in the Digital Age: Whose Game is it Anyway* Mainstream, Edinburgh (2000)

Hamil, S, Michie, J and Oughton, C (Eds) *A Game of Two Halves? The Business of Football* Mainstream, Edinburgh (1999)

Hamil, S, Michie, J, Oughton, C and Warby, S *The Changing Face of the Football Business: Supporters Direct* Frank Cass, London (2001)

Holt, M, Michie, J, Tacon, R, Oughton, C and Walters, G [Annual] *The State of the Game: The Corporate Governance of Football Clubs 2001 through 2006* Birkbeck, University of London

Hornby, N *Fever Pitch* (1992)

Horton, E *Moving the Goalposts: Footballs Exploitation* Mainstream, (1997)

Kelly, S (Ed) *A Game of Two Halves* Hamlyn, London (1997)

King, A *The End of the Terraces: The Transformation of English Football in the 1990s* Leicester University Press, Leicester (2001)

Morrow, S *The New Business of Football: Accounting and Finance in Football* Macmillan, London (1999)

Morrow, S *The Peoples Game? Football Finance and Society* Palgrave MacMillan, Basingstoke (2003)

Rippon, A *Soccer: The Road to Crisis* Moorland (1983)

Redhead, S *Post-Fandon and the Millenial Blues* Routledge (1997)

Simmons, R 'The Demand for English League Football: A Club-Level Analysis' *Applied Economics* Vol 28 pp. 139–155 (1996)

Shawcross, W *Murdoch: The Making of a Media Empire* (1997)

Szymanski, S and Smith, R 'The English Football Industry: Profit Performance and Industrial Structure' *International Review of Applied Economics* Vol 11, No1 pp. 135–153 (1997)

Szymanski, S and Kuypers, T *Winners and Losers: The Business Strategy of Football* Penguin Books, London (2000)

Taylor, C *The Beautiful Game: A Journey Through Latin American Football* Victor Gollancz, London (1998)

'When Saturday comes' *The Half Decent Football Book* Penguin, London (2005)

'The Future of Football' *Soccer and Society* Vol 1, No1 (Spring 2000)

Vialli, G and Marcotti, G *The Italian Job* Bantam Press (2006)

Watt, T *A Passion for the Game: Real Lives in Football* Mainstream, Edinburgh (1995)

Williams, J and Wagg, S (Editors) *British Football and Social Change* Leicester University Press, Leicester (1991)

Zimbalist, A 'Sport as Business' *Oxford Review of Economic Policy* Vol 19 pp. 503–511 (2003)

Globalisation

Armstrong, G, Giulianotti, R.and Toulis, N *Entering the Field; New Perspectives on World Football* (2007)

Dicken, P *Global Shift, Reshaping the Global Economic Map in the 21st Century* Sage Publications, London (2003)

Finn, G *Football Culture: Local Conflicts Global Visions* Frank Cass (2000)

Foer, F *How Football Explains the World: An Unlikely Theory of Globalisation* Arrow (2006)

Giulianotti, R and Williams J (Eds) *Game Without Frontier: Football, Identity and Modernity* Arena, Aldershot (1994)

Giulianotti, R (Ed) *Globalisation and Sport* (2007)

Goldblatt, D *The Ball is Round: A Global History of Football* Viking (2006)

Harris, N *The Foreign Revolution* Aurot (2006)

Lanfranchi, P and Taylor, M *Moving with the Ball: The Migration of Professional Footballers* Berg, Oxford (2001)

Sandy, R, Sloane, P J and Rosentraub M S *The Economics of Sport: An International Perspective* Palgrave, Macmillan (2004)

Sklair, L 'The Transnational Capitalist Class and Global Politics' *International Political Science Review* 23, 2 pp. 159–174 (2002)

Stiglitz, J *Globalization and its Discontents* Allen Lane, London (2002)

Stiglitz, J *The Roaring Nineties: Seeds of Destruction* Allen Lane, London (2003)

Stiglitz, J and Charlton A *Making Globalization Work* Allen Lane, London (2006)

Sugden J and Tomlinson A *Great Balls of Fire: How Big Money in Hijacking World Football* Mainstream (1999)

Westerbeek, H and Smith A *Sport Business in the Global Marketplace* Palgrave, Basingstoke (2002)

Yallop, D *How They Stole the Game* Poetic Publishing, London (1999)

Ownership and Finance

Arnold, A J *Finance and Ownership: A Business History of Professional Football in Bradford* Duckworth, London (1998)

Arnold, A J 'An Industry in Decline? The Trend in Football League Gate Receipts' *The Service Industries Journal* Vol 11, No 2 pp. 43–52 (1991)

Arnold, A and Beneviste, I 'Producer Cartels in English League Football' *Economic Affairs* Vol 8, Pt 1 pp. 18–23 (1987a)

Arnold, A and Beneviste, I 'Wealth and Poverty in the English Football League' *Accounting and Business Research* Vol 17, No 67 pp. 195–203 (1987b)

Arnold, A and Beneviste, I 'Cross Subsidisation and Competition Policy in English Professional Football' *Journal of Industrial Affairs* Vol 15, No1 pp. 2–14 (1988)

Arnold A and Webb B J 'Aston Villa and Wolverhampton Wanderers 1971/ 2 to 1981/2: A Study of Finance Policies in the Football Industry' *Managerial Finance* Vol 12, No1 pp. 11–19 (1986)

Arthur Anderson & Co'*The Financing and Taxation of Football Clubs*' Football Association and Football League (1982)

Burns, J *BARCA: A Peoples Passion* Bloomsbury, London (1999)

Dept of Education and Science 'Report of the Committee on Football' *Chester Report*, HMSO (1968)

Deloitte (Formerly Deloitte and Touche) *'Annual Review of Football Finances'* (1992 through 2007)

Fitch Ratings-Reports on Public Finance, Project Finance, and US Sports Facility Finances, New York

Football League (Chairman Sir N Chester) *Report of the Committee of Enquiry into Structure and Finance*, Lytham St Annes (1983)

Frampton, P, Michie, J and Walsh A *Fresh Players, New Tactics, Lessons from the Northampton Town Supporters Trust* Football Governance Research Centre, Birkbeck College, London (2001)

FSF News, Football Supporters Federation, London

Glanville, R *Chester FC: The Official Biography* Headline Press (2005)

Green, C *The Sack Race: The Story of Football Gaffers* Mainstream, Edinburgh (2002)

Harris, H *The Chelsea Revolution* John Black, London (2003)

Jackson, M and Maltby, P (Eds) *Trust in Football* Institute for Public Policy Research, London (2004)

King, A 'New Directors, Customers, and Fans: The Transformation of English Football in the 1990s' *Sociology of Sport Journal* Vol 14 pp. 224–240 (1997)

Midgley, D and Hutchinson, C *Abramovich, The Billionaire From Nowhere* Harper Collins (2006)

Sloane, P, 'The Economics of Professional Football: The Football Club as a Utility Maximiser' *Scottish Journal of Political Economy* June pp. 121–146 (1971)

Smith, Sir John 'Football – its Values, Finances and Reputation' *Report to the Football Association* by Sir John Smith (1997)

Tomas, J *Soccer Czars* Mainstream, Edinburgh (1996)

Competitive Balance

Borland J and McDonald R 'Demand for Sport' *Oxford Review of Economic Policy* 19, 4 pp. 478–502 (2003)

Dobson, S and Goddard J 'Revenue Divergence and Competitive Balance in a Divisional Sports League' *Scottish Journal of Political Economy* 51, 3 pp. 359–376 (2004)

Fort, R and Fizel J (Eds) *International Sports Economics Comparisons* Praeger, Connecticut (2004)

Fort, R 'European and North American Sports Differences' *Scottish Journal of Political Economy*, 47, 4 pp. 431–455 (2000)

Gladden, J M, Irwin, R I and Sutton W A 'Managing North American Major Sports Teams in a New Millennium: A Focus on Building Brand Equity' *Journal of Sport Management* 15 pp. 297–317 (2001)

Hoehn, T and Szymanski S 'The Americanization of European Football' *Economic Policy* 28 pp. 205–40 (1999)

MacCambridge, M *America's Game* Random House, New York (2004)

Michie, J and Oughton, C *Competitive Balance in Football: Trends and Effects*

Football Governance Research Centre, Birkbeck (2004)

Neale, W 'The Peculiar Economics of Professional Sport' *Quarterly Journal of Economics* 78, 1 pp. 1–14 (1964)

Ozanian, M *Football Fiefdoms* Forbes (9/3/04)

Quirk, J and Fort R *Pay Dirt The Business of Professional Team Sports* Princeton University Press, Princeton (1997)

Schmidt, M B and Berri, D 'Competitive Balance and Attendance: the Case of Major League Baseball' *Journal of Sports Economics* 2 pp. 145–167 (2001)

Sherony, K and Haupert M 'The Demand for Major League Baseball: A Test of the Uncertainty of Outcome Hypothesis' *The American Economist* 36 pp. 72–80 (1992)

Sloane, P J 'The Economics of Professional Football; The Football Club as a Utility Maximiser' *Scottish Journal of Political Economy* 18 pp. 121–146 (1971)

Szymanski, S 'Income Inequality, Competitive Balance and the Attractiveness of Team Sports' *Economic Journal* 111 pp. 69–84 (2001)

Szymanski, S and Zimbalist, A *National Pastime* Brookings Institution, Washington DC (2005)

Szymanski, S 'Economic Design of Sporting Contests' *Journal of Economic Literature* pp. 1137–1187 (2003)

Zimbalist, A S 'Competitive Balance in Sports Leagues: An Introduction' *Journal of Sports Economics* 3 pp. 111–121 (2002)

Governance

'Arnaut Report', *The Independent European Sports Review* (2006)

Antonini, P and Cubbin J 'The Bosman Ruling and the Emergence of a Single Market in Soccer Talent' *European Journal of Law and Economics* Vol 9, No 2 pp. 157–173 (2000)

Bull, D and Campbell A *Football and the Commons People* (1994)

Butler, B *The Official History of the Football Association* Queen Anne Press, London (1991)

Conn, D 'Lessons to be Learned from Wembley's Woes' *The Guardian* (8/3/06)

Edworthy, N *The Second Most Important Job in the Country* Virgin Publishing (1999)

Foster, K 'Can Sport be Regulated by Europe? An Analysis of Alternative Models' in Caiger, A and Gardiner, S (Eds) *Professional Sport in the EU: Regulation and Re-Regulation* TMC Asser Press, The Hague (2001)

Freddi, C *Complete Book of the World Cup 2006* Harper Sport, London (2006)

Gibson, A and Pickford W *Association Football and the Men who made it* [Four volumes] Caxton Publishing, London (1905) and (1911)

Granville, B *The History (Story) of the World Cup* Faber and Faber, London (1973) and (2005)

Greaves, J and Giller, N *Don't Shoot the Manager: The Revealing Story of England Soccer Bosses* Boxtree (1993)

Greenfield, S and Osborn G *Regulating Football: Commodification, Consumption and the Law* Pluto Press, London (2001)

Hardaker, A *Hardaker of the League* (1977)

Harding, J *For the Good of the Game: History of the Professional Footballers' Association* Robson Books, London (1991)

Hayil, S, Michie, J, Oughton, C and Warby *The FA Structural Review: Submission to Lord Burns Consultant Documents* (2005)

Horrie, C *Premiership* Pocket Books, London (2002)

Holt, M *A Fit and Proper Test for Football? Protecting and Regulating Clubs* Football Governance Research Centre, Birkbeck (2003)

Holt, M, Michie, J and Oughton, C *The Role and Regulation of Agents in Football* The Sports Nexus (2006)

Houlihan, B *The Government and Politics of Sport* Routledge, London (1991)

Houlihan, B *Sport, Policy and Politics: a Comparative Analysis* Routledge, London (1997)

Inglis, S *League Football and the Men Who Made It* Collins Willow, London (1988)

Lovejoy, J *Sven Goran Eriksson* Collins Willow, London (2002)

Jennings, A *Foul: The Secret World of Fifa* Harper Sport, London (2006)

McArdle, D *From Boot Money to Bosman: Football Society and the Law* Routledge-Cavendish, London (2000)

Michie, J 'The Governance and Regulation of Professional Football' *Political Quarterly* 71, 2 pp. 184–191 (2000)

Michie, J and Oughton, C *FA: Fit for Purpose?* The Sports Nexus (2005)

Murphy, P and Waddington, I *Soccer Review 2004* Facilitated by the Professional Footballers Association

Rous, S *Football World: A Life in Sport* Faber and Faber, London (1978)

Sugden, J and Tomlinson A *Fifa and the Contest for World Football: Who Rules the Peoples Game?* Polity Press, Cambridge (1998)

Sugden, J and Tomlinson A *Badfellas; Fifa Family at War* Mainstream, Edinburgh (2002)

The Blueprint for the Future of Football The Football Association (1991)

One Game, One Team, One Voice: Managing Footballs Future The Football League (1990)

Vision Europe (UEFA's Strategy Document Approved) UEFA (21/4/05)

Yallop, D *How They Stole the Game* (1999)

Success

Argenti, J *Corporate Collapse: The Causes and Symptons* McGraw Hill (1976)

Berri, D, Schmidt, M and Brook, S *The Wages of Wins* Stanford University Press, Palo Alto (2006)

Cannon, T and Hamil, S 'Reforming Footballs Boardrooms' in *Football in the Digital Age* Hamil, S, Michie, J, Oughton, C and Warby, S (Eds) pp. 36–46 Mainstream, London (2000)

Carter, N *The Football Manager: A History* Routledge

Finkelstein, S and Hambrick, D *Strategic Leadership* West Publishing, Minneapolis (1996)

Grundy, A 'Managing Strategic Breakthroughs – Lessons from the Football Industry' *Strategic Change* 7 pp. 127–138 (1999)

Grundy, A 'Strategic and Financial Management in the Football Industry' *Strategic Change* pp. 405–422, December (2004)

King J and Kelly J *The Cult of the Manager: Do They Really Make A Difference* Virgin, London (1997)

Reilly, T (Ed) *Science and Soccer* E & FN Spon, London (1996)

Sonnenfield, J 'What Makes Great Boards Great' *Harvard Business Review* September (2002)

Dark Side

Armstrong, G and Giulianotti R *Fear and Loathing in World Football* Berg, Oxford (2001)

Bent, I, McIlroy, R, Mousley, K and Walsh P *Football Confidential* BBC Books, London (2000)

Campbell, D, May, P and Shields, A *The Lad Done Bad – Scandal, Sex and Sleaze in English Football* Penguin Books, London (1996)

Collins, T and Vamplew, W *Mud, Sweat and Beers: A Cultural History of Sport and Alcohol* Berg (2002)

Claridge, S and Ridley, I *Tales from the Boot Camp*

Conn, D, Green, C, McIlroy, R and Mousley, K *Football Confidential 2* BBC, London (2003)

Collymore, S *Tackling My Demons* Collins Willow, London (2004)

Dunning, E, Murphy, P and Williams, J *The Roots of Football Hooliganism* Routledge, London (1988)

Flynn, A, Guest, L and Law, P *The Secret Life of Football* Queen Anne Press, London (1989)

Foot, J *Calcio: A History of Italian Football* Fourth Estate (2006)

Gregg, H and Anderson, F *Harrys Game* Mainstream, Edinburgh (2002)

Inglis, S *Soccer in the Dock: A History of British Football Scandals 1900 to 1965* Willow, London (1985)

Jackson, N I *Association Football* George Newnes, London (1899)

Johnson, G *Football and Gangsters: How Organised Crime Controls the Beautiful Game* Mainstream, Edinburgh (2007)

Lilley, P *Dirty Dealing: The Untold Truths about Global Money Laundering* Kogan Page, London (2006)

McGill, C *Football Inc How Soccer Fans are Losing the Game* Vision, London (2001)

Murphy, P, Williams, J and Dunning, E *Football on Trial* Routledge, London (1990)

Orakwue, S *Pitch Invaders* Victor Gollancz, London (1998)

Sharpe, G *Gambling on Goals – A Century of Football Betting* Mainstream, Edinburgh (1997)

Sugden, J *Scum Airways* Mainstream, Edinburgh (2003)

Thomas, D *Foul Play: The Inside Story of the Biggest Corruption Trial in British Sporting History* Bantam Press, London

'When Saturday Comes' *Power, Corruption and Pies* Mainstream, Edinburgh (1999)

Williams, R *Football Babylon* Virgin Books, London (1996)

Wilson, J *Behind the Curtain* Orion, London (2006)

Players and Managers

Adams, T and Ridley, I *Addicted* Collins Willow, London (1998)

Blanchflower, D *The Double and Before* Four Square Books, London (1961)

Bose, M *False Messiah: The Life and Times of Terry Venables* Andre Deutsch (1996).

Charlton, J and Byrne, P *Jack Charlton: The Autobiography* Partridge-Press, London (1996)

Clough, B and Sadler, J *Clough: The Autobiography* Corgi, London (1994)

Clough, B and Sadler, J *Clough: Walking on Water* Headline, London (2002)

Crick, M *The Boss: The Many Sides of Alex Ferguson* Simon and Schuster, London (2002)

Derbyshire, O *John Terry, Captain Marvel* John Blake (2007)

Dunphy, E *Only a Game* Viking and Penguin, London (1976) and (1987)

Dunphy, E *A Strange Kind of Glory: Sir Matt Busby and Manchester United* London (1991)

Ellis, D *Deadly Doug* John Blake (2005)

Ferdinand, R and Custis, S *Rio: My Story* Headline, London (2006)

Ferguson, A and McKvanney, H *Managing My Life: My Autobiography* Hodden and Stoughton, London (1999)

Gascoigne, P and Davies, H *Gazza, My Story* Headline, London (2004)

Graham, G *George Graham: The Glory and the Grief* Andre Deutsch, London (1995)

Greaves, J *This One's on Me* Coronet, London (1979)

is, H and Curry, S *Venables: The Inside Story* Headline, London
994)

Hill, J *Striking for Soccer* London (1961)

Hill, J *The Autobiography of Jimmy Hill* (1998)

Holden, J *Stan Cullis, The Iron Manager* Breedon Books, Derby (2000)

Jones, V *Vinnie: The Autobiography: Confessions of A Bad Boy* Headline, London (1998)

Keith, J *The Essential Shankly* (2001)

Kelly, S *Bill Shankly: 'Its much more important than that'* Virgin (1997)

Keane, R and Dunphy, E *Keane, The Autobiography* Michael Joseph/ Penguin, London (2002)

Keegan, K *Kevin Keegan: My Autobiography* Little, Brown, London (1997)

McAllister, G and Clarke, G *Captains Log: The Gary McAllister Story* Mainstream, Edinburgh (1995)

McGrath, P *Back From the Brink* Century, London (2006)

McManaman S and Edworthy, S *El Macca: Four Years with Real Madrid* Simon and Schuster, London (2004)

Moynihan, L *Gordon Strachan* Virgin Books, London (2005)

Nelson, G *Left Foot Forward* Headline, London (1995)

Norvick, J *In a League of their Own: Footballs Maverick Managers* Mainstream, Edinburgh (1995)

O'Leary, D *Leeds United on Trial* Little, Brown, London (2002)

Redknapp, H and McGovern D *Harry Redknapp: My Autobiography* Collins Willow, London (1998)

Robson, B and Hayward, P *Bobby Robson, Fairwell But Not Goodbye* Hodder and Stoughton, London (2005)

Robinson, G *The Unconventional Minister* (2000).

Shackleton, L and Jack, D *The Clown Prince of Soccer* (1956) and (2005)

Vasili, P *The First Black Footballer – Arthur Wharton 1865–1930* Frank Cass, London (1998)

Venables, T *The Best Game in the World* Century Books, London (1996)

Clubs

Ballague *A Season on the Brink: A Portrait of Rafael Benitiz's Liverpool* Orion (2005)

Bose, M *Manchester Unlimited: The Rise and Rise of the Worlds Premier Football Club* Orion Business, London (1999)

Bose, M *Manchester Unlimited: The Money, Egos and Infighting behind the worlds Richest Soccer Club* (2000)

Bowler, D and Bains, J *Samba in the Smethwick End* Mainstream, Edinburgh (2000)

Boyden, M *Brums the Word* The Parrs Wood Press, Manchester (2003)

Brady, K *Brady Play the Blues* (1995)

Conner, J *The Lost Babes: Manchester United and the Forgotton Victims of Munich* Harper Sport (2006)

Crick, M and Smith, D *Manchester United: The Betrayal of a Legend* Pelham Books, London (1989)

Garry, J *Manchester City, The Complete Record* Breq (2006)

Goodyear, D and Matthews, T *Aston Villa, A Complete Record 1874–1988* Breedon Books (1988)

Geroski, R *Staying Up: A Fan Behind the Scenes in the Premiership* Little, Brown, London (1998)

Goodwin, B *The Essential History of Tottenham* Headline, London

Hill, J and Williams J (Eds) *Sport and Identity in the North of England* Keele University Press, Keele (1996)

Hutchinson, R *The Toon: A Complete History of Newcastle United* Mainstream, Edinburgh (1997)

Joannou, P *United: The First 100 Years; The History of Newcastle United* ACL Publishing, Leicester (1991)

Johnson, A *The Battle for Manchester City* Mainstream (1994)

Liversedge, S *Liverpool, From the Inside* Mainstream, Edinburgh (1995)

Matthews, T *West Midlands Football* Tempus Publishing (2004)

Matthews, T *Birmingham City, A Complete Record (1875–1989)* Breedon Books (1989)

McOwan, G *The Essential History of West Bromwich Albion* Headline Books, London (2002)

Morris, P *West Bromwich Albion* Heinemann (1965)

Mourant, A *Leeds United, The Glory Years* The Bluecoat Press, Liverpool

Mourant, A *The Essential History of Leeds United* Headline, London (2000)

Rippon, A *The Aston Villa Story* Breedon Books (1993)

Scholar, I and Bose, M *Behind Closed Doors: Dreams and Nightmares at Spurs* Orion Business, London (1992)

Rostron, P *Leeds United: Trials and Tribulations* Mainstream, Edinburgh (2004)

Soar, P and Tyler, M *The Official History of Arsenal 1886–1995* Hamlyn, London (1995)

Soar, P *The Official History of Tottenham Hotspur* Hamlyn (1996)

Ward, A and Griffin, J *The Essential History of Aston Villa* Headline, London (2002)

Williams, J *Liverpool FC and the Changing Face of English Football* Mainstream (2000)

Whitehead, R *Children of the Revolution: Aston Villa in the 1970s* Sports Projects, Smethwick (2001)

Index

425

Arsenal (*cont.*)
    foreign players 41, 54
    Kroenke, Stan 381n8, 383–4n24,
        410–11n14
    marketing success 275
    Usmanov, Alisher 411
Ashby, Eddie 351
Ashley, Mike 316, 383n24, 408n1
Association of European Professional
        Football Leagues (EPFL) 142–3
Aston Villa 44, 225, 285
    1992–3 success 15
    attendance figures 278, 307
    Collymore's criticisms of treatment by
        22–3
    competitive balance and 60
    Cup final 1904–5 game against
        Manchester City 226
    Doug Ellis and 181, 281–2
    lack of successful leadership 171,
        280–2
    market value 50, 62, 245
    marketing failure 275, 276
    Midlands football and 257–8, 259,
        260–1, 265, 266, 267, 270, 275, 280–2,
        283, 284–5
    under a luxury tax model 85
    under a wages and salaries cap model
        83
    NTL acquisition 99
    stock market experience 95, 96
    under-borrowing 267
    see also Villa Park
Atkinson, Ron 243
Atlanta Braves 73
Atlético Madrid 190

Banks, Simon 289, 290
Banks, Tony 145
Barcelona football club 20, 122
Barnard, John Jervis 322
Barnes, John 202
Barnsley football club 206
Barton, Joey 396n8
Barwick, Brian 152, 159, 373nn2 and 27
baseball 31, 65
    dominance by New York Yankees 68
    salary capping 69, 78
basketball 60, 65, 73, 145, 198, 269
Bates, Ken 96, 107, 108, 155, 179, 241–2,
        382n19
Bayern Münich 20, 21, 22, 75–6, 121

Bean, Graham 154, 388n22
'beautiful game' 309, 369n3
Beckham, David
    2003 US tour 27
    2007 signing to US team 375n13,
        406n12
    Ferguson and 201
    media treatment 193
    playing for Real Madrid 55
Beitar 113
benefactors 100–4
Benfica 22
Benitez, Rafael 342
Berezovsky, Boris 114
Bergara, Danny 393–4n12
Bergkamp, Dennis 360
Berlusconi, Silvio 88, 120, 142, 216, 298–9
Bernstein, David 229
Berry, Johnny 236
Best, George 196, 197, 202
    tributes to 17
betting 219–20
    see also match fixing
Birch, Trevor 330, 404n19
Birmingham and Aston Tramway
        Company 265
Birmingham City football club 83, 85,
        86, 307, 401n1, 402n2
    leadership failure 279–80
    Midlands football and 257–8, 266, 270,
        278
Birmingham, city of 262–3, 264, 268, 275
Birmingham Evening Dispatch 265
Birmingham Football Association 219
Blackburn Rovers 60, 109, 373n1
Blair, Tony 17, 144, 145, 146
Blanchflower, Danny 171, 280, 281
Blanchflower, Jackie 236
Blatter, Philippe 386–7n13
Blatter, Sepp 13, 38, 130, 131, 132–3,
        134, 385n6
    Annan and 295
    Blair and 146
    on dealing with racial abusers 192–3
    Platini and 141
Blunkett, David 107
BMB 207
Boa Morte, Luis 392n31
Bobroff, Paul 347, 349
Boisseau, Pascal 207
Boisseau, Sebastian 207
Boler, Stephen 228

426

428

430

see also luxury tax model
Faye, Amby 397n20
Al-Fayed, Mohamed 102, 109, 207–8, 381n9, 396–7n15
Ferdinand, Rio 4, 26, 158–9, 199–200, 392n30, 396n13
Ferguson, Duncan 328, 396n8
Ferguson, Sir Alex 248–50
  and agency services 205
  attempts to stop drinking culture 197
  BSkyB and 47
  on Cantona's departure from United 177–8
  Ferdinand and 26
  on the Glazers 252–3
  on Martin Edwards 246–7
  on 'player power and ego' 201
  and United success 232
  United's early years with 241, 243–4
Fiat 88
FIFA (Fédération Internationale de Football Association)
  commercialism 127, 287
  competitive balance and 13–14
  corruption 13, 24, 130–2, 386n9
  criticisms of 9, 124, 129–33
  ethics committee 296
  finances 130, 385–6n8
  football governance and 124–5, 126–36
  G14's case against 124, 294
  and the globalisation of football 42
  high talking whilst under investigation 9
  licensed agents 210–11
  Lord Coe and the watchdog committee 313–14
  organisational structure 133–6, 294
  president 6, 147
  racism and 192
  taskforce 'For the good of the game' 24
  vision for the future 295
  World Cup broadcasting rights 5
  World Cup finals as world's biggest sporting event 32–3
  World Cup reservations 23
  see also World Cup
finance 87–123
  benefactors 100–4
  foreign investors 109–20, 404–5n20 see also foreign investors

globalisation 45–54
secret money 105–9
stock market see stock market
strategic investment 99–100
supporters trusts 89, 104–5 see also supporters trusts
financial gearing 53, 267
Financial Service Authority (FSA) 94, 108–9
Financial Times 279, 316, 317
Fiszman, Danny 355, 359, 383n24
Flintoff, Freddie 274
Foot, John 214, 215–16
Foot, Michael 144
Football Association see FA
football environment
  business and the 'people's game' 17–18, 39, 124–5, 255, 287–8 see also commercialisation of football
  the consumers 28–33 see also consumers; fans
  future scenarios 290–1, 293–312
  the game at a crossroads 288–93
  growth in demand 26–8
  health of the game 20–6
  in the Midlands see Midlands football
  performance see club performance
  present state of play 18–20, 288–93
  the producers 38–9
  pyramid structure of football 23, 25, 76, 290
  scenario of a rival league 311–12
  scenario of commercialism slowing down 304–6
  scenario of commercialism with more equal revenue division 303–4
  scenario of continuing growth with a new super league 298–301
  scenario of increased commercialism with modest change 293–8
  scenario of less globalisation 310
  scenario of market led growth with intervention 301–3
  scenario of supporter disillusionment 306–9, 407nn14 and 18
  television 33–8, 288–9, 373n27 see also television
  the way forward 312–14
Football Foundation 80
Football League
  creation by businessmen 17–18, 264
  FA and 148–9

431

434

Proactive Sports Management 205, 206, 329
Professional Footballers Association (PFA) 55, 192, 372n19
Professional Game Match Officials (PGMO) 218
Putin, Vladimir 111
Pye, Freddie 229
pyramid structure of football 23, 25, 76, 290

Queens Park Rangers 117–18
Quirk, James and Fort, Rodney 67

racism
    FIFA's discussions on 295
    racial abuse of players 191–3, 395nn5–6
    in Spanish football 295, 395nn5–6
Ranson, Ray 400n5, 404n20
rape 196
Reading football club 91, 404n20
Real Madrid 20, 22, 27
    Beckham and Woodgate as players for 55
    Franco and 222–3
Redknapp, Harry 177, 220
Reebok 38
referees
    abuse of 195, 249
    scandals 8, 19, 214, 219
regulation 39
Reid, Peter 228, 258, 273
Reid, Robert 154
restrictive practices
    and the Americanisation of European football 73–9
    schemes for Europe 79–84
    NFL 65–6, 67
    salary capping see salary capping
retained profits 89
revenue sharing
    future scenario of commercialism with more equal revenue division 303–4
    lack of success in baseball 78
    luxury tax model 84–6
    NFL 22, 62
Reynolds, George 103
Richards, David 159
Richardson, Arthur 346
Richardson, Bryan 208, 258
Ridsdale, Peter 117, 206, 271

Rioch, Bruce 363
Robins, Derrick 278
Robinson, Peter 172–3, 333, 335
Robson, Bryan 259
Robson, Sir Bobby 204, 408n3
Rodriquez, Alex 409n8
Roeder, Glenn 393n12
Roma football club 21, 120
Romanov, Vladimir 118–19
Rooney, Wayne 19, 204, 206, 256, 329–30, 331
Rossi, Guido 216
Rous, Sir Stanley 1, 127, 150, 152–3, 298, 393n12
Royle, Joe 229, 324
Rozelle, Pete 70–1
Rugby League 74–5
Rummenigge, Karl-Heinz 75–6
Rysaffe Ltd 107

salary capping 11, 12, 74–9, 299, 301–2
    baseball 69, 78
    model scheme for Europe 79–84
    NFL 21–2, 62–3, 71–2, 84–5, 303, 377n7
    NHL 78–9
    Rugby League 74–5
    UEFA 301
Sampdoria football club 120
Samuelson, Christopher 330, 331
San Francisco 49ers 68
Saunders, Ron 228
Sawyer, Eric 335
Schmeichel, Peter 205, 362
Schmidt, Martin B and Berri, David 60
Scholar, Irving 101–2, 346–50
Scolari, Luiz 159
Scudamore, Richard 33–4, 35, 145–6, 296, 370n13, 372n24, 374n8
Seattle Seahawks 68
secret money 105–9
Segars, Hans 220
Sensi, Francesco 120
Setanta 36
Sexton, Dave 243, 358
Seymour, Stan 318, 319
Shackleton, Len 174, 184
Shankly, Bill 173, 334–6, 357
shareholders
    agents' fees and 205
    debt finance and 53–4

438

440

professional sport 'above the law' 64–6

Usmanov, Alisher 411

Valencia football club 21
Vasili, Phil 171
Venables, Terry 172, 173–4, 175, 273, 333
  Scholar and 348–9
  Sugar and 350–2
venture capital companies 98–9
Vialli, Gianluca 408n21
Villa Park 60, 278, 280
Villa, Ricardo 376n17
Villarreal football club 20, 136
violence
  mafia 395n7
  organised crime 395n7, 399n26
  player 193–5, 396n8
  rape 196
  spectator 191–3, 236–7, 395n7

Wale, Sidney 346
Walker, Jack 100, 102, 109
Walker, Michael 280–1, 324
Walvin, James 17, 39
Wardle, John 228–9, 230
Warner, Jack 128
Washington Redskins 61–2, 68
Wembley National Stadium Limited (WNSL) 155–7
Wembley Stadium 29, 30, 145, 146, 155–7
Wenger, Arsène 135–6, 177, 200, 363, 371n7, 394nn14 and 23, 410n14
Werder Bremen 21
West Bromwich Albion
  conservative board 282
  end of 2004–5 season 6, 258
  marketing failure 275
  Midlands football and 257, 259, 260, 261, 265, 266, 270, 278, 404–5n20
West Ham United 61, 114–16, 369–70n6, 390–2n30
W.H. Holdings 116
Whelen, Dave 12, 75, 99–100, 109
Whelen, Ken 279
Whiteside, Norman 243

Whittaker, George 237
Whittaker, Tom 356, 357, 361
Wigan Athletic 99–100, 109
Wigan Warriors 74–5
Wilkinson, Howard 273
Williams, T.V. 334
Williamson, Howard 394n15
Wilson, Jonathan 382n22, 399n26, 407n15
Wimbledon Football Club 7
Winters, Jeff 249
wire tapping 217
Wiseman, Jack 279
Wiseman, Keith 154
Wolverhampton Wanderers 81, 82
  Midlands football and 257, 259, 260, 261, 266, 270, 272
  post-Cullis decline 170
  sale to Morgan 381n13, 409n7
Woodgate, Jonathan 55, 194–5
Woods, Jon 331
Woodward, Sir Clive 36
World Cup
  1966 10
  1970 127
  2006 5, 18
  2010 6
  Blair and 2006 Cup 146
  broadcasting success and competitive balance 5–6
  Coca-Cola and 2, 20, 128–9
  as commercial enterprise 18, 129
  world's biggest sporting event 32–3
  ticket allocations 23
  Warner and 128
World Trading Organisation 310
Wrexham football club 103
Wright, Billy 357
Wright, Chris 117

Yeltsin, Boris 110–11
Yeung, Carson 404n20
York City football club 105

Zahavi, Pini 113, 154, 210, 397n20
Zen-Ruffinen, Michael 130
Zimbalist, Andrew 59–60